Russia Survival Guide: Business & Travel

Russia Survival Guide is not a tourist's guide to Russia. Instead, it is a practical, comprehensive and up-to-the-minute *travel* guide to the complexities of independent travel and business (*especially* business) in a country that is undergoing profound and rapid change.

Tourist guides (which usually are updated every couple of years and take 12-18 months to get from finished manuscript to bookstores) are fine for those parts of the equation which are not in flux. But for what constitutes reality in Russia today, that covers very little. *Russia Survival Guide*, now in its seventh annual update, covers the rest. And since we go from manuscript to bookstores in less than two months, our information is rarely more than a year old.

Russia Survival Guide answers questions you won't find addressed elsewhere: how to get cash in a crunch in Yekaterinburg, how to avoid committing cultural *faux pas*, how to register your business in Russia, how to select a partner or management personnel, where to get government funding for an investment project, where to get medical aid in Omsk, where to look for the best books, maps and periodicals on Russia, what to take with you when you go, where to go to study Russian, where not to go to keep from getting mugged. And much, much more.

Our **Russia City Guide**, covering Russia's 80 largest cities, is alone worth many times the price of this guide.

This guide is the product of many person's unflagging efforts, including Stephanie Ratmeyer, Mikhail Ivanov, Clare Kimmel, Oksana Gusarova, Robert Greenall, Elena Kuznetsova, Irina Tonkikh, Lena Gorb, Anastasia Ivanova, Vladimir Ovchinnikov, Scott D. McDonald, Anne Griffin and countless others.

Corrections and comments are enthusiastically encouraged. Please contact RIS or KZR at either of the addresses on the page facing.

Russia Survival Guide is just one of a series of publications of Russian Information Services. Other publications include: *Russian Life magazine, Where in Moscow, Where in St. Petersburg, The New Moscow: City Map and Guide, The New St. Petersburg: City Map and Guide, Bilingual Wall Map of Russia and the Republics* and *Business Russian.* Through our exclusive *Access Russia* catalog, we also distribute over 250 invaluable books, periodicals and products related to doing business and traveling in Russia.

All information in this guide is the most authoritative information available at the time of printing.

The Publisher
November 1996

Что русскому здорово, то немцу смерть.

What is healthy for a Russian, is deadly for a foreigner.

— Russian proverb

RUSSIA
SURVIVAL GUIDE

Paul E. Richardson

The
definitive
guide to
doing
business
and traveling
in Russia

EDITION 7

Russian Information Services, Inc.
Montpelier, VT

Every attempt has been made to make this guide the most up-to-date collection of business and travel information available. Given the swift rate of change in Russia and the new Commonwealth, mistakes in phone numbers, addresses, and on other points of fact are inevitable. The authors, editors and publishers accept no liability for any consequences which may arise from the use of information in this guide.

First edition: October 1990
Second edition: August 1991
Third edition: March 1992
Fourth edition: March 1993
Fifth edition: March 1994
Sixth edition: March 1995
Seventh edition: November 1996

Published by:
Russian Information Services (RIS Publications)
89 Main Street, Suite 2
Montpelier, VT 05602 USA
phone: 802-223-4955
fax: 802-223-6105
email: 73244.3372@compuserve.com
WWW: http://www.friends-partners.org/rispubs/

In cooperation with:
Издательство КЗР (KZR Publications)
Pokrovsky bulvar 8, #305
Moscow 109817
phone: 095-917-2613
fax: 095-917-9148
email: 74754.3234@compuserve.com

Russian Information Services, Montpelier, VT USA

Library of Congress Catalog Card Number: 96-068793
ISBN 1-880100-30-4

Table of Contents

8. Doing Business — 169

9. Russian Business Law — 183

Index — 224

Tables, Graphs & Illustrations

Facts & Reference

Russia Facts*

Percentage of the Russian GDP produced by the private sector: 76%

Inflation in Russia, 1993; 1994; 1995; 1996 (est.): 840%; 215%; 131%; 80%

Rate of industrial growth, same years: -16%; -21%; -3%; 4%

Number of Russians expected to visit the Riviera in 1996: 300,000

Amount spent by foreign tourists in Russia, 1995 (bn $): 1.4

...in Hungary, China and South Korea: 1.6; 8.3; 5.7

Rank of US among Russia's export markets: 4

...of Germany, UK and Switzerland: 1,2,3

Number of joint ventures in Russia: 14,600

Rank of US, Germany and China as j.v. partners: 1,2,3

Estimated pct. of Russian companies that do not pay taxes: 40%

Pct. of energy delivered to Russian consumers in 1995 not paid for: 33%

Percentage of Russian drivers insured: 2%

Percentage of Russian companies with insurance: 40%

Insurance services as pct. of GNP in Russia; in US: 1.5%; 10%

Number of web sites found when searching for "Russia": 500,000

Price of prime office space, per ft., per year, Moscow: $98

...price in Hong Kong; in Tokyo: $125; $131

Ice cream consumed in Russia, per year (tons): 350,000

Cash holdings of Russian citizens (est.): $18,000,000,000

Of which in $100 bills (est.): $14,400,000,000

Number of counterfeit $100 bills per Russian citizen: 20

Pct. of household savings kept in hard currency, 1992; 1995: 3.2%; 61.6%

Pct. of Russians earning less than subsistence income: 20%

Russian import duty on whirlpool baths: 5% ...on textiles: 25-30%

Number of Russian air passengers in 1991; 1995 (mn): 132; 35

Current Russian bus./econ. leaders that were CPSU members: 78%

Est. pct. of banks controlled by organized crime: 50-80%

See first page of index for sources

Arctic Ocean

Norwegian Sea

North Sea

Franz
Joseph
Islands

Barents
Sea

Novaya Zemlya

Kara Sea

•D

•Murmansk

Baltic
Sea

Vorkuta •

Salekhard •

Kaliningrad•
(Russia)

Latvia Tallinn
Riga

Estonia

•Vyborg
Lake Petrozavodsk
Ladoga
St. Petersburg *Lake Onega*

Arkhangelsk •

Urengoy •

Lithuania
•Vilnius

Pskov

•Novgorod

•Syktyvkar

•Brest

Minsk •

Smolensk

Cherepovets
•Vologda

Belarus

•Tver

•Lvov

Ukraine

Gomel•

Moscow

Rostov

Yaroslavl
Kostroma
Ivanovo

•Vyatka

Russian Federation

Kaluga

Kiev• Bryansk

Oryol

Vladimir

Moldova
Chisinau

Cherkassy

Tula

Ryazan

Nizhny Novgorod

•Kursk

Lipetsk

•Cheboksary

•Izhevsk

Perm

Nizhevartovsk •

Odessa Kharkov

•Belgorod

Saransk

Kazan

Yoshkar-Ola

Dnepropetrovsk

Voronezh

Tambov

Naberezhnye Chelny

Nizhny Tagil

•Zaporozhe

Penza

Ulyanovsk

Donetsk

Tolyatti

Yekaterinburg

Tyumen

*Black
Sea*

•Saratov

Samara

Ufa

•Rostov-on-Don

•Krasnodar

Volgograd

Oral

Magnitogorsk

•Chelyabinsk

Kurgan

Tomsk •

•Sochi

Elista

Astrakhan

Orenburg

•Kustanay

Omsk•

Novosibirsk•

Aqtobe

Kokchetav

Georgia
Tbilisi Grozny

•Guriyev

Kazakhstan

Aqmola

Pavlodar•

Barnaul

Armenia
Yerevan

Makhachkala

Karaganda

Semey

•Dzhezkazgan

Azerbaidzhan Baku

*Aral
Sea*

*Lake
Balkhash*

*Caspian
Sea*

Azov
Sea

•Kzyl-Orda

Taldy-Kurgan
•

Turkmenistan

Uzbekistan

Dzhambul

Chimkent

Almaty

•Ashgabat

Bukhara

Tashkent

Bishkek

Samarqand

Kyrgizistan

Dushanbe

Tadzhikistan

Chukchi Sea

Wrangel Island

Provideniya

East Siberian Sea

Cherskiy

Anadyr

Bering
Sea

Severnaya Zemlya

New Siberian
Islands

Laptev
Sea

Norilsk

Tiksi

Magadan

Petropavlovsk-
Kamchatskiy

Okhotsk

Sea of
Okhotsk

(Russia)

Yakutsk

Lensk

Sakhalin Island

Yuzhno-Sakhalinsk

Krasnoyarsk

Bratsk

Lake
Baykal

Khabarovsk

Blagoveshchensk

erovo

Novokuznetsk

Angarsk

Irkutsk

Ulan-Ude

Chita

Nakhodka

Vladivostok

Sea of
Japan

Russia and the Independent States

⭐ National capital

Izhevsk ● City

Latvia Country

🕐 Local time when
12:00 in Moscow

——— International Boundary

------- Time zone Boundary

0   Miles   800

994, Russian Information Services, Inc.

Average Year-Round
Temperatures in Russia (Celcius)

		Jan	Feb	Mar	Apr	May	Jun	Jul	Aug	Sep	Oct	Nov	Dec
Moscow	Hi	-10	-7	-2	6	16	20	22	20	13	7	-2	-8
	Lo	-15	-13	-10	-2	6	10	12	11	6	1	-6	-12
St. Petersburg	Hi	-5	-4	1	7	15	19	22	19	14	7	1	-3
	Lo	-11	-11	-8	-1	6	11	14	12	7	3	-3	-8
Black Sea	Hi	4	5	7	12	18	24	26	26	22	17	10	6
	Lo	-1.1	0	2	6	11	16	18	18	14	10	4	2
Caucasus	Hi	0	2	12	20	26	31	36	34	29	21	11	3
	Lo	-9	-8	1	6	11	15	18	18	13	7	2	-3
Far East	Hi	-11	-5	1	8	12	17	21	25	20	13	2	-7
	Lo	-18	-15	-7	1	6	11	16	18	13	6	-4	-13
Siberia -- East	Hi	-18	-14	-6	2	11	20	21	19	11	3	-16	-16
	Lo	-24	-21	-13	-3	5	11	15	12	4	-3	-23	-22
Volga basin	Hi	-7	-5	-1	6	11	17	19	18	13	6	0	-4
	Lo	-13	-12	-8	-1	7	10	13	11	6	1	-7	-11

Notes: *Temperatures are given in degrees celcius (for fahrenheit, use the conversion table at right), based on average daily temperatures for the month in question. 'Wet Months' indicate that these are the months of greater precipitation (rain during more than 25% of the days of a given month).*

Wet
Month

RUSSIAN TIME CHANGES

Russia changes to and from Summer Time on different weekends from much of the West. Between Moscow and New York, the time differences during the year are:

From the last Sunday of March to the first
   Sunday of April: 9 hours.
From the last Sunday of September to the last
   Sunday of October: 7 hours
All other times: 8 hours.

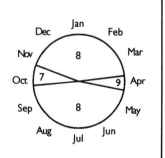

Metric Conversion Chart

LENGTH

1 centimeter	0.394 inches
1 inch	2.540 centimeters
1 foot	0.305 meters
1 meter	3.281 feet
1 yard	0.9144 meters
1 kilometer	0.6214 mile
1 mile	1.6094 kilometers
1 verst (Russia)	1.067 kilometers

WEIGHT

1 gram	0.03527 ounce
1 ounce	28.35 grams
1 pound	0.4536 kilos
1 kilogram	2.2046 pounds
1 met. ton	0.9842 Eng. ton
1 Eng. ton	1.016 metric ton

SQUARES AND AREA

1 sq. centimeter	0.1550 sq. inch
1 sq. inch	6.452 sq. centimeters
1 sq. meter	10.764 sq. feet
1 sq. foot	0.09290 sq. meters
1 sq. meter	1.196 sq. yards
1 sq. yard	0.8361 sq. meters
1 sq. kilometer	0.386 sq. mile
1 sq. mile	2.59 sq. kilometers
1 hectare	2.47 acres
1 acre	0.405 hectares

VOLUME

1 tsp.	5 ml
1 cup	0.24 liter
1 liter (dry)	0.908 quart
1 quart (dry)	1.101 liters
1 liter (liquid)	1.0567 quarts
1 quart (liquid)	0.9463 liters
1 US gal. (liquid)	3.785 liters
1 Imp. gal. (lqd)	4.546 liters
1 liter (liquid)	0.264 US gal.
1 liter (liquid)	0.220 Imp. gal.

CLOTHING SIZES

WOMEN

Suits and Dresses

American	8	10	12	14	16	18
British	10	12	14	16	18	20
Russian	36	38	40	42	44	46

Stockings

American & British	8	8½	9	9½	10	10½
Russian	0	1	2	3	4	5

Shoes

American	6	7	8	9
British	4½	5½	6½	7½
Russian	36	37	38	40

MEN

Suits/Coats

American	36	38	40	42	44	46
Russian	46	48	50	52	54	56

Shirts

American & British	15	16	17	18
Russian	38	41	43	45

Shoes

American & British	5	6	7	8	9	10	11
Russian	38	39	41	42	43	44	45

TEMPERATURE

(°F - 32) x 0.56 = °C
(°C x 1.8) + 32 = °F

°F	°C
100	40
90	35
80	30
70	25
60	20
50	15
40	10
30	5
20	0
10	-5
0	-10
-10	-15
-20	-20
-30	-25
-40	-30
	-35
	-40

*Russian **hat sizes** are based on the measurement, in centimeters, of the circumference of one's head, at mid-forehead level.

City Codes Within the CIS

To direct-dial long distance within the Commonwealth of Independent States, dial 8, wait for a dial tone, then dial the city code as listed below and then the local number. You will need to add zeroes or twos between the city code and the local number to make a total of 10 digits if the number of digits do not already equal ten.

Almaty	327	Kursk	07100
Arkhangelsk	818	Lipetsk	0740
Ashkabad	363	Lvov	322
Astrakhan	85100	Magadan	41300
Baku	8922	Magnitogorsk	35137
Barnaul	3952	Minsk	0172
Bishkek	331	Moscow	095
Blagoveshensk	41622	Mozhaisk	238
Borodino	39168	Murmansk	815
Bratsk	39531	Nikolaev	510
Brest	01622	Nizhny Novgorod	8312
Bryansk	08322	Noginsk	251
Bukhara	365	Novgorod	8160
Cheboksari	8350	Novosibirsk	3832
Chelyabinsk	351	Odessa	48
Cherkassy	472	Omsk	38122
Chita	30222	Orel	0860
Dagomys	8620	Orenburg	35300
Dnepropetrovsk	562	Pavlodar	3182
Donetsk	622	Penza	8412
Dushanbe	3772	Perm	3422
Fergana	373	Petropavlovsk	3150
Gomel	2322	Petrozavodsk	81400
Grozny	8712	Pinsk	01653
Irkutsk	3952	Poltava	05322
Ivanovo	09322	Pskov	81122
Izhevsk	3412	Rostov	08536
Kaliningrad	01122	Rostov-on-Don	8632
Kaluga	08422	Rovno	360
Karaganda	3210	Ryazan	0912
Kaunas	0127	St. Petersburg	812
Kazan	8432	Samarkand	366
Kemerovo	38422	Saransk	8342
Khabarovsk	4210	Saratov	8452
Kharkov	572	Semipalatinsk	3222
Kiev	44	Sergeyev Posad	254
Kirov	833	Sevastopol	690
Kostroma	09422	Simferopol	6522
Krasnodar	8612	Smolensk	08100
Krasnoyarsk	3912	Sochi	8620
Kuybyshev	8462	Stavropol	86522
Kurgan	35222	Sukhumi	88122

Sumgait	89264
Suzdal	09231
Syktyvkar	82122
Taganrog	86344
Tambov	07522
Tashkent	3712
Tbilisi	8832
Termez	37622
Tomsk	38222
Tula	0872
Tver	08222
Tyumen	3452
Ufa	3472
Ulan-Ude	30122
Ulyanovsk	84222
Uralsk	31122
Vitebsk	02122
Vladimir	09222
Volgograd	8442
Vologda	81722
Volokolamsk	236
Voronezh	0732
Vyborg	278
Yakutsk	41122
Yalta	600
Yaroslavl	0852
Yekaterinburg	3432
Yerevan	8852
Zaporozhe	612
Zhitomir	041

☑ For other cities, or if you have difficulties with dialing, or if you want the number for directory assistance for a certain city (some are listed in Chapter 4), call 07.

☑ Note that several CIS and FSU countries now have their own country dialing codes (see chart on the following page).

International Country and City Codes

To dial an international call from Russia, first dial 8, wait for a dial tone, then 10, then the country code, then the city code and local number.

Country/City	Code	Country/City	Code	Country/City	Code
Albania	355	Georgia	995	Korea, South	82
Algeria	213	Germany	49	Seoul	2
Argentina	54	Berlin	30	Kuwait	965
Buenos Aires	1	Bonn	228	Latvia	371
Armenia	374	Dusseldorf	211	Riga	2
Australia	61	Frankfurt	69	Liberia	231
Melbourne	3	Munich	89	Libya	218
Sydney	2	Greece	30	Liechtenstein	4175
Austria	43	Athens	1	Lithuania	370
Vienna	1	Guatemala	502	Vilnius	2
Azerbaidzhan	994	Haiti	509	Luxembourg	352
Bahrain	973	Honduras	504	Malawi	265
Belarus	375	Hong Kong	852	Malaysia	60
Belgium	32	Hong Kong	5	Mexico	52
Brussels	2	Hungary	36	Mexico City	5
Bolivia	591	Budapest	1	Moldova	373
Santa Cruz	33	Iceland	354	Chisinau	2
Canada	1	India	91	Monaco	3393
Montreal	514	Bombay	22	Morocco	212
Ottawa	613	New Delhi	11	Namibia	264
Toronto	416	Indonesia	62	Nepal	977
Vancouver	604	Jakarta	21	Netherlands	31
Cameroon	237	Iran	98	Amsterdam	20
Chile	56	Teheran	21	The Hague	70
Santiago	2	Iraq	964	New Zealand	64
China	86	Baghdad	1	Nicaragua	505
Beijing	1	Ireland	353	Nigeria	234
Columbia	57	Dublin	1	Norway	47
Bogota	1	Israel	972	Oslo	2
Costa Rica	506	Jerusalem	2	Oman	968
Croatia	385	Tel Aviv	3	Pakistan	92
Cyprus	357	Italy	39	Islamabad	51
Czech Republic	42	Florence	55	Panama	507
Prague	2	Milan	2	Peru	51
Denmark	45	Rome	6	Phillipines	63
Copenhagen	1 & 2	Venice	41	Manila	2
Ecuador	593	Ivory Coast	225	Poland	48
Egypt	20	Japan	81	Warsaw	22
El Salvador	503	Tokyo	3	Portugal	351
Estonia	372	Yokohama	45	Lisbon	1
Tallinn	2	Jordan	962	Qatar	974
Ethiopia	251	Amman	6	Romania	40
Finland	358	Kazakstan	7	Bucharest	0
Helsinki	0	Kenya	254	Russia	7
France	33	Kirgizistan	7	Moscow	095
Paris	1			St. Petersburg	812

Country/City	Code
Saudi Arabia	966
Senegal	221
Singapore	65
Slovak Republic	42
South Africa	27
Spain	34
Barcelona	3
Madrid	1
Sri Lanka	94
Suriname	597
Sweden	46
Stockholm	8
Switzerland	41
Geneva	22
Zurich	1
Tadzhikistan	7
Taiwan	886
Thailand	66
Bangkok	2
Tunisia	216
Turkey	90
Istanbul	1
Turkmenistan	993
Ukraine	380
United Arab Emirates	971
UK	44
Belfast	232
Cardiff	222
Glasgow	41
London	171 or 181
United States	1
Boston	617
Chicago	312
Dallas	214
Detroit	313
Houston	713
Los Angeles	213
Montpelier	802
New York	212
San Francisco	415
Seattle	206
Washington	202
Uruguay	598
Uzbekistan	7
Vatican City	396
Venezuela	58
Yemen Arab Republic	967
Yugoslavia	381
Belgrade	11

Administrative Divisions of Russia

Arctic Ocean

Norwegian Sea

Franz Joseph Islands

Barents Sea

Novaya Zemlya

Kara Sea

Taymy

• Murmansk

• Dudink

Baltic Sea

liningrad ussia)

KARELIA

• Pskov

Lake Ladoga • Petrozavodsk
• St. Petersburg *Lake Onega* • Arkhangelsk • Naryan-Mar

Nenetsiya AOk

• Novgorod

• Syktyvkar

• Salekhard

• Smolensk • Tver
• Vologda

KOMI

Yamalo-Nenets AOk

• Urengoy

Moscow ⭐
• Kaluga
Bryansk •
• Oryol • Tula • Vladimir
• Kursk • Lipetsk
• Belgorod • Saransk
• Voronezh • Tambov
• Yaroslavl
• Kostroma
• Ivanovo
• Nizhny Novgorod
③ • Cheboksary • Yoshkar-Ola
① • Kazan ④
②
TATARSTAN
• Penza
• Ulyanovsk

Komi-Permyat AOk

• Perm

Khanty-Mansi AOk
• Khanti-Mansisk

KRAS

• Ryazan
• Vyatka

• Saratov • Samara
• Yekaterinburg
• Tyumen

• Rostov-on-Don
asnodar
• Volgograd
• Ufa
• Chelyabinsk
BASHKIRIA
• Kurgan

⑤
• Elista
⑥
⑦ ⑪ • Astrakhan
⑧ ⑨
• Grozny
Orenburg

• Omsk

• Tomsk
• Kemerovo
• Novosibirsk

⑩ • Makhachkala

• Barnaul

KH

Aral Sea

• Gorno-Alta
GORNO-ALTAI

Caspian Sea

Administrative Divisions of Russia

⭐ National capital

Izhevsk • Oblast/regional center

▨ **AUTONOMOUS REPUBLIC**

——— International Boundary

——— Autonomous republic, oblast or kray boundary

············ Autonomous oblast (AO) or autonomous okrug (AOk) boundary

Miles

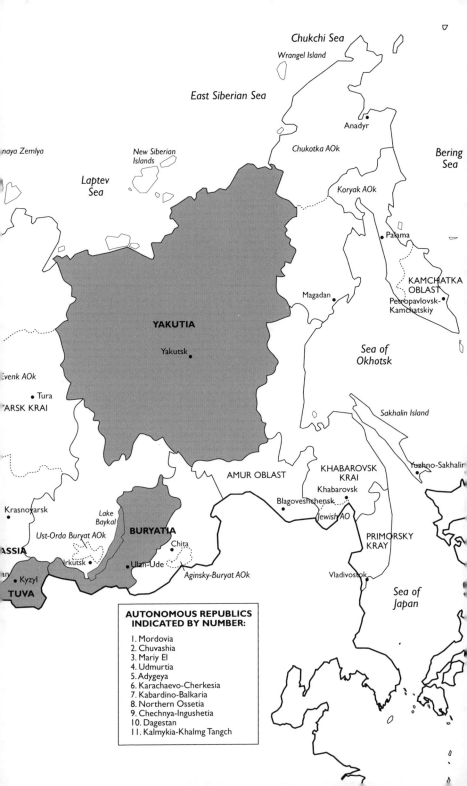

Chukchi Sea

Wrangel Island

East Siberian Sea

naya Zemlya

New Siberian
Islands

Laptev
Sea

Anadyr

Chukotka AOk

Bering
Sea

Koryak AOk

Palama

YAKUTIA

KAMCHATKA
OBLAST

Magadan

Petropavlovsk-
Kamchatskiy

Yakutsk

Sea of
Okhotsk

Evenk AOk

Tura

ARSK KRAI

Sakhalin Island

Yuzhno-Sakhalir

Krasnoyarsk

AMUR OBLAST

KHABAROVSK
KRAI

Lake
Baykal

Khabarovsk

Blagoveshchensk

Ust-Orda Buryat AOk

BURYATIA

Jewish AO

ASSIA

Chita

Irkutsk

PRIMORSKY
KRAY

Ulan-Ude

Kyzyl

Aginsky-Buryat AOk

Vladivostok

TUVA

Sea of
Japan

**AUTONOMOUS REPUBLICS
INDICATED BY NUMBER:**

1. Mordovia
2. Chuvashia
3. Mariy El
4. Udmurtia
5. Adygeya
6. Karachaevo-Cherkesia
7. Kabardino-Balkaria
8. Northern Ossetia
9. Chechnya-Ingushetia
10. Dagestan
11. Kalmykia-Khalmg Tangch

Information Resources

The number of new publications and information resources on Russia each year continues to grow. At times the flood of information can be overwhelming and confusing. This section strives to provide a concise and reasonably comprehensive survey of the various types of information resources (at least those relating to business and travel) available in printed, electronic and other formats. Inasmuch as is possible, we try to focus on the better publications and products, as well as on those which have had, or show promise of having, lasting power in a turbulent market.

BOOKS

Past editions of the Survival Guide have listed here over a hundred recommended books, maps and directories. Many of them are hard-to-find and not readily available through local bookstores. With this edition we have limited the listing of titles to reference and business titles of greatest interest to businesspersons and independent travelers. **For a more complete listing of language, business, general interest, travel and other books related to Russia and the FSU, you will want to request a free copy of the catalog** *Access Russia, Central Europe and Points Between* **(from the publishers of this guide).** Call 1-800-639-4301 or fax 802-223-6105 (or write to the publisher's address opposite the title page) to get a copy of the free catalog. **Most all of the books listed below are available through the** *Access Russia* **catalog.**

Cultural Topics

A Taste of Russia: A Cookbook of Russian Hospitality, by Darra Goldstein. *User-friendly, with plenty of detail on how to "simulate" native Russian foodstuffs, for the most authentic results. Home bartenders will love the table of recipes for making flavored vodkas. (HarperCollins Publishers; ISBN 0-06-097385-4; $16.00; 306 pp.; 1983)*

A Dictionary of Russian Gesture, by Barbara Monahan. *This entertaining introduction and guide to the wide variety of Russian gestures illustrates the critical non-verbal component so often left out of courses on language and culture. Even pages contain descriptions of (or prescriptions for) common gestures while odd pages bear photographic illustrations. The book is fully indexed, so you can find just the sentiment you're looking for. The language of gestures is far from universal. Avoid a myriad of cultural faux paus with this handbook. (Hermitage; ISBN 0-938920-38-3; $10.50; 180 pp.; 1983)*

From Nyet to Da, by Yale Richmond. *An insightful look at the Russian character by a veteran foreign service officer. Includes pertinent reflections on Russian national character and how understanding it can lead to more effective negotiation and social/business interaction. This should be on the bookshelf of anyone with a serious business interest in Russia. (Intercultural Press; $17.95; 200 pp.; 1996)*

Negotiating with the Soviets, by Raymond E. Smith. *Ignore the word "Soviets" in this title. But for a handful of pages on soviet ideology, this book is about Russians. It is about the historical, social and cultural factors that inform their negotiating behavior. And it should be required reading for anyone who will ever negotiate a business deal, bargain for a rental contract, or bluster oneself into a restaurant in Russia. Written by* a career US diplomat with over a dozen years experience negotiating with Russian diplomats, politicians, waiters and business people, this book is a storehouse of invaluable insights, anecdotes and analyses. More than just a description of how Russians negotiate, it hones in on the more important question: why Russians negotiate the way they do. (Indiana University Press; ISBN 0-253-20535-2; $11.95; 148 pp.; 1989)

Russian Folk Belief, by Linda J. Ivanits. *This is a comprehensive look at the many aspects of Russian folk beliefs, from the pagan background to Christian personages, to devils, spirits and sorcery. Ivanits seeks to demonstrate that Slavic pagan beliefs are overlaid with popular Christianity, first through extensive historical and social analysis, then through presentation (in English translation) of many classic folk narratives. (M.E. Sharpe, Inc.; ISBN 0-87332-889-2; $22.95; 276 pp.; 1989)*

The Russian Way, by Zita Dabars. *This concise and readable guide to Russian culture is a must for students of Russian, for travelers and business people. It covers 73 separate topics in alphabetical order (from advertising to hygiene to mushrooms to language) that help illuminate some of the traits that make Russians Russian. Complete with a bibliography and index, this book will help break the culture barrier and let you better understand the Russian way of doing things. (NTC Publishing Group; ISBN 0-8442-4296-9; $12.95; 128 pp.; 1994)*

The Russian's World: Life and Language, by Genevra Gerhart. *Best described as a compilation for non-Russians of what Russian common knowledge might be, this is the information one Russian assumes another has when they are talking together. It is a description of the Russian's world from the Russian's point of view. Primarily a language text, it is full of useful, contextual readings, translations and commentary. But it is also a reference book, containing everything from notes on Russian holidays and dress, to The Table of Ranks, the Russian Morse Code table and the Russian Periodic Table. In all, it is a cultural road map that should be on the reference shelf of anyone who wishes to navigate in Russian culture, language and history. (Harcourt Brace; ISBN 0-1550-1053-0; $37.00; 419 pp.; 1995)*

The Xenophobe's Guide to the Russians (...to the Americans),. *The last thing these provocatively-titled books promote is xenophobia. Rather, their intent is to cure xenophobia through humor and honesty. Published in the UK (and hard to find in the US), these concise guides are frank, irreverent and intensely funny guides to the culture, beliefs, traditions and foibles of nations. Get the Russian guide for yourself, and give a gift of the American guide to your foreign partner. Then exchange copies. (Associated Publishers Group; ISBN 1-85304-737-6; $5.95; 64 pp.; 1993)*

General Business & History

A History of Russia, 5th Edition, by Nicholas V. Riasanovsky. *Widely acclaimed as the best one-volume survey of Russian history anywhere, this new 5th edition has been revised and expanded to cover glasnost, perestroika, the dissolution of the Soviet Union, and the events of 1992. For anyone interested in the main themes of Russian history, this is the most authoritative, readable, and well-balanced study available. (Oxford University Press; ISBN 0-19-507462-9; $38.00; 710 pp.; 1993)*

Free Enterprise Moves East: Doing Business from Prague to Vladivostok, by Carter Henderson. *If you are looking for a lucid, readable review of the business atmospheres in Russia, the CIS and Central Europe, this is the book. Henderson, former Wall Street Journal London Bureau Chief, offers a street-level, journalist-style view of the developing business environment amongst 400 million born-again capitalists in the former communist states. Easily mixing political and economic reportage with inter-*

views and case studies of successful businesses, he paints a realistic and mainly optimistic picture of the region's capitalist future. (ICS Press; ISBN 1-55815-325-X; $24.95; 286 pp.; 3/96)

Land of the Firebird: The Beauty of Old Russia, by Suzanne Massie. *One of the best, easy-reading historical tomes available. Full of beautiful photographs of art and architecture and great as a gift. (Heart Tree Press; ISBN 0-671-46059-5; $23.00; 495 pp.; 1995)*

The Russian Far East: A History, by John J. Stephan. *A monumental survey of the history of Russia's Far East. The result of over 25 years of research and study, Stephan's new book reveals vibrant, cosmopolitan lifestyles in this vast, rugged and supposedly insular region. He examines all facets of the region's history: its Chinese and Mongol roots, its role on the edge of the Russian and Soviet empires, and its repeated thrusts for autonomy. (Stanford University Press; ISBN 0-8047-2311-7; $45.00; 482 pp.; 1994)*

For Russian Colleagues

American Phrasebook for Russians, by Vadim Blagowidow. *The only phrasebook designed specifically to address the needs of Russian-speaking visitors to America. This extensive introduction to American society anticipates real-life concerns such as arrival and customs, public transport, personal information, telephone conversations, important signs and services, renting an apartment, shopping, schools, health problems, food, driving a car, and even getting into arguments- always with an eye on American culture. An ideal gift for colleagues, visiting exchange groups, and newly-arrived emigres. (Hippocrene Books, Inc.; ISBN 0-7818-0054-4; $8.95; 200 pp.; 1992)*

Conversational English for Russian Speakers. *Designed for those who have already studied English in some detail, this is a cassette tape series (four 60-minute tapes) to help build critical conversational vocabulary and idioms. Using dialogues and explanations in both English and Russian, the course helps intermediate to advanced students make that critical step from speaking in English to thinking in English. Each tape includes fold-out transcripts of lessons. (Random House, Inc.; ISBN 0-517-59855-8; $25.00; 1994)*

Russian Yellow Pages 1995-6. *Printed in Russian, this unique 800-page book (now in an all-new second edition) is the definitive how-to guide to life in the United States for newly-immigrating, or visiting, Russian speakers. Covering everything from how to return defective goods to how to find work, make up a resume, rent an apartment, pay taxes and use the post office (and much more), this makes a great gift for frequent visitors or newly-arriving friends (or spouses). Also includes a state-by-state historical, informational and yellow-pages section, making it the most comprehensive compendium of Russian-related activity in the US. (Liberty Publishing House; ISBN 0-914481-72-X; $18.00; 544 pp.; 1992)*

Language and Dictionaries

Business Russian, by Svetlana Aleksandroff. *A practical guide to learning the Russian you need for doing business in the new Russia! This essential text for the intermediate to advanced student is appropriate for either classroom or individual use. It is intensely practical, which means you'll not only learn important business vocabulary and usage, but also become knowledgeable about business operations, customs and behavior. Full of examples of documentation and contemporary conversations, this book includes chapters on important subjects like business travel, correspondence, exhibitions, negotiations, agreements and contracts, and formation of businesses. Includes a complete*

Russian-English business dictionary as well. (*Russian Information Services; ISBN 1-880100-14-2; $16.00; 182 pp.; 1993*)

Dictionary of Russian Slang and Colloquial Expressions, by Eve Adler and Vladimir Shlyakhov. *Some 4500 words and their popular meanings — definitions you won't find in standard Russian-English dictionaries. This is language as it is actually spoken: street language, criminal jargon, teenagers' slang, army and police expressions. Informal and vernacular words and phrases are listed alphabetically in cyrillic, followed by their translations and meanings in English. (Barron's Educational Series, Inc.; ISBN 0-8120-9085-3; $11.95; 336 pp.; 1995)*

English-Russian, Russian-English Dictionary, by Kenneth Katzner. *This is the only dictionary on the market that is based on American (rather than British) English. Compact but comprehensive and now in paperback. (John Wiley & Sons, Inc.; ISBN 0-471-01707-8; $32.50; 904 pp.; 1994)*

Oxford Russian Dictionary. *This single-volume hardcover Oxford dictionary quite simply has no equal. It contains over 180,000 words and phrases and 290,000 translations in over 1300 crisply typeset pages (surely the most comprehensive and authoritative English-Russian/Russian-English dictionary anywhere available). (Oxford University Press; ISBN 0-19-864189-3; $49.95; 1300 pp.; 1994)*

Pimsleur Russian Language Program (tapes). *Dr. Paul Pimsleur found that language learning is most effective when taken in 30 minute doses. His series of language programs are built around this philosophy and this four tape set (8 half-hour lessons) is a progressive, basic introduction to Russian that requires no workbook or reading material. The package includes a certificate for $25 off the full 30 lesson Russian program. (Simon & Schuster; ISBN 0-671-52166-7; $25.00; 4 hrs pp.; 1995)*

Russian-English/English-Russian Dictionary of Business & Legal Terms, by Shane DeBeer. *This unique and invaluable reference work for business people, lawyers, students, translators, diplomats and anyone else dealing with business and legal terminology in Russian, contains over 40,000 entries. Includes pronunciation guides, extensive usage notes, grammatical notes and listing of legal and business terms. (Hippocrene Books, Inc.; ISBN 0-7818-0163-X; $50.00; 800 pp.; 1995)*

Tricky Accents (Kaverznye udareniya), by David Elianov. *No student of Russian can afford to be without this book. It fills an important gap in language learning by cataloguing Russian homographs — words that are spelled the same but have different stress, leading to often very different meanings (e.g. mUka — torment and mukA — flour). In Russian, proper or improper use of stress is one of the most obvious indicators of native vs. foreign speakers. This book will help alleviate difficult, and often embarrassing, stress problems. (Hermitage; ISBN 1-55779-080-9; $10.00; 100 pp.; 1995)*

Maps and Atlases

Atlas of Russia and the Post Soviet Republics. *This new atlas was two years in the making. It is the first comprehensive, post-Soviet atlas in English of the former Soviet Union. Includes maps of Russia, the Baltics, Transcaucasia, Ukraine, Moldova and the*

Central Asian states. Plus five large-scale street plans of the new states' capital cities. Nearly 8000 places are indexed on the maps and the full-color maps show topography, hydrography, political boundaries and much more! A must-have resource for map lovers and a vital reference tool for business people and tourists. (Arguments and Facts International; $72.00; 64 pp.; 1994)

Map of Russia and the Republics. Over a year in the making, this is the first-ever map of Russia and the FSU using the latest in GIS mapping technology and digital publishing. The result is a highly accurate, crisp, clean and colorful map of 1/6th of the Earth's surface. A unique feature of this map is that it is actually two identical maps — on one side it is entirely in Russian, on the other entirely in English. It shows all population centers over 30,000 inhabitants, geographic features (shaded relief) and administrative regions. Cities are indexed right on the map and there is an enlarged Moscow region map and administrative divisions map. Measures a full 3' x 4'; folds to 6" x 9". Laminated Wall Map Version: $25. (Russian Information Services; $10.00; 1996)

The New Moscow City Map and Guide. This map has repeatedly met with with rave reviews ('meticulously accurate...user friendly' - TIME Magazine) and has been used by senators, diplomats, tourists, businesspeople and even President Clinton and Vice President Gore on trips to Russia's capital. This revised and updated third edition includes hundred of significant street and feature revisions to account for recent changes. Features include an expanded city center map, a regional map and a bilingual metro map. Restaurants, hotels, business centers, currency stores, and other important locations are all featured and meticulously indexed. This is, quite simply, the most up-to-date, accurate, and user-friendly map of Moscow available! Decorate your home or office with the laminated wall map version! (Russian Information Services; ISBN 1-880100-33-9; $6.95; 1996)

The New St. Petersburg City Map and Guide. This is the most current and useful map of the 'Venice of the North' anywhere available. One side features a full city map, the other side includes an expanded city center map, a walking map of Nevskiy prospekt, a metro and regional map. All this plus a feature and city street index! For hanging at home or the office, be sure to order the laminated version. Second edition. (Russian Information Services; ISBN 1-880100-34-7; $6.95; 1996)

Reference

Baltic Information Business Directory. This is the best and most current business and travel directory to the three Baltic states available. Includes phone, fax and address information on government offices, important businesses, service enterprises and entertainment for each of the three republics, plus a nice collection of useful travel phrases. (New Horizons Trading Network; $14.00; 320 pp.; 1994)

CIS Publishing Guides to the Former Soviet Union, A series of five guides, each updated twice annually, to important sectors of the FSU economies: Foreign Transport Guide, Capital Markets Guide, Banking Guide, Oil & Gas Guide, Telecommunications Guide. Each guide offers extensive company directories, plus essays on investment in the sector (CIS Technical Publishing Institute; $390 per volume, or $680 per year per guide).

Jobs in Russia and the Newly Independent States, by Moira Forbes. This one-of-a-kind guide provides essential information on finding work in Russia and the NIS. It surveys current and emerging opportunities in more than 25 employment areas, from advertising to communications, from banking to law, teaching to health care. It also *includes useful tips on traveling to and living in the region, general tips on useful approaches to finding work there and how to contact major international employers (complete with contact information). (Impact Publications; ISBN 1-57023-004-8; $15.95; 235 pp.; 1994)*

Major Ports of the Russian Far East. *A reference resource on the RFE's nine major ports, with maps, contact information, information on port specialization, infrastructure and regional trends. (Russian Far East Update; $49.00; 12 pp.; 1994)*

Petroleum Business Handbook for the Former Soviet Union, by Joseph A. Kliger. *Outlines the 'do's and don'ts' for doing business in this sector. Some 100 real-life examples covering everything from dress to discourse. (Pennwell Books; ISBN 0-87814-428-5; $64.95; 180 pp.; 1994)*

Russian Far East Directory. *The all-new edition of this city-by-city yellow pages type business directory to the Russian Far East helps you find everything from hotels to foreign businesses, railway stations to stock exchanges, banks to barbers, airlines to translators. Includes easy-to-read English language maps of all major cities featured, plus regional maps and quadrilingual (English, Russian, Korean, Japanese) headings, this is a vital business or travel resource for the Russian Far East. Cities covered: Birobidzhan, Khabarovsk, Kholmsk, Korsakov, Magadan, Nakhodka, Okha, Petropavlovsk-Kamchatsky, Port Vanino, Sovetskaya Gavan, Vladivostok, Yelizovo, Yuzhno-Sakhalinsk. (Register Inc.; $20.00; 216 pp.; 1995)*

Russian Regions Today: Atlas of the Russian Federation. *Basic, raw data is often the most difficult to find on Russia. This new reference work provides a wealth of new and useful material not elsewhere available. It is a region-by-region survey of the Russian Federation, with overview essays and regional maps for each of the 88 administrative divisions. Includes, for each town in each region, data on: population, longitude and latitude, postal codes, industrial output and workforce. There is also an exhaustive index to the towns listed. (Russian Info and Business Center; $149.00; 400 pp.; 1995) The publisher also has a full range of industrial directories on Russia, plus a CD-ROM,* **Russian Regional Explorer** *which provides most all the information of Russian Regions Today for $169.*

The Cambridge Encyclopedia of Russia and the Former Soviet Union, Archie Brown, et al eds. *Over 130 scholars contributed to this voluminous work that covers history, art, politics, language, culture, warfare, society and much more. Divided topically and indexed meticulously, the book allows the reader to easily locate and investigate areas of individual interest. (Cambridge University Press; ISBN 0-521-35593-1; $49.95; 592 pp.; 1994)*

The Interflo Index of Organizations Doing Business in the FSU, 7/89-9/94. *An invaluable index to over five years of business activity in the FSU. A company-by-company listing referenced to abstracts from Interflo newsletter (see Periodicals section). Also available on disk for $125. (Paul Surovell; $75.00; 173 pp.; 1994)*

The Ross Register of Siberian Industry, Robert E. Ross, ed. *Siberia forms a critical part of Russian industry. This is a detailed reference directory of 450 large Siberian enterprises, including contact information, list of major products produced and export activity. It also includes a very useful introductory description of Siberia, its mineral wealth and the factors influencing its future development. (Norman Ross Publishing, Inc.; ISBN 0-88354-125-4; $119.00; 180 pp.; 1995)*

The Russian Far East: A Business Reference Guide, Elisa Miller, ed. *Packed with critical information. Informative tables and graphs give exclusive economic statistics on natural resources, population, industry and construction, communications and trans-*

portation, quality of life, agriculture and trade. There are maps by district, listings of RFE officials, a history of the RFE, an exclusive chapter on Russian business law, and city maps for major RFE cities. Also contains chapters on travel and communications for the business traveler. (Russian Far East Update; ISBN 0-9641286-1-6; $37.50; 260 pp.; 1996)

Travel Guides

An Explorer's Guide to Moscow, by Robert Greenall. *This new volume by the Managing Editor of* Russian Life *magazine is ideal for the first time and frequent traveler alike. Oriented to the cost-conscious and independent-minded traveler, this book gives you plenty of survival information (from food to visas), plus the historical and travel information you need to understand what you are seeing. (Zephyr Press; ISBN 0-939010-51-8; $14.95; 272 pp.; 8/95)*

An Explorer's Guide to Russia, by Robert Greenall. *This is a current and useable guide to the 'Heart of Russia.' For those traveling to the Western regions of Russia and seeking to escape bland tours and overpriced accommodations, this is the ticket. Includes useful tourist and travel information (including B&B info) for some 20 cities and regions, from Murmansk to Ryazan, including maps and reference information. (Zephyr Press; ISBN 0-939010-41-0; $17.95; 416 pp.; 1994)*

Central Asia: The Practical Handbook, by Giles Whittell. *The first guide to independent travel to the new republics of Central Asia. Wonderfully designed and packed with essential tourist information, the book also features color country and region maps, walking maps for major cities, useful words and phrases in the local tongues, and all the historical and cultural information you'll need. (The Globe Pequot Press; ISBN 1-56440-227-4; $15.95; 330 pp.; 1993)*

Knopf Guide to St. Petersburg. *A compact, colorful, artistic and engaging guide to Russia's Imperial City. An ideal gift for someone who has or will be traveling to St. Petersburg, this book is a treat to pore over. Each colorful and information-rich page of this handsome guide is full of history, colorful social and cultural details and invaluable travel information. (Random House, Inc.; ISBN 0-679-76202-7; $25.00; 324 pp.; 1995)*

Russia by River, by Howard Shernoff & Tanya Samofalova. *River cruises between St. Petersburg and Moscow are one of the best ways to see Russia. With this book, the traveler has detailed descriptions of all the stops along the way, inclusive of history, places to see, plus an "inside scoop" on each locale, providing insider information on seeing the hidden side of Russia. (Russia By River; ISBN 5-87490-007-1; $13.00; 208 pp.; 1995)*

The Russian Far East, by Erik & Allegra Harris Azulay. *A brand-new, comprehensive travel guide to this wild and intriguing region of Russia. Complete with maps, walking tours for major cities, descriptions and ratings of accommodations, tips for restaurant-hunting and getting around, and details on the best sites to see and how. (Hippocrene Books, Inc.; ISBN 0-7818-0325-X; $18.95; 250 pp.; 1995)*

The Trans-Siberian Rail Guide, by Robert Strauss. *The ultimate guide to the ultimate train ride, just released in a new 4th edition. This book is crammed full of facts and information on traveling the several lines of the trans-sib. Contains easy-to-follow strip maps of railway routes, essential Russian, Mongolian and Chinese phrases, traveler's anecdotes from the turn of the century to the present day, essential information on gateways to the trans-sib and useful tips on security, officialdom, climate, food and much more. (Compass Star; ISBN 0-9520900-0-7; $17.95; 275 pp.; 1995)*

Where in Moscow. *Where can the Westerner in Moscow take their dry cleaning, find accounting and legal advice, rent a car, or buy a tennis racket? All at an acceptable level of quality and service? Turn to this pathbreaking guide to find out. Includes concise and invaluable yellow and white pages directory information to the essential goods and services that business people, students and independent travelers need. Address, phone and fax numbers are listed for each entry, and a newly-updated 30-page indexed city street map helps you find what you need. No other resource is as current, comprehensive or easy to use. (Russian Information Services; ISBN 1-880100-31-2; $13.50; 248 pp.; 1996)*

Where in St. Petersburg. *Featured in Travel & Leisure Magazine for being the first-ever yellow pages for St. Petersburg, the current edition of this pathbreaking guide contains more information and is designed to give you a better handle on Russia's fast-changing second city than any other city guide. Includes yellow and white page directories, a bilingual metro map, and a colorful city street map — with all three elements cross-referenced, putting all the essential information in one handsome, easy-to-access package. A must for independent travelers. (Russian Information Services; ISBN 1-880100-32-0; $13.50; 176 pp.; 1996)*

PERIODICALS

This section is restricted to periodicals which mainly or exclusively focus on the former Soviet Union, with particular reference to business and travel issues. Thus, unless they have a particular bearing on business, travel and trade activity, they are excluded.

Publications are sorted by subject category. Each listing cites frequency of the publication, its average length, and the price for an annual subscription, unless otherwise stated. Ordering information is also provided.

Agriculture

AgExporter. Superintendent of Documents, ATTN: AGEXPORTER, PO Box 371954, Pittsburgh, PA 15250-7954, ph. 202-783-3238, fax 202-512-2250. *Monthly agricultural trade magazine, providing information on overseas trade opportunities, reports on marketing activities, and how-tos of agricultural exporting. ($18; Monthly; 50 pp.)*

Agriculture Report. Interfax-US News Agency, 1675 Larimer, Ste. #600, Denver, CO 80202, ph. 303-825-1510, fax 303-825-1513. *A weekly round-up of news from Russia and the CIS on Agriculture issues. ($160; Weekly; 4 pp.)*

World Perspectives: AG Review. World Perspectives, Inc., 1150 18th St., N.W., Suite 275, Washington, DC 20036, ph. 202-785-3345, fax 202-659-6891. *An extensive and current analysis of US agriculture policy and international agriculture market trends. Aimed at agri-business, government and institutional readers. ($495; Monthly; 40 pp.)*

Construction & Real Estate

Construction Market Intelligence: Russia. R.S. Means Company, 100 Construction Plaza, PO Box 800, Kingson, MA 02364, ph. 617-585-7880, fax 617-585-7099, email <tomdion3@aol.com>. *A bimonthly newsletter on the risks and rewards of working in the Russian real estate and construction markets. Includes loads of data, projections and trade show information. Shorter on news items. ($195; Bimonthly; 8 pp.)*

Eurobuild Russia. Bredgade 35B, Copenhagen, Denmark, ph. 45-33-162-100, fax 45-33-162-700, email <ecr@cybernet.dk>. *Covering the Russian real estate scene. ($60 per month; Monthly)*

The Moscow Report. The Western Group, 3400 Peachtree Rd., NE, Ste 635, 3715 Northside Parkway, Atlanta, GA 30326, ph. 404-816-9775, fax 404-816-9795, email <7232323@mcimail.com>. *A free publication focusing on real-estate related issues. Covers corporate real estate market opportunities. (Free; Irreg.; 10 pp.)*

The Redee Report (7 Reports, by country). Interforum Services, Ltd., 565 Fulham Road, London, SW6 1ES UK, ph. 44-71-386-9322, fax 44-71 381-8914. *Special reports on the real estate markets of the countries of Russia and Eastern Europe. Prices and recency vary.*

Conversion & Military

Conversion. Center for Int'l Security and Arms Control, Stanford University, Galvez House, 320 Galvez Street, Stanford, CA 94305-6165, ph. 415-723-9344, fax 415-723-0089, email <jlehrer@leland.stanford.edu>. *A good concise daily overview of political and economic events, reviewing both Western and Eastern media and sources. Also includes daily exchange rates for the ruble. (Free; Quarterly; 16 pp.)*

Military Parade. Zigzag Venture Group, Olympic Tower East, 645 Fifth Avenue, 7th Floor, New York, NY 10022, ph. 212-725-6700, fax 212-725-6915. *Illustrated information and analyses of Russian military and defense production, including technical data related to conversion and development of the aerospace industry. ($360; Bi-monthly; 200 pp.)*

Post-Soviet Nuclear & Defense Monitor. Exchange Monitor Publications, 1826 Jefferson Place NW, #100, Washington, DC 20016, ph. 800-776-1314, fax 202-296-2805, email <72254.1457@compuserve.com>. *A good roundup of industry-specific news, government contracts on offer and lots of good news in brief. ($595; Biweekly; 20 pp.)*

Employment

Home and Away. Home and Away, Expats House, 29 Lacon Road, East Dulwich, London SE22 9HE, England, ph. 81-299-4986, fax 81-299-2484. *Expatriate news monthly for those who are, or would like to be, working outside their native land. Includes international job listings. ($150; Monthly; 1000 listings)*

International Employment Gazette. International Employment Gazette, 220 North Main Street, Suite 100, Greenville, SC 29601, ph. 800-882-9188, fax 864-235-3369. *A bi-weekly listing of jobs available overseas. ($95; Bi-weekly; 64 pp.)*

Overseas Employment Newsletter. Overseas Employment Services, PO Box 460, Mount Royal, Quebec H3P 3C7, Canada, ph. 514-739-1108, fax 514-739-0795. *Covers over 300 international jobs every two weeks. The company also offers a line of related books. ($105; Biweekly; 16-18 pp.)*

Finance & Securities

Capital Markets Report. Independent Media, ul. Vyborgskaya 16, Moscow, ph. +7-095-232-9272, fax +7-095-232-1769. *Weekly, up-to-the-minute coverage of developments in the debt, equity and currency markets, from the people that bring you The*

Moscow Times *and* Russia Review. *New investment opportunities, investment funds, jvs and privatization sales are all covered in great detail. ($1,495; Weekly; 8 pp.)*

Russia Portfolio. Global Investor Publishing, 50 Follen Street, Suite 216, Cambridge, MA 02138, ph. 617-864-4999, fax 617-864-4942, email <75107.2343@compuserve.com>. *A comprehensive overview of activity in the Russian securities market. Offers solid data and mainly brief news items — easy to digest in an hour or so. Early warnings of stock and bond issues, updates on securities laws and regulations, company news and more. ($1,195; Biweekly; 16-20 pp.)*

The Russian Companies Service. CIS Information Publishing, 11-13 Charterhouse Buildings, London, EC1M 7AN, ph. 44-171-490-3774, fax 44-171-490-5371. *The first compendium of independent company profiles. At roll-out, included in-depth financial information on 150 top Russian companies, with more to come and updates to existing information every 2 months. ($1,195; B-monthly updates)*

General & Business

BISNIS Bulletin. US Department of Commerce, Room 7413, US Dept. of Commerce, 14th & Constitution Ave., NW, Washington, DC 20230, ph. 202-482-4655, fax 202-482-2293. *These two free publications of the Department of Commerce contain useful information on government programs, legal developments, calendars of upcoming events, financing information, etc. on the NIS (Newly Independent States). Search for Partners contains lists of NIS firms seeking partnership with US investors, and contains full contact and some background information on the firm. (Free; 4-8 pp.)*

BNA's Eastern Europe Reporter. Bureau of National Affairs, Inc., 1231 25th St., NW, Washington, DC 20037, ph. 202-452-4577, fax 202-452-7583, email <beer@bna.com>. *A very comprehensive and high-quality bi-weekly publication, EER features much in-country reporting and a unique and useful governmental perspective. Reporting often features input and reactions from government officials and private practitioners. A 'deals concluded' section covers the whole region and the publication features full texts of important legislation. ($895; Twice-monthly, indexed; 40 pp.)*

Business America. US GPO, International Trade Association, 14th & Constitution Ave., NW, #3418, Washington, DC 20230, ph. 202-482-3251, fax 202-482-5819. *General interest publication on exporting which frequently provides useful information on US trade policies as well as contact information and listings of conferences and trade shows. Frequently covers Russia. ($43; Monthly ($53.75 foreign))*

Business Eastern Europe. Business International, 111 West 57th Street, New York, NY 10019, ph. 212-554-0600, fax 212-586-0248. *A pricey weekly publication which focuses on the entire region, utilizing the broad resources available to Business International and the Economist Intelligence Unit. Includes spotlights on certain industries, profiles, consideration of legal, taxation and economic issues and even some business travel. ($1,100; Weekly; 12 pp.)*

Business Update Russia. Broadfax S.A., 59 Route des Jeunes, 1227 Geneva, Switzerland, ph. 41-22-300-2951, fax 41-22-300-2948. *A concise, top-of-the-news, single-page, twice-weekly fax letter that covers business, politics, legal developments and statistics. Exchange rates and commodity prices are also provided. A good way to keep on top of the latest developments without drowning in information. ($690; Twice weekly; 1 pp.)*

Central European. Euromoney Publications, Nestor House, Playhouse Yard, London EC4V 5EX, ENGLAND, ph. 71-779-8597, fax 71-779-8689. *A monthly magazine covering business and finance (mainly the latter) in Central and Eastern Europe. A mix of brief focus articles and shorter 'deals done' pieces. Also features brief announcements of new joint ventures. ($460; 10 issues/year; 40-80 pp.)*

Central European Economic Review. Wall Street Journal Europe, Blvd. Brand Whitlock 87, Brussels, 1200 BELGIUM, ph. 32-2-741-1211, fax 32-2-732-1102. *This tabloid-sized publication covers the region with the depth and style you'd expect from the Wall Street Journal. Readable, informative articles and useful data, at a price that won't break the bank. ($95; 10 issues/year; 38 pp.)*

Cold War International History Project Bulletin. Woodrow Wilson Center, 1000 Jefferson Drive, SW, Washington, DC 20560, ph. 202-357-2967, fax 202-357-4439. *A suberb periodic publication that catalogs and publishes some of the most interesting materials just uncovered from Soviet archives. (Free; Irreg.)*

Commersant Weekly (in Russian). WorldTrade Executive, PO Box 761, Concord, MA 01742, ph. 508-287-0301, fax 508-287-0302, email <73361.3427@ compuserve.com>. *Russia's leading business daily also produces a weekly edition (in Russian, of course). Covers all aspects of business and commerce, with the distinctively irreverent style that has made Commersant famous. ($425; Weekly; 24 pp.)*

Countertrade Outlook. DP Publications, Box 7188, Fairfax Station, VA 22039, ph. 703-425-1322, fax 703-425-7911. *Provides intelligence on financing trade, projects and opportunity finance in Russia and other forex-short markets through such reciprocal trade forms as barter, counterpurchase, buyback, clearing, switch, build-operate-transfer, debt-for-equity swaps, offset, etc. ($488; 24 issues/yr.; 8 pp.)*

Country Report: Russia. Economist Intelligence Unit, 111 West 57th Street, New York, NY 10019, ph. 212-554-0600, fax 212-586-0248. *A quarterly round-up of political, foreign policy and economic developments in the Commonwealth. Astute and cogent analyses, with clear presentations of economic information. More space given to larger economic and political issues, less to business developments. Subscription also includes country profile. Economist also publishes three other Country Reports, on the Baltics, Central Asia and Ukraine. ($315; Quarterly; 25-40 pp.)*

Current Digest of the Post-Soviet Press. Current Digest of the Post-Soviet Press, 3857 N. High St., Columbus, OH 43214, ph. 614-292-4234, fax 614-267-6310, email <sgoodric@osu.edu>. *A weekly publication which translates articles from the Russian and Commonwealth press and/or abstracts them. The translations are specifically intended for teaching and research, and although translations typically appear about 6 weeks after publication in Russia. Indexed quarterly. ($850; Weekly; 20-40 pp.)*

Current Russian Press. Panorama of Russia, PO Box 44-1658A, Somerville, MA 02144, ph. 617-625-3635, fax 617-628-0338, email <panoramrus@aol.com>. *A monthly journal which is an index of articles appearing in the most important Russian journals and newspapers. ($220; Monthly; 310 pp.)*

Daily Report on Russia and the Former Soviet Republics. Intercon International, 888 17th Street NW, Suite 1200, Washington, DC 20006, ph. 800-348-7519, email <75144.3347@compuserve.com>. *A good concise business daily overview of political and economic events, reviewing both Western and Eastern media and sources. Also includes daily exchange rates for the ruble and a monthly editorial by former KGB Major General (ret.) Oleg Kalugin. ($895; Daily by fax ($495 by mail weekly); 4 pp.)*

Delovie Lyudi. 1560 Broadway, Ste. 511, New York, NY 10036, ph. 212-221-6700, fax 212-221-6997. *A monthly magazine that covers the Russian/CIS business scene. ($85; Monthly; 100 pp.)*

East European Investment Magazine. Dixon & Co., 119 Fifth Ave., 8th Floor, New York, NY 10003, ph. 212-388-1500, fax 212-254-3386. *Covering the entire region, including the former Soviet Union, this magazine includes articles on finance, conversion, trade and investment. But the majority of the publication is given over to a listing of deals done, joint ventures signed, acquisitions and other new foreign investments in the region. Publishes much important data not available elsewhere. ($580; Quarterly; 250 pp.)*

East European Statistics Service. East-West SPRL, 10 Boulevard Saint-Lazare, 1210 Brussels, BELGIUM, ph. 02-218-4349, fax 02-218-1985. *Trade and economic statistics on EE and the FSU. ($355; Monthly; 12 pp.)*

East-West Business Analyst. Debos Oxford Publications, Ltd., Kennett House, Suite 2, 108-110 London Road, Oxford, OX3 9 AW ENGLAND. *As the title indicates, this monthly publication focuses on all of Eastern Europe. Typically an issue focuses on a single country and is very 'econometric' in approach, relying on presentation of tables and graphs, as well as several pages of news. ($125; Monthly; 8-10 pp.)*

East-West Business and Trade. Welt Publishing, 14 W. Mount Vernon Place, Baltimore, MD 21201, ph. 800-898-4685, fax 410-783-8438. *One of the oldest periodicals in the field, this bi-weekly has a distinctive 'deals concluded' format. Concise and very eclectic in the news items it covers. Lots of brief news items. ($459; Biweekly; 8-12 pp.)*

East-West Fortnightly Bulletin. East-West SPRL, 10 Boulevard Saint-Lazare, 1210 Brussels, BELGIUM, ph. 02-218-4349, fax 02-218-1985. *Mainly a listing of deals done and overviews of general business news and developments. Heavily weighted to coverage of Eastern Europe, but also covers Russia and the FSU. ($1,250; Bi-weekly; 16 pp.)*

East-West Investment News. Economic Commission for Europe, United Nations, Palais des Nations, CH 1211 Geneva 10, SWITZERLAND, ph. 41-22-917-2364, fax 41-22-917-0036. *Monitors and analyzes legislative acts and other regulations on foreign investors' access to and activities in the countries of Central and Eastern Europe. Also contains statistical reports on foreign investment in the region, reviews of recent publications and announcements of upcoming meetings of interest to investors. ($80; Quarterly)*

East/West Commersant. WorldTrade Executive, PO Box 761, Concord, MA 01742, ph. 508-287-0301, fax 508-287-0302, email <73361.3427@compuserve.com>. *This 12-page biweekly offers exclusive English language translations from Commersant (see above for Russian version), plus details of the latest business transactions in all areas of EE and the FSU. ($425; Biweekly; 20 pp.)*

East/West Executive Guide. WorldTrade Executive, PO Box 761, Concord, MA 01742, ph. 508-287-0301, fax 508-287-0302, email <73361.3427@ compuserve.com>. *Each bi-weekly issue is packed with detailed information on doing business in Russia, with a concerted emphasis on the 'how-to's'. Excellent coverage of privatization, legal developments and the business climate. Much of the content is comprised of contributions by practicing professionals. ($596; Monthly; 40 pp.)*

East/West Letter. Okno Group, 1217 Olivia Avenue, Ann Arbor, MI 48104-3934, ph. 313-995-5934, fax 313-995-5934, email <info@okno.com>, web <www.msn.com/~okno>. *A mix of long and short analytical articles, data and news briefs on* *business and politics throughout Eastern Europe and the former USSR. ($40; Bimonthly; 16 pp.)*

Eastern Europe Finance. DP Publications, Box 7188, Fairfax Station, VA 22039, ph. 703-425-1322, fax 703-425-7911. *A very good biweekly publication devoted to money and money-related issues in Eastern Europe and the FSU, with particular emphasis on currencies, trade, finance, banking and insurance. Updates on who is getting money from World Bank, EBRD, other sources public and private, and for what ends. ($437; Bi-weekly; 8-16 pp.)*

Eastern Europe Monitor. Business Monitor International, Ltd., 56-60 St. John Street, London, EC1M 4DT England, ph. 71-608-3646, fax 71-608-3620. *A bimonthly overview of the region on a country-by-country basis. ($395; Monthly; 12 pp.)*

Eastern European Markets. Financial Times Newsletters, 14 East 60th Street, Penthouse, New York, NY 10022, ph. 212-888-3469, fax 201-729-9598. *Consists of mainly medium length articles, analyzing events and deals concluded. Focuses on the entire region. Has a nice back-page feature chronicling events of the past two weeks in the region. ($870; Biweekly; 16 pp.)*

Economic Life of the Russian Far East. Marketing Data Research, 8103 104th St., SW, Tacoma, WA 98498, ph. 206-588-4149, fax 206-588-4366, email <mktg@ ix.netcom.com>. *Focuses on market developments in the Russian Far East, including product availability and prices. Contains market leads and is available in print or email form. ($340; Weekly; 7-10 pp.)*

Ecotass. ITAR-TASS USA, Inc., 50 Rockefeller Plaza, Ste 501, New York, NY 10020, ph. 212-664-0977, fax 212-245-4035. *Authoritative weekly summary of the leading Russian wire service. Available by mail, fax or email. ($150; Weekly; 25 pp.) Also available:* **Ecotass Daily** *($250; Daily; 35 pp.)*

Export Finance Weekly. Trade Reports International Group, 2104 National Press Building, NW, Washington, DC 20045, ph. 301-946-0817, fax 301-946-2631. *Brief articles on country-related finance issues, plus xerox copies of ExImBank minutes (announcing various guarantees). ($475; Weekly; 12 pp.)*

FBIS Daily Reports: Central Eurasia. NTIS, 5285 Port Royal Road, Springfield, VA 22161, ph. 703-487-4630. *This daily compendium of translations from the Russian and Commonwealth press and media provides a wealth of useful information for the specialist, but will drown you in information if you do not have the time to get through it all (Interflo, abstracted below, reviews the contents of this for its subscribers). Also available is a publication called simply Central Eurasia, which is published twice weekly and costs $550/yr. ($625; Daily)*

Finance Eastern Europe. Financial Times Newsletters, 14 East 60th Street, Penthouse, New York, NY 10022, ph. 212-888-3469, fax 201-729-9598. *Reporting the financial side of reforms and business developments in the region. Excellent analytical reportage and current citings of deals done. ($700; Biweekly; 16-20 pp.)*

Financing Foreign Operations: Russia. Business International, 111 West 57th Street, New York, NY 10019, ph. 212-554-0600, fax 212-586-0248. *A review of the political and economic environment plus detailed financial information and advice on foreign exchange regulations, sources of capital, short-, medium- and long-term financing techniques, equity financing, capital incentives, cash management, trade finance and insurance. ($150; Twice-yearly; 25 pp.)*

Glas: New Russian Writing. Zephyr Press, 13 Robinson Street, Somerville, MA 02145, ph. 617-628-9726, fax 617-776-8246, email <edhogan@world.std.com>.

The best, most current Russian fiction in translation. Editions come out 2-3 times a year and cost $9.95 to $13.95 apiece. Subscriptions also available.

Global Forecasting Service. Economist Intelligence Unit, 111 West 57th Street, New York, NY 10019, ph. 212-554-0600, fax 212-586-0248. *A wide range of quality information products are published periodically by EIU and its American partner, Business International. These include Global Forecasting Service, Country Risk Service, Regional Reference, and Offices and Agencies in Eastern Europe. They also publish one-off research studies of certain sectors of the Russian/FSU economy and/or analyses of investment options. On the whole, the quality of the analyses is quite high, with prices to match.*

Interfax News Bulletin. Interfax-US News Agency, 1675 Larimer, Ste. #600, Denver, CO 80202, ph. 303-825-1510, fax 303-825-1513. *A daily fax news service covering economic and political news from around the CIS. Interfax publishes three other daily bulletins: Daily Business Report, Diplomatic Panorama and Baltnews, costing $240 and $210 per month, respectively. Interfax also publishes nine weekly journals: Weekly Business Report, Petroleum Report, Mining Report, Agriculture Report, Financial Report, Viewpoint, Ukraine Business Review, Statistical Report, and Business Laws. Each sells for $160-250 monthly, with an extra charge for fax delivery. All are informed by Interfax correspondents spread throughout the FSU. Discounts for multiple and long-term subscriptions. ($290/month; Daily)*

Interflo. Paul Surovell, P.O. Box 42, Maplewood, NJ 07040, ph. 201-763-9493, fax 201-763-9493. *For over 10 years, Interflo has been the leading chronicler of deals done, contracts concluded and trade conducted in the FSU. This is a monthly overview of usually 250+ articles from journal articles, wire services, press releases and government publications. Unquestionably one of the best periodical values on the market. Also includes excerpts or full reprints of short legal acts or US government compiled economic data of interest. Available on floppy disk for $424 per year. ($172; Monthly; 30-40 pp.)*

International Economic Review. US International Trade Commission, Office of Economics, Trade Reports Division, 500 E St. SW, Washington, DC 20436, ph. 202-205-3270, fax 202-205-2340. *Focuses more generally on international economic issues and trends, but also covers events and trends in Russia and the CIS. Also issues quarterly report on trade with the former Eastern Bloc and China. (Free; Monthly; 12-16 pp.)*

Mars. Metro Area Russian Services, P.O. Box 53305, Washington, DC 20009. *With a specific focus on Russophiles in the Baltimore and DC area, this monthly is gossipy and light. Sometimes has job opportunities listed. Its 'Beets and Pieces' section features useful tidbits for persons living in the DC area. ($20; Monthly; 8 pp.)*

Moscow Letter, The. Interforum Services, Ltd., 565 Fulham Road, London, SW6 1ES UK, ph. 44-71-386-9322, fax 44-71 381-8914. *A collection of short news items, a few longer articles and directory info related to business and travel in Moscow. ($330; Monthly; 8 pp.)*

Moscow Times Russia Review, see **Russia Review**

Ost-Markt. GSA Publications, Box 430, Bound Brook, NJ 08805, ph. 908-457-9070, fax 908-457-0908. *A new English language monthly newsletter, based on the German newsletter of the same name. Short news items and notes on deals done. ($345; Monthly; 12 pp.)*

Passport to the New World. Zigzag Venture Group, Olympic Tower East, 645 Fifth Avenue, 7th Floor, New York, NY 10022, ph. 212-725-6700, fax 212-725-6915. *A thick and glossy bi-monthly with beautiful photography and informative directories.*

Which makes up for roughly-edited text that is often a near literal translation from Russian. ($70; Bi-monthly; 200 pp.)

PlanEcon Business Report. PlanEcon, 1111 - 14th St., NW, Suite 801, Washington, DC 20005-5603, ph. 202-898-0471, fax 202-898-0445. *This bi-monthly newsletter focuses on the entire Eastern Europe and Commonwealth region with sections on privatization, legislation, the economy and foreign trade. Industry by industry reportage of developments and deals. Includes a modicum of economic data. PlanEcon also publishes two specialized quarterly publications, PlanEcon Energy Report and PlanEcon Chemical Report, which are 60-80 pages in length and sell for $800/yr, and a semiannual publication, PlanEcon Review and Outlook, which summarizes economic performance and forecasts for the future on a country-by-country basis, typically devoting 20-40 pages to each country and selling for $850 per country, $1500 for Russia. PlanEcon Report focuses on major macroeconomic and trade developments throughouth Eastern Europe and the CIS and is of most interest to academics. Typically, each 30-40 page issue will focus on particular countries or sectors and treat them in great detail. ($1600) ($800; Bi-monthly; 20 pp.)*

Political and Economic Update. The Atlantic Council of the United States, 910 17th Street, NW, Suite 1000, Washington, DC 20006, ph. 202-463-7226, fax 202-463-7241, email <info@acgate.acus.org>. *Examines the current political dynamics and economic trends in Russia, Ukraine and other FSU countries. ($4; Quarterly; 4 pp.)*

Problems of Economic Transition. M.E. Sharpe, Inc., 80 Business Park Drive, Armonk, NY 10504, ph. 914-273-1800, fax 914-273-2106. *A compilation of articles by and interviews with economists and policy-makers on the nature and direction of economic reform in Russia, translated from the Russian. ($725; Monthly; 96 pp.)*

Problems of Post-Communism. M.E. Sharpe, Inc., 80 Business Park Drive, Armonk, NY 10504, ph. 914-273-1800, fax 914-273-2106. *A bimonthly analysis of politics, economics and international issues, as they impinge on the former communist states. The journal, which took up the baton from Problems of Communism, has a somewhat academic tone, but certainly not a weighty one, and offers excellent treatment of important political issues in particular. ($45; Bimonthly; 64 pp.)*

Russia Briefing. Eastern Europe Newsletter, 87 Duke Road, London W4 2BW, UK, ph. 081-995-3860, fax 081-747-8802. *Political and economic analyses of the events and players shaping the Russian scene. Invaluable profiles of individuals, articles on special topics and readable synopses of recent events. ($505; Monthly; 14-18 pp.)*

Russia Express Executive Briefing & Russia Express Contracts. International Industrial Information, Ltd., PO Box 12, Montmouth, Gwent NP5 3YL, UK, ph. 1-600-890-274, fax 1-600-890-774. *This bi-weekly includes a few in-depth articles, but the majority of the publication focuses on shorter blurbs. Also a list of new opportunities and upcoming trade and exhibition events. Included is a subscription to Russia Express Contracts, a monthly upcoming trade and exhibition events. Included is a subscription to Russia Express Contracts, a monthly update to a huge database of trade opportunities, grouped by 100 project classifications under eleven major headings. ($600; Bi-weekly; 28-32 pp.)*

Russia: A Country Report. Political Risk Services, 6320 Fly Rd., Ste 102, PO Box 248, Syracuse, NY 13057-0248, ph. 315-431-0511, fax 315-431-0200, email <polrisk@aol.com>, web <www.polrisk.com>. *This country report offers unparalleled political and economic risk forecasting by the world's largest private-sector network of country risk analysts. Each report features up-to-date political, economic and*

The ✤ Moscow Times

PUBLISHED BY INDEPENDENT PRESS © 1992

If it's not in The Moscow Times, it's not in the news.

The Moscow Times is Russia's favorite English language daily newspaper, providing accurate and detailed information of all the latest news from Moscow and abroad.

The ✤ Moscow Times
Капитал

The paper every professional Russian is reading

Kapital is a weekly Russian language newspaper printed every Wednesday. It covers all aspects of business and success, from news and company profiles to Management techniques and Job Opportunities. If you want the best, you want Kapital.

For more information about subscriptions and advertising in The Moscow Times & Kapital, please call us at 913-2937/49/40/41/42/43/44/45, or fax us at 913-2938/46

demographic data, 12-month chronological listings of events critical to business, pertinent geographic and histrorical details, profiles of political actors, 18-month forecasts of business conditions and five-year political and economic forecasts. ($335; Yearly; 50 pp.)

Russia Review, *In North America:* RIS Publications, 89 Main St., Ste 2, Montpelier, VT 05602, ph. 802-223-4955, fax 802-223-6105, email <73244.3372@ compuserve.com>; *In Europe/Asia:* Novamedia, Van Eeghenstraat 93, 171 EX Amsterdam, Holland, ph. 31-20-664-0978, fax 31-20-676-0701, email <nova@euronet.nl>; *In Russia:* Independent Media, ul. Vyborgskaya 16, ph. 095-232-9272, fax 232-1769 *The definitive business newsmagazine on Russia. Forty-eight pages every two weeks of business news, stock market indicators, political and social news impinging on business and more. Includes some reportage from the daily edition of the Moscow Times, but mainly stories exclusive to this publication — stories focused on business success and how it is being achieved in Russia. If you only get one subscription publication on business in Russia, this should be it. ($295; Biweekly; 48 pp.)*

Russian and East European Finance and Trade. M.E. Sharpe, Inc., 80 Business Park Drive, Armonk, NY 10504, ph. 914-273-1800, fax 914-273-2106. *Compendiums of academic-style articles, translated from Russian and East European journals, covering issues related to international trade, finance and reform in the former Comecon states. ($572; Bimonthly; 100 pp.)*

Russian Commerce News. Russian-American Chamber of Commerce, 3025 South Parker Road, Ste 735, Aurora, CO 80014, ph. 303-745-0757, fax 303-745-0776, email <russianbus@aol.com>. *Profiles of members, announcements of the Chamber's activities and coverage of topical issues related to business and trade to Russia. Free to members. (Free; Quarterly; 28 pp.)*

Russian Customs News and **Russian Customs Tariffs Service.** CIS Information Publishing, 800 Summer St., Ste 315, Stamford, CT 06901, ph. +44-1424-774-433, fax +44-1424-773-334. *The former is a monthly, 8-page newsletter covering the month's developments in the Russian customs environment. The latter is a continually updated listing of goods with their customs tarriffs, with commentary. ($595 and $1770/yr; Monthly; 8 pp.)*

Russian Far East News. Alaska Center for International Business, Business Education Bldg. 203, 3211 Providence Drive, Anchorage, AK 99508, ph. 907-786-4300, fax 907-486-4319, email <74164.1345@compuserve.com>. *Focused exclusively on the Russian Far East, this concise monthly is organized by region and industry. Coverage includes politics and business as well as environmental and native issues, from a businessperson's perspective. ($100; Monthly; 12 pp.)*

Russian Far East Update. Russian Far East Update, PO Box 22126, Seattle, WA 98122, ph. 206-447-2668, fax 206-628-0979, email <rfeupdate@russianfareast. com>. *Exclusive focus on the Far Eastern regions of Russia. Unquestionably the most up-to-date and comprehensive resource for persons and companies with a specific interest in this region. Short news items as well as longer reports and special features. ($295; Monthly; 16 pp.)*

Russian Gospel Messenger. Russian Gospel Ministries, PO Box 1188, Elkhart, IN 46515, ph. 219-522-3486, fax 219-293-1932. *A free bimonthly distributed by a nonprofit Evangelical Baptist group, dedicated to relating the circumstances and experiences of the Christian church in Russia and Ukraine. (Free; Bi-monthly; 4 pp.)*

Russian Life. Russian Information Services, 89 Main Street, Suite 2, Montpelier, VT 05602, ph. 800-639-4301, fax 802-223-6105, email <73244.3372@compuserve.com>, web <www.friends-partners.org/rispubs/>. *The monthly magazine of Russian history, culture, business and travel. Celebrating its 40th anniversary in 1996, the magazine features fine feature and news stories and photo journalism on all aspects of life in the new Russia. Regular departments include Practical Traveler, Travel Journal, Russian Calendar (important events in Russian history that month), Russian Cuisine and Survival Russian – a guide to the Russian you really need to know. ($25; Monthly; 32 pp.)*

Surviving Together. ISAR, 1601 Connecticut Ave., NW, Suite 301, Washington, DC 20009, ph. 202-387-3034, fax 202-667-3291, email <isar@igc.apc.org>. *Subtitled "A Quarterly on Grassroots Cooperation in Eurasia," this is a good general information publication for the business person as well. It is a valuable resource for picking up on important events, deals and happenings occurring outside 'the mainstream'. Strong emphasis on environmental issues. ($25; Quarterly; 64 pp.)*

The Harriman Review. The Harriman Institute - Columbia University, 420 West 118th St., Rm. 1218, New York, NY 10027, ph. 212-854-8454, fax 212-666-3481. *This publication treats contemporary issues with an analytical/academic bent. Published by a leading Russian studies institute in the United States, the Forum can be counted on to be thought provoking and of a high caliber. ($35; Quarterly; 56 pp.)*

The Russia Desk (fax & email delivery). Commerce Publishing International, 4001 N 9th Street, Ste 904, Arlington, VA 22203-1962, ph. 703-524-7750, fax 703-524-1630, email <edhazelwood@interramp.com>. *A biweekly fax newsletter focusing on business opportunities and financing arrangements in civil aviation, space and defense conversion in the FSU. Lost of brief news items, plus a few longer articles in each issue. ($695; Bi-weekly; 8 pp.)*

The Siberian Business Review. Research Triangle World Trade Center, PO Box 13487, Research Triangle Park, NC 27709, ph. 919-828-7778, fax 919-828-7749, email <75453.102@compuserve.com>. *A new quarterly newsletter covering business and investment activity in the region. Includes data, notes on business travel, region profiles, calendars of events and longer feature articles. ($100; Qrtly; 8 pp.)*

The Wild East. 14 East 60th Street, Penthouse, New York, NY 10022, ph. 212-888-3469, fax 201-729-9598. *A monthly look at the practical side of doing business in Russia, with the idea being that the best business advice is that direct from the trenches. ($179; Monthly; 8 pp.)*

Together in Europe. East-West SPRL, 10 Boulevard Saint-Lazare, 1210 Brussels, BELGIUM, ph. 02-218-4349, fax 02-218-1985. *Mainly features coverage of the EU, but also some articles and data on Eastern Europe and Russia, as it impinges on the EU. ($465; Monthly; 12 pp.)*

Tracking Eastern Europe. A.M.F. International Consultants, 812 N. Wood Ave., Linden, NJ 07036, ph. 908-486-3534, fax 908-486-4084. *A collection of brief news items related to business and investment in the region, plus usually one longer piece. Heightened focus is given to Poland. Includes lists of trade events in the region, country-by-country exchange rates and investment opportunities. ($445; Biweekly; 12 pp.)*

Transition. Open Media Research Institute, Motokov Building, Na Strzi 63, 14062 Prague, 4 Pankrac, Czech Republic, ph. 42-2-6114-2114, fax 42-2-6114-3323, email <info@omri.cz>, web <www.omri.cz>. *One of the best deals going. Monthly newsletter published by the World Bank which chronicles countries of the former Eastern* *bloc making the transition to free market economies. Excellent analytical articles; more than just the clearinghouse of information on World Bank activities which the letter claims to be. ($175; Semi-monthly; 72 pp.)*

Transition. The World Bank, Policy Research Dept., Room N-1103, The World Bank, 1818 H Street, NW, Washington, DC 20433, ph. 202-473-6982, fax 202-676-0439, web <http://www.worldbank.org/html/prddr/trans/>. *One of the best deals going. Monthly newsletter published by the World Bank which chronicles countries of the former Eastern bloc making the transition to free market economies. Excellent analytical articles; more than just the clearinghouse of information on World Bank activities which the letter claims to be. (Free; Monthly; 16 pp.)*

Hi-Technology/Computers

Eastern European & Former Soviet Telecom Report. International Technology Consultants, 1724 Kalorama Rd., Ste# 210, Washington, DC 20009, ph. 202-234-2138, fax 202-483-7922. *This monthly is exactly what the title suggests. It provides a well-organized, comprehensive country by country reporting of political, regulatory and business developments and trends in the telecom, information processing and broadcasting sectors in the region. Each issue features an interview with a leading figure in the field, as well as company and country profiles. ($679; Monthly; 25 pp.)*

JPRS Serials Reports. NTIS, 5285 Port Royal Road, Springfield, VA 22161, ph. 703-487-4630. *Translations of Russian and former USSR republics' media relating to a wide range of scientific, technology, aviation and military subjects are available on a periodical basis. Prices range from $150-850 per year, with frequency of reports ranging from less than weekly to monthly. Contact NTIS for a list of current subject headings.*

Russian Telecom Newsletter. Information Gatekeepers, 214 Harvard Avenue, Boston, MA 02134, ph. 800-323-1088, fax 617-734-8562. *Tracks the history and current state of CIS telecommunications through news, features and commentary. Regular profiles of CIS companies and joint venture opportunities. ($575; Monthly)*

Legal & Accounting

Business and Commercial Laws of Russia: Translations with Expert Commentary. Shepard's/McGraw-Hill, Inc., 555 Middlecreek Pkwy, Colorado Springs, CO 80921, ph. 800-458-8811, fax 800-525-0053. *The most current, comprehensive, and authoritatively analyzed collection of post-Soviet Russian business and commercial laws. Designed to meet the real world information needs of attorneys and business people, this three volume set is arranged topically. ($840; Quarterly updates)*

Butterworth Central and East European Business Law Bulletin. Butterworth Legal Publishers, Butterworth Legal Publishers, 90 Stiles Road, Salem, NH 03079, ph. 800-544-1013, fax 603-898-9858. *This quarterly publication looks at doing business in the region from a strictly legal point of view, with equal emphasis on theoretical examinations of legal issues and developments and the practice of doing business in light of these same issues. Includes lists of recent legislation. ($385; Quarterly; 16-24 pp.)*

CIS Law Notes. Patterson, Belknap, Webb & Tyler, 1133 Avenue of the Americas, New York, NY 10036-6710, ph. 212-336-2107, fax 212-336-2222, email <pbwt@pbwt.com>. *This is a must for anyone interested in legal aspects of investment in Russia. Don't let the price fool you, this offers some of the most useful overviews of major business legislation and regulations in Russia and Eastern Europe. (Free; Bimonthly; 20-28 pp.)*

East European Business Law. Financial Times Newsletters, 14 East 60th Street, Penthouse, New York, NY 10022, ph. 212-888-3469, fax 201-729-9598. *Features extracts from recent business and trade legislation passed throughout Eastern Europe and the CIS and a modicum of commentary to illuminate the texts. With a country-by-country treatment, commentaries of recent developments are concise and useful. ($796; Monthly; 24-30 pp.)*

Intelprop News. Interforum Services, Ltd., 565 Fulham Road, London, SW6 1ES UK, ph. 44-71-386-9322, fax 44-71 381-8914. *A monthly newsletter covering intellectual property developments and legislation in Central Europe and the former Soviet Union. Includes articles contributed by Western and Eastern specialists and practitioners as well as news briefs, joint venture announcements and texts of legislation. ($390; Monthly; 12 pp.)*

Laws of the CIS: The Bottom Line. Chadbourne and Parke, 30 Rockefeller Plaza, New York, NY 10112, ph. 212-408-5190, fax 212-541-5369. *This quarterly publication (along with periodic papers) is written and edited by practicing lawyers of Chadbourne and Parke and its Russian office and can provide a useful practitioner's view. (Free; Quarterly; 8-12 pp.)*

NTIS Legal Texts: Russia and Independent States. NTIS, 5285 Port Royal Road, Springfield, VA 22161, ph. 703-487-4630, . *A selective translation service of major Russian and East European legislation. Subscribers place a deposit with NTIS and this deposit is debited when laws are translated and delivered. ($150; Irregular)*

Review of Central and East European Law. Martinus Nijhoff Publishers, Inst. of East European Law and Russian Studies, Leiden University, PO Box 921, 2300 RA Leiden, Netherlands, ph. 31-71-527-7814, fax 31-71-527-7732, email <r.verheul@law.leidenuniv.nl>. *Covers theory and practice of the legal systems of Central and Eastern Europe, including all the republics of the former USSR. ($268.50; Bi-monthly)*

Russia and Commonwealth Business Law Report. LRP Publications, Ste 140, 580 Village Blvd, West Palm Beach, FL 33409-1904, ph. 407-687-1220, fax 407-687-9410. *Each issue includes in-depth articles on timely legal topics, English texts of key documents, round-ups of recent laws and decrees in the CIS, and in-depth analysis of legal developments that affect foreign investment and business activity. ($970; Bi-weekly; 12 pp.)*

Russia and the Republics Legal Materials. Juris Publishing, Inc., One Bridge St., Irvington-on-Hudson, NY 10533, ph. 914-375-3400, fax 914-375-6047. *Translations of legislation on business, investment, taxation and trade, with digests by the editors, summarizing legal acts. ($550; Updated bimonthly; Looseleaf pp.)*

SEEL—Survey of East European Law. Juris Publishing, Inc., One Bridge St., Irvington-on-Hudson, NY 10533, ph. 914-375-3400, fax 914-375-6047. *A concise and readable monthly overview of legislative changes in the region. Includes commentaries by practicing professionals and leading academics and texts of some laws. ($295; monthly; 16-20 pp.)*

Oil/Petrochem

Russian Oil & Gas Monitor, Moscow, ph. 095-149-7245, fax 095-149-5045. *A monthly analytical overview of the industry. Covers purchase and sale activity, stock market performance, production activity and changes within the industry. ($1,000; Monthly)*

Neft i Kapital (in Russian). Russian Petroleum Investor, 18455 Burbank Blvd., Ste 310, Tarzana, CA 91356, ph. 818-343-8474, fax 818-343-8475. *Billed as a monthly analytical journal for CIS decisionmakers, this color magazine offers authoritative reading (in Russian) on Russia's oil and gas sphere. ($120; Monthly; 80 pp.)*

Nefte Compass. The Oil Daily Co., 1401 New York Ave., NW, Suite 500, Washington, DC 20005, ph. 202-662-0700, fax 202-662-0751. *A weekly briefing on the oil and gas sectors in Eastern Europe and the FSU. Good concise articles. Available by fax, mail and online. ($1,725; Weekly; 12 pp.)*

Russian Petroleum Investor. Russian Petroleum Investor, 18455 Burbank Blvd., Ste 310, Tarzana, CA 91356, ph. 818-343-8474, fax 818-343-8475. *An excellent, in-depth monthly covering the Russian oil & gas sectors, with independent reporting, interviews, data and analysis. Incisive tone and style; very readable. Unfortunately, priced for the oil specialist. ($2,500; 10 issues/yr; 60-80 pp.)*

Regional

Armenian International Magazine. The Fourth Millenium Society, PO Box 10793, Glendale, CA 91209-3793, ph. 818-246-7979, fax 818-246-0088, email <aim4@aol.com>. *A monthly magazine of Armenian culture, history and life. Covers everything from important personages (from Alex Manoogian to Andrei Agassi) to language and history, to events in Armenia and the diaspora. ($45; Monthly; 48 pp.)*

Azerbaijan International. Azerbaijan International, PO Box 5217, Sherman Oaks, CA 91413, ph. 818-785-0077, fax 818-997-7337, email <ai@artnet.net>. *A quarterly magazine covering contemporary issues and trends related to Azerbaijan. Cover international relations, business, music, science, oil etc. ($36; Quarterly; 88 pp.)*

Baltic Business Report. Baltic Ventures, Inc., 1075 Washington St., West Newton, MA 02165, ph. 617-527-2550, fax 617-527-2823, email <bvi@igc.apc.org>. *A comprehensive monthly survey of business, investment, trade and economic news for the Baltic states. Interviews, in-depth articles analyzing recent legislation and events, and industry briefs highlighting recent deals and decisions. ($260; Monthly; 12 pp.)*

Country Report: Ukraine. Political Risk Services, 6320 Fly Rd., Ste 102, PO Box 248, Syracuse, NY 13057-0248, ph. 315-431-0511, fax 315-431-0200, email <polrisk@aol.com; http://www.polrisk.com>. *See Country Report: Russia, above. ($335; Yearly; 50 pp.)*

Eastern Economist (on Ukraine). Eastern Economist, 2229 W. Iowa Street, Chicago, IL 60622, ph. 312-278-8662, fax 312-278-4051. *A business investment weekly focused on Ukraine. Profiles, news briefs and longer news and analysis. ($565; Weekly; 24 pp.)*

Raiduha. Ukrainian Business Bulletin, PO Box 30134, Cleveland, OH 44130, ph. 216-237-1721, fax 216-230-1556, email <ec525@cleveland.freenet.edu>. *General business and investment news on Ukraine, including information about legislation and deals done. ($40; Monthly; 8 pp.)*

The Kiev Letter. Interforum Services, Ltd., 565 Fulham Road, London, SW6 1ES UK, ph. 44-71-386-9322, fax 44-71 381-8914. *A monthly report on business in Ukraine. ($330; Monthly; 16 pp.)*

Tajikistan Report. Americans for Democracy in Russia, 57 Winfield St., San Francisco, CA 94110. *A quarterly tabloid on the Tadzhik business environment, companies active there, politics and more. (Free; Quarterly; 4 pp.)*

Ukrainian Business Digest. International Information Systems, 21 Bridge Square, PO Box 3127, Westport, CT 06880, ph. 203-221-7450. *A thorough information resource on business developments in Ukraine. Features good in-country reporting. Each month's issue contains 8-10 medium-length articles on current developments, tables and occasional listings of companies active in Ukraine. ($245; Monthly; 12 pp.)*

Ukrainian Business Review. The Ukraine Business Agency, Vigilant House, 120 Wilton Road, London SW1V 1JZ, ENGLAND, ph. 71-931-0665, fax 71-873-8633. *($400; Monthly; 20 pp.)*

Ukrinform Daily Fax Service — Fax on Demand, 718-796-2691. National News Agency of Ukraine, UN Secretariat Building, 405E 42nd Street, Room 453A, New York, NY 10017, ph. 718-796-4820, fax 718-796-0261. *Monthly report of public opinion polls, data and analysis of the attitudes of opinion leaders. ($120; Daily, by fax)*

US-Kazakhstan Monitor. US-Kazakhstan Council, 2000 L Street NW, Suite 2000, Washington, DC 20036, ph. 202-416-1624, fax 202-416-1865. *In-depth articles and reportage on business in Kazakhstan, international aid, conversion, trade and more. A must if you are interested in business in this region. The publication is provided free to members of the Council. ($100; Bimonthly; 16-20 pp.)*

Travel

International Travel News. 2120 28th Street, Sacramento, CA 95818, ph. 916-457-3643, . *A good source for listings of offbeat travel itineraries and programs, teaching ESL programs and student programs. ($18; Monthly; 170 pp.)*

Russia and China Travel Newsletter. International Intertrade Index, Box 636 Federal Square, Newark, NJ 07101, ph. 908-686-2382, fax 201-622-1740. *A monthly publication with a target audience of travel professionals, this can also be a useful newsletter for frequent travelers to Russia and the Commonwealth. ($62; Weekly; 4 pp.)*

Russian Life. *See listing under General Interest/Business above.*

Travel Security Intelligencer. 437 Grosevenor, Suite 12, Westmount, QUEBEC, H3Y 2S5, ph. 514-933-6314, fax 514-933-6314, email <tsi@connectmmic.net>. *A monthly overview of travel-security related issues worldwide. Gives current information on travel advisories and analysis of the "real" situation related to traveling to specific countries that may pose hazards. ($80; Monthly; 6-10 pp.)*

Traveling Healthy. 108-48 70th Road, Forest Hills, NY 11375, ph. 718-268-7290, fax 718-261-9082. *While not focused exclusively on Russia or the NIS, it does cover important travel issues which have extreme salience for the frequent traveler and does periodically feature travel issues/problems related to this region. Covers what to eat, immunizations, pollution problems, avoiding accidents and sources of information. Ask for the back issues on Eastern Europe and the FSU. ($33; Bi-monthly; 8 pp.)*

RUSSIAN LANGUAGE RESOURCES

Russian language programs are listed near the end of this chapter. For persons who already have a good grasp of the language, here are some places to find Russian language books, newspapers and contacts.

Newspapers

Most of these are for the emigre community (there are, of course, many more; these are just some of the larger ones).

Автограф (Autograph). PO Box 101951, Denver, CO 80250-1951, ph. 303-399-7299, fax 303-399-7299, email <olegzel@aol.com>. *A bilingual monthly magazine targetted at Russophiles, business people and travelers alike. Most ads and much information is Colorado-focused. ($86; Monthly; 36 pp.)*

Бостонский Курьер, 387 Harvard St., Brookline, MA 02146, ph. 617-566-2197, fax 617-734-8802 (biweekly newspaper)

Вестник, 6100 Park Heights Ave., Baltimore, MD 21215, ph. 410-358-0900, fax 410-358-3867 (bi-weekly magazine)

Новое Русское Слово, 519 8th Ave., New York, NY 10018, ph. 212-564-8544

Панорама, 501 S. Fairfax Ave., Suite 206, Los Angeles, CA 90036, ph. 213-931-2692 (weekly newspaper)

Русский Голос, 130 E. 16th Street, New York, NY 10003, ph. 212-475-7595

Русский Бюллетень, ph. 617-277-5398

Publishers/Distributors of Russian Language Books and Periodicals

Access Russia, 89 Main St., Ste 2, Montpelier, VT 05602, ph. 800-639-4301, fax 802-223-6105. *(Twice-yearly catalog of publications on Russia, including some Russian language materials and publications of Great Encyclopedia of Russia.)*

Ardis, 2901 Heatherway, Ann Arbor, MI 48104, ph. 313-971-2367

East View Publications, 3020 Harbor Lane North, Minneapolis, MN 55447, ph. 800-477-1005, 612-550-0961, fax 612-559-2931 *(general interest Russian language books, Russian-language maps, military literature and many major Russian periodicals, esp. academic and scientific)*

Effect, 501 Fifth Ave., Room 1612, New York, NY 10017, ph. 212-557-1321, fax 212-697-4835 *(Kommersant Daily and Weekly editions, as well as several other major Russian newspapers)*

Firebird Publications, 27 Dubon Court, Farmingdale, NY 11735, ph. 800-854-9595 *(dictionaries, literature)*

Focus, 10 State Street, Newburyport, MA 01950, ph. 508-462-7288, fax 508-462-9035, web <www.pullins.com> *(graded readers, language texts and Russian language editions of Russian classics)*

Kontext, 475 5th Ave., Suite 511, New York, NY 10017, ph. 212-213-2125

Kubon & Sanger, Hessstrasse 39/41, Munich, Germany, ph. +49-89-54-218-109, fax +49-89-54-218-218. *The largest European distributor of Russian language publications.*

Liberty Publishers, 475 Fifth Ave., Ste 511, New York, NY 10017, ph. 212-213-2126, fax 212-447-7558

Lukomorye, PO Box 161, Bay Station, Brooklyn, NY 11235, ph. 718-891-1927

Forum, 1405 Avenue Z, Suite 173, Brooklyn, NY 11235, ph. 718-745-2370

N&N Books International, 63-73 110th Street, Forest Hills, NY 11375, ph. 718-896-2665, fax 718-896-2778 *(literature, history, poetry and prose, both published in Russia and in the diaspora)*

Pacific BVL, 1329 Sixth Ave., San Francisco, CA 94122, ph. 415-681-2332, fax 415-753-6961

Russian Information Services, 89 Main Street, Suite 2, Montpelier, VT 05602, ph. 802-223-4955 (*language books and instructional materials*)

Russian Language Specialties, PO Box 711, Pullman, NI 49450, ph. 616-236-5880 (*literature, tshirts, maps*)

Russian Press Service, 1805 Crain Street, Evanston, IL 60202, ph. 708-491-9851, fax 708-491-1440 (*fiction and non-fiction published in Russia and the FSU*)

Russian Book Stores

Black Sea Bookstore, 3175 Coney Island Ave., Brooklyn, NY 11235, ph. 718-769-2878

Book Shelves, 501 S. Fairfax Ave., Ste 206, Los Angeles, CA 90036, ph. 213-931-9787.

Kamkin Books, 925 Broadway, New York, NY 10010, ph. 212-673-0776, fax 212-673-2473; 4950-56 Boiling Brook Pkwy, Rockville, MD 20852, ph. 301-881-5973, fax 301-881-1637

Russian, Central & East European Bookshop, 28 Denmark St., London WC2H 8NJ, ph. +44-171-379-6253, fax +44-171-240-6975

Shoroshim, 1566 Coney Island Ave., Brooklyn, NY 11230

Znania Books, 5237 Geary Blvd, San Francisco, CA 94118

ELECTRONIC MEDIA

In the past two years, there has been an explosion of information on Russia made available on the Internet, through private database vendors, commercial on-line services and electronic newsletters. This new section of the Survival Guide is an attempt to catalog this information. This type of media changes much more rapidly than print media. This is a snapshot taken in mid-1996.

Where to start

If you read Russian and plan to navigate the Internet (especially the WWW), the first thing you need to do is get Russian font support. The on-line standard is something called KOI-8. Head for one of the main Russophile servers listed below and look for sections titled language or software support. Then follow the directions, download and install the necessary fonts, and you are off and running.

Given the vast amount of resources available on the internet (especially on international business, trade and travel), we have been highly selective here, focusing in many cases on good starting places that will point you to areas of more specific interest. We are particularly greatful to Sergei Naumov for his assistance in pointing us to Russia-based WWW servers.

The following are good crossroads from which to begin navigating the much-feted information superhighway. For more specific interests, see the listings below.

Compuserve. Of the major on-line services (Prodigy and America-Online being the other two), this is clearly the strongest for business purposes, and has a very active and courteous clientele. The wealth of information resources, forums and ease of use of this service (particularly via the free CIM and Navigator software) makes it invaluable. Plus the email system is easy-to-use. **On-line Service:** Customer Services, PO Box 20212, Columbus, OH 43220, ph. 800-848-8990.

Dazhbog's Grandchildren. The brainchild of Sergei Naumov, this is a well-connected and well-conceived WWW site and should be one of your first stops,

---

GET ON THE INTERNET NOW

References to internet resources below assumes a modest familiarity with navigating the internet (i.e. gopher, WWW, anonymous ftp, usenet).

If you have yet to connect to the internet, get hooked up right away. There is just too much out there to believe. Get a fully enabled SLIP or CSLIP account to gain easy, user-friendly access to the WWW, which is the fastest-growing part of the internet. Pick up one of the many book/disc package products currently on sale. They include plenty of information about access providers. Or try calling an access provider that offers a full software solution (we like Netcom, ph. 1-800-353-6300 and Glasnet, 1-415-948-5753 or IGC, 415-442-0220). The three largest on-line services (Prodigy, Compuserve and America.Online) are also in the process of integrating such direct access into their services. Prodigy had a WWW browser at the time of publication.

---

particularly if you need KOI-8 software (see the software section just off the main home page.) **Internet-WWW:** http://sunsite.unc.edu/sergei/vnuki.html.

Friends and Partners. This internet resource encompasses so much and is so well inter-connected with other Web sites, that, if you are not already familiar with it, it should be your first stop, no matter what your interest. Everything, from travel, to language, to business and services is here (our *Access Russia* catalog home page is connected to the services sub-section here — see Business and Trade below). **Internet-WWW:** http://solar.rtd.utk.edu/friends/home.html. Subscribing to the mailing list is a must: **Internet-listserv:** listproc@solar.rtd.utk.edu, leave subject line blank, type in the message section: subscribe friends YOUR NAME

Little Russia is a Web site with loads of useful general information about Russia. Its presentation is simple and attractive. And its links to other sites are often quite unique. Check out the link to the Kizhi Museum of Wooden Architecture (in Karelia), and the on-line CD catalog. **Internet-WWW:** http://mars.uthscsa.edu/Russia/

REESWEL Virtual Library. This WWW server maintained by the University of Pittsburgh offers some of the best links and most comprehensive listings on the web. **Internet-WWW:** http://www.pitt.edu/~cjp/rees.html

Russian servers. You may be surprised to learn how many WWW servers are currently on-line in Russia. Some we have listed in special sections below. But if you want a good overview, head to the map of Russian servers maintained by the Russian Academy of Sciences. You just point your mouse to a server of interest shown on the map and click! It links you to all the major servers, from Krasnoyarsk to Petersburg. **Internet-WWW:** http://www.ac.msk.su/map.html

AEROSPACE

Russian Aerospace Guide is an email newsletter that is free for researchers and amateurs interested in Russian aerospace. **Internet:** to subscribe, send an email message to dennisn@comm.mot.com.

AGRICULTURE

Russian Agricultural Newsletter is available on-line. **Internet-listserv:** listserv@umd.umd.edu, leave subject line blank, type in the message section: subscribe rusag-l YOUR NAME

BUSINESS & TRADE

A&G News From Russia is a series of seven weekly newsletters in English that can be sent to your email account (in compressed ARJ format). Newsletters cover privatization, legislation, finance and investment, real estate, commodity markets, business activity, and politics and cost $2 per month per newsletter. **Internet:** to subscribe, send an email message to ag@panix.com with your name, company and billing address, as well as the newsletters you would like to receive.

Access Russia on-line catalog of over 250 business and travel books, maps, directories and products (including many mentioned in the resource section of this guide). **Internet-WWW:** http://solar.rtd.utk.edu/friends/services/access-russia.

American Business Centers offer a wide range of business support and information services in Russia and the NIS. See their home page for the latest information. **Internet-WWW:** http://www.itaiep.doc.gov/bisnis/abc/abc.html

Analytica is a series of three weekly on-line newsletters (economics, politics & general news) that are delivered by email, after passing through the fine editing net of the Institute of Central/East European and Russian Area Studies of Carleton University. The cost is just $150 per newsletter per year. **Internet:** to subscribe, send an email message to dwestman@ccs.carleton.ca.

Businessman's Library. Includes an electronic archive of *Ekonomika i Zhizn*, a legal database, information on banks and banking, and an electronic Russian dictionary. **CD-ROM:** $548/yr. EastView Publications, 3020 Harbor Lane North, Minneapolis, MN 55447, ph. 612-550-0961, fax 612-559-2931

East European Database. A CD-ROM product that includes information on over 50,000 enterprises in Eastern Europe and the FSU, plus information on trade, finance and aid programs and more. **CD-ROM:** $395. Contact Erie-Raiduha, PO Box 30134, Cleveland, OH 44130, ph. 216-237-1721, fax 216-230-1556.

Eastern Europe Business Network is a listserv devoted to building contacts between business people in the East and West. **Internet-listserv:** listserv@pucc.princeton. edu, to subscribe, send an email message with the subject line blank and type in the message: subscribe e-europe YOUR NAME

Exchange rates and information on currency futures trading is available on the RCRME (Russian Commodities and Raw Materials Exchange) home page. **Internet-WWW:** http://www.fe.msk.ru/infomarket/rtsb/ewelcome.html

Kommersant Database is CD-ROM database of some 40,000 joint ventures, banks, stock exchanges and small businesses in Russia. Includes contact info and area of activity. Also includes texts of over 1300 laws. **CD-ROM:** $148. EastView Publications, 3020 Harbor Lane North, Minneapolis, MN 55447, ph. 612-550-0961, fax 612-559-2931. Also ask about the **General Register** CD-ROM database ($485) which in cludes information on over 46,000 companies, and **Officials and Business People** CD-ROM, a directory of executives of all state and major private companies ($105).

Relcom Home Page. You can also get here from Friends and Partners, but if you want to go direct to what is one of the main WWW home pages in Russia (to be compared only to the St. Petersburg home page), start here. Includes everything from an on-line dictionary to security market data to on-line art. Get Russian KOI-8 fonts before going in too deep here (instructions and automatic download available on this server). **Internet-WWW:** http://www.kiae.su/www/wtr/.

Russian-American Chamber of Commerce. A fine homepage of this leading trade group. Includes excellent links to other important sites. **Internet-WWW:** http:/ /www.nar.com/racc/.

Russian Far East Update. Samples of the monthly newsletter (see Periodicals section above for description). **Internet-WWW:** http://www.russianfareast.com/ wistar.homepage.html>

Russica Databases feature some of the best on-line, searchable resources available for business. There are databases of English translations of the Russian press: Russian Press Digest, BizEkon Report and Russian Far East Report. There is also a Public Association Directory, Business Directory, and an extensive Who's Who. The database server is amazingly fast. See also the listing below under Law. **On-line Database:** IRI USA, PO Box 3535, Albuquerque, NM 87190, ph. 505-262-2062, fax 505-255-1662, email <iri-usa@rt66.com>, web <www.rt66.com/~iri-usa/>. Also accessible via Lexis/Nexus, Communicate, Datastar and GBI.

St. Petersburg Business News offers daily digests of the news focused on business issues, and is available in either English or Russian. **Internet:** to subscribe, send an email message to aag@cfea.ecc.spb.su.

Who's Who in Russia is a database of over 50,000 local and federal officials in Russia. **Database:** D.N. Young and Associates, 203 W. Ascension, Gonzales, LA 70737, ph. 504-644-8605, fax 504-644-1663.

COMPUTING

Russian Computing Newsletter is dedicated to discussion of Russo-focused word-processing, computing, etc. **Internet-listserv:** listserv@ubvm.cc.buffalo.edu, leave subject line blank, in the message, type: subscribe rustex-l YOUR NAME. Another closely affiliated newsletter focuses on connecting Russia and the NIS to the internet. **Internet-listserv:** listserv@ubvm.cc.buffalo.edu, leave subject line blank and type in message: subscribe suearn-l YOUR NAME.

Russian Encyclopedia of Information and Telecommunicaton is a database of thousands of databases available in Russia. The database is available in Russian or English. **Database:** The Socium Company, PO Box 390334, Mountain View, CA 94039, ph. 415-691-9721, fax 510-651-0606, BBS 415-691-9092. Cost: $265 plus $6 s&h.

DEMOGRAPHY

1989 USSR Census on CD. Twelve volumes of all the demographic information you'd ever want to have. In both Russian and English. **CD-ROM:** $707.50. EastView Publications, 3020 Harbor Lane North, Minneapolis, MN 55447, ph. 612-550-0961, fax 612-559-2931

New World Demographics database includes map and demographic data by administrative divisions. Also in book form. **Database:** $399. New World Demographics, PO Box 866, Shady Side, MD 20764, ph. 410-867-3767, fax 410-867-0549.

GOVERNMENT SOURCES

BISNIS trade and investment leads for the FSU are on-line in a section of the government's Economic Bulletin Board, much of which is a paid on-line service. Check out the trade promotion section. **Internet-telnet:** ebb.stat-usa.gov; use guest as your login name. **On-line service:** Direct log-in is available at 9600 baud at 202-482-2584, at 14.4k baud at 202-482-2167. **Internet-WWW:** http://www.itaiep.doc.gov/bisnis/bisnis.html

CIA World Factbook is available on-line in many different places. **Internet-WWW:** http://www.ic.gov/94fact/country/200.html

FedWorld offers a good front door to most all the important government pages on the Web. **Internet-WWW:** http://www.fedworld.gov.

National Trade Databank offers a wealth of trade-related information resources. Unlike most government resources, there is a fee for WWW access. Gopher access is free. Still, you can view some of the information and get a taste for it for free. **Internet-WWW:** http://www.stat-usa.gov/BEN/services/ntdbhome.html. **Internet-gopher:** gopher://gopher.stat-usa.gov

USAID Procurement and Contracting Opportunities are publicized on-line. **Internet-gopher:** gopher.info.usaid.gov. **Internet-WWW:** http://www.info.usaid.gov

HEALTH

NIS HEALTH Clearinghouse is maintained by the Department of Internatioanl Projects at the National Public Health and Hospital Institute. It provides information on health and health-care assistance in the NIS and Central and Eastern Europe. Includes country studies and project reports. **Internet:** to subscribe, send an email message with your vitae to nphhi@igc.apc.org. **Internet-WWW:** http://solar.rtd.utk.edu/friends/health/health.html

HISTORY

H-RUSSIA is a moderated internet listserv devoted to discussion of Russian and Soviet history and encompasses over 350 academics worldwide. **Internet-listserv:** listserv@uicvm.uic.edu, leave the subject field blank, in the message, type: subscribe h-russia YOUR NAME, YOUR INSTITUTION.

Soviet Archives includes on-line English translations of documents from recently opened Soviet archives. **Internet-gopher:** gopher.virginia.edu, choose Library Services, University Library GWIS, Alphabetic Organization, then Soviet Archive Exhibit. **Internet-anonymous ftp:** ftp.loc.gov, path /pub/exhibit.images/russian.archive.exhibit.

LANGUAGE

Russian-English, English-Russian On-line Dictionary. Look it up on-line! **Internet-WWW:** http://www.elvis.msk.su/cgi-bin/mtrans. Also try http://www.stack.serpukhov.su:70/7wr/dict/index/dictionary.inv

Russian Chat Channel allows you to chat on-line with other Russian speakers, although, as with many on-line news and chat services, don't expect high-brow stuff here. **Internet-Relay Chat (IRC):** channel is #russian.

Russian for Travelers. Includes sound! You can dowload tons of files, by subject, to hear pronunciation via your computer's sound board. **Internet-WWW:** http://insti.physics.sunysb.edu/~mmartin/languages/russian.html

Russian Practice News Group covers lots of language-related topics and can be a good list to subscribe to if you want to communicate with other Russophiles. **Internet-usenet:** k12.lang.russian.

Russian Word Lists. First is a list of over 31,000 Russian words in alphabetical order. You decide what to do with it. **Internet-WWW:** http://www.pitt.edu/~cjp/rslang.html. Ditto with the archive of Russian curse words (мат). **Internet-gopher:** infomeister.osc.edu, path /pub/central_eastern_europe/russian/obscenities/

LAW

Russian Laws. This is a real gem. Over 10,000 laws, in Russian (you'll need a KOI-8 font set), which you can read on-line or copy to your hard disk. A good menuing system helps you navigate through alphabetical and subject listings. There is also a quick review section that allows you to view legislation passed/published in the last 7 or 30 days. **Internet-WWW:** http://www.inforis.nnov.su. Also try http://www.dux.ru/kodex/KodexHome.html.

RusLegisline. If you need your laws to be in English, this is a very fast searchable on-line database of current and past Russian legislation. This dataset is the raw data used to create the respected Shepards-McGraw Hill publication, *Business*

and Commercial Laws of Russia (see Periodicals, Law section above). **On-line Database:** IRI USA, PO Box 3535, Albuquerque, NM 87190, ph. 505-262-2062, fax 505-255-1662, email <iri-usa@rt66.com>, web <www.rt66.com/~iri-usa/> $145/year, plus $39 per hour connect time and about $2 per page for laws downloaded. Also accessible via Lexis/Nexus, Communicate, Datastar and GBI.

Russian Law CD put out by Access Innovations includes full texts of most major Russian legislation. **Database:** Access Innovations, Inc., PO Box 40130, Albuquerque, NM 87196, ph. 505-265-3591, fax 505-256-1080, $1500.

MAPS

CIA City Maps. Head to this web site to access over 230,000 maps, including maps of Russian regions, CIS states, Moscow, St. Petersburg and the capitals of other former soviet republics. These are all very big files. **Internet-WWW:** http://www.lib.utexas.edu/Libs/PCL/Map_collection/Map_collection.html. For city maps, go to City Net. **Internet-WWW:** http://www.city.net.

Russian Computer Maps and Data are available from Russian Info & Business Center (ph. 202-547-3800, fax 202-546-4784). Includes geographic and statistical data that interfaces with administrative regional maps. A relatively new product, Russian Regional Explorer, collates some of the company's data onto a CD-ROM.

NEWS, GENERAL

Compuserve's Soviet Crisis Newsclips (GO USSRCLIPS) features articles retrieved from UPI, Reuters, ITAR/TASS and others, covering the latest-breaking news from the former Soviet Union. See Compuserve contact information at the beginning of the section.

East Europe Daily Brief, from Oxford Analytica, draws on the talents of 700 Oxford University academics and specialists, which can be delivered daily by fax or email. Database of past articles also available. **On-line News Service:** 1501 M Street, NW, Ste. 600, Washington, DC 20005, ph. 202-739-0290, fax 202-659-8287.

Ecotass Daily and Weekly Reports. If you thrive on information, subscribe to either or both of these wire services, which can be delivered straight to your email inbox. The reporting is authoritative and comprehensive, and focuses mainly on business and economic issues. **On-Line News Service:** ITAR-TASS USA, 50 Rockefeller Plaza, Suite 501, New York, NY 10020, ph. 212-664-0977, fax 212-245-4035. Cost of the weekly is $150 per year, for the daily, $250 per year.

EVPNet offers on-line access to full texts of two Russian newspapers, *Sevodnya* and *Delovoi Mir*. Of special interest, however, is the company's free *EVP Press Digest*, which is a daily on-line newsletter that can be sent to you by email (about 50-70k per day), and a separate, fee-based service ($10/month) that lists the major articles in Russian newspapers that are available for delivery in Russian or translated. **On-line Database:** EastView Publications, 3020 Harbor Lane North, Minneapolis, MN 55447, ph. 612-550-0961, fax 612-559-2931. **On-Line News Service:** To receive EVP Press Digest, send an email message to: online@eastview.com

Federal News Service is a news wire service offering the latest news direct from the Kremlin. Press releases, statements, schedules, you name it. Available as subscription (price based on circulation) or document on request. FNS can also offer a Media Digest clipping service and translation services. FNS, 620 National Press

Building, NW, Washington, DC 20045, ph. 202-347-1400, fax 202-393-4733, email fednews@pipeline.com.

FSUBIZ is a closed, moderated listserv devoted to discussion of business and professional issues related to doing business in the NIS. **Internet-Listserv:** listserv@bankrupt.com, to subscribe, send an email message with your email address in it in the format: subscribe fsubiz email@my.com.

Moscow Times offers selected stories on-line at the Russia Today web page. **Internet-WWW:** http://www.russiatoday.com/

Network of East-West Women is a networking and information resource for women doing business and involved in the non-profit sector in Russia, the NIS and Eastern Europe. **Internet-WWW:** http://www.igc.apc.org/neww

NewsNet offers access to a number of useful news and information services, including Russia Express, Russia Express Contracts, Federal News Service and others. **On-line Service:** NewsNet, 945 Haverford Road, Bryn Mawr, PA 19010, ph. 800-345-1301 or 215-527-8030. Cost is $15 per month, plus $1.50 per minute connect time. Special starter kit costs $79.95.

OMRI Daily Report is a must. If you subscribe to nothing else or get nothing else online, at least subscribe to OMRI. It brings some of the best and most current political and economic reportage to your inbox every day and costs not a penny. **Internet-Listserv:** listserv@ubvm.cc.buffalo.edu, to subscribe, send an email message with the subject line blank and write in the message section: subscribe omri-l YOUR NAME.

Russian Business News Update, is an on-line newsletter published monthly and distributed free by email. Send an email message to jzander@ix.netcom.com.

Russian Life magazine, from the publishers of this guide. Includes samples of this leading magazine of Russian culture, history, business and travel. **Internet-WWW:** http://www.friends-partners.org/rispubs/

St. Petersburg News (that city's English language weekly) is on-line each week on the internet. The next best thing to actually being there! But what is even better is that this Web site will connect you to loads of other invaluable and interesting Russo-Web sites. **Internet-WWW:** http://www.spb.su/sppress.

Trade Show Central provides a searchable database of trade shows worldwide. **Internet-WWW:** http://www.tsentral.com/html/tsc-search.cgi

OTHER CIS/NIS STATES

Armenian newspaper in English. Internet-WWW: http://office.aic.net/news.html

Azerbaidzhan Newsletter is a weekly newsletter direct from Baku and is available by subscription. Is sent to your email address in ARJ compressed format. **Internet:** to subscribe, send a normal email message to root@centre.baku.az.

Azerbaizhan Home Page. Internet-WWW: http://www.friends-partners.org/azerbaijan/

Baltic Republics. There are two good starting places. First is a listserv on the Baltics. **Internet-listserv:** listserv@ubvm.cc.buffalo.edu, to subscribe, send an email message with the subject line blank and write in the message section: subscribe balt-l YOUR NAME. There is also a Web site with informatoin on the baltics. **Internet-WWW:** http://www.viabalt.ee/News/

Belarus Home Page. Internet-WWW: http://faraday.clas.virginia.edu`ana4a/

Georgian News Agency has a home page. **Internet-WWW:** http://www.sonet.gc/bgi/bgi.html

Kazakh history and culture, **Internet-WWW:** http://www.ricc.kz/

Kyrgyzstan Infohub, Internet-WWW: http://www.infohub.com/TRAVEL/TRAVEL-LER/ASIA/Kyrgyzstan.html

Tadzhikistan information, **Internet-WWW:** http://www.soros.org/tajkstan.html

The Global Monitor: Kazakhstan is a CD-ROM disc with legal, economic, energy and general business and travel information. Contains full texts of laws. **Database:** In+Sync Imaging, 2323 S. Voss, Suite 230, Houston, TX 77057, ph. 800-801-2342 or 713-975-6691. Price: $785 or $1685 for an annual subscription.

Turkmenistan information, **Internet-WWW:** http://www2.hawaii.edu/`abichel/

Ukraine Home Page, is a new web site, but one which could well become an important starting point for interest in this region. **Internet-WWW:** http://www.osc.edu/ukraine.html

Uzbekistan information, **Internet-WWW:** http://www.uni.uiuc.edu/`krasavin/sk/

RELIGION

Orthodox Christianity Listserv. A moderated listserv devoted to discussion of Russia's dominant religion. **Internet-listserv:** listserv@iubvm.ucs.indiana.edu, to subscribe send an email message with the subject field blank and write in the message section: subscribe orthodox YOUR NAME, also see the Orthodox Church in America Homepage. **Internet-WWW:** http://www.oca.org

TRAVEL & OTHER

Access Russia on-line catalog of over 100 travel and business related books, maps, directories and products (including many mentioned in the resource section of this guide). **Internet-WWW:** http://www.friends-partners.org/rispubs/

Aeroflot. The Russian airline has on-line information including flight schedules at this web site. **Internet-WWW:** http://www.seanet.com/RussianPage/Aeroflot/Aeroflot.html

City Net. Includes travel and business and government information on world cities. **Internet-WWW:** http://www.city.net

Compuserve Travel Forum (GO TRAVEL) is very dynamic and the libraries are bursting with files for the first time or repeat traveler. **On-line BBS:** See Compuserve contact information at the beginning of the section. The other major commercial on-line services, Prodigy and America-Online also have active travel forums, but we like Compuserve's best.

Foreign Relations is not really travel related, except in a tangential way. It kind of a singles web page that seeks to bring together Western men and Russian women. **Internet-WWW:** http://www.kiss.com/fr/

Hermitage CD-ROM. An electronic tour of the Hermitage, in three volumes, featuring hundreds of digital reproductions of the museum's holdings. **CD-ROM:** $49.95 each (3 volumes). Cascade Marketing, ph. 509-663-9523.

Kremlin Tour. A multi-media excursion highlighting the sights and sounds of Moscow's most famous tourist site. Take a right turn off the Relcom server. **Internet-WWW:** http://www.kiae.su/www/wtr/kremlin/begin.html

Russian City/Regional Information. The growing list of Russia-based WWW servers means there are lots of sites providing local information on business, travel and tourism. They have varying reliability, but are worth checking out if you are going to the region/city indicated (or if you want to look up a phone number in Simbirsk or say you visited a server in Chelyabinsk). For the most up-to-date connections, go to the sensitive map noted in the introduction of this section. **Internet-WWW:**

> Chelyabinsk: http://www.chel.su
> Izhevsk: http://www.mark-itt.ru/
> Krasnoyarsk: http://www.sable.krasnoyarsk.su/
> Moscow: http://www.kiae.su/
> Nizhny Novgorod: http://www.inforis.nnov.su/
> Pskov: http://www.queen.ru/
> Simbirsk: http://www.stc.simbirsk.su/
> St. Petersburg: http://www.spb.su/
> Yekaterinburg: http://www.mplik.ru/

Russian Consulate. The Russian Consulate in Seattle has a home page offering visa application information. **Internet-WWW:** http://www.vldbros.com/consul/rfcons.html

Russian National Tourist Office has a homepage now. **Internet-WWW:** http://www.interknowledge.com/russia

Russian President's Homepage is just what it says it is. **Internet-WWW:** http://www.gov.ru

The Virtual Tourist features tourist guides to many destinations, including Russia and the CIS. **Internet-WWW:** http://wings.buffalo.edu/world/vt2

US Department of State Travel Advisories are published on-line and you can subscribe to a listserv that delivers all new advisories to your email address. **Internet-gopher:** gopher.stolaf.edu. **Internet-listserv:** email to: travel-advisories-request@stolaf.edu; leave the subject line blank and entire the following in the message line: subscribe travel-advisories YOUR NAME. Also available on Compuserve (GO STATE) and other on-line services.

FAX RETRIEVAL SERVICES

This technology allows the user to dial from his/her fax machine or phone, enter a document code, and receive a document back by fax. You pay only the cost of the phone call.

Flashfax BISNIS Bank: *Maintained by the Business Information Service for the Newly Independent States (BISNIS) at the US Department of Commerce, this service includes trade opportunities, calendars of trade events, market information and aid/investment support opportunities. To access the service, dial* **202-482-3145** *from any touch tone phone and follow the instructions.*

Russian Embassy: *Visa application forms and the latest information on requirements. Call* **800-634-4296** *from any touch tone telephone and follow the instructions.*

The Export Hotline: *Maintained by International Strategies, Inc. and underwritten by AT&T, KPMG Peat Marwick, Business Week, Delta Airlines and others. Call from the phone on your fax machine to* **617-248-9393** *and follow instructions.*

Ukrinform Fax Service. *A fax information service, updated daily, covering the latest news from Ukraine. Call* **718-796-2691** *from your fax machine and follow the menus.*

US Centers for Disease Control: *Runs a fax retrieval service on issues of concern to travelers, including regional health alerts and immunization recommendations. Call* **404-332-4559** *from any touch-tone telephone and follow the instructions.*

US Department of State Travel Advisories: *You can receive copies of the most current advisories by fax by dialing* **202-647-3000** *and following the directions.*

UNITED STATES GOVERNMENT: INFORMATION AND RESOURCES

For the sake of brevity, the addresses of government organizations which provide various kinds of information are listed immediately below, with any specific phone numbers or offices noted within references:

[BISNIS]   Business Information Service of the Newly Independent States, US Department of Commerce, Room H-7413, Washington, DC 20230, ph. 202-482-4655; fax 202-482-2293.

[DoS]   Department of State, 2201 C St. NW, Washington, DC 20520, ph. 202-647-9086.

[DoC]   Department of Commerce, 14th St. and Constitution Ave., NW, Washington, DC 20230, ph. 202-482-2000.

[E/IB]   Export/Import Bank, 811 Vermont Avenue, NW, Washington, DC 20571, ph. 202-565-3200; fax 202-565-3210.

[ITC]   International Trade Commission, 500 E St. SW, Washington, DC 20436, ph. 202-205-2000.

[OPIC]   Overseas Private Investment Corporation, 1100 New York Ave., NW, Washington, DC 20527, ph. 202-336-8799; fax 202-408-9859.

[USAID]   United States Agency for International Development, SA-2, Room 100, Washington, DC 20523, ph. 800-872-4348, fax 202-663-2670

Adoption

Current law allows adoptions in Russia and Ukraine, although most US citizens attempting the procedure have faced a steep uphill battle, particularly in Russia. If you seek the most current information on adopting a child from any of the countries of the former USSR, contact the DoS' Office of Consular Services at 202-736-7000 or American Citizen Services, ph. 202-647-5225.

Export Licensing

ELECTRONIC APPLICATION FILING

• Electronic communication is speeding export control processes. The Department of Commerce's ELAIN system allows for electronic filing of license applications. Within the ELAIN system there is also a system known as EXPERT, which helps exporters determine if a given technology is export controlled.

For more information on Electronic Filing of Export License Applications, contact IBEK Corporation, 202-463-0904 or OCR International, 301-208-0700. Both are officially licensed with DoC.

EXPORT ADMINISTRATION REGULATIONS
• The regulations are a publication of the Department of Commerce, and may be ordered from the Superintendent of Documents, U.S. Government Printing Office, Washington, DC 20402, ph. 202-783-3238, fax 202-512-2233. The price is $87 per year (stock # 903-017-00000-7).

OTHER USEFUL NUMBERS
• **Bureau of Export Administration**, DoC, 714-660-0144
• **Export License Voice Info System:** 202-482-4811
• **Tracking Export License Applications:** 202-482-4811

Export Financing and Insurance

PUBLICATIONS
• The publication of BISNIS, *Sources of Finance for Trade and Investment in the Newly Independent States,* is the most informative and detailed resource available on this subject. Free publication. Call 202-482-4655.

HOTLINE
• The **E/IB** operates an Export Financing Hotline at 800-565-3946.

FINANCE
• The **E/IB** offers: medium and long term loan guarantees with repayment protection against both political and commercial risks for private sector loans; medium and long term direct loans to foreign buyers of US exports and intermediate loans to responsible parties that extend loans to foreign buyers – at up to 85% of the export value. In the case of the latter financing options, the buyer must approach a Russian bank designated by E/IB as a sovereign borrower (i.e. VneshTorgBank and Vnesheconombank or a private bank which E/IB has established a guarantee arrangement with, i.e. Tokobank and International Moscow Bank). E/IB is also now considering project finance proposals for the oil and gas sector and, under a new Oil and Gas Framework Agreement allowing E/IB financing for sales of US oil and gas equipment based on assignment of the receipts of oil or gas contracts.
• **OPIC** offers: direct loans of $500,000 to $6 mn to small and medium-sized companies for up to 50% of the cost of a new venture and 75% of the cost of an expansion; investment finance (loan guarantees) of $200 mn for investors with significant equity and management stake in a Russian venture.
• The **Small Business Administration** offers: loan guarantees to small businesses for fixed assets and working capital; a guaranteed, one-year rolling line of credit to support financing of labor and materials for manufacturing or wholesaling for export, for developing foreign markets, for financing foreign accounts receivable, and, in come cases, for funding foreign business travel and trade show participation; loan guarantees for the purchase or upgrading of facilities or equipment within the US, for production of export oriented goods and services. To locate the SBA office nearest you, call 800-U-ASK-SBA, or fax 202-205-7064.
• The **International Finance Corporation** (IFC) provides loans for up to 25% of the cost of large ($25-400 mn) ventures oriented to private investment. Call IFC Corporate Relations Unit at 202-473-9331. IFC also has a new $20mn agency

guarantee with ABN-Amro Bank to help Russian banks establish LCs with lower cash collateral exposure.

- **The European Bank for Reconstruction and Development** (EBRD), of which the US Government is a founder, offers equity investment and debt guarantees to "foster the transition toward open market-oriented economies and to promote private and entrepreneurial initiative." Target industries (with emphasis on privatization) are telecom, energy, infrastructure, goods and services distribution, banking and financial services. EBRD will typically finance up to 35% of a project and will lend no less than $5 mn for a project. Contact EBRD in London at +44-71-338-6569, fax +44-71-338-6487.

INSURANCE

- **OPIC** now offers investment insurance to protect US firms against currency inconvertibility, expropriation and political violence. The government corporation has specialized programs for financial institutions, leasing, oil and gas, natural resources and for contractors and exporters. They also have a small business insurance package which offers streamlined application procedures.
- **E/IB** offers short and medium-term export credit insurance, through loans or reimbursement, protecting investors against losses should a foreign buyer default. It also offers working capital guarantees, to encourage local lenders to make loans to US businesses for various export activities.
- **Multilateral Investment Guarantee Agency** (MIGA) offers guarantees to investors against losses caused by non-commercial risks, ph. 202-473-0179.

INSURANCE AND FINANCE INFORMATION

- **Finance and Countertrade Div.**, DoC, Rm 1104, ph. 202-482-4434.
- **USDA** has established an alternative export arrangement division to help stimulate non-conventional agricultural trade. Call 202-720-6211.
- **American Association of Importers and Exporters**, 11 W. 42nd Street, New York, NY 10036, ph. 212-944-2230, fax 212-382-2606.
- The **E/IB** holds periodic seminars on ways to start exporting to the CIS. Call 202-565-3200 for more information.

Geographical Information

- Declassified **CIA maps** on the former USSR can be ordered through the NTIS order desk at 703-487-4650. But first get a copy of the free catalogue by calling the Public Affairs office at 703-351-2053.
- Defense Mapping Agency **nautical maps** and **aeronautical maps** of the former Soviet Union can be had for a song. Reap the peace dividend and call and ask for a catalogue to be sent to you: 301-436-6990.
- For **current city maps of Moscow and St. Petersburg**, and **the best maps of Russia and the FSU**, call RIS at 802-223-4955.

Information, General

- **American Business Centers:** For an updated list of ABC locations and contact numbers in Russia and the NIS, call 202-482-4655, option 21.
- **BISNIS, DoC:** 202-482-4655, fax 202-482-2293. Ask for a current and complete package of information on accessing the Russian/CIS market. Also ask to be put on the mailing list for their free newsletter.
- **Commerce Business Daily**, published by the DoC, it includes Requests for Proposals, and Requests for Applications relating to export contracts. To subscribe,

call the Superintendent of Documents at 202-512-1800, fax 202-512-2233 (cost is $324 per year, or $275 for second class delivery).
- **DoC Russia and Independent States Desk:** 202-482-2354, fax 202-377-8042.
- **DoS Russia and Independent States Desk:** 202-647-9806; Commercial Visas/ Exchange Department: 202-647-8956
- **Eastern European Business Information Center:** 202-482-2645
- **Export Hotline** (Fax Retrieval Service), fax 617-248-9393
- **Flashfax BISNIS Bank,** fax 202-482-3145
- **OPIC** offers advisory services, investment missions, and an Opportunity Bank (buyer-seller database), as well as an Investor Information Service.
- **USAID** has a very helpful Trade Information Center at 800-USA-TRADE.
- Information on **World Bank** and **EBRD** aid activities and tender possibilities are included in the Flashfax BISNIS Bank (see above). Detailed information in this area is also available by calling the DoC liaison at the World Bank 202-458-0118.
- For information on the activity of non-governmental organizations in Russia and the NIS, contact **Citizens Democracy Corps** at 800-394-1945.

CIA PUBLICATIONS

To subscribe to all CIA declassified publications, the annual subscription fee is just $375. To order, call 202-707-9527 or write to DOCEX, Exchange and Gifts Division, Library of Congress, Washington, DC 20540-4230. Among these are directories of leaders, maps, economic data resource and reference publications.

Market Studies, Contacts and General Reports

- **American Business Centers,** with (at press time) 13 centers in major cities of Russia and the NIS, can offer excellent on-the-ground support and information services to US companies traveling to these cities and regions. For updated contact information on the centers, call 202-482-4655, option 21, or use the Flashfax faxback service at 202-482-3145, requesting document #7022.
- **Country Market Studies:** A market study of Russia ("Industry Sector Analysis") or any of the other Commonwealth states, based on research by the International Trade Administration, is available through DoC district offices. Call 202-482-5291 for the closest district office, or use the fax-back service at 800-872-8723.
- **Finding Russian contacts:** The DoC's Agent/Distributor Service (ADS) is now available for Russia via DoC district offices. First, contact your local district office (call 800-872-8723 to get the coordinates of the closest one), where they will review your product literature. This will be forwarded on to DoC officials in Moscow, who will locate and contact potential agents and distributors. Within 60-90 days, you will receive a list of up to six of the best qualified and most interested contacts, along with relevant contact and background information. The cost is $250.
- **OPIC** has a Project Development Program for funding up to $150,000 (50-75%) of the cost of feasibility studies of proposed investments in the region. This program is administered by Ernst & Young, 1225 Connecticut Ave., NW, Washington, DC 20036, ph. 202-327-6439, fax 202-327-6399.
- **US Trade and Development Program,** SA-16, Room 309, Washington DC, 20523-1602, ph. 703-875-4357; fax 703-875-4009. Funds feasibility studies, training programs, etc. which have priority status in the CIS and relate to US Export potential and have untied financing. Feasibility studies to be funded are typically listed in *Commerce Business Daily*. Prior to conduct of feasibility studies, TDA contracts with private consultants to do Definitional Missions (DM) or desk studies of the project, to see if it meets TDA criteria. For current tenders, call the DM line at 703-875-7447.
- *See also Technical Assistance below.*

EAST-WEST TRADE

• **DoC** can provide some statistics on trade and investment for a fee. Contact DoC at 202-482-5291 to get connected with your district office Trade Specialist. BISNIS can also provide general info.

Technical Assistance

CONVERSION

• **BISNIS** issues a publication *Russian Defense Business Directory*, which lists key converting enterprises and summarizes important legislation and activity in this area. See the Books, Directories and Reference section above.

• **DoC** has established, together with the Russian government, an Intergovernmental US-Russian Business Development Committee, which has a subcommittee on Defense Conversion. Contact ph.: 202-482-3701.

• The **Geonomics Institute**, while not a governmental organization, has begun a project under its Breadloaf Charter to encourage and assist US and Russian conversion processes. Contact: Geonomics Institute, 14 Hillcrest Ave., Middlebury, VT 05753, ph. 802-388-9619, fax 802-388-9627

• The **US Department of Defense** has allocated some $800 million in funding for conversion assistance. Contracts which may be bid on are published in *Commerce Business Daily* (see General Information above).

COUNTERTRADE

• The **Financial Services and Countertrade Division** (FSCD) of DoC provides assistance to companies seeking to get started in barter and other countertrade operations. Call 202-482-4434, fax 202-482-5702.

• Two **publications** prepared by FSCD are available from the Superintendent of Documents, ph. 202-512-1800, fax 202-512-2233: *International Countertrade: A Guide for Managers and Executives* (#003-009-00613-9), and *Individual Country Practices in International Countertrade* (#003-009-00614-7).

• See *Countertrade Outlook* in periodicals section above.

ENVIRONMENT

• **ISAR**, a private, not-for-profit organization, has established an **International Clearinghouse on the Environment**, to facilitate and enhance communication on environmental issues. The project involves setting up centers for such transnational communication in Russia and the US. For more information, contact ISAR at 1601 Connecticut Ave., NW, Suite 301, Washington, DC 20009, ph. 202-387-3034.

EXPORT ASSISTANCE

• The **CABNIS** program begun by DoC (Consortia of American Businesses in the Newly Independent States) seeks to encourage companies in an industry area to establish consortia that will provide economies of scale for businesses seeking to do business in and export to the NIS. A consortia, established with the help of a CABNIS grant, will provide members with export information, marketing and promotion services, and establish an on-the-ground presence in the NIS.

• The DoC has extended its **Office Away from Home** service to Moscow. This service allows US companies, for a very modest fee, access to office space and support services while traveling in Moscow, including an answering service, international phone and fax, and meeting rooms. Contact them in advance by dialing direct to Moscow at 011-7-502-224-1105, fax 011-7-502-224-1106. From Moscow, their number is 255-4848, fax 230-2101.

- The DoC also has extended its **Gold Key Service** to Russia. This service uses DoC specialists to help American companies develop a market strategy for Russia, and to set up appropriate meetings with the government, firms and individuals prior to your arrival in Moscow. Six key contacts are identified for $300. For each day's meetings there is a $100 charge. Three week advance notice is required to use this service. Contact BISNIS or the US Commercial office in Moscow (see previous note for more information.

FOREIGN AID/INVESTMENT FUNDS

Good newsletter sources on the activity of new and existing investment funds are listed earlier in this chapter. Unless otherwise specified, contact information for these funds is in the Important Associations and Organizations listing below.

- **USAID** has set up several programs, in areas from health care to private sector development to environmental protection to energy efficiency to encouraging democratic pluralism, all under its Bureau for Europe and the NIS, Center for Trade and Investment Services, ph. 202-663-2667, fax 202-663-2670. Proposal and Application Requests are published regularly in *Commerce Business Daily* (see General Information above).
- **Agribusiness Partners International**, capitalized at $100 mn offers debt/equity financing for the NIS, in the agricultural/food sector, in the $10 mn range.
- **Allied Capital International Small Business Fund**, is a $20 mn equity fund that focuses on basic manufacturing and service industries sponsored by qualifying US small businesses.
- **CARESBAC**, is capitalized at $3.5 mn and provides debt/equity financing for Russian companies in St. Petersburg in the $75-250,000 range.
- **CEE/NIS Property Fund**, capitalized at $240 mn, with target basic industries as well as light industrial and manufacturing industries, as well as retail properties.
- **The Central Asian-American Enterprise Fund**, founded with USAID funding, seeks to aid companies in the Central Asian republics.
- **The Croesus Russia Funds**, expects to raise some $50 mn for share investment in Russian private companies, and is managed by Croesus Capital Management Corp., ph. 212-593-1881, fax 212-593-3054.
- **The EBRD** is setting up five small regional funds, the first targetted at Smolensk and captialized at $12 mn. The fund will help restructure local industry through equity investments. The Smolensk Fund is being managed by Siparex (France).
- **The Eurasia Foundation**, a new privately-managed organization financed by USAID, supports, through grants (generally $50-75,000), activities designed to develop the private sector, reform the public sector, or develop and support media and communications.
- The **Fleming Russia Securities Fund** is a UK-based $54 mn fund that focuses on equity investments in oil & gas, mining, utilities, automotive and telecom industries. Contact ph. +44-71-382-8869.
- **First Russian Frontiers Trust Fund** is a $60 mn fund that will make 10 year invstments in securities throughout Russia, the FSU and Eastern Europe. Contact Pictet Asset Management, ph. +44-71-972-6800, fax +44-71-972-6868.
- **The First Russia-NIS Regional Fund** is a $160 mn fund managed by Baring International Investment Management and was invested partly by EBRD and IFC and partially guaranteed by OPIC. The majority of targetted enterprises will be in infrastructural industries.

- **Framlington Russian Investment Fund** was one of the first European funds focusing on Russia and was capitalized by the EBRD and IFC, as well as other private sources. It typically makes minority-stake investments of $500,0000 to $4 mn (total capitalization of the fund is $66 mn).
- **Global Environment Emerging Markets Fund**, is an equity investmetn fund for the NIS, with focus on environmental infrastructure and environmental municipal services.
- **The Major Projects Fund**, administered by American International Group, focuses on large infrastructure projects and is capitalized at $300 mn.
- **New Europe East Investment Fund** is capitalized at $130 mn and targets its investments at Western-managed private compnaies in Russia and Eastern Europe. The typical size of investment is $5-15 mn.
- **The Newstar Fund** is targetting smaller companies with investments of half amillion dollars to $5 mn. Of prime interest are heavily undervalued companies and companies with Western management.
- **The Pioneer Fund** seeks to raise $100 mn to place in small ($500,000) investments in Russia, building on the company's success in Eastern Europe. Contact Pioneer at 617-742-7825.
- **The Red Tiger Investment Co.** is a $15+ UK-based fundthat targets investment in publicly-trade securities. Contact Regent Fund Management at +44-71-332-0360, fax +44-71-332-0341.
- **Russia Value Fund** is managed by San Antonio Capital and capitalized at $50 mn. It has invested mainly in securities in the telecom and oil and gas industries.
- The **Russian Partners Fund** is a $100-200 mn investment fund to provide equity investment in larger newly-formed or privatized enterprises in Russia. It is fully ensured by OPIC. It will focus on joint ventures with ties to the US economy or that will generate hard currency income through exports (primarily in mining, oil and gas). It is administered by Paine Webber.
- **The US-Russia Investment Fund** was created through the merger of (1) **The Fund for Large Enterprises in Russia**, capitalized by USAID at $100 mn and offers a range of investment and loan options to medium and large enterprisesand (2) **Russian-American Enterprise Fund,** created in 1993 by USAID (with $340 mn for the next 4-5 years) with the aim of providing loans and/or investments in small- and medium-sized businesses in the Russian Federation, including in US-Russian joint ventures.
- **Western NIS and Baltics Enterprise Fund**, funded by USAID and capitalized at $250 mn, is managed by NCH Advisers and focuses on financing ventures in Western NIS states.

TRAINING

- The **International Executive Service Corps** (a non-governmental organization) sends retired US business persons to Russia to aid and consult with privatizing and reforming enterprises. IESC, Stanford Harbor Park, 333 Ludlow St., Stanford, CT 06902, ph. 203-967-6000, fax 203-324-2531.
- **The Business Development Program**, founded with USAID funding, and overseen by Deloitte Touche Tohmatsu, offers resources, associations and service organizations to stimulate the growth of emerging private sector companies. Moscow contact number: ph 931-9662, fax 931-9663.
- **SABIT**, the Special American Business Internship Training program run by the DoC, provides subsistence grants for Russian internees in American businesses. Priority sectors are energy, pharmaceuticals, agribusiness, telecom, financial ser-

vices, housing, medical equipment, conversion, and the environment. Phone 202-482-0073, fax 202-482-2443.
• **Citizen Democracy Corps** (a private organization) offers volunteer opportunities in Russia and the former USSR. Call 800-394-1945.
• **USIA** programs include support for NIS graduate, undergrad and non-degree students to study in the US, exchange programs, visiting professorships and professionals in residence in the NIS. Contact USIA at ph. 202-619-4420, fax 202-619-6988.
• **The Morozov Group**, founded with USAID funding, operates in over 30 Russian cities and works with local universities and institutes to foster the growth of a nationwide business-training network. Contact, in Moscow, ph. 564-8185.
• The **Peace Corps** has started sending volunteers to work in the NIS. To find out how to serve, talk to the Peace Corps' Russia desk at 202-606-3973.

Travel Information

PASSPORT INFORMATION
• For information on getting a passport, call 202-647-0518.

TRAVEL ADVISORY INFORMATION
• For the latest **travel advisories,** call 202-647-5225, or write to Overseas Citizens Services, Bureau of Consular Affairs, DoS, Room 4800. This is also valid for emergency information, such as the death of a US relative while that person is abroad. Advisories are also accessible on Compuserve (GO STATE) and via a fax back service (call 202-647-3000).
• The **Bureau of Diplomatic Security** at DoS operates an electronic bulletin board, updated daily, providing useful information about security risks and emergencies involving Americans abroad. As well, it gives current information on entry requirements for visiting other countries and information about foreigners visiting the US. Dial, by modem, 202-647-9225.
• *See periodicals section above, especially **Russian Life.***

Important Associations and Organizations

Only organizations dealing with Russia or the entire CIS are listed here. For associations and organizations related to other NIS states, get the listing from BISNIS Flashfax (see above under Fax Retrieval Services).
• **Allied Capital Corporation**, 1666 K Street, NW, 9th floor, Washington, DC 20006, ph. 202-331-1112, fax 202-659-2053.
• **American Business Centers**, US&FCS/Office of International Operations, Russia/NIS Program Office, Washington, DC 20230, ph. 202-482-2902, fax 202-482-2456.
• **American Chamber of Commerce in Russia**, Riverside Towers, Moscow, ph. 095-941-8435, fax 095-941-8437.
• **American International Group**, 70 Pine Street, New York, NY 10270, ph. 212-770-7000, fax 212-809-3581
• **American-Russian Business Council of Southern California**, 1250 Sixth Ave., Ste 234, San Diego, CA 92101, ph. 800-428-9308
• **American-Russian Chamber of Commerce**, 929 Merchandise Mart, Chicago, IL 60654, ph. 312-494-6562, fax 312-275-2250.
• **American-Russian Cultural Cooperation Foundation**, Mt. Vernon College, 2100 Fox Hall Rd., NW, Washington, DC 20007, ph. 202-625-9454.

- **American-Uzbekistan Chamber of Commerce**, 1413 K Street, NW, Box 181, Washington, DC 20005, ph. 202-637-0466, fax 202-637-0467.
- **Bridges**, PO Box 4663, Englewood, CO 80155, ph. 303-220-5397.
- **California-Russia Trade Association**, 865 S. Figueroa St., 29th floor, Los Angeles, CA 90017-2571, ph. 213-892-9335, fax 213-680-4518.
- **CARESBAC**, 1150 Connecticut Ave., NW, Suite 715, Washington, DC 20005, ph. 202-737-8463, fax 202-737-5536.
- **CEE/NIS Equities**, 372 Washington St., Wellesley, MA 02181, ph. 617-431-2600, fax 617-431-7749.
- **Central Asian-American Enterprise Fund**, 1634 Eye St., NW, Ste 200, Washington, DC 20006, ph. 202-737-7000, fax 202-737-7077.
- **CIS-America Chamber of Commerce**, 8707 Katy Fwy., Ste 208, Houston, TX 77024, ph. 713-464-4800, fax 713-464-5511.
- **Citizen Democracy Corps**, 1400 Eye St NW, St 1125, Washington, DC 20005, ph. 202-872-0933 or 800-394-1945, fax 202-872-0923. Information on aid and service organizations active in the CIS.
- **Defense Enterprise Fund**, 104 Crofton Rd., Waban, MA 02168, ph. 617-527-3307, fax 617-527-2722.
- **Eurasia Foundation**, 1527 New Hampshire Ave., NW, Washington, DC 20036, ph. 202-234-7370, fax 202-234-7377.
- **First Russia NIS Regional Fund**, 1221 Avenue of the Americas, 24th flr., New York, NY 10020, ph. 212-730-4868, fax 212-730-2871.
- **Former Soviet Union Florida Chamber of Commerce**, 1717 N. Bayshore Drive, Ste 2000, Miami, FL 33132, ph. 305-539-5117, fax 305-539-5111.
- **Framlington Asset Management**, 155 Bishopgate, London EC2M 3FT, ph. +44-71-374-4100, fax +444-71-382-9116.
- **Foundation for Russian-American Economic Cooperation**, 1932 First Ave., Suite 803, Seattle, WA 98101, ph. 206-443-1935, fax 206-443-0954
- **Global Environment Fund**, 1201 New York Ave., NW, #200, Washington, DC 20005, ph. 202-789-4500, fax 202-789-4508.
- **Moscow Chamber of Commerce**, ul. Chekhova 13, Moscow 103050, Russia, 095-299-7612.
- **NCH Advisors**, 712 Fifth Ave, 46th floor, New York, NY 10022, ph. 212-308-4343, fax 212-308-4398
- **New England East-West Trade Council**, PO Box 60, Boston, MA 02130
- **New Europe East Investment Fund**, Capital Research International, 25 Bedford St., London WC2E 9HN, ph. +44-71-236-3514, fax +44-71-257-6767.
- **Newstar**, 1200 G St., NW, Ste 800, Washington, DC 20004, ph. 202-783-4155, fax 202-628-5986.
- **Paine Webber Russia Partners Fund**, 1285 Avenue of the Americas, 14th flr., New York, NY 10019, ph. 212-713-2000, fax 212-713-1087.
- **Russia Society of New Hampshire**, 17 Tulley Street, Windham, NH 03087, ph. 603-434-0343
- **Russian Agency for International Cooperation and Development**, ul. Vozdvizhenka 18, Moscow, Russia ph. 095-290-0903, fax 095-975-2253.
- **Russian-American Chamber of Commerce**, The Market Place, Tower II, 3025 South Parker Road, 7th Flr., Aurora, CO 80014, ph. 303-745-0757, fax 303-745-0776.
- **Russian Chamber of Commerce and Industry**, ul. Kuybysheva 6, Moscow K-5 103684, Russia, ph. 095-921-0811, telex 411126.
- **Russian National Tourist Office**, 800 3rd Ave., Ste 3101, New York, NY 10022, ph. 212-758-1162, fax 212-758-0933.
- **Russian Trade and Cultural Center**, 35th floor, West, One World Trade Center, New York, NY 10048, ph. 212-432-2989

WHO WENT TO BAT FOR AMERICAN BUSINESS WHEN THE RUSSIAN GOVERNMENT DECIDED TO TAX LOANS AS REVENUES?

SINCE DECEMBER 1993
THE AMERICAN CHAMBER OF COMMERCE IN RUSSIA HAS BECOME THE MOST INFLUENTIAL ORGANIZATION SUPPORTING AMERICAN BUSINESS IN RUSSIA.

Russia's nascent free market and constantly evolving legal system pose barriers to investment that are more easily overcome through a common effort. That's why over 230 US companies have joined the Chamber - to present the unified voice of American investment before the main decision makers in all branches of the Russian government. If your company is beginning operations in Russia, minimize your start up time, get the assistance and support you need in the American Chamber of Commerce.

The Chamber works closely with the Russian and US governments to eliminate obstacles to American investment in Russia. Frequent meetings with high-level officials provide an important link with key policy makers.

You will have an opportunity to participate in industry-specific committees which determine Chamber policy positions. The Chamber offers you an opportunity to meet with the most influential members of the American business community in Moscow and develop crucial business ties.

Working to improve Russian policy toward investment.

American Chamber of Commerce in Russia

For membership information please contact Elizabeth Szatmari (7095)-941-8435 or send a fax to (7095)-941-8437.

Why the Road to Russia Leads through Vermont...

 ## RIS Publications
Montpelier, Vermont
800-639-4301

Since 1990, publishing and distributing quality books, maps and periodicals for persons traveling to and doing business in Russia.

Books
Russia Survival Guide: Business & Travel
Where in Moscow
Where in St. Petersburg
Business Russian
KZR Illustrated Russian-English Dictionary
(by RIS' parent company, KZR Publications)
Marco Polo Travel Guides (in Russian) to USA, Paris, London,
Grand Canary and the Turkish Coast (KZR Publications)
Survival Russian

Maps
The New Moscow City Map and Guide
The New St. Petersburg City Map and Guide
Bilingual Wall Map of Russia and the Republics

Periodicals
Russian Life – a 40-year-old monthly magazine of
Russian history, culture, business and travel
Russia Review (published by Independent Media,
RIS is North America distributor)

Catalog
Access Russia & Central Europe
– with over 300 books, maps, periodicals and products
related to travel and doing business in Russia.

- **San Antonio Capital (Russia Value Fund),** 15750 IH 10, West, San Antonio, TX 78249, ph. 210-694-4400, fax 210-561-3316.
- **Smolensk Regional Venture Fund (c/o Siparex),** 139 rue Vendome, 69477 Lyon Cedex 06, France, ph. +33-78-524-107, fax +33-785-26163.
- **St. Petersburg American Business Association,** St. Petersburg, Russia, ph. 812-275-4587.
- **St. Petersburg Chamber of Commerce,** nab. Krasnovo Flota 10, St. Petersburg 190000, Russia, ph. 812-314-9953.
- **Trade Representation of the Russian Federation,** 2001 Connecticut Ave., NW, Washington DC 20008, ph. 202-232-5988; fax 202-232-2917.
- **US-Armenian Business Council,** Embassy of the Republic of Armenia, 2225 R St., NW, Washington, DC 20008, ph. 202-319-1976, fax 202-319-2982
- **US-Azerbaidzhan Council,** 1030 15th St., NW, Suite 444, Washington, DC 20005, ph. 202-371-2288, fax 202-371-2299.
- **US-Kazakhstan Council,** 2000 L Street, NW, Suite 200, Washington, C 20036, ph. 202-416-1624, fax 202-416-1865.
- **US-Kirgiz Business Council,**1000 Thomas Jefferson St., NW, Ste 500, Washington, DC 20007, ph. 202-347-6540, fax 202-347-6537
- **US-NIS Chamber of Commerce and Industry,** PO Box 1178, Central Islip, NY 11722.
- **US-Russia Business Council & Business Forum,** 1701 Pennsylvania Ave., NW, Suite 650, Washington, DC 20006, ph. 202-739-9180, fax 202-659-5920.
- **US-Russia Investment Fund,** 17 State Street, 26th flr, New York, NY 10004, ph. 212-483-1177, fax 212-483-0999.
- **US Information Agency,** Washington, DC 20547, ph. 202-619-5055, fax 202-619-5958.
- **Western NIS Enterprise Fund,** 15 W. 39th Street, 11th floor, New York, NY 10018, ph. 212-556-9320, fax 212-556-9321

BRITISH GOVERNMENT/PRIVATE OFFICES & SERVICES
Government offices

- **Department of Trade and Industry,** Ashdowne House, 123 Victoria Street, London SW1E 6RB, ph. 71-215-5000, fax 71-828-3258, telex 8813148 DIHQ G.
- **Foreign and Commonwealth Office,** King Charles Street, London SW1A 2AH, ph. 71-270-3832, fax 71-270-3282.

Private Associations and Organizations

- **Britain-Russia Chamber of Commerce,** 42 Southwark St., London SE1 1UN, ph. 71-403-1706, fax 71-403-1245. *Provides in-depth assistance for members. They maintain a Moscow office which supports members in their visits to Russia, and organize seminars and group visits to Russia. Members receive a monthly internal newsletter and the BSCC Journal. Members are also entitled to discounts on individual accommodations while in Moscow.*
- **The Britain-Russia Centre,** 14 Grosvenor Pl., London SW1X 7HW, ph. 71-235-2116, fax 71-259-6254. *The British East-West Centre is a subsidiary of the above. Based from the same location, they deal with non-Russian republic concerns.*

•**European Bank for Reconstruction and Development,** One Exchange Square, London EC2A 2EH, ph. 71-338-6000, fax 71-338-6122

CANADIAN GOVERNMENT/PRIVATE OFFICES & SERVICES
Government

• **Department of Foreign Affairs and International Trade**, Russia Trade Development Division, 125 Sussex Drive, Ottawa, K1A OG2, ph. 613-996-6324, fax 613-995-1279.

EUROPEAN AND JAPANESE CHAMBERS OF COMMERCE

All of the following are very active agents for their members, liaisoning with both Russian and home governments. Most all have offices in Moscow.

FINLAND: Finnish-Soviet Chamber of Commerce, Annankatu 32A, 00100 Helsinki, ph. 90-693-1066, fax 90-693-1442, telex 121589 FISOP.

FRANCE: French-Russian Chamber of Commerce, 22 Avenue Franklin Roosevelt, 75008 Paris, ph. 1-42-25-9710, fax 1-43-59-7473, telex 615909

GERMANY: Association of German Chambers of Industry and Commerce, Adenauer Allee 88, 53113 Bonn, Germany, ph. 228-104-188, fax 228-104-179 •**Ost-Ausschuss der Deutschen Wirtshaft**, Gustav Heinemann Ufer 84, 50968 Koeln, ph. 221-3708-417, fax 221-3708-540 •**Bundesstelle fuer Ausenhandles Information,** Agrippa Strasser 7893, 50676 Koeln 1, ph. 221-20571, fax 221-2057-212

ITALY: Italian-Soviet Chamber of Commerce, via San Tomaso 5, 20121 Milano, ph. 720-04-008, fax 805-2009, telex 333821.

JAPAN: Japan-Russia Trade Association, Sanko Building 6-4-3, Kojimachi Chiyodaku, Tokyo, ph. 03-3262-8401, fax 03-3262-8403, telex J 27213

NETHERLANDS: Nederlands-Russische Kamer van Koophandel, Lange Voorhout 86, Apt. #5, 2514 EA Den Haag, Netherlands, ph. 70-345-1600, fax 70-362-5231

Russian Embassies in Foreign Countries

AUSTRALIA: *Embassy:* 78 Canberra Avenue, Griffith A.C.T. 2603, Canberra, ph. 6-295-9033, fax 295-1847; (Consular Dept.) 295-9474, telex 62239. *Consulate:* 7-9 Fullerton Street, Woollahra, Sydney, N.S.W. 2025, ph. 2-327-5065, telex 7173606

AUSTRIA: *Embassy:* Reisnerstrasse 45-47, A-1030 Wien, ph. 1-713-1215, 712-12-29, fax 1-712-3388, (Consular Dept.) 712-32-33, telex 136278. *Consulate*: Burgelsteinstrasse 2, 5020 Salzburg, ph. 624-184, fax 621-7434.

BELGIUM: *Embassy:* 66 Avenue De Fre, B-1180 Bruxelles, ph. 2-374-6886, 374-3406, fax 2-374-2613, telex (Consular Dept.) 65272. *Consulate*: Della Faililaan 20, 2020 Antwerpen, ph. 3-829-1611, telex 4435779.

CANADA: *Embassy:* 285 Charlotte Street, Ottawa, Ontario, K1N 8L5, ph. 613-235-4341, 236-1413, fax 613-236-6342, telex 533332. *Consulate:* 52 Range Road, Ottawa K1N 8J5, ph. 613-236-6215, fax 613-238-6158. *Consulate*: 3655 Avenue du Musee, Montreal, P.Q., H1W 1S1, ph. 514-843-5901, 882-9041, telex 5560071.

CHINA: *Embassy:* Dong Zhi Men Wai 4, Zhong Jie, Beijing 100600, ph. 1-532-2051, fax 1-532-4853.

CZECH REPUBLIC: *Embassy:* Pod Kastany 1, CZ-16000 Prague, ph. 2-381-940, fax 2-373-800; *Consulate:* ul. Klinky 142b, CZ-60300 Brno, ph. 5-334-427, fax 334-429; *Consulate:* ul. Petra Velikeho 18, CZ-36001, Karlovy Vary, ph. 17-22-609, fax 17-26-261.

DENMARK: *Embassy:* Kristianiagade 5, DK-2100 Copenhagen, ph. 31-42-55-85, 42-55-86, fax 31-41-37-41, telex 5516943.

FINLAND: *Embassy:* Tehtaankatu 1B, FIN-00140 Helsinki, ph. 0-66-18-76, 66-18-77, 60-70-50, fax 0-66-10-06 (Consular) 0-66-14-49, telex 125577.

FRANCE: *Embassy:* 40-50 Boulevard Lannes, F-75016 Paris, ph. 1-450-40550, (Consular Dept.) 450-40501, fax 450-41765; *Consulate:* 8 Rue de Prony, F-75017, Paris, ph. 444-32900, fax 444-32994; *Consulate:* 3 rue Ambroise-Pare, F-13272 Marseille, ph. 917-71525, telex 440272.

GERMANY: *Embassy:* Waldstrasse 42, D-53132 Bonn, ph. 228-312-085, 312-087, 312-074, fax 228-311-563, (Consular Dept.) 312-075, telex (Consular Dept.) 885615. *Consulate:* Unter-den-Linden 63-65, Berlin 1080, ph. 30-229-1110, fax 30-229-9397; *Consulate:* Reichensteiner Weg 34-36, D-14195, Berlin, ph. 30-832-7004, fax 30-832-5049; *Consulate:* am Feeteich 20, D-22085 Hamburg, ph. 40-229-5201, fax 40-229-7727; *Consulate:* Seidelstrasse 18, D-80355 Munich, ph. 89-592-528, fax 89-523-039; *Consulate:* Kickerlingsberg 18, D-04105 Leipzig, ph. 341-592-203, fax 341-524-04; *Consulate:* Tuehnenstrasse 3, D-18057 Rostok, ph. 381-227-42, fax 381-227-43

GREAT BRITAIN: *Embassy:* 13 Kensington Palace Gardens, London W8 4QX, ph. 171-229-3628, fax 171-727-8624; *Consulate:* 5 Kensington Palace Gardens, W8 4QR, ph. 171-229-8027, fax 171-229-3215; *Consulate:* 9 Coates Crescent, Ediburgh E113 7RL, ph. 131-225-7098, fax 131-225-9587.

GREECE: *Embassy:* Palais Psychico, 28 Nikiforou Litra, Athens, ph. 1-672-5235, fax 1-647-9708

ICELAND: *Embassy:* 33 Gardastraeti, Reykjavik, ph. 1-1-51-56, 62-04-55, fax 62-06-33 telex (Consular Dept.) 5012200.

INDIA: *Embassy:* Shantipath, Chanakyapuri, New-Delhi 110021, ph. 11-687-3799, fax 11-687-6823; *Consulate:* 42 Jamogandas Marg (Old Nepean Sea Road), Bombay: 40006, ph. 22-363-3627; *Consulate:* 31 Shakespeare Sarani, Calcutta 700017, ph. 33-44-20-06; *Consulate:* 14 Santhome High Road, Madras 600004, ph. 44-83-23-20.

IRELAND: *Embassy:* 186 Orwell Road, Rathgar, Dublin 14, ph. 1-92-35-25, 92-20-48, telex (Consular Dept.) 50033622.

ISRAEL: *Embassy:* 120 Rehov Hayarkon, Tel Aviv 63573, ph. 3-522-6744, fax 3-522-6713

ITALY: *Embassy:* via Gaeta 5, 00185 Roma, ph. 6-494-1681, 6-494-1649, fax 6-491-031, telex (Consular Dept.) 622310; *Consulate:* via Sant'Aquilino 3, I-20148, Milano, ph. 2-487-059-12; *Consulate:* via Ghirardelli Perscetto 16, Genova, ph. 10-31-54-10.

JAPAN: *Embassy:* 1-1 Azabudai, 2-chome, Minato-ku, Tokyo, 106, ph. 3-3583-4224, 3483-4445, fax 3505-0593; *Consulate:* Osaka-fu Toyonakashi Nishi Midorigaoka 1-2-2, ph. 6-848-3452, fax 6-848-3453; *Consulate:* 826 Nishi 12-chome, Minami 14-jo, Chuo-ku, Sapporo, 064, ph. 11-561-3171, fax 11-561-8897

MEXICO: *Embassy:* Jose Vasconselos 204 (Condesa), Delegacion Cuanthema, 06140, ph. 5-273-1303, fax 5-273-1545; *Consulate:* Avenida Vicitimas, 5 y 6 de Julia N 1045, Veracruz.

NETHERLANDS: *Embassy:* Andries Bickerweg 2, NL-2517 JP Den Haag, Holland, ph. 70-345-1300, fax 70-346-7940.

NEW ZEALAND: *Embassy:* 57 Messines Road, Karori, Wellington, ph. 4-476-6113, (Consular Dept.) 4-476-6742, fax 4-476-3843.

NORWAY: *Embassy:* 0271 Oslo 2, Drammensveien 74, ph. 2-255-3278, 255-3279, (Consular Dept.) 260-3035, fax 2-255-0070.

POLAND: *Embassy:* Belvederska 49, PL-00-761 Warsaw, ph. 22-213-453, fax 2-625-3016.

SWEDEN: *Embassy:* Gjorwellsgatan 31, S-11260 Stockholm, ph. 8-130-440/441, fax 8-618-2703. *Consulate:* St. Sigfridsgatan 1, Box 5093, 40222 Goteborg, ph. 31-40-80-84, 40-84-00, 20-60-93, telex 6182703.

SWITZERLAND: *Embassy:* Brunnadernrain 37, CH-3006 Bern, ph. 31-352-0566, (Consular Dept.) 31-352-6460, fax 31-352-5595; *Consulate:* Brunnadernrain 53, CH-3006, Bern, ph. 31-352-0567, fax 31-352-6460. *Consulate:* Rue Schaub 24, 1202 Geneve, ph. 22-734-7955. UN Mission: 15 Ave de la Praix, CH-1202, Geneva 20, ph. 22-733-1870, fax 22-734-4044.

TURKEY: *Embassy:* Karyagdi Sok 5, Cankaya TR-06692, Ankara, ph. 31-440-8217, fax 312-438-3952.

UNITED STATES: *Embassy:* 2650 Wisconsin Ave., NW, Washington, DC 20007, ph. 202-298-5770; *Consulate:* 1825 Phelps Place, Washington, DC 20008, ph. 202-939-8907, 8913, 8918; Information dept.: 202-232-6020 *Consulate:* 2790 Green Street, San Francisco, CA 94123, ph. 415-202-9800, fax 415-929-0306, telex 184945. *Consulate:* 9 East 91st St., New York, NY 10128, ph. 212-348-0926, fax 831-9162. *Consulate:* 2323 Westin Building, 2001 Sixth Ave., Seattle, WA 98121, ph. 206-728-1910, fax 206-728-1871. UN Mission: 136 East 67th St., New York NY 10021, ph. 212-861-4900, fax 212-628-0252.

Newly Independent States' Embassies in the US

Due to space limitations, only embassies in the United States can be listed here. The Russian embassy in any other country can give you addresses of the embassies of other former Soviet republics. You may also, of course, inquire via the republic's embassy in the US, at the address below.

ARMENIA: Embassy of the Republic of Armenia, 2225 R St., NW, Washington, DC 20008, ph. 202-319-1976, fax 202-319-2952

AZERBAIDZHAN: Embassy of Azerbaidzhann, 927 15th Street, NW, Ste. 700, Washington, DC 20005, ph. 202-842-0001

BELARUS: Embassy of Belarus, 1619 New Hampshire Ave., NW, Washington, DC 20009, ph. 202-986-1604, fax 202-986-1805

ESTONIA: Embassy of Estonia, 1030 15th St., NW, Ste 1000, Washington, DC 20005, ph. 202-789-0320, fax 202-789-0471.

GEORGIA: Embassy of Georgia, 1511 K St. NW, #424, Washington, DC 20005, ph. 202-393-5959, fax 202-393-6060

KAZAKHSTAN: Embassy of Kazakhstan, 3421 Massachusetts Ave., NW, Washington, DC 20007, ph. 202-333-4504, fax 202-333-4509

KIRGIZISTAN: Embassy of Kirgizistan, 1511 K Street, NW, Suite 706, Washington, DC 20005, ph. 202-347-3732, fax 202-347-3718

LATVIA: Embassy of Latvia, 4325 17th St. NW, Washington, DC 20011, ph. 202-726-8213, fax 202-726-6785

LITHUANIA: Embassy of Lithuania, 2622 16th Street NW, Washington, DC 20009, ph. 202-234-5860, fax 202-328-0466; Consulates: 41 W. 82nd St., Apt. 5B, New York, NY 10024; 3959 Franklin Ave., Los Angeles, CA 90027, ph. 805-496-5324

MOLDOVA: Moldovan Embasssy, 1511 K St. NW, #329, Washington, DC 20005, ph. 202-783-3012, fax 202-783-3342

TADZHIKISTAN: Direct inquiries c/o Russian Embassy

TURKMENISTAN: Turkmenistan Embassy, 2207 Mass. Ave., NW, Washington, DC 20008, ph. 202-588-1500, fax 202-588-0697

UKRAINE: Embassy of Ukraine, 3350 M St., NW, Washington, DC 20007, ph. 202-337-0293, fax 202-342-3874

UZBEKISTAN: Uzbekistan Embassy, 1511 K St. NW, #619, Washington, DC 20005, ph. 202-638-4266, fax 202-638-4268

US and UK Diplomatic Representations

Listed below are the US and UK embassies and consulates in Russia and the Newly Independent States of the former USSR, plus, for the latter and where available, each state's chamber of commerce for the encouragement of foreign trade. See Chapter 2 for a list of these states' embassies in Moscow.

RUSSIA
Moscow
US Embassy: Novinskiy bulvar 19-23, Moscow, ph. 095-252-2450, fax 095-255-9965, telex 413160 [after hours ph. 095-252-1898] *Commercial Office:* Novinskiy bulvar 15, *International:* ph. 502-224-1105, fax 502-224-1106, telex 413205; *from Moscow:* 095-255-4848, fax 095-230-2101.

UK Embassy: Sofiyskaya nab. 14, ph. 956-7200, fax 956-7420, telex 413341. *Commercial Office:* Kutuzovsky prosp. 7/4, ph. 956-7477, fax 956-7480, telex 413341.

St. Petersburg
US Consulate: Furshtadtskaya ul. 15, St. Petersburg, ph. 812-274-8235, telex 64121527. *Commercial Office,* Hotelship Peterhof, Nab. Makarova, V.O., ph. 812-119-6045, fax 812-213-6962, telex 005831401452. *American Business Center,* Bolshaya Morskaya 57, ph. 110-6042, fax 311-0794, email <abcspb@sovam.com>

UK Consulate: pl. Proletarskoy Diktatury 5, ph. 119-6036, fax 119-6037, telex 1445136.

For other cities, see Chapter 4.

OTHER NEWLY INDEPENDENT STATES

ARMENIA: US Embassy, Gen Bagramian 18, Yerevan, ph. 885-215-1144, fax 885-215-1122; **Armenian Chamber of Commerce,** Kutuzov st. 24, Yerevan, ph. 885-277-390.

AZERBAIDZHAN: US Embassy, Hotel Intourist, Baku, ph. 8922-926-306. **UK Embassy**, Hotel Intourist, room 214, ph. 8922-917-986.

BELARUS: US Embassy, Starovilenskaya 46, Minsk, ph. 0172-347-642, fax 0172-347-853; **Belarus Chamber of Commerce,** Ya Kolasa 65, Minsk, ph. 0172-660-460; **UK Embassy** (c/o German Embassy), ul. Sacharova 26, Minsk, ph. 0172-368-916, fax 0172-368-552.

ESTONIA: US Embassy, Kentmanni 20, Tallinn, ph. 2-455-313, international via Finland (358): 49-303-182, fax 49-308-17; **UK Embasssy,** Kentmanni 20, Tallin, ph. 3726-313-353, fax 3726-313-354; **Estonian Chamber of Commerce,** Toom-Koolo 17, Tallinn, ph. 2-444-929, fax 2-443-656, telex 173254.

GEORGIA: US Embassy, Antonelli 25, Tbilisi, ph. 8832-989-967, fax 8832-742-052; **Chamber of Commerce,** Chavachavadze pr. 1, Tbilisi, ph. 8832-222-554.

KAZAKHSTAN: US Embassy, Seyfullina 551, Almaty, ph. 3272-631-375, fax 3272-633-883; Commercial Office, ul. Furmanova 99, ph. 3272-631-770, fax 3272-633-883, telex 251375; **UK Embassy,** ul. Furmanova 173, Almaty, ph. 3272-506-191, fax 3272-506-260.

KYRGYZSTAN: US Embassy, Erkindick 66, Bishkek, ph. 3312-222-270, fax 3312-223-551; **Kirgiz Chamber of Commerce,** Frunze st. 435, Bishkek, ph. 3312-264-942.

LATVIA: US Embassy, Raina bulvaris 7, ph. 2-210-005, fax 2-220-502, telex 161211, international via Finland (358): ph. 49-311-348, fax 49-314-665; **UK Embassy,** Elizabetes Iela 2, 3rd flr., Riga, ph. 371-320-737, fax 371-322-973; **Latvian Chamber of Commerce,** Brivibas bulvaris 21, ph. 2-332-205, fax 2-332-276.

LITHUANIA: US Embassy, Akmenu 6, Vilnius, ph. 2-628-049, fax 2-222-779; **Chamber of Commerce,** Algirdas 31, ph. 2-661-550, fax 2-661-542; **UK Embassy,** Antakalnio Gatve 2, Vilnius, ph. 370-222-070, fax 370-357-579.

MOLDOVA: US Embassy, Strada Alexei Mateevich 103, Chisinau, ph. 2-233-494, fax 2-233-494.

TADZHIKISTAN: US Embassy, Hotel Independence, Ainii st. 39, Dushanbe, ph. 3772-248-233; **Tadzhik Chamber of Commerce,** Sh. Rustaveli st. 31, ph. 3772-226-968.

TURKMENISTAN: US Embassy, Yubileynaya Hotel, Ashgabat, ph. 3632-244-925.

UKRAINE: US Embassy, Vul. Yuriy Kotsubinskoho 10, Kiev, ph. 044-244-7349, fax 044-244-7350, telex 131142; **Commercial Office,** Kudryavskiy Uzviz 7, 2nd floor, ph. 044-417-2669, fax 044-417-1419; **UK Embassy,** Desyatinna 9, Kiev, ph. 044-228-0504, fax 044-228-3972; **Ukranian Chamber of Commerce,** Bol. Zhitomirskaya st. 133, Kiev, ph. 044-222-911.

UZBEKISTAN: US Embassy, Chilanzarskaya 82, Tashkent, ph. 3712-776-986; **Consulate,** Chilanzarskaya 55, ph. 3712-771-407, fax 3712-776-953; **UK Embasssy,** ul. Akad. Nurmukhamedova 13, Tashkent, ph. 3712-533-685, fax 3712-447-221; **Uzbekistan Chamber of Commerce,** Pr. Lenina 16a, Tashkent, ph. 3712-336-282.

Travel Agents/Visa Services

While any travel agent can arrange travel to Russia, some companies have built a specialty on, or have specific experience with, travel to Russia. Many also can provide visa expediting services. Those with more experience and good contacts in Russia can also set up ground transportation and qualified translators.

AUSTRALIA

Intourist, Underwood House, 34-49 Pitt Street, Sydney NSW 2000, ph. 02-277-652, telex INTAUS AA 176604

Red Bear Tours, 320B Glenferrie Rd., Melbourne, Victoria 3144, ph. 3-824-7183, fax 3-822-3956, telex AA38615 Kewtel

Gateway Travel, PO Box 451, Strathfield N.S.W. 2135, ph. 2-745-3333, fax 2-745-3237

AUSTRIA

Intourist, Schwedenplatz 3-4, 1010 Wien, ph. 63-95-47; telex 114524

CANADA

Canadian Gateway, 7077 Bathurst, Unit 204, Toronto, Ontario L4J 2J6, ph. 800-668-8401; fax 416-660-7004; telex 06-964737 (visa expediting and both group and individual travel arrangements)

Carlson Wagonlit Travel, 4 King St. West, Suite 805, Toronto, Ontario, M5H 1B6, ph. 416-862-8020; fax 416-862-2390.

ENGLAND

Alpha-Omega, Bordin House, 6 Beaconsfield Ct., Garforth, Leeds, L5251QH, ph. 113-286-2121, fax 113-286-4964

East-West Travel Limited, 15 Kensington High St., London W8 5NP

Goodwill Holidays, Manor Chambers, The Green, School Ln., Wellyn, Hargeshire AL6 9EB, UK, ph. 438-716-421, fax 438-840-228

Intourist, Intourist House, 219 Marsh Wall, Isle of Dogs, London E14 9FJ, ph. 71-538-3202, fax 71-538-5967, telex 27232 INTMOS

Intravel Ltd., World Trade Centre, International House, 1 St. Catherine's Way, London E1 9UN

Overseas Business Travel, Ltd., 117-119 Leman St., London E1 8EX

Russia House, Ltd., 37 Kingley Ct., Kingley St., London W1R 5LE, UK, ph. 71-439-1271, fax 71-434-0813

Visa Shop, The, 44 Chandos Place, London, WC2N 4HS, ph. 71-379-0419

FRANCE

Intourist, 7 Boulevard des Capucines, 75002 Paris, ph. 47-42-47-40; telex 680180 INTOUR.

FINLAND

Area, Pohjoisesplanadi 2, Helsinki, ph. 90-7661-491

Intourist, Etela Esplanaadi, 14, 00130 Helsinki 13, ph. 90-631, telex 124654 INTOUR.

GERMANY

Intourist, Friedrichstrasse 153A, 1080 Berlin, ph. 229-1948, 228-1492, telex 115173 INTOUR • 1000 Berlin, Kurfurstendamm 63, ph. 030-88-00-70, telex 185392 INTOUR • Stephanstrasse 1, 6000 Frankfurt am Main 1, ph. 069-28-57-76, telex 414232 INTOUR.

ITALY

Intourist, Piazza Buenos Aires 6/7, 00198 Roma, ph. 86-38-92; telex 626367 INURSS.

JAPAN

Intourist, Roppongi Heights, 1-16, 4-chome Roppongi, Minato-ku, Tokyo, ph. 03-584-6617, 03-584-6618, telex 27645.

SWITZERLAND

Intourist, Usteristrasse, 9 Lowenplatz, 8001 Zurich; ph. 01-211-3335; telex 813005 TOSU CH.

UNITED STATES

American International Homestays, PO Box 1754, Nederland, CO, 80466, ph. 800-876-2048, fax 303-642-3365

AmeriRuss Cruises, 384 East 1300 South, Orem UT 84059, ph. 800-279-4454, fax 801-226-1881. (Russian river cruises)

Barry Martin Travel, 16 East 34th St., 3rd fl., New York, NY 10016, ph. 212-422-0091, fax 212-344-1997.

Bolshoi Cruises, 379 N. University Ave., Suite 301, Provo, UT 84601, ph. 800-769-8687, fax 801-377-8800. (Volga river and Karelia cruises)

Cruise Marketing International, 1601 Industrial Way, Ste. A, Belmont, CA 94002, ph. 800-578-7742. (Cruises and ship-hotel in Moscow)

East-West Discovery, PO Box 69, Volcano, HI 96785, ph. 808-985-8552.

East-West Tours & Travel Consulting, 10 E. 39th St., 8th flr., New York, NY 10016, ph. 212-545-0737, fax 212-889-2009

Express Visa Service, Inc., 2150 Wisconsin Ave., Suite 20, Washington, DC 20007, ph. 202-337-2442, fax 202-337-3019. (visa expediting).

IBV Bed and Breakfast Systems & Capital Visa, 13113 Ideal Drive, Silver Spring, MD 20906, ph. 301-942-3770, fax 301-933-0024.

Intourist, 610 Rockefeller Center, #603, New York, NY 10120, ph. 212-757-3884, 757-3885, fax 212-459-0031, telex REP INTUR 62614 UW.

ITS Tours and Travel, 1055 Texas Ave., Suite 104, College Station, TX 77840, ph. 800-533-8688, 409-764-9400

Mountain Travel/Sobek, 6420 Fairmount Ave., El Cerrito, CA 94530, ph. 800-227-2384, fax 510-525-7710. (Adventure travel)

New Solutions, 513 N. Missouri Ave., Roswell, NM 68201, ph. 800-768-9535.

Pioneer East/West Initiatives, 203 Allston St., Cambridge, MA 02139, ph. 800-369-1322, fax 617-547-7304.

Rahim Travel, 12 South Dixie Highway, 2nd flr., Lake Worth FL 33460, ph. 800-556-5305, fax 407-582-1353, telex 362788.

REI Adventures, PO Box 1938, Sumner, WA 98390, ph. 800-622-2236 (Adventure travel: from trekking in the Altai to biking Baikal).

Russia and Beyond, 1201 Third Ave., Suite 1800, Seattle, WA 98101, ph. 800-841-1811 or 206-205-4848, fax 206-205-4711.

Russia Travel Bureau, 225 East 44th Street, New York, NY 10017, ph. 212-986-1500, fax 212-490-1650.

Tour Designs, Inc., 616 G Street, SW, Washington, DC 20024, ph. 202-554-5820, fax 202-479-0472, telex 904266.

Visa Advisors, 1801 Connecticut Ave. NW, #300, NW, Washington, DC 20009, 202-797-7976, fax 202-667-6708 (visa expediting).

Your Own World, 796 Crestmoor Dr., San Jose, CA 95129, ph. 800-473-6165 or 408-255-9041, fax 408-255-9541

Other Services

Access to certain types of professional services and opportunities may be faciliated by the following lists of firms active in Russia and the CIS. Due to space limitations, mainly US addresses are listed.

ACCOUNTING FIRMS

Arthur Andersen, 1345 Avenue of the Americas, New York, NY 10105, ph. 212-708-4125.

Coopers & Lybrand, 1251 Avenue of the Americas, New York, NY 10020, ph. 212-536-2000, fax 212-536-3038.

Deloitte & Touche, 1001 Pennsylvania Ave., NW, Washington, DC 20004-2505, ph. 202-879-5600, fax 202-879-5607.

Ernst & Young, International Business Services, 787 Seventh Ave., New York, NY 10019, ph. 212-773-3000.

Price Waterhouse, 1616 N. Ft. Meyer Dr., Arlington, VA 22209, ph. 703-741-1000, fax 703-741-1616.

EXECUTIVE SEARCH SERVICES

Antal International, Shropshire House, 1 Capper Street, London, WC1E 6JA, ph. +44-171-637-2001, fax +44-171-637-0949.

Ernst & Young, International Business Services, 787 Seventh Ave., New York, NY 10019, ph. 212-773-3000.

Eurospan, ul. Baumanskaya 43/1, Ste 106, Moscow, ph. 095-261-5228

Gilbert & Van Campen, 420 Lexington Ave., New York, NY 10170, ph. 212-661-2122, fax 212-599-0839.

Preng & Associates, 211 Picadilly, London W1V 9LD, ph.+44- 71-548-9860, fax +44-71-895-1361.

EXHIBITION SERVICES

Arche International F.R.L., via Valassina 24, Milan, Italy, 20159, ph. +39-2-6680-4640, fax +39-2-6680-4710.

Comtek International, 43 Danbury Road, Wilton, CT 06897, ph. 203-834-1122, fax 203-762-0773.

Glahe International, PO Box 2460, Germantown, MD 20875, ph. 301-515-0012, fax 301-515-0016.

International Trade and Exhibitions, Ltd., Byron House, 112A Shirland Road, London W9 2EQ, ph. +44-71-286-9720, fax +44-71-286-0177.

Messe und Ausstellungs Gesellschaft, Heinickestrasse 2, D2000 Hamburg 20, Germany, ph. +49-40-460-3001, fax +49-40-460-4276.

Nowea International, PO Box 320203, Stockumer Kirchstrasse 61, D4000, Dusseldorf 30, Germany, ph. 211-456-002, fax 211-456-0740.

LAW FIRMS

While thousands of Western lawyers are active in Russia, for the sake of brevity, the list below (as with the lists of accountants and executive search firms) lists US addresses of firms that have been consistently involved over the past several years. Most have offices in Russia (see our Where in Moscow *or* Where in St. Petersburg *for addresses of these offices).*

Akin, Gump, Strauss, Hauer & Feld, 1333 New Hampshire Ave., NW, Suite 400, Washington, DC 20036, ph. 202-887-4000, fax 202-887-4288.

Arnold & Porter, 555 12th Street NW, Washington, DC 20036, ph. 202-942-5999, fax 202-942-5926.

Baker & McKenzie, 2 Embarcadero Center 24th floor, San Francisco, CA 94111, ph. 415-576-3000, 415-576-3099.

Chadbourne & Parke, 30 Rockefeller Plaza, New York, NY 10112, ph. 212-408-5100, fax 212-541-5406.

Cole, Corette & Arbutyn, 805 15th St., Suite 900, NW, Washington, DC 20005, ph. 202-872-1414, fax 202-296-8238.

Coudert Brothers, 200 Park Avenue, New York, NY 10166, fax 212-880-4400.

Davis, Graham and Stubbs, 370 17th Street, Ste. 4700, Denver, CO 80202, ph. 303-892-9400, fax 303-893-1379.

Debevoise & Plimpton, 875 Third Ave., New York, NY 10022, ph. 212-909-6000, fax 212-909-6836.

Hale & Dorr, 60 State Street, Boston, MA 02109, ph. 617-526-6000, fax 617-526-5000.

Heller, Ehrman, White & McAuliffe, 333 Bush St., San Francisco, CA 94104, ph. 415-772-6000, fax 415-772-6268.

Holmes, Roberts & Owen, 1700 Lincoln St., Ste. 4100, Denver, CO 80203, ph. 303-861-7000, fax 303-866-0200

Hughes, Thorsness, Gantz, Powell and Brundin, 550 West 7th Ave., ste 1100, Anchorage, AK 99501, ph. 907-274-7522, fax 907-263-8320.

Latham & Watkins, 520 South Grand Ave., Suite 200, Los Angeles, CA 90071, ph. 813-891-1200, fax 813-891-7123.

Leboeuf, Lamb, Leiby & Macrae, 125 West 55th St., New York, NY 10019, ph. 212-424-8000, fax 212-424-8500.

Milbank, Tweed, Hadley & McCloy, One Chase Manhattan Plaza, New York, NY 10005-1413, ph. 212-530-5000, fax 212-530-5219.

Pepper, Hamilton & Scheetz, 1300 19th St. NW, Ste. 700, Washington, DC 20036, ph. 202-828-1200, fax 202-828-1665.

Salans, Hertzfeld and Heilbron, 750 Lexington Ave., 14th floor, New York, NY 10022, ph. 212-644-0800.

Steptoe & Johnson, 1330 Connecticut Ave., NW, Washington, DC 20036, ph. 202-429-3000, fax 202-429-3902.

Tuttle, Taylor & Hebron, 1025 Thomas Jefferson St., NW, Washington, DC 20007, ph. 202-342-1300, fax 202-342-5880.

Vinson and Elkins, 1455 Pennsylvania Ave., NW Suite 700, Washington, DC 20004, ph. 202-639-6500, fax 202-639-6604.

Vorys, Sater, Seymour and Pease, Suite 1111, 1828 L Street, 11th fl., NW, Washington, DC 20036, ph. 202-467-8800, fax 202-467-8900.

White & Case, 1155 Avenue of the Americas, New York, NY 10036, ph. 212-819-8200, fax 212-354-8113.

RUSSIAN BUSINESS CARDS

As mentioned several times in this book, it is a real plus, if you are traveling to Russia on business, to have business cards printed in both Russian and English. The following firms have some experience in typesetting and printing such cards, as well as more complicated jobs.

Exclusively Russian!, 87 Windwhisper Ln., Annapolis, MD 21403, ph. 800-473-9517, fax 410-263-2878

Hermitage, PO Box 410, Tenafly, NJ 07670, ph. 201-894-8247, fax 201-894-5591.

Russian Language Services, 1801 E. 27th Ave., Anchorage, AK 99508, ph. 907-272-0327, fax 907-274-6999.

Tangent Graphics, 9609 49th Ave., College Park, MD 20740, ph. 301-441-1880, fax 301-441-1910.

• If you want to try typesetting cards yourself and all you need are Russian fonts, the best sets are available through the *Access Russia* catalogue, ph. 800-639-4301.

RUSSIAN LANGUAGE STUDY PROGRAMS

Learning Russian can be the best investment a business person makes in their Russia-based ventures. Listed below are programs for Russian language study offered by or associated with universities, either for study in Russia or the United States.

American Council of Teachers of Russian, 1776 Massachusetts Avenue, NW, Suite 300, Washington, DC 20036, ph. 202-328-2287 *(summer and year-long programs)*

Council for Scholarship in Russia, 1456 Corcoran Ave., NW, Washington, DC 20009, ph. 202-342-2642. (summer program in St. Petersburg)

Dept. of Russian and Slavic Languagues, 340 Modern Languages, Univ. of Arizona, Tucson, AZ 85721, ph. 602-621-7341. (course in Moscow and St. Petersburg)

Intensive Summer Language Program. Dept. of Russian, 235 Jessup Hall, Univ. of Iowa, Iowa City, IA 52242. (intensive summer language program at MGU).

Middlebury College, American Collegiate Consortium, 14 Hillcrest Ave., Middlebury, VT 05753, ph. 802-388-0222. (summer and year-long programs)

Moscow Internship Program, Boston University, Div. of International Programs, 232 Bay State Road, Boston, MA 02215, ph. 617-353-9888. (summer program with business internships in Moscow and St. Petersburg)

Norwich University, The Russian School, Northfield, VT 05663, ph. 802-485-2165. (summer program in Vermont)

People To People International, 501 E. Armour Blvd., Kansas City, MO 64109-2246, ph. 816-531-4701(summer internships in Moscow)

Perelingua Sprachreisen, Varziner Str. 5, D12159 Berlin, ph. 30-851-8001, fax 30-851-6983. (in Moscow, St. Petersburg and other cities)

Pushkin House, 1634 Armacost Ave., #3, Los Angeles, CA 90025, ph. 310-826-4094, fax 310-473-7435

Red Bear Tours, 320B Glenferrie Rd., Malvern, Victoria, 3144 Australia, ph. 3-824-7183. (four week intensive courses in Moscow, year-round)

Rostov-on-Don Summer Program, UNC-CH Study Abroad Office, 12 Caldwell Hall, CB 3130, Chapel Hill, NC 27599-3130, ph. 919-962-7001. (summer study program in Rostov-on-Don)

Russian Language Institute, Bryn Mawr College, 101 North Merion Ave., Bryn Mawr, PA 19010-2899, ph. 610-526-5187. (eight week, two semester program in Bryn Mawr)

Russian School, The, Middlebury College, Middlebury, VT 05753, ph. 802-388-3711 x5533. (summer programs in Vermont)

Russian Summer Language Institute, Department of Slavic Languages and Literatures, University of Pittsburgh, 1417 CL, Pittsburgh, PA 15260, ph. 412-624-5906, fax 412-624-9714. (summer program, through fourth year, in Pittsburgh)

Summer in St. Petersburg Program, Center for Slavic, Eurasian & East European Studies, 121 Allen Blvd., Durham, NC 27708, ph. 919-684-2174. (summer language study in St. Petersburg)

Summer Intensive Russian Program, Slavic Languages and Literature, University of Washington, Seattle, WA 98195, ph. 206-543-6848. (summer program, 1st through 4th year, in Seattle)

Summer Intensive Russian Program, Monterey Institute of International Studies, 425 Van Buren St., Monterey, CA 93940, ph. 408-647-4115. (summer program in Monterey)

SWEEL, Dept. of Slavic Languages & Literature, Ballantine Hall 502, Bloomington, IN 47405, ph. 812-855-1648. (10 week intensive summer workshop in Russian and other Slavic Languages, in Bloomington)

SALES AGENTS & REPRESENTATIVES

One of the best ways to access the Russian market, if you have something you feel would sell there, but don't know where to start, is to use the services of agents who can represent your product in Russia and the CIS and provide you with office space while you are there. Moscow addresses are given for some of the longer-established firms of this type. The law and accounting firms listed above will also be able to make some suggestions, and can perform important tasks like due diligence on prospective clients.

Argus Trading Ltd., ul. Skakovaya 9, floor 4, ph. 945-2777, fax 945-2765, telex 612171 *(general trading)*

Axel Johnson AB, Kutuzovskiy pr. 13, kv. 131-132, ph. 243-5025, fax 230-6348, telex 413154 *(representation)*

Camco, Krasnopresnenskaya nab. 12, office 1340, ph. 253-1575, fax 253-1340, telex 413523 *(oilfield equipment)*

FMC Corporation, Gruzinskiy per. 3, kv. 201-202, ph. 254-4119, fax 200-2291

Ipatco, ul. Petrovka 15, office 19-20, ph. 924-5893, fax 200-1228, telex 413310 *(representation)*

Overseas Marketing Corporation Limited (OMC), Krasnopresnenskaya nab. 12, office 1405, ph. 253-1701, fax 253-9487, telex 413672 *(trading)*

RCMI, Inc. (Research Consultation Management Intl.), ul. Chekhova 15, ph. 209-9814, fax 209-1398 *(representation, market research)*

Satra Corporation, Tryokhprudny per. 11/13, ph. 299-9169, fax 200-0250, telex 413360 *(aerospace, automotive)*

Scott-European Corporation, Krasnopresnenskaya nab. 12, office 502, ph. 253-1048, fax 253-9382, telex 411813 *(hospital/medical equipment, pharmaceuticals, construction, mining and oilfield equipment)*

ZigZag Venture Group, Plotnikov per. 12, ph. 241-3593, fax 244-7235, telex 411636 *(consulting, trading)*

Preparations & Visas   2

What to Do Before You Leave

BUSINESS TRIPS

The most important thing to do is to gather information. The previous section of this book details the sources and types of information available. Since the direct costs and opportunity costs of a business trip to Russia are quite great, you should do everything you can to make your trip as worthwhile as possible. You cannot over prepare. To summarize the advised preparation:

• **Talk to people who have made the same type of trip** – find out what went right and what went wrong, and why. Travel essay books also provide useful insights. See Chapter 1.

• **Study up** on the state of development of the area of the economy you are interested in. This is relatively easy to do if you have access to a major university or city library. Review the types and sources of business information surveyed in Chapter 1 to select those of most use to you.

• **Check if your local city chamber of commerce has resources** it can provide (for a list of international chambers of commerce, see Chapter 1). State commercial and development offices can also often be of assistance.

• **Apply early for a visa** (see section below, *Visas and Visa Support*).

• **Be certain your contacts will be in Russia** when you are there. July to September is vacation time. Late December to early January is also slow, as is the first week of May (see the table below on Russian holidays).

• **Arrange meetings with Russian contacts before you leave.** Use government agencies to help where applicable and possible (see the previous section). Private Russian companies and Western law and consulting firms with offices in Moscow or St. Petersburg can also be of assistance (see the Yellow Pages in our *Where in Moscow* or *Where in St. Petersburg*, plus the listings in Chapter 1). It is best to arrange at least a few meetings before you leave.

• **Arrange transport support, accommodation and other services** (i.e. translators) before you leave. See Chapter 3, Accommodation & Travel, for information on hotels and other accommodation and travel alternatives. See also the list of travel agents in Chapter 1.

• **Prepare and bring along any draft documents, agreements**, etc. It is also best to have such documents translated before you go, by a translator who has your best interests at heart.

THINGS TO TAKE ALONG

If you have not left already, you should consider including some or all of the following items to make your trip more pleasurable, successful, comfortable, etc. Most everything on this list can now be found in Moscow and often in St. Petersburg (rarely in the provinces). But you usually need to know where to look. It's best to save time and bring your own.

 PACKING CHECKLIST

TOILETRIES, MEDICATIONS AND PERSONAL ITEMS

Over the counter drugs are still often hard to come by. Bring the basics: **Pepto-Bismol**, antacids, aspirin, acetominophen, Sudafed or other cold medicine. Also try to get some disposable syringes in case of health emergencies. Bring along **proof of health insurance coverage** and some **claim forms** if you are staying for a long time. Pocket-pack tissues and wet-wipe type **towelettes** always come in handy. If you are staying in an apartment, bring along a small tube of **laundry soap** and a universal flat bathtub **stopper** (or golf ball) in case you need to wash out a shirt or socks. Be certain to bring along any **prescription medication**. If you suffer from dry skin, bring some **lotion** in winter, indoors it will be very warm and dry. An extra pair of **glasses or contact lenses** is also a good idea. Don't forget a **power converter** for your hair dryer, shaver, etc. *Russia is on 220 volts, 50 Hz*, the plug is a two-pin, thin European plug.

CLOTHING, ACCESSORIES AND OUTERWEAR

Check the temperature chart in Chapter 1 to get an idea of average daily temperatures for the region you are traveling to. In any event, bring a **portable umbrella** if you are traveling between March and October. Pack **galoshes** or bring shoes you do not mind soiling (city sidewalks are grimy in summer, icy, salty and slushy in winter). Bring very **warm clothes** if traveling October-April (including a hat and overcoat), and a warm **trench coat** for May and September.

FOR BUSINESS TRIPS

You will make a good impression with **business cards** that have Russian on one side (see Chapter 1 for some typesetters). Also bring some small, **business gifts**, i.e. pocket calculator, pens. Blank business **letterheads** are always useful for typing an unexpected letter to a Ministry or an invitation to visit your home country. A personal and/or business **checkbook** will help you get cash in a crunch (see Chapter 5). Finally, pack a **telephone plug adaptor** if you plan to bring a laptop with modem and send faxes or Email (available at 1-802-223-4955, ask for item A710).

ESSENTIAL EXTRAS FOR ALL TRIPS

Be sure to have a couple of **spare one-dollar bills** in your pocket for a luggage cart at the airport. A good **pocket dictionary** of Russian-English (or relevant first language) is invaluable. Documents: bring two copies of all relevant, local phone numbers; pack **a list of credit cards** and their numbers and carry them in a separate place; make a **photocopy of your passport and visa**, and keep them separately from the originals in case of loss or theft. If you are in the US, call **Magellan's** (800-962-4943) and get their travel catalogue. It will provide other ideas (money belts, water filters, etc.). Last, but not least, don't forget to pack your *Russia Survival Guide, Where in Moscow* and *Where in St. Petersburg*.

Visas and Visa Support

Nearly all foreigners must have a visa to enter and exit Russia. Your visa, along with your passport, will be carefully inspected each time you enter and leave the country.

If you do not have a passport, get one immediately. You cannot get a visa without a passport. In the US, you can make application at most local courthouses and/or post offices.

A visa is a sheet of paper which lists information about you, including your name, year of birth, passport number, etc., and indicates the dates during which you may be in Russia, which cities you intend visit (though this is not a limiting factor any longer), the purpose of your visit, and which organization has sponsored your visa. **Four different types of visas exist for non-diplomats: tourist visas, private individual visas, transit visas and business visas.** Each type can be valid for various lengths of time.

TOURIST AND PRIVATE VISAS

A **tourist visa** is arranged through a tourist agency when booking travel to Russia. You will fill out a visa application form like that printed in this chapter, and your travel agent will submit this on your behalf. Many travel agencies now offer not only packaged group tours, but also individualized travel packages (see list of travel agents in Chapter 1). In both cases, agents should arrange for your visa as part of their services.

A **private individual visa** is based on an invitation issued on your behalf by a Russian citizen, through their local UVIR (visa registration) office. This is a *comparatively long and tortuous process* and not recommended as a first option. Most Russians have contacts with a local business that will agree to sponsor your visa (see below), and it is advised to go that route first, as business visas are easier and quicker to obtain.

If, however, you seek a private individual visa, you will need to obtain three applications from the Russian embassy. Attach a passport photo to each completed application and send two of them to your Russian friend. They will take these to UVIR or their local militia for approval and for issuance of official permission (извешение – *izveshcheniye*). Once this has been issued, send the application you retained to the Russian consulate or embassy, along with two more passport photos and a photocopy of the identification pages of your passport.

Both tourist and private visas are typically single-entry visas good for a specified period of time.

TRANSIT VISAS

If you are only planning on passing through Russia on your way to another destination (including to another republic of the former USSR), you can obtain a transit visa relatively easily.

You must submit to the Russian embassy/consulate a visa application form, as printed on the following page (you can enlarge this form on a good copier or call the Russian consulate's fax-back service, see Ch. 1), a copy of your passport identification page, a xerox copy of the visa for the country which is your destination (if such a visa is required), and a copy of your airline tickets showing your booking to your final destination. A transit visa will allow you to spend 24 hours in the transit city, usually Moscow. See below on *Airport Visas* for extending a transit visa.

BUSINESS VISAS

Persons visiting Russia on business are granted **business visas** by the Ministry of Foreign Affairs. In order to obtain a business visa, you must be sponsored by a Russian organization that can "support" your visa, i.e. demonstrate to the Ministry of Foreign Affairs (MFA) that it is necessary for you to visit Russia and that it is in a position to be responsible for helping to facilitate your stay in the country. Only ministries, state organizations, joint ventures and/or enterprises which are officially registered in the city soviet (city council) and with MFA can support visas.

Single-Entry Business Visa

This is the predominant, recommended and simplest type of visa to obtain. And until you have an established reason for a long term business relationship (be it a joint venture or other activity requiring multiple-entries), this is the type of visa you will receive. What follows is a description of the process you and your Russian contacts must go through each time you need a single-entry business visa.

Inform your business contacts or partners that you wish to visit Russia. It is best to give at least one month's notice of your desire to visit, if this is possible. The major difficulty in getting a visa is that the process can be slow the first time. When you and your Russian contacts have agreed on a date for your visit, add a couple of days onto each end of the time period to allow for slow arrival of the visa and possible extensions of your visit.

Send your contacts/partners:

❶ *Your passport data: number, date of birth, date and location of passport issuance and expiry. Your passport must be valid at least three months beyond the date of your planned departure from Russia.*

❷ *The dates of your visit and a list of the cities you will need to visit.*

❸ *The name of the city from which you will be departing immediately before entering Russia. If, for example, you are flying to Moscow via Helsinki, you will list Helsinki as the departure city, even if your travels originated somewhere else. Your departure city is the last stop before landing in Russia.*

After your sponsoring organization has received all the required information from you, it should send you a written invitation via telex, fax or letter, inviting you for a business visit for the time period specified (and specifying the information listed above). *If you are being invited by a private company, be sure to have your contacts also send a copy of their company's registration certificate.*

When you receive your invitation, you must send the following items to the nearest Russian embassy or consulate (see addresses in Chapter 1):

SAMPLE VISA APPLICATION FORM ☑

КОНСУЛЬСТВО (консульский отдел посольства) Росии в ___С Ш А___
страна

Place photograph here

Questionnaire
В И З О В А Я   А Н К Е Т А

	Nationality	Национальность
	Present Citizenship / If you ever had Soviet or Russian citizenship, when and why did you lose it?	Гражданство (если вы имели советское или российское гражданство, то когда и в связи с чем его утратили)
	Surname (in Capital Letters)	Фамилия
	First and Middle Names	Имя, отчество
	Day, Month, Year of Birth Sex	Дата рождения Пол
	Purpose of Trip Business ☐ Pleasure ☐	Цель поездки Бизнес ☐ Туризм ☐
	Department or organizations to be visited. Tourist or Travel Agency Reference.	В какое учреждение. Регистрационный номер.
	Destinations (cities)	Маршрут следования (в пункты)
	Date of Entry Date of Departure	Дата въезда Дата выезда
	Profession	Профессия
	Position	Должность
	Place of Birth. If born in USSR or Russia, when and where emigrated?	Место рождения. Если вы родились в СССР или России, то куда и когда эмигрировали?
	Passport No. Expiration Date	Категория Вид и кратость визы
	Maiden Name	Девичья фамилия
	Spouse's Name	Фамилия мужа
	Dates of previous visits to USSR or Russia	Даты ваших поездок в СССР или Россию
	Do you have medical coverage valid in Russia? (check one) Official Medical Protection Plan Purchased ☐ Paid by Host ☐	
	Place of work or study, address (Место работы) Office Tel. No. (Рабочий тел.)	
	Permanent Address (Адрес постоянного места жительства) Home Tel. No. (Домашняя тел.)	

	Surname Фамилия	First Name, Patronymic Имя Отчество Имена	Date of Birth Дата рождения	Permanent Address Адрес местожительства
Children under 16 traveling with you Дети до 16 лет следующие с вами				
Relatives in Russia or former USSR Ваши родственники в России				

I declare that the data given in this Questionnaire are correct and comprehensive.
Я заявляю, что все данные, указанные в анкете, являются правильными и полными.

Signature:
Подпись:

❶ *A completed visa application form;*

❷ *A copy of your invitation and the inviting company's registration certificate;*

❸ *A xerox copy of the identification page(s) of your passport,* trimmed to the size of the original and stapled to the upper left hand corner of the application form;

❹ *Three passport-size photos.* One of these should be stapled to the marked box in the upper-right corner of the application form, the other two stapled to the copy of your passport identification page. Photos can be black and white or color, preferably on matte paper. Write your name on the backsides of the photos;

❺ *A cover letter from you or your company,* explaining who is going, where, when and with what purpose;

❻ *A processing fee of $40 (money order or company check); £10 in the UK;*

❼ *A self-addressed, stamped return envelope.* In the US, if you include a prepaid airbill (i.e. for Fedex), your visa will be express mailed back to you. Otherwise it will be sent by certified mail.

You now wait until this embassy or consulate issues your visa. This may end up being the most time consuming part of the process. The turnaround time of visa applications has become much shorter and more predictable in the last couple of years. Processing typically takes no more than 10 working days.

You can speed the visa issuing process by enclosing a rush fee, instead of the $40 fee noted above and by including a return express mail waybill, addressed to yourself. The cost is $50 (£40) for one-week service, $80 (£60) for next day, and $120 for same day service (if delivered prior to 11 am). Allow an extra day for processing if you are applying by mail.

It does happen that permission for a visa is denied. This can be because the invitation was issued by a non-registered Russian organization or company (registration must be with the local city soviet, i.e. it must be a legally functioning enterprise or organization). But it can also be because the Russian government has identified a problem in your record.

While it is rare that an explanation accompanies a specific visa refusal, in the past, illegal currency exchange and/or other types of interaction

☑	RUSSIAN NATIONAL HOLIDAYS
January 1-2	New Year's
January 7	Russian Orthodox Christmas
March 8	International Women's Day
May 1-2	Holiday of Spring Labor
May 9	Victory Day (WWII)
June 12	Independence Day
November 7	Anniversary of the October Revolution

with the black market during previous visits to Russia were grounds for refusal. Other possible reasons for refusal are previous violation of visa rules, violations of customs regulations and/or criminal behavior.

If something happens to disrupt your travel plans and you, for some reason need to extend the duration of your visa before you depart, you will need a new invitation from your host organization. Send this and your visa with a $10 fee to the consulate or embassy and your visa will be extended.

Dual-Entry Visa

The breakup of the Soviet Union has led to widespread use of this type of visa. If your itinerary requires you to exit and reenter Russia (i.e. Moscow – Riga – St. Petersburg), you can apply for a dual-entry visa instead of having to get an exit and reentry visa when you are in Moscow (see below for procedures). You simply must specify your itinerary as such in your cover letter and application. See below for information on visa requirements of the other republics of the former USSR.

Multiple-Entry Business Visa

If you foresee traveling frequently, you may wish to seek a multiple-entry (многократная—*mnogokratnaya*) visa. These visas are now issued for a one-year period and allow the bearer to enter and exit at will, without getting a new visa for each visit.

This visa, however, is a bit more difficult and time consuming to obtain. Your contact in Russia, instead of sending you the invitation letter directly, must apply at the Ministry of Foreign Relations, and the latter must send a telex to the embassy in your home country for that embassy to clear a multiple-entry visa request.

If permission from the Ministry of Foreign Relations is granted, your contact/sponsoring organization should notify you of same, at which point you send in your application to the Russian embassy (follow the application procedures listed in the section on Single-Entry Visas; note that **the cost for processing a multiple-entry visa is $140).** You will not necessarily need to send in a copy of the invitation letter, merely state that you have been informed that your visa was approved by the Ministry of Foreign Affairs.

If you are just beginning to develop a business relationship with people in Russia, you will find it much easier to simply get a single-entry business visa, as described above, for each trip to the country. If you find later that a multiple-entry visa is necessary, it is suggested that you seek to have one issued while you are in Moscow for a business trip (see below for procedures). With a bit of pushing and savvy on the part of your Russian partner, this can also be achieved while you are in-country.

Airport Visas

In 1993, Moscow and St. Petersburg authorities announced the availability of airport visas for persons arriving in these cities without visas.

Since this announcement, Russian consulates in the West have repeatedly repudiated this reality. While there has been anectdotal evidence of successful and unsuccessful attempts to use this avenue to gain entry, this is not a reliable, adviseable or safe way to enter Russia. Follow the advice of the Russian consulate, avoid problems, and get your visa before departure. Which leads into a summary of how to avoid visa headaches, in general.

Avoiding Visa Headaches

There are two things you can do to avoid the headache and worry over a late issue of a visa.

❶ As suggested above, request that your visa be valid from a few days prior to your scheduled departure date.

❷ After receiving your visa support letter from your Russian contacts, send all your materials to a company that specializes in expediting visas. These companies deliver your documents to the correct offices, make follow-up calls to check on the status of your visa, and will express mail it to you the day it is issued. See Chapter 1 under *Travel and Visa Agencies* for a short list of such organizations.

Alternatively, by enclosing an additional fee (see above under *Single Entry Business Visa*), you can receive "rush service" from the Russian embassy itself. As well, you can enclose a return express mail waybill, addressed to yourself.

Registration Upon Arrival

You are required to register with UVIR within 72 hours of your arrival in Russia. If you are staying in a hotel, the hotel will hold your passport for 1-2 days and take care of the registration for you (if the hotel is authorized to do such registrations). If you are not staying in a hotel, make sure that someone in your sponsoring organization takes your passport to UVIR and registers you. **You are not recommended to visit UVIR yourself.** In repeated interviews, Moscow UVIR officials have specifically stated that registration at UVIR should be done by foreigners' Russian sponsors/ contacts. This attitude, of course, may differ in other cities. In Moscow, UVIR is located at ul. Pokrovka 42, in St. Petersburg it is at ul. Saltykova-Shchedrina 4. **Foreigners are no longer required by law to register with the militia.**

If you are planning a stay longer than a week, and particularly if you plan on traveling outside the capitals, it is advisable to register with your embassy. It usually takes just a few moments and, at the very least, can often make things go smoother if you lose your passport during your trip.

Length of Visa

It is unwise to stay in Russia past the expiration date on your visa. It is simple enough to have your partners extend your visa dates (see the following section). If your visa does expire before you leave the country and you have not extended it, you may be required to pay a fine and open yourself to harassment, bribery and potential detainment. Further, the next time you try to get a visa to enter the country, you could face difficulties and long delays. It could also place your sponsoring organization in a difficult position.

CHANGING YOUR VISA STATUS

Once you are in Russia, you may wish to change your visa status. This section focuses on how to extend a visa, how to change a visa sponsor, and how to obtain a multiple-entry visa if you already have a single-entry visa. The information (prices in particular) was valid at the time of publication.

Extending a Visa

To extend your current visa, you will need to have the organization that invited you (your current visa sponsor) write a letter asking for your visa to be extended to a particular date. The letter *must include all your current passport and visa information and exactly correspond to the format and wording requested by UVIR* – if you have any questions on this latter score, there are sample letters on the wall at UVIR. UVIR will not process a request accompanied by a non-standard support letter. Your contact then goes to UVIR, taking along your passport and current visa. At UVIR, they will provide a form to fill out on the spot which asks for the basic information on your visa and passport. This form is submitted with your passport, visa and letter. *No payment is necessary for this procedure*. Your visa should be ready to be picked up the next working day. Don't be surprised, however, if several visits to UVIR are required.

Changing a Visa Sponsor

If you are seeking to change your visa sponsor, you must start from scratch (see above). You need to exit and re-enter the country on a visa sponsored by the new organization/company. In the past it has been possble to have a new sponsor write a letter extending a visa issued under sponsorship of another organization, but that practice seems to have ended.

☑ GENERAL VISA REGISTRATION INFORMATION

UVIR (the Office of Visa Registration for Foreigners), is located at ul. Pokrovka 42 in Moscow, and ul. Saltykova-Shchedrina 4 in St. Petersburg. The office is open on Mondays, Tuesdays and Thursdays from 10-18:00 and on Friday from 10-17:00 with lunch each day from 13-15:00.

You can go to UVIR by yourself, but it is *highly recommended* that you take along your Russian visa sponsor or a Russian friend.

Sberbank: For some operations related to extending your visa or changing your visa status, you will be required to make payment to UVIR's Sberbank (Savings Bank) account. You can make payment at any Sberbank (in Moscow, there is a Sberbank branch directly across the street from UVIR) to UVIR's account, which is: Kommercheskiy Narodny Bank account number **101-308-02**. To make payment you fill in a *kvitantsiya* (квитанция) or receipt form. This receipt is your proof of payment for services anticipated and will accompany your letter/application for different operations.

Obtaining a Multiple-Entry Visa

First and most importantly, to get a multiple-entry visa, *the organization/sponsor on your current visa must be the sponsor for your multiple-entry visa.*

Have the organization which sponsored your original, single-entry visa, and which will also sponsor your multiple-entry visa write a letter containing all current visa and passport information. In the letter, be sure to *note your local address of residence and include in which region it is located. Have your organization stamp the letter with their registered round stamp.*

At this point, you go to any Sberbank (see General Visa Registration Information), and fill out a *kvitantsia* or receipt form. You must *pay a nominal ruble fee to UVIR's account* (check at UVIR first to get the current fee). The teller will give you a receipt.

Have your Russian contact take this receipt from the bank teller, along with your passport, current visa, two passport photos, and the stamped letter, to UVIR. At UVIR, they will get a form to fill out on the spot which asks for the basic information found on your visa and passport. This is submitted with your passport, visa, photos and letter. Technically speaking, your visa should be ready within ten working days.

Again, UVIR will not give you a multiple-entry visa if the sponsoring organization in your letter is different from your original visa sponsor (the one printed on your current visa). In this case, they will only extend your visa, but not change it to a multiple-entry. The only proven way to change sponsors and get a multiple-entry visa is to leave the country and reenter on a new single-entry visa from your new sponsor. You can then change it over to a multiple-entry visa when in Russia.

TRAVELING TO OTHER CITIES IN RUSSIA

It used to be that, by law, foreigners could only travel to those cities which were indicated on their visa. This is no longer true. Visas are not required for any cities, and foreigners can travel to any city which is not "closed" (for security reasons). There is also no longer a restriction on foreigners forbidding travel outside a 40 kilometer limit from the city which they are visiting. For detailed travel contact information on over 80 Russian cities, see Chapter 4.

VISAS TO STATES OF THE FORMER USSR

Whereas in Soviet times, one visa served all 15 republics of the Soviet Union, now each republic/country is setting its own requirements. If you are transiting Russia or visiting it first, your best bet (except perhaps for travel to the Baltics) may be to get a Russian visa while in the West and deal with a visa to the other CIS country, if need be, once in Moscow (most consular services accept applications weekday mornings). Fees will be lower and waits shorter. If you do seek to get a visa directly from the country's embassy in the US, contact them at the number listed in Chapter 1 and get the low-down on what you need to submit.

Most all states require a completed visa application, which can be obtained from the embassy in Moscow or abroad (again, see Ch. 1). You are also advised to submit 2 passport-size photos, a letter of invitation, where required, a copy of the information page of your passport and a letter on company letterhead, describing the purpose of the visit.

An abbreviated, republic-by-republic wrap-up of what you need for a visa to the republics is provided in the table at right.

THE RE-ENTRY VISA

If you need to leave Russia for a period of time and then reenter, the organization sponsoring your visa must write a letter which includes all your present passport and visa details. The letter *must cover where you are going, the date you are leaving and the date you are coming back to Russia.* You then go to any Sberbank (see previous section), and fill out a *kvitantsia* or receipt form. There you must *pay a nominal ruble fee to UVIR's account* (check at UVIR first for the current fee) and the teller will then give you a receipt.

Your Russian contact then takes this receipt, two passport photos, your passport, current visa and the letter to UVIR (see previous section). At UVIR, they provide a form to fill out on the spot which asks for the basic information found on your visa and passport. You then hand this in with your passport, visa, photos and letter. Usually, your green exit-entry visa will be ready within three to four working days. You will get back your original visa, so for a time you will have both. When you leave the country, the border passport control officer will take half of the new green visa. They will take the other half when you return. While you do not need your current (original) visa, it is best to keep it with you, should questions arise.

Reportedly there is no need for a reentry visa if you are visiting a former USSR republic that accepts the Russian visa, but it is best in these changing times not to take risks and go through this procedure in any case.

Russians Traveling Abroad

If you decide that it is necessary to meet with your Russian partners or contacts in your home country, they will have to get international passports before they can leave Russia. The new law on emigration and foreign travel no longer requires Russian citizens to have an exit visa. Russians now approach the embassy of their destination country directly. For that, however, they must have an international passport.

Every country has different procedures regulating visitor or business visas. Here we cover only the US requirements.

First you must invite your associates by means of an official "Letter of Invitation" on your company letterhead. This letter must include the following information in your own language (Russian is optional):

❶ The full name, address and passport number of the person being invited;

❷ The full name of your company;

❸ The full address and phone numbers of your company inside the country your guests will visit, plus a short description of the nature

---

☑	**EMBASSY ADDRESSES IN MOSCOW**

(bolded number is consular department)

Armenia: Armyansky per. 2, ph. 924-1269; **925-0765**
Azerbaidzhan: Leontyevsky p. 16, ph. 229-1649; **229-4525**
Belarus: ul. Maroseyka 17/6, ph. 924-7031; **924-7095**
Estonia: Maly Kislovsky p. 5, ph. 290-5013; **290-3178**
Georgia: ul. Nozhovy 6, ph. 291-6602; **241-5214**
Kazakhstan: Chistoprudny bulvar 3a, ph. 208-9852; **927-1836**
Kirgizistan: ul. Bolshaya Ordynka 64, ph. 237-4882; **237-4481**
Latvia: ul. Chaplygina 3, ph. 925-2707; **923-6666**
Lithuania: Borisoglebsky p. 10, ph. 291-2643; **291-1501**
Moldova: Kuznetsky Most 18, ph. 924-6342; **928-1050**
Tadzhikistan: Skatertny p. 19, ph. 290-6102; **290-5736**
Turkmenistan: Philippovsky p. 22, ph. 291-6636; **202-0278**
Ukraine: Leontyevsky p. 18, ph. 229-2804; **229-0784**
Uzbekistan: Pogorelsky p. 12, ph. 230-0076; **230-0054**

Note that this table is provided as a general guideline only. Visa requirements have been known to vary over time. For the most authoritative information, call the embassy prior to submitting your application materials.

Prices are based on the cost for a basic single-entry visa. Often business visas are priced separately. Multi-entry visas, longer-term visas and visas that must be processed quickly incur surcharges. Costs and times vary between Moscow and at embassies outside Russia.

See the notes at left for more general application information.

Country	Visa required?	Russian visa valid	Airport visas?	Invitation req'd?	Transit visa req'd?	Price	Processing time (days)
Armenia	✓			✓	✓	$50	5
Azerbaidzhan	✓			✓		$40	3
Belarus	✓			✓	✓	$60	5
Estonia	*					$10	7
Georgia	✓		✓	✓	✓	$60	1
Kazakhstan	✓			✓	✓	$30	1
Kyrgyzstan	✓	✓		✓	✓	$40	1
Latvia	✓		✓	✓		$10	10
Lithuania	*		✓			$20	10
Moldova	✓		✓	✓	✓	$40	5
Tadzhikistan	✓			✓	✓	$50	5
Turkmenistan	✓			✓		$10	7
Ukraine	✓			✓		$50	1
Uzbekistan	✓			✓		$50	1

* - For some European citizens, not required for US or UK citizens of your business (your company address cannot be in Canada if your guests will be going to the United States);

❹ An outline of planned meetings or conferences, with as exact an itinerary as possible and an exact statement of the purpose of the trip;

❺ Dates of the trip.

The letter must be notarized. This is very important. The easiest way to do this in Moscow is at your embassy or consulate. Go letter in hand (call ahead to find out when you can get such a letter notarized) and have it notarized on the spot.

The US Embassy in Moscow has a special service for easy processing of entry visas for Russians invited on business to the US by US companies. Your contact must take the invitation letter, a letter confirming his/her relationship with the company, his or her passport, two photographs, a typed, completed visa application (available from the embassy), and a $20 processing fee to the US Embassy (Novinsky bulvar 19/23, in Moscow) between 8-10 am on weekdays. For more information, contact the US Embassy in Moscow at 255-9555/6/7/8/9 between 2-4 pm.

NON-BUSINESS VISAS

In response to bad press in Russia, the US Embassy has made getting a non-immigrant travel visa to the US much easier for Russian nationals. It has designated several local travel agents who can get visas for clients without the dreaded interview process. It has also opened an express-service window for certain individuals: persons over 60, persons who have close relatives who are US citizens, students and participants of exchange programs, persons who have traveled two or more times to the US. These persons must bring to the Embassy their passport, two photographs and a completed visa application form. The $20 application fee is payable at the time of receipt of the visa.

Customs Regulations

ARRIVING BY PLANE

You will know you are in Russia when you begin the process of passport control, baggage collection, and customs. The process is slow, has long lines, and can be arbitrary and chaotic.

At passport control, your visa and passport will be scrutinized by young border guards. If your visa is in order and you have not arrived outside the effective dates of your visa, you should have no problems and be through in about 15-30 minutes, depending upon lines.

The arrival of your bags on the conveyer belts can take anywhere from 10 minutes to an hour. While you are waiting for your bags to come, you can track down a customs declaration form if you were not given one on the plane, and fill it in. You may not be able to locate one in your native language. For this reason, and to let you know what to look for, a sample form is printed in this chapter. You will be asked to declare all money, jewelry, videotapes, electronic items, and other objects of value. *Write down everything* of this sort. The obvious implication of this declaration procedure is that, upon leaving, you should not be taking anything out with you that you cannot prove to have brought in with you or purchased in a hard currency shop (save your receipt), nor should you have more currency than you came in with (unless you have proper receipts for wire transfers, credit card cash advances, etc.).

If your luggage is lost *en route*, report immediately to the lost luggage office off to the side of the baggage claim area. This is a frequent enough occurrence anywhere in the world, much less Russia, to suggest that the traveler have in a carry-on what is needed to survive for a day or two. It should be noted, however, that significant technological improvements have been made in the past year that allow the Moscow lost baggage service desk to immediately track lost bags. Such waylaid luggage is now even delivered to travelers' local residence, usually within 24 hours.

Note: Problems with baggage theft and "pillaging" have been on the rise. Valuables should therefore be in a carry-on, and *a hard sided suitcase that can be locked is recommended* for check-through.

Upon collecting your baggage, you proceed to customs. There are now green (nothing to declare) and red (something to declare) channels. The lines for the red channel are always long. If you want to be able to progress through the green channel you should not have more than $500 worth of hard currency (including cash and travelers' checks) with you. There is no limit to the amount of money a foreigner can bring into the country (for Russians there is a $2000 limit without bank documentation), and there are no longer any limits on "luxury items" such as cigarettes, perfume or alcohol (although there are limits on taking them out).

In reality, passing through the green channel means you will not be able to take *out* more than $500. If you plan to spend all the cash you have brought with you, pass through the green channel. Be certain, however, that any personal possessions of value (personal computer, diamond rings, Rolex watch) are indicated on the second side of your customs declaration form and duly noted by the customs officer (they will circle the items noted in such a manner that additional items cannot be written in later).

There is a duty free shop before you go through customs at Sheremetevo (Moscow) or Pulkovo (St. Petersburg) and you can buy some luxury items there if you want to bring them in as gifts or for personal consumption.

If you are traveling on a business visa, you are probably less likely to have your baggage searched, particularly if you travel light. Those who

 TRAVEL ADVISORY INFORMATION

US Dept. of State Travel Advisories, ph. (202) 647-5225
Fax-back service (dial from a fax phone): (202) 647-3000

Sample Customs Declaration

A. Cleared on entry to (exit from) the Russia

No.	Description of objects	Quantity (in words)

I—6
Анга.

Keep for the duration of your stay in the Russia or abroad. Not renewable in case of loss.

Persons giving false information in the Customs Declaration or to Customs officers shall render themselves liable under laws of the Russia.

broad

CUSTOMS DECLARATION

Full name

Citizenship

Arriving from

Country of destination

e of Bank

Purpose of visit(business, tourism, private, etc.)

My luggage (including hand luggage) submitted for Customs inspection consists of   pieces.

With me and in my luggage I have:

I.   Weapons of all descriptions and ammunition

II. Narcotics and appliances for the use thereof

III. Antiques and objects of art (painting, drawings, icons, sculptures, etc.)

IV. Russian rubles, Russian State Loan bonds, Russian lottery tickets   999M

V. Currency other than Russian rubles (bank notes, exchequer bills, coins), payment vouchers (cheques, bills, letters of credit, etc.), securities (shares, bonds, etc.) in foreign currencies , precious metals (gold, silver, platinum, metals of platinum group) in any form or condition, crude and processed natural precious stones (diamonds, brilliants, rubies, emeralds, sapphires and pearls), jewery and other articles made of precious metals and precious stones, andscrap thereof, as well as property papers:

| Description | Amount/quantity | | For official use |
	in figures	in words	

VI. Russian rubles, other currency, payment vouchers, valuables and any objects belonging to other persons

I am aware that, in addition to the objects listed in the Customs Declaration, I must submit for inspection: printed matter, manuscripts, films, sound recordings, postage stamps, graphics, etc. plants, fruits,seeds, live animals and birds, as well as raw foodstuffs of animal origin and slaughtered fowl.

I also declare that my luggage sent separately consists of   pieces.

Date   Owner of luggage (signed)

Finnair 861 A-ADL

look suspicious (unfortunately this is often judged by skin color) or who travel heavy seem to have their bags checked more closely (Russian citizens are also subjected to greater scrutiny than are foreigners). On the way out of Russia, the same general rules apply, but with recent customs crackdowns it is more often that an outgoing passenger's bags are checked, at least cursorily.

The customs officer will verify your customs declaration (if you go through the red channel) and make some marks on it. Your customs declaration will then be given back to you. *Your customs declaration is a very important document. Do not lose it.* Keep your declaration slip with you and/or your passport at all times. You will have to fill in another declaration upon leaving the country.

If you lose your incoming declaration you, theoretically, will not be allowed to take out any of the money or goods on your export declaration, because you will be unable to prove you came in with them. In reality, however, this situation has relaxed greatly in the last year and, at worst, you will probably be treated as if you came in through the green channel – you will not be allowed to take out more than $500 cash. It is probably not likely that your personal valuables will be scrutinized, if they are not somehow "suspicious" (i.e. if you have lots of gold rings). Still, all of this is heavily subject to the mood and demeanor of the customs official you will be dealing with. As in all things of this nature in Russia, it is best to be forthright, apologetic and humble (and, when that does not work, resort to loud and unrepentant self-righteous indignation). Still, avoid any behavior that might suggest you are trying to "get away with something."

You could request that your embassy write a letter to Central Customs, Komsomolskaya ploshchad 1a, Moscow, requesting issuance of a duplicate declaration, but this is really not worth your time.

It does happen that customs officials ask to see the wallets of travelers in order to verify the amount of money being brought in or out. In other words, lying about this figure is not in your interest. It will only cost you grief and probably bring you little gain.

For departure from Russia, *allow 60-90 minutes for customs before check-in time at your airline.* Thus, it is good practice to arrive at the airport about two hours before your flight time. If you are flying Aeroflot, it is advisable to arrive closer to three hours in advance of the flight time.

ARRIVING BY TRAIN

If you come into Russia from Helsinki or elsewhere by train, you will want to be very mindful of the customs regulations just mentioned and those discussed below. Whether arriving in or departing from Russia by train, it is logical and true that the customs officers will have more time and opportunity for customs inspection. Expect more customs difficulties when traveling by train. Expect to have your papers and belongings subjected to much closer scrutiny. Not that any of this must happen, but the likelihood is higher when traveling by train.

CUSTOMS RESTRICTIONS AND LIMITATIONS

Recent legal acts have drastically limited the number of items subject to import duties. Still, there are certain items subject to different types of restrictions and limitations. These are summarized below.

ART, ICONS AND PRECIOUS METALS

Objects of art, gold, precious stones, icons, and the like are all being monitored tightly at exit customs control. Be sure that anything like this which you buy can be taken out of Russia duty free.

Anything which may be deemed of historical or cultural value is forbidden from export. Items of historical or cultural value are (for example): sculpture, graphics and paintings by outstanding artists of any period or country, icons and other religious items, Russian and foreign manuscripts, books dating before 1977, porcelain and crystal, rugs and tapestries, coins and jewelry, restored furniture. If you are in doubt about a specific purchase, Russian customs authorities can be consulted at Komsomolskaya ploshchad 1a, ph. 975-4460.

Objects of art can be exported if you go through the proper procedures. This requires registration of the object with the Ministry of Culture to obtain a *spravka*, which can take up to a month (as any item must be examined by an expert committee responsible for that sort of item). If the Ministry of Culture determines that the object may be exported, a letter is prepared for customs with the tax to be charged (100 percent of the value of the item). To have the object evaluated and obtain a *spravka* (or to get more information), take the object to the Ministry of Culture at ul. M. Dmitrovka 29 (open Tuesdays 10-14) in Moscow (on Thursdays, go to ul. Neglinnaya 8 between 11-14), ph. 921-3258. The Ministry of Culture requires three photographs of the object. Get them done ahead of time.

Do not worry about declaring souvenirs (but be sure they are souvenirs and not valuable works of art) you have picked up on the Arbat, Izmailovo Park or other open-air markets. But do not try taking out a suitcase-full of Palekh lacquered boxes. Items purchased for hard currency can be taken out without limit, so long as you retain the receipt (see *Gifts* below).

AUTOMOBILES

Individuals can import one car duty-free for personal use and keep it in Russia for one year. You cannot sell or transfer the car without payment of the duty (5 ECU/cc) as penalty. Individuals can import duty-free one car that was made in Russia or the FSU each calendar year, but can sell the car only after it has been in-country for two years. The duty payable on such cars is 2 ECU/cc. Russians that have resided abroad for more than six months can import a car duty-free (excluding cars less than a year old or driven less than 20,000 km, with an engine capacity of greater than 1800 cc).

CAVIAR AND CONSUMER GOODS

Russian customs regulations state that the export of sturgeon and salmon caviar by foreign citizens is permitted without limitation on condition of presentation of a receipt that the caviar was purchased for hard currency "according to established procedures." Caviar obtained through other channels (i.e. for rubles) is not permitted for export.

Regulations also limit the export of other consumer items. The value of consumer goods (and presumably gifts, but this is not so strictly enforced) purchased for rubles which may be taken out of the country may not exceed 300,000 rubles. In effect, this makes export of foodstuffs, medicines, etc. completely forbidden (unless purchased for hard currency).

No more than 5 liters of vodka and 1000 cigarettes may be taken out (this can be overridden by considerations of what you may have brought in and stated on your declaration, or by goods you can prove to have purchased at hard currency stores – there is no limit on such items if purchased in Duty Free stores). Russians who have lived abroad for more than six months can bring in up to $5000 worth of goods duty free.

COMPUTERS AND ELECTRONICS

There is some confusion as to whether personal computers and other consumer electronics can be brought in duty free. As with many things, the law is inconsistently applied. There is a law which requires you to pay a deposit upon entry with such items, and the deposit is refunded if you leave with the items.

In reality, this deposit requirement is not being applied. You should resist its application in the case of a personal laptop computer or shortwave radio, etc. (see Personal Use Doctrine below) If, however, you are bringing in consumer electronics to sell (which is legal) you should be prepared to pay the duty. If you can prove you are bringing in electronics as gifts, you will have a $2,000 duty-free allowance.

Even though Russia is now a member of CoCom, there are still come CoCom restrictions on exporting computers into Russia from member countries. For the most part, any off-the-shelf type computer may be exported under General License. Only larger, mainframe-type or super-mini type computers require special licensing procedures.

By way of guidelines, the US Bureau of Export Administration says that computers with a "CTP" of less than 2000 do not need an export license and can be exported under General Destination. A computer with a CTP of greater than 2000 that is being used for civiliam purposes needs a GCTP, which is a variation on a Validated License. A computer with >2000 CTP that is to be used for military purposes must have a Validated License. So what is a CTP? The Bureau answers only that is a standard measure of computing power which can be supplied by a computer manufacturer.

You may wish to contact your Department of Commerce or Foreign Trade (or relevant chamber of commerce – see Chapter 1) for the most up-to-date information. In the United States call the Bureau of Export Administration at 202-482-4532 (Operations Division, PO Box 273, Washington, DC 20044).

Private individuals cannot bring into the country radio-telephones and certain other high-frequency devices.

CURRENCY AND MONETARY INSTRUMENTS

Import and export of rubles is no longer forbidden. Yet, you cannot take more hard currency or rubles out of Russia than you brought in (you can bring in or out R500,000 if it is on your declaration). Technically you are required to write down on your customs declarations (in and out) all travelers' checks and any monetary instruments made payable to you, but many people do not. You cannot export cancelled securities. There is no limit on the amount of foreign currency cash you may bring into the country, provided it is for personal use.

GIFTS

The law states that foreign citizens can bring in up to $2,000 worth of goods in gifts without duty (Russians that have been abroad for more than six months and non-residents coming to stay in Russia for more than 6 months can bring in $5000 worth of goods duty free). Expect this law, as with many Russian laws, to be applied erratically and arbitrarily. Likewise, you can send in, via the post if you dare, a package with less than $200 in merchandise and can send out a package with less than the equivalent of five minimum monthly salaries in merchandise.

Meanwhile, the law also says that an individual non-resident may only export goods worth 50 minimal monthly salaries along with your personal property that was reported upon entry. Gifts in excess of this amount are to be dutied at 60% of the value of the goods. Again, expect this law to be applied erratically.

NARCOTICS AND FIREARMS

Narcotics and firearms may not be imported into or exported from Russia.

PRESCRIPTION DRUGS

Many Western over-the-counter drugs theoretically require permission from the Ministry of Health to be brought into the country, but allowance for personal use is given.

PRINTED AND RECORDED MATERIAL

The new customs code forbids the import or export of published products "which contain information that could cause harm to the political or economic interests of the country, to the security of the state, to social order, to the protection of the health and morality of the population."

Admittedly, this is casting the net a bit wide. This could easily be construed to encompass everything from pornography to Amnesty International reports. But it gets better.

In its desire to stem to outward flow of priceless Russian manuscripts, the Russian government in 1994 brought into force regulations that put greater scrutiny on books and printed matter taken out of the country. The law requires that anyone leaving the country produce a detailed listing of any personal book collection they wish to take with them. This list must be submitted to the Committee on the Export of Publications Abroad at the Russian State Library. Books published prior to 1945 are forbidden from export and reference literature can be subject to taxation, due to its relatively low price in Russia. In reality, individuals taking out a couple of current publications need not worry about this regulation. Older books bought at a local used book store could cause problems, however.

Other precautions: Don't bring in original manuscripts or documents without leaving a copy at home. If you are carrying into or out of the country internal (Russian) government documents which might be deemed of a sensitive nature, you should have a letter from the appropriate ministry or department which gave you the documents, vouchsafing the fact that you have proper authority to be carrying these papers on your person. Current regulations allow import of up to five video cassettes for personal use. Leave these sealed if you can for entry, so there will be no chance they will be seen as recorded material. Customs regulations forbid import into Russia of recorded video cassettes (meaning commercial movies, not personal recordings).

TRADE SAMPLES

You can take trade samples both into and out of Russia without much problem, provided you have the proper documentation and provided the samples do not infringe any of the restrictions mentioned above. To exit with trade samples, have the company which has given you the samples prepare a letter in Russian, with the appropriate stamps, attesting to the fact that these are samples and should not be subject to export restrictions. If you feel the need, you can prepare a similar letter for samples which you are importing.

A FINAL CONSIDERATION

A guiding principle for what you should or can bring in with you without any difficulty or duty could be called the **Personal Use Doctrine**. If you can reasonably claim that the items you are bringing in with you are for your personal use, whether they be cosmetics, film, a laptop computer, or books, then you should have no problem. If you are bringing in 10 pairs of new jeans or 40 blank video cassettes (keep blank video cassettes wrapped when entering), it will be very difficult to claim these are for personal use (unless perhaps you are staying for an extended period). In keeping with this, expatriates coming to stay in Russia for six months or longer are extended a $5000 duty free allowance on all personal items.

CONFISCATION

In the event you have something confiscated upon entry, you will normally be issued a receipt for the item. This receipt, or *kvitantsiya* allows you to reclaim the item on your way out (in theory). Undeclared currency or undeclared valuable property may be subject to permanent confiscation. If the items confiscated are considered "contraband", a protocol detailing the reasons for the seizure will also be made out. Contraband and items confiscated upon exit will not likely be returned to you.

Travel & Accommodations 3

Getting to Russia

There are any number of options and travel combinations for getting to Russia. And new ways are constantly opening up. The most common path of entry, of course, is by air.

There are direct flights to Moscow and St. Petersburg from the US, Canada, and most European countries. In the US, only Delta and Aeroflot have non-stop flights into Russia. From Europe, most all major carriers, e.g. Lufthansa, British Airways, Air France, SAS and Finnair, have non-stop scheduled flights, as does Aeroflot. As well, these European carriers (and others) have direct flights via Europe out of New York, Washington, Miami, Seattle, Los Angeles, Chicago, and other major North American cities. Lufthansa is taking an early lead with the greatest number of flights and destinations into Russia.

The obvious advice, of course, is to seek the learned input of your travel agent or one of those listed in Chapter 1 of this book. They should know how to get you the best fares. And unless you are traveling at the last moment, there is no reason you should pay full fare to get to Russia. Even with recent increases in travel to Russia, there are empty seats on nearly all flights to Russia. This makes it a buyer's market.

One alternative, whether you are going for business or pleasure, is to travel with a group. Often the package group fares (airfare, accommodations and food included), can be less than a standard airfare. Certainly if you factor in hotel room costs that you would pay traveling alone, this can be a good way to travel. Of course, you will want to be very careful about the hotel(s) the group is staying in (make sure it is centrally located), and will want to gain the assent of the group leader for your departure from the planned itinerary – something totally acceptable now, but unthinkable in soviet times. Again, see the list of travel agents in Chapter 1.

If you are traveling from North America, consider the option of a flight with a European stopover. European airlines have run special deals which include a free overnight in Frankfurt, Prague or London, or which offer special arrangements with Russian and East European hotels (such as Lufthansa's Eastern Europe Program – ph. 800-645-3880).

"Taking the train in" is becoming an increasingly popular way to traverse the Russian frontier. The Helsinki-St. Petersburg route is particularly well-traveled. The seven hour trip gets you into St. Petersburg by dinner time and costs just $122 (first class berth; second class is $72). The next best (translation: next shortest) route, excepting entry via the Baltic states, is Berlin-Moscow. The trip takes 36 hours and a first class ticket runs $273 ($179 for second class). If you are interested in booking train travel into Russia or within Russia before your go, RailEurope is your best bet, ph. (800) 438-7245 or (914) 682-2999 and ask for the Russia desk.

There are also ferries and boats into St. Petersburg (or the Baltic capitals) from Helsinki and Stockholm, depending on the time of year. Again, talk to your travel agent.

Accommodations

The situation with travel accommodations in Russia is improving. First, the growth of private enterprise has led to a flourishing of private tour agencies and bed and breakfast operations. Second, the activity of joint ventures and Western investment has led to renovation of a handful of landmark Moscow and St. Petersburg hotels. Space is less and less often hard to come by. As opposed to even a year or two ago, accommodation choices have become better and more numerous.

If you or your host have not already arranged for accommodation, it is suggested you begin settling this issue well in advance of any travel to Russia. And even if you have traveled to Russia frequently, you will want to survey some of the newer alternatives now open to you. Whereas in years past all bookings for independent travel had to go through Intourist, now booking a room can be as easy as sending a fax or telex to a hotel, or contacting a Western representative of a Russian hotel or bed and breakfast service (or booking through a travel agent).

As elsewhere in the world, there are basically two accommodation choices: hotels and lodging in private apartments.

HOTELS

There are essentially two types of hotels in Russia today: renovated and un-renovated. Renovated hotels include former state-owned hotels that are now operated as joint ventures or are being managed by a Western hotel management company. Also included are the newer breed of hotels owned and run by private Russian companies, and those renovated and run by city and state governments. The common thread is that, to varying degrees, these hotels' living, dining and service facilities have been renovated and their staff have been retrained to meet or approach international service standards.

The un-renovated hotels are the soviet-era behemoths that the reno-vated hotels are trying to distance themselves from. Often dim and cavern-ous, usually shoddily maintained and always offering lackluster service at best, these tend to be state- or enterprise-owned hotels or hotels recently privatized. It is here that you can still view relics of the soviet era: surly waiters, intrusive maids and matrons, cockroaches the size of small house pets and plumbing not upgraded since the revolution. While such hotels still predominate in the provinces, there are fewer and fewer un-renovated hotels in Moscow and St. Petersburg.

The renovated hotels generally offer some measure of business and support services, easy access to money changing (with more plentiful supplies of rubles), the best restaurants and bars, and better locations. Because of their relative prosperity, however, they are more inclined than less-well-off hotels to attract street urchin-pickpockets, conniving cab drivers and prostitutes.

The un-renovated hotels, obviously, offer lower prices. And, true enough, not all un-renovated hotels are undesireable. It simply is more difficult to know what you will be facing in such hotels. By all means, if you have a good recommendation for an older hotel from a trustworthy source, you may have stumbled upon a diamond in the rough. One that may well be on the brink of renovation.

The table on the following pages summarizes the relative quality, size and prices of major Moscow and St. Petersburg hotels. Both renovated and un-renovated hotels (usually 1-2 stars) are listed. Booking or fax numbers for these hotels are provided. Some of these numbers are in the West (especially in the case of chains); some (those preceded by the country code 7) are the hotel's number in Moscow or St. Petersburg. For addresses and locations, see our *Where in Moscow* or *Where in St. Petersburg*. If you don't find a hotel listed in the table, it is because foreigners very rarely stay there, because the hotel opened after this edition of *Russia Survival Guide* was printed, or because the hotel has yet to be renovated. *If you book a room independently, always get a confirmation or reservation number.*

ACCOMMODATION IN APARTMENTS

Accommodation in private apartments is often somewhat more flexible and inexpensive than lodging in hotels, and can be a better option for longer (> one week) stays. This option runs the gamut from bed and breakfast arrangements, to staying with friends and acquaintances, to long-term apartment rental, which were all illegal just a few years ago.

When staying with friends, you will be responsible for dealing with visa registration yourself; read up on this in Chapter 2 under *Visa Support*.

Bed and breakfast and apartment rental alternatives offer a refreshing alternative to hotel stays. A number of Western companies have solid Russian counterparts they work with to arrange these types of accommodation. As well, Moscow or St. Petersburg-based travel companies or apartment leasing companies (see the Yellow Pages in our *Where in Moscow* or *Where in St. Petersburg*) can offer such services. The terms, prices and procedures of each varies. The Apartment Accommodation Checklist and list of companies on pages 90-91 ought to be useful in picking the service provider that best suits your needs.

	Class	No. Rooms	Cost Single	Cost Double	For reservations (* = fax)
Main Moscow Hotels					
Aerostar	★★★★	413	$235-335	$275-375	1-800-843-3311
					7-095-213-9001*
Arbat (Oktyabrskaya II)	★★	107	$130	$160	7-095-244-7628
Baltschug-Kempinsky	★★★★★	234	DM490	DM540	1-800-426-3135
					7-095-230-6503*
Belgrade	★	450	$84	$96	7-095-248-2716
Danilovskiy	★★	100	$200	$230	7-095-954-0750*
Inflotel (Aleksandr Blok)	★★	71	$75	$77-202	7-095-253-9578*
Intourist	★★	434	$130	$135	7-095-956-8450*
Kosmos	★★	1777	—	$110	7-095-215-8880*
Leningradskaya	★	347	$70-85	$120	7-095-975-1802*
Marco Polo Presnya	★★★★	68	$228	$271	1-800-735-5470
					7-095-926-5402*
Metropol	★★★★★	375	$340	$350	1-800-462-6686
					7-501-927-6001*
Mezhdunarodnaya I	★★★	565	$205	$215-250	7-095-253-2051*
Minsk	★	240	$50	$77	7-095-299-1213
Moscow Renaissance	★★★★★	488	$235	$275	1-800-468-3571
					7-095-931-9076

NOTE:

The information in this table was gathered just prior to publication. Room rates do not include VAT (20-25%) and are subject to change without notice.The ratings for hotels are based on a polling of travel agents and business people who travel frequently to Russia and use the following parameters:

★★★★★   **Highest class hotel.** The finest restaurants in the city; unsurpassed support services; modern amenities.

★★★★   **High class hotel.** Would be a first-class hotel in any world capital. Fine restaurants, customer service and business services.

★★★   **Very good to excellent hotel.** Good restaurants. Good to excellent customer service and business services. Comfortable, but either a bit inconveniently located or a bit "soviet" in its style of service.

★★   **Average to good hotel.** Restaurants OK but not consistent. Customer service standards low; few or no business services.

★   **Passable hotel.** Restaurants not suggested. Customer service is poor to non-existent. No business services.

	Class	No. Rooms	Cost Single	Cost Double	For reservations (* = fax)
Moskva	★★	993	$36	$44	7-095-925-0155
National	★★★★★	231	$255	$295-335	7-095-258-7154*
Novotel	★★★★	488	$211	$242	1-800-221-4542
					7-095-926-5903*
Palace Hotel	★★★★★	221	$354	$390	1-800-735-5470
					7-503-956-3151*
Pekin	★★	80	$95	$120	7-095-200-1420*
President	★★★	210	$200	$230	7-501-230-2318*
Rossia	★★	3091	$63	$84	7-095-232-6262*
Savoy	★★★★	86	$360	$390	7-095-929-8665*
Slavyanskaya-Radisson	★★★★	416	$245	$265	1-800-333-3333
					7-095-941-8000*
Sofitel-Iris	★★★★	195	$245	$295	1-800-221-4542
					7-095-488-8844*
Tverskaya	★★★★	122	$230	$260	7-095-258-3099*
Ukraine	★★	1013	$90	$120	7-095-243-3093*

Main St. Petersburg Hotels

	Class	No. Rooms	Cost Single	Cost Double	For reservations (* = fax)
Astoria	★★★★	436	$195	$220	7-812-210-5133*
Clarion North Crown	★★★★	257	$215	$265	1-800-424-6423
					7-812-329-7001*
Grand Hotel Europe	★★★★★	300	$295	$335	1-800-843-3311
					7-812-329-6002*
Helen (in Sovietskaya)	★★	120	$94	$115	7-812-113-0860*
Sankt Peterburg	★★	410	$75	$95	7-812-542-9064*
Moskva	★★	740	$65	$80	7-812-274-2130*
Nevskiy Palace	★★★★★	287	$288	$342	1-800-735-5470
					7-812-275-2001*
Okhtinskaya	★★★	300	$70	$78	7-812-227-2618*
Peterhof	★★★	109	$80	$140	41-55-272-755
					7-812-325-8889*
Pribaltiyskaya	★★	1200	—	$160	7-812-356-0094*
Pulkovskaya	★★★	1600	$120	$140	7-812-264-6396*

☑ APARTMENT ACCOMMODATION CHECKLIST

❑ If this is your first time visiting Russia or arranging a stay in an apartment, it is recommended to work through a Western partner of a bed and breakfast or rental venture.

❑ Try to work only with an agent that can also arrange for your visa support, thus taking care of two problems at once.

❑ Ask and request written verification that the apartment will have a phone that you can use, if you require one.

❑ Ask if the agent's apartment has an individual water heater. Hot water turn-offs are common in Russia, particularly in summer months, and you don't want to pay thousands of dollars to get over there and not be able to have a hot shower.

❑ Get specific directions and a map of the apartment's location before you go, in the event you cannot meet up with your contact.

❑ Use these directions and this map and ask past travelers about the desireability of this location from a range of perspectives (i.e. proximity to metro stations).

❑ Quiz your agent on how, in the case of B&B arrangements, acceptable families are selected. Know what your options are if you and your host family are incompatible.

❑ Quiz your agent in detail about security precautions *vis-a-vis* the apartment. Know in advance who will have keys, when and under what circumstances they will be allowed to enter during your stay. Ask for a statement in writing of what responsibility the agent accepts for the apartment's security. If the agent does not have such a statement and cannot produce one, look elsewhere.

❑ Ask the agent for a list of past customers you can contact about the service they provided.

❑ Finally, discuss with the agent any and all health and environment (smoking, noise, water, etc.) concerns you have, before you leave.

This checklist only provides suggestions.Obviously your needs and itinerary will be very specific. Use this as a starting point for discussions to assure that your service provider can meet your special needs.

THE *Classic*
FLIGHT

148 points to 102 countries

Information: (095) 155-5045.
Booking of tickets: (095) 245-0017.
Cargo transportation: (095) 155-6644,
(095) 578-7940.
Passenger charter: (095) 578-7089.
Cargo charter: (095) 578-8568.
Fax: (095) 155-6647. Telex: (095) 411969
125836 Moscow,
Leningradsky Prospekt 37, bld. 9.

AEROFLOT
Russian International Airlines

Bed & Breakfast and Apartment Rental Agents

American International Homestays, PO Box 1754, Nederland, CO 80466, ph. 800-876-2048, fax 303-642-3365. [Moscow, St. Petersburg, major Russian cities, plus Ukraine, Central Asia and Baltics].

Cultural Access Network, Box 4410, Laguna Beach, CA 92652, ph. 714-497-6773, fax 714-497-6809. [Moscow, St. Petersburg, ph. $75 per night].

East-West Ventures, Inc., P.O. Box 14391, Tucson, AZ 85732, ph. 800-833-4398. [Moscow, St. Petersburg, Kiev, Sochi, ph. $42-64 per night; also offer visa support, driver and translator services]

I.B.V. Bed and Breakfast Systems, 13113 Ideal Drive, Silver Spring, MD 20906, ph. 301-942-3770, fax 301-933-0024.

International Bed and Breakfast, P.O. Box 823, Huntington Valley, PA 19006, ph. 800-422-5283, fax 215-663-8580.

New Solutions, 513 N. Missouri Ave., Roswell, NM 68201, ph. 800-768-9535

Pioneer East/West Initiatives, 88 Brooks Ave., Arlington, MA 02174, ph. 617-648-2020, fax 617-648-7304.

Progressive Tours, 12 Porchester Pl., Marble Arch, London W2 2B5, England, ph. 71-262-1676.

Red Bear Tours, 320B Glenferrie Road, Melbourne, Victoria 3144, Australia, ph. 3-824-7183, fax 3-822-3956, telex AA38615 Kewtel [Moscow and St. Petersburg, $25 a night with meals; also visa support, translators].

YOUTH HOSTELS

Youth hostels have begun operating in both Moscow and St. Petersburg. Both are clean, safe and recommended as cheap alternatives to hotel stays. Both offer an admirable mix of services, ranging from nightly movies to visa support, to ticket purchasing for the Transsiberian and the ballet.

St. Petersburg International Hostel, 3rd Sovyetskaya ul. 28, ph. +7-812-277-0569, fax +7-812-277-5102, email ryhtcaron@glas.apc.org. US Reservations: 409 N. Pacific Coast Hwy, 106/390, Redondo Beach, CA 90277, ph. 310-379-4316, fax 310-379-8420. [visas, library, travel services, close to city center and main train stations]

Travellers' Guest House (Moscow), Bolshaya Pereyaslavskaya ul. 50, ph. +7-095-971-4059, fax +7-095-280-7686, email <tgh@glas.apc.org>. [$30/single, $35/double, $15/dormitory, offer visa support, travel services, close to three major train stations]

The Two Capitals

Most visitors to Russia begin their travels in one of the two capitals: Moscow (the current capital) or St. Petersburg (the imperial capital). One of the first problems to be faced when arriving in these or any Russian city is arrangement of transport. If this is not something a host organization is handling, then you should bone up on the range of options open to you. But first, you should get the lay of the land.

GETTING ORIENTED IN MOSCOW

It always helps to get an understanding of the geography of a city before trying to get around it. It also makes the place seem a bit less foreign.

Moscow is a city founded on a river. Actually, it is founded on three rivers, but two have been put largely underground. The Moscow (Москва) river is the most important geographical feature in the city, but it can also provide the greatest source of confusion in navigation. This is because it does not flow in a straight line through the city, but snakes its way north and south, forming something of a tongue and groove feature in the city center (where the Kremlin lies in the center of the tongue).

Your best bet is not to use the river as a source of orientation, except in the city center. You are better off orienting to the fact that the major city roadways are a series of concentric rings with major arteries intersecting them and stretching outward. The two major rings are the Boulevard Ring and the Garden Ring. Navigating with respect to these two rings (and sometimes the outer Ring Road) and a major cross road will help you remember which end is up. It is helpful to remember that the metro system is similarly organized around a main ring line. For a detailed, current map of Moscow, see *The New Moscow City Map and Guide*, which is also printed in page format in our *Where in Moscow* (see the ordering information in the back of the book).

Sightseeing in Moscow

Should your trip allow sightseeing time, your best bet is to have a native (either one of your hosts or even a taxi driver) give you a drive through the center of Moscow. There are more than enough attractions to see in and around Red Square and the Kremlin. For further points of interest, check your more conventional tourist guide books (see the notes on *Books* in Chapter 1) or ask the service bureau at your hotel for some help (be prepared in the latter case to pay hard currency).

A further interesting way of sightseeing can be via trams. More frequently than buses they allow you to sit down and see out (except in winter when the windows are usually fogged up). Their routes can take you through some of the more interesting, older neighborhoods of Moscow (as this was the first form of public transport in Moscow), and they offer you the advantage of being able to get off at virtually any stop, cross the tracks and take the same numbered tram back to where you started.

Boat rides on the Moscow river in summer are also a relaxing way to see the city and the outlying areas. Boats stop at many landings along the river and run fairly frequently during daytime hours. For a good half-day trip, start at the Kievsky Train Station stop and ride around the peninsula to get off at Gorky Park and go for a stroll there.

The view from Sparrow Hills (formerly Lenin Hills) on a clear day is also not to be missed. For a quiet afternoon in a park atmosphere, try a stroll around Novodevichy or Danilovsky monastery, Kolomenskoye, Sokolniki, the Botanical Gardens, Tsaritsyno or Izmailovo Park.

If you are interested in hitting the pavement and stopping in shops, we recommend Pyatnitskaya, Tverskaya and Petrovka Streets, and the Arbat, for their high shop-density and uniqueness. The old section of town known as Kitay Gorod (Chinese City), where foreigners lived under the Czars, was a major commercial center and may pose some interest for that reason. Likewise, the section near and around Novokuznetsky metro station has much charm.

The Pushkin Museum and Tretyakov Museum (recently reopened) are considered to be the best the city has to offer. But there are also many specialized museums and newer, private galleries. See our *Where in Moscow* for the most current listings. Current exhibits are listed in *The Moscow Times*, which is available free in hotels throughout the city.

For serious shopping for souvenirs, the place to go is the Vernisage at Izmailovo Park (weekends only, go to Izmailovo Park metro station). Everything and anything, it is said, is on sale at Izmailovo, and there are always deals to be had.

If you are looking for a day trip outside the city, there are a number of places in close driving range to visit. Most notable are Sergeyev Posad (formerly Zagorsk), Arkhangelskoye, Abramtsevo, and Gorkiy Leninskiye. A bit farther off are Klin and Borodino.

GETTING ORIENTED IN ST. PETERSBURG

St. Petersburg, for over 200 years Russia's capital, is a city founded on a river delta with the specific purpose of being a maritime city. The river Neva is therefore the most important geographic feature of this "Venice of the North." But the plethora of bridges and canals between the city's 44 islands in the Neva's delta are enough to create significant confusion for the first time visitor.

Your best bet is to focus on the "half-circle" of the city center which is bordered by the river Fontanki on its round edges and the river Neva along its "straight" edge. This half-circle can then be seen as divided into wedges by the three major avenues, Nevsky prospekt, ul. Dzerzhinskovo, and Prospekt Mayorovo. Nevsky prospekt is the most important area of commercial activity in the city.

There are two major islands which form the other half of the circle, on the other side of the Neva. These are Vasilevsky island, where the University is located, and Petrogradsky island, to which Peter-Paul Fortress is attached. Both are mainly residential, and most industrial activity is in the southern regions of the city near the airport, or on the "Vyborg side," also across the river from the main commercial center.

Two key points for orientation in St. Petersburg are the spires of Peter-Paul Fortress and the Admiralty, which can both be seen from most places near the center. The Admiralty spire, golden with a silhouette of a sailing ship at its peak, is the true center of the city and is the apex of the three main avenues in the "half-circle." The taller spire of Peter-Paul Fortress is topped with a cross.

The metro is not as central a part of public transport in St. Petersburg as is the case in Moscow, particularly in navigating the city center. Many points are easily accessible by trolley buses. If you have a lot of ground to cover, rent a car or stick to cabs. For maps and the most up-to-date directory information on St. Petersburg, pick up a copy of our *Where in St. Petersburg*, which includes, in page format, the most current and useful city street map of St. Petersburg, *The New St. Petersburg City Map and Guide* (see the ordering information in the back of the book).

Sightseeing in St. Petersburg

St. Petersburg is more compact than Moscow and easier to navigate on foot. Aside from that, you cannot get the flavor of the canals or the beautifully decorated facades from driving around in cars or trams, so sightseeing on foot is a necessity.

Be sure to see St. Isaac's Cathedral, Peter-Paul Fortress and Palace Square (дворцовая площадь – *dvortsovaya ploshchad*). If you have a spare day in the city, spend it at the Hermitage and/or the Russian Museum, with a side trip to the restored Menshikov Palace across the river from the Winter Palace. But these are just some highlights; St. Petersburg is filled with points of artistic, architectural and historical interest, all of which are detailed in conventional tourist guides (see the notes on *Books* in Ch. 1).

Boat rides on the canals (except in winter) are an inexpensive and interesting way to see the city. Boats depart every 15 minutes from Anichkov bridge (where Nevsky Prospekt meets Fontanka embankment) or opposite the entrance to the Hermitage.

If you are interested in shopping, a walk up and down Nevsky Prospekt is the recommended itinerary. Start at Palace Square and walk up one side at least to Gostiny Dvor, then cross and walk back. You'll get your fill. Klenovy (Maple) alley is the newest venue for street souvenir sales.

For a quiet afternoon in a park, try Kirov Park on Yelagin island. It has walking paths, boating, a bathing beach as well as an exhibition hall and theaters. Boating is also possible at Park Pobedy (Victory Park). Lenin Park and the Botanical Gardens, on opposite sides of Petrogradsky ostrov (island), are also nice.

If you want to get outside the city, visit the former Imperial palaces in Petrodvorets, Pushkin or Pavlovsk, all in close range. Boats and trains service these palaces, or you can rent a car and drive.

PUBLIC TRANSPORT

In general, given the loads it must carry, public transport in both Moscow and St. Petersburg is good. And because it is ridiculously inexpensive, it is crowded and not always your best bet for getting places in a hurry. As well, bus and tram routes are not easily understandable to the non-Russian speaker or non-resident. The metro, however, can be a good way to get around on your own if you can read some Cyrillic (or simply count stops).

The metro system dates from the 1930s in Moscow and from the 1950s in St. Petersburg. Trains run, during daytime hours, about every 2-3 minutes (usually more frequently). The metro is to be avoided at all costs during rush hours, between 7-10 a.m. and 4-7 p.m., unless you have a deep yearning to "get close" to Russia.

One pays for the metro ride by depositing a metro token (which you can buy at a change window, sometimes a few at a time when supplies are short) in automated entry gates inside metro stations. Buses and trams require you to purchase *talony* (талоны) or tickets at metro stations, kiosks, or on the buses and trams themselves, and to validate them by stamping them in punches hanging on the inside of the cabin. Prices for public transport have risen incredibly (by a factor of ten) in the past year, and this trend will continue. Still, in real dollar terms, the fare will likely stay under 50 cents per ride for the foreseeable future.

You can also buy a **monthly pass** good for unlimited travel on all public transport (again prices are constantly changing, but are usually pegged at around 100 times the price of a single ride). If you plan on riding public transport often, have your Russian contact buy this *yediny bilet* (единый билет) for you before your arrival as they are only on sale at selected metro stations beginning the middle of a month for the coming month. They can save a lot of hassle waiting in line to buy tokens.

Metro, Buses and Trolleybuses operate from 6 a.m. to 1 a.m.; Trams 05:30 to 01:30. Metro transfer stations (переходы– *perekhodi*) close at 00:30. Note that these are "official" hours. Given fuel shortages and ever-rising operating costs, expect that many less-busy stations and routes will close down somewhat earlier (and run less often).

TAXIS

The taxi cab, as it is known in other world capitals, virtually disappeared from Moscow and St. Petersburg in the mid-nineties. The predominant form of cabs in these and many other major Russian cities became "gypsy cabs." Among this category are both self-employed drivers (they will often have a little green light in the passenger side of the windshield) and your average Russian who is looking for extra money to meet petrol bills, and is willing to drive you somewhere if it is not too far out of his way (the masculine is accurate usage when speaking about driving, as very few women in Russia drive).

Certainly you can still chance across the odd official cab, the dusty black or yellow Volgas whose meters have been ticking off ten-kopek kilometers since the 1970s. And private companies and municipalities are starting to build up fleets of cabs. But it will be some time before taxi fleets – like the yellow Mercedes in Frankfurt or the sedans in London, rule the roads.

All's fare. This lack of a centralized system makes for a fairly free-wheeling taxi market. All fares are negotiated. The only exceptions are set-rate fares (which can be based on the destination, e.g. the airport, or mileage: rubles/kilometer). These are the rule for hotel-based services and private companies that have appeared in recent years. See our *Where in Moscow* or *Where in St. Petersburg* for listings of the latter, many of which offer quite competitive rates and allow booking by telephone.

As a foreigner catching a gypsy cab on the streets, you should simply expect to pay more for taxis than would the average Russian. Particularly if you do not speak Russian. Nevertheless, despite inflation, the rate for taxi rides (for foreigners) has remained pretty constant vs. the dollar, despite dramatic falls in the ruble/dollar exchange rate. Expect a 10-20 minute cab ride to cost you the ruble equivalent of $3-5 or thereabouts.

While it is less and less likely as time goes on, being recognizable as a foreigner can still infrequently open you to demands of hard-currency payment for rides, particularly late at night, and particularly around foreign tourist hotels and from the airport. Refuse this. As an aside, it is *highly* recommended to use a private "limo" service from the airport to your hotel (expect to pay $40-50). In Moscow, just go up to one of the taxi counters at the airport or call or fax ahead of your arrival – see the Yellow Pages in our *Where in Moscow* or *Where in St. Petersburg*. Of note: In Moscow (at the time of printing) a shuttle bus service from Sheremetevo airport to the city center was being started.

No matter the means of payment, be cautious about flashing lots of money around (something that can be quite inadvertent when you are rooting through a wad of money, trying to discern a 100 from a 10,000 ruble note). As a point of safety, it is wise to keep a sufficient, but not excessive, amount of ruble notes for cab fares in an easy-to-reach pocket and leave your wallet untouched. See the section on *Crime* in Chapter 5 for some further consideration of this issue.

You may also want to consider hiring a cab for the day, the going rate starting at about $10 in rubles per hour for extended periods. Call and compare the rates of private cab companies listed in the Yellow Pages in our *Where in Moscow* or *Where in St. Petersburg*. Or, if you are feeling really lucky, try striking up a conversation with the random gypsy cab driver. Occasionally, if the price is right, you can convince a freelancer to drive you around for a few hours.

More tips. If riding shotgun with a private driver, you are required to wear a seat-belt, or at least drape it across your shoulder. This is not the case if you happen to catch a ride with an official taxi.

Given the recent rise in crime against foreigners, you are advised to be somewhat wary about riding "gypsy-style."

In general, taxis are a good way to get around, if you are willing to brave excessive speeds and exhaust fumes. It is cheaper, faster and more direct than public transport.

CAR RENTAL

The spread of private enterprise to Russia has widened the alternatives for car rental services. Some good deals can be found, but some real rip-offs also need to be avoided. Most agencies offer cars either with or without

---

TIPS ON BEING TAXI SAVVY

Here are some tips for riding wisely in Russian taxis, reprinted with permission from Russian Life magazine (to subscribe, call 800-639-4301, fax 802-223-6105)

- Cars waiting in front of hotels, train stations, and airports charge extremely inflated prices and usually have dubious affiliations. If you find yourself at one of these places and want to pay a lot less, walk around the corner, out of sight, and hail a car there.
- If you don't speak any Russian, don't expect the driver to speak English or any other foreign language. Learn Russian numbers and how to pronounce your destination. It will save you money.
- If you are with a Russian friend or colleague, let them do the flagging and talking. You're more likely to get a better price. If you really feel savvy and have lots of places to go, try negotiating an hourly or daily rate.
- Know the best driving route to your destination (study a map if you have to). Cross the street or hike around the corner if that will place you more in the path of the most direct driving route to your destination.
- You can tip off the driver that you're not a novice by addressing him as шеф (*shchef* – chief, boss) or командир (*komandir* – commander, captain)
- If you are not in a big hurry and don't like the price you are quoted, just close the car door and hail another. Agree on a price before getting into the car, and don't be afraid to haggle or just let them go.
- Set aside your fare money in a separate pocket ahead of time. Don't display large wads of cash, especially hard currency.
- Women alone, especially at night, might want to wait for an official taxi, which are required to post driver identification in the car.
- There is still the option of calling the central taxi booking office (see *Where in Moscow* or *Where in St. Petersburg* for numbers) and ordering a taxi, which is more reliable than it used to be.
- If the driver looks like a hooligan, don't assume it's the occupation. Send him on his way.
- Never get into a car with more than one passenger in it. NEVER! Look carefully in the back seat. If you have any suspicions, send them on their way.
- Never allow the driver to stop for groceries or cigarettes along the way.
- If you chat with the driver, talk about neutral topics. No personal details.
- Use only official taxi agencies from airports.
- Most importantly, relax and enjoy the game. The worst that is likely to happen is that you will wind up paying what you would at home.

---

drivers. See our *Where in Moscow* and *Where in St. Petersburg* for agency listings.

Two points (warnings?) ought to be to kept in mind when choosing to rent a car to drive yourself. First, Russian drivers make New York cab drivers look tame. And the astronomical increase in the number of cars on Moscow and St. Petersburg roads means there are many more of them out there than there used to be. Second, neither Moscow nor St. Petersburg are, in any sense, easy cities to navigate. Street signs are sparse and well-hidden, making it very easy to commit traffic violations. Left turns and right turns are often prohibited by an obscure, unlit sign. And your inevitable transgressions of traffic laws are, particularly at intersections, closely monitored by the ubiquitous GAI traffic officers (ГАИ – pronounced "guy-ee"), who, increasingly, look on Western drivers in the manner of sharks eyeing wounded prey.

And then there is the latest hazard: the smoked-glass Mercedes and Volvo sedans that drive as if they own the road. In point of fact, they just might. Many a hapless driver of late has been unlucky enough to collide with one of Russia's less-than-genteel *nouveau-riche*. The less charitable seem to subscribe to "your-fault insurance" policies, with rather unforgiving damage appraisals. This is why you see humble Moskvitches and Ladas given foreign cars wide berths.

In sum, if you know your way around Moscow or St. Petersburg already, read Russian, and do not mind a bit of added tension on your trip, car rental may be the way for you. Otherwise, stick to taxis or rental cars furnished with a driver. If you do decide to rent a car, here is what you need to know.

License: You must have an International Drivers License (obtained from AAA in the United States) to drive in Russia, and your home country license as well, although GAI rarely get beyond your International License. You can, of course, also drive with a Russian license.

If you do not have an International license, you can get a Russian one (which you must do if you are a resident) by taking your valid license from your home country (along with two passport photos and a nominal fee) to the GlavUPDK Spetsavtotsentr in Moscow at ul. Kievskaya 8, ph. 240-2092. You may have to pass a written test and simulation (complete with model cars), plus a driving test.

Insurance: Most insurance policies can be extended to cover, if they do not already, car rental in Russia. Talk to your insurance agent. Of course, car rental agents also offer insurance when you rent the car, and some may require it. To avoid any problems, you may want to bring proof of insurance coverage. Insurance can also be purchased in Moscow or St. Petersburg (see our *Where in Moscow* or *Where in St. Petersburg*. One note: Russian law allows the company to refuse compensation for damage if a driver is pronounced by authorities to have been under the influence of alcohol at the time of an accident. Such determinations can be arrived at without the benefit of documentable tests.

Traffic violations: In the event you are pulled over for a traffic violation, the usual fee is nominal, and can be paid on the spot. More serious violations, such as driving under the influence of alcohol (which is very strictly punished), or inflicting serious human or property damage in an accident can bring heftier fines and land you in jail. Middle range violations, such as driving without a license or not stopping when signalled to by a militia (GAI) officer (this consists of a flick of the baton and signalling you over toward the curb), usually include a lecture and some haggling before payment of a nominal fee. There have been sporadic incidents of harassment of foreign drivers, yet this has been on the decline of late (see the notes on *Crime*, Chapter 5). In general, to avoid difficulties, if stopped for a traffic violation, remind yourself that you are at a distinct disadvantage and opt to pay the nominal cost of roadside justice, taking heart in the fact that you are probably helping to supplement the miserly salary of a public servant.

☑ MILEAGE CONVERSION	
US	**Russia**
20 mpg	12 liters/100k
30 mpg	8 liters/100k
40 mpg	6 liters/100k

If you are stopped for suspicion of drinking and driving, GAI will give you a breathalizer test on the spot. If the breathalizer shows green, you can dispute the test (at which point you can be taken in for a blood test) or accept the results on the spot (your license will be confiscated) and agree to show up at the GAI office at a later date, at which time GAI will decide your case.

Accidents: If you should get in an accident, the law is that none of the vehicles in the accident may be moved until a GAI officer comes around and takes measurements and writes up a report. This policy is the cause of most traffic jams. The reality is that, if both parties agree who is at fault in the accident, that person will often offer to settle the situation "directly" (i.e. by paying cash for damages) to avoid a run-in with the bureaucracy and demerits on one's driving record. Be wary, however, of any offer of delayed settlement.

An accident ensures an unhappy and bureaucrat-filled visit, so drive carefully. If you do get in an accident, you will be instructed by the GAI officer where you will need to go to fill out necessary accident report papers. This will depend upon where your vehicle is registered. Take all potentially relevant paperwork (license, registration, insurance papers) and a translator if you need one.

Street signs: Street names are in Russian (Cyrillic) and are usually posted on the corners of buildings. Road signs are mainly in keeping with internationally accepted graphical signage, but there are enough important signs in Russian that you should have a reading knowledge of Russian if you want to drive safely.

Rules of the road: Some important driving rules should be noted. Always wear your seat-belt (you will be stopped if you don't). Horns are for emergencies only. Headlights are never used in city limits except in dimmed position, *even at night* (this is slowly changing, however). The speed limit within the city limits is 60 kph (37 mph); outside the city it is 90 kph (56 mph). Turning right on red lights is prohibited. Even in the daytime, headlights must be turned on (in dimmed intensity) when entering tunnels and turned off when exiting. If there isn't a street sign saying you can turn right or left at an intersection, technically you cannot. Just because the guy in front of you just drove up on the sidewalk, it does not make it right. Left turns are almost never possible on major roads; you drive on to a U-turn lane, then come back and make a right turn. Drinking and driving is a very serious offence.

Gas Stations: Three types of gasoline are available: 76 octane, 93 octane, and 95 octane. Most stations have the former two. Do not use 76 octane unless you are told the car has been adapted for this, and in this event use only 76 octane. If you are driving a foreign-made car, use only 95 octane. To avoid waiting in line at gas stations, you can buy gas "by the canister" (10-30 liters) from private speculators, who sell gas at prices well above the normal retail price. Beware, however, such vendors often water down the gas they sell, which can immobilize your vehicle without warning.

In the Yellow Pages of our *Where in Moscow*, you will find a list of Moscow city gas stations by region and a list of stores that sell oil and grease for Russian cars. For St. Petersburg gas stations, consult *Where in St. Petersburg*.

Travel Beyond The Capitals

The same guidelines that apply in Moscow and St. Petersburg are also true for other major cities in Russia. Usually, however, the quality of accommodation and availability of goods and services is far better in the two capitals than in other cities. Especially if you are traveling east, it can be much more difficult to make an international phone call or find a competent translator.

With the exception of a few direct international flights to major cities like Tallinn, Vilnius, Riga, Almaty, St. Petersburg, Yekaterinburg and Kiev (and Khabarovsk, Vladivostok and Magadan from Anchorage and Seattle), it is necessary to travel via Moscow to most points within Russia and the former Soviet Union.

Since October 1992, the only areas "closed" to foreign travel are selected "sensitive" military sites. Further, there is no need to notify authorities about one's itinerary for trips throughout Russia (yet it is wise to leave word with friends or your embassy if you are planning extended solo travel in the hinterlands).

It is advised to have your accommodation reserved in advance. The travel agents listed in the Yellow Pages of our *Where in Moscow* can arrange this, as can some of the travel agents listed in Chapter 1 (see also the *Russian City Guide*, Chapter 4). Regarding travel to cities in other states of the Commonwealth, see the notes on *Visas* in Chapter 2.

As a final general note about traveling within Russia and the Commonwealth, it is highly advisable not to bring with you items that you cannot bear to lose, or that are irreplaceable. Remember, you and your luggage will stand out as being clearly "foreign" and will be a more tempting target for thieves. Keep your passport and all valuable documents with you (and not in your luggage) at all times.

AIR TRAVEL

If the organization that is sponsoring your visit does not arrange the booking and purchase of your air tickets, and you have not done so from your home country, you can book your internal travel through travel agencies listed in the Yellow Pages of our *Where in Moscow* or *Where in St. Petersburg* or through the travel desk of a major hotel. You can also deal directly with Aeroflot to book a flight, but if you do not speak Russian and do not enjoy waiting in long lines, it is simpler to avoid this.

It is often *very* difficult to get tickets for internal travel with less than 72 hours advance booking, so the earlier you start working on it, the better your chances are of traveling. In general, you will have a better chance and less hassle getting the flight or train you want if you book through a travel agency than if you try to book the travel directly. Travel agencies usually have direct contacts that help speed up the process of confirming bookings.

Aeroflot is dead. Once the world's largest airline, the international division was spun off (now known as Aeroflot–Russian International Airlines) and the domestic division has disintegrated into over 300 regional or municipal-based airline companies, most flying jets bearing the old Aeroflot logo. For ease of reference, everyone still calls most of these airlines Aeroflot (as we do in our City Guide, Chapter 4).

Many of these small air fleets are irregularly maintained and flown (often for lack of fuel), undependable and obscenely dangerous. It is not recommended to fly on any domestic airline that is not subject to rigorous licensing and inspection standards. While the Russian government is taking steps to put unsafe airlines out of business and provide oversight for all the others, for the time being the best guideline is to only fly on airlines that have international certification. It is also worth singling out one airline that enjoys a particularly good record for flight safety and comfort: Transaero (Moscow phone: 578-0537/8/9).

What this all means is that the traveler should place a premium on a knowledgeable, savvy local travel agent (see *Where in Moscow* and *Where in St. Petersburg* for listings) who is up on the most recent changes and knows which routes/flights/companies are dependable and safe.

Ruble prices for internal flights (and rail tickets) have skyrocketed with recent price liberalization. Still, on a per mile basis, even with occasional two-tier pricing (higher fares for foreigners) fares are well under Western rates for similar flights.

Book in-country: It is wisest to book tickets for domestic air travel *after* arriving in Russia. Otherwise, you may book a flight from abroad and arrive in Moscow, only to find that your flight has been cancelled or discontinued. Again, rely on a domestic travel agent (see the Yellow Pages in our *Where in Moscow* and *Where in St. Petersburg*) for bookings on internal air travel. If you do book an internal flight from abroad, be certain to use a highly knowledgeable agent and to reconfirm your reservation upon your arrival in-country.

It is also wise to make a note of the reference number you will be given for your travel reservations, and to keep this with your tickets when they have been issued. This is especially true for flights. There is a chance that when you arrive at the airport with tickets in hand, you will be informed that your name is not on the passenger list and you therefore will not be allowed to board the plane. This occurs because flights are regularly over-booked (especially as fuel shortages have restricted their number). If this happens to you, it is best to simply dig in your heels and fight like a dog.

Caveat: if the flight is oversold to the point of passengers buying their way on the flight and sitting in aisles, get off that flight. It is a sorry commentary on the state of the industry that this practice, as well as serious cargo overloading, is a less than rare occurence and one of the most common causes of current Russian air disasters. Don't put your safety and life at risk if you fear overloading. Get off the plane and go catch the train.

It used to be that, for air and rail travel within the former USSR, arrival and departure times were given in Moscow time. This convention has shattered with the assertion of the former republics' independence. Even Russian cities have begun discarding this admittedly odd standard. It is the exception, rather than the rule, that Moscow time is used to denote local arrival and departure times. In any case, check the time differences chart on the map at the front of the book (or the city-by-city clocks in the section following) to calculate local arrival and departure times *vis-a-vis* Moscow time. Then check locally to see which standard is being used.

Moscow has four airports, Sheremetevo I and II, Domodedovo and Vnukovo, so it is very important to find out from which airport your flight is scheduled to leave. Sheremetevo I is for flights to the North and West, including St. Petersburg; Sheremetevo II is for international flights; Domodedovo (Russia's largest airport) is for Eastern destinations; Vnukovo is for southern destinations. All of the airports are quite a distance outside the city; allow one hour traveling time to get to the airport by car or taxi; allow one and a half hours to get to Domodedovo (a 46 km drive).

St. Petersburg has two airports, Pulkovo and Rzhevka. Pulkovo has two terminals. Pulkovo I services domestic flights, Pulkovo II services international flights. Rzhevka handles short distance domestic flights.

Be sure to arrive at the airport at least one hour before your flight is scheduled to depart, and be warned that if you do not allow yourself that much time you stand a chance of not getting on the flight. Check-in and boarding take longer in Moscow or St. Petersburg than in most Western cities.

When you arrive at the airport, keep in mind that foreigners often still must go to a separate check-in desk, usually located somewhat apart from the main check-in hall. You usually locate this desk by looking for a blue and white "Intourist" sign. Your taxi driver or your Russian hosts will almost certainly know where it is located. After you have presented your ticket and checked your baggage (weight limit is 44 lbs.), you will be directed to a waiting room until it is time to board the plane.

When the plane is ready for boarding, an airline representative will escort you to the plane. Often foreigners are driven out to the plane and seated in the front of the forward cabin before the other passengers come aboard – this is considered First Class. Do not expect to be extremely comfortable during the flight. "First Class" and "Business Class" as you may know them do not exist for internal flights (this is coming, however, and was first offered in late 1994 on the Moscow-St. Petersburg route). All of the seats are very close together and there is little room for carry-on luggage. The cabins are also generally not as clean or well-maintained as they are on other airlines.

Unless the flight is more than several hours long, food and drink may not be served. Check with your travel agent ahead of time on this score. In any case, if you suspect that you will be hungry or thirsty during the flight, it is best to bring your own provisions (bottled water is highly advised).

It is essential to always reconfirm the next flight on your itinerary as soon as possible at the Intourist or other travel desk of your hotel.

TRAIN TRAVEL

Many foreigners find that travel by train is easier, more comfortable and more convenient than air travel if the destination is relatively close to Moscow or St. Petersburg. For example, a common way for a business person to travel between Moscow and St. Petersburg is by the night train, which leaves either city at just before or after midnight and arrives in the other city between 8:00 and 9:00 am. In the summer months, it is even light early enough to allow for a view of the countryside. And there is also a day express train that makes the trip in about six hours.

One of the advantages of traveling by train is that you depart and arrive in the center of a city, instead of 30-40 minutes outside of it. And, unless you have more than 77 lbs. of luggage with you, you do not need to wait to collect it when you arrive at your destination (although this is rarely enforced). Train travel can also be more relaxing because you have more room to move around and stretch out than you have on a plane. In the winter months, when airports are often closed due to bad weather conditions, train travel is also more reliable. And with recent fuel shortages causing huge delays with air travel, train travel, while slower, is a more certain mode of transport.

If you plan to eat on the train, it is advisable to bring your own food. Dining cars are showing more plentiful supplies of food these days (this, plus a growth in walkabout vendors), but this is relatively speaking, and it is best to pack what suits your tastes. *Definitely bring your own supply of water* (bottled water can now be bought in most major Moscow and St. Petersburg hotels), even for brushing your teeth. It is advisable to bring your own toilet paper or tissues. If you travel "soft class" (see below), sheets, blankets and towels will be provided, but you may have to pay a small fee for these after you board the train or when you buy your ticket.

Which class? Several different classes are available for train travel, and you must specify what you want when you request your reservation. *By all means travel first class.* There are two types of cabins available. A *coupé* cabin has four berths, two up, two down. A soft class (*myagky*) cabin has two berths and is a hair bigger. A first class compartment has cushioned berths, a small table, reading lamps and a radio. Restroom facilities are located at the end of the car. In no case should you agree to ride by *platzcar*, which is an open bunk car. There are also sitting (*sideniye*) cars, which are acceptable only for short rides. On overnight trips, it is preferable to have a cabin in the middle of the train car as they are less noisy.

If you do not buy the whole compartment for yourself (which you should always try to do), you will share it with others. If you buy out a whole cabin and travel alone (or as a twosome in a four-berth cabin) the train conductor, if she finds out, will insist you cannot do this, and will say they must put someone else in your cabin. This problem can usually be resolved with a small "gift." Note also that it is not a convention to assign persons of the same sex to a sleeping compartment, so if you do not already have a traveling companion, be prepared to share a compartment with either males or females.

You can buy train tickets through any good travel agency (see listings in our *Where in Moscow* and *Where in St. Petersburg*). You can also simply go to the train station where the train will leave from (or to the Advance Ticket Sales office – in Moscow at ul. Petrovka 15 and nab. Kanala Griboyedova in St. Petersburg) and buy a ticket, if it is more than 48 hours or less than 24 hours before the train leaves. See the Yellow Pages in our *Where in Moscow* or *Where in St. Petersburg* for telephone numbers you can call to order tickets from your home/office and have them delivered to you there. Usually if you order tickets 3-4 days in advance you will not have trouble with availability. *One caveat:* given the steep hikes in air fares, which will continue, expect relative overcrowding of rail transport for the foreseeable future.

Passengers must now have their name printed on the ticket they use, and must show identification (often photo ID) both when buying the ticket and when boarding. Still, linguistic ability, the mood of train officials (to say nothing of train station cashiers' ability to deal with currency payments), and the amount of foreigner traffic on a route tends to determine how consistently this is enforced. The advised route is to buy tickets through a travel agent, through Intourist or at the "foreigners' desk" of the locations given above. You will pay a bit more but expedite your travels.

It is best to be at your train at least 30 minutes before departure time – trains tend to leave more promptly than planes. The conductor will ask for your ticket (and identification) before you will be allowed to board the train. Be sure you get the ticket booklet, including the cover, back if you have other tickets in it. Once the train is underway, the conductor will usually serve hot tea before you leave and in the morning on overnight trains. At various train stops budding capitalists will board the train selling food; on well-traveled routes, vendors will walk the train pretty much constantly, selling everything from colas to ice cream to *buterbrody* (open-faced sandwiches).

Crime on trains has been on the rise of late. See the notes on how to protect yourself when traveling by train in Chapter 5.

Both Moscow and St. Petersburg have more than one train station, so be sure to find out from which station your train will leave. As a general guide:

In Moscow: Byelorussky Station serves Belarus, Poland and the West; Kievsky Station is for the Ukraine; Leningradsky Station is for the North and St. Petersburg and Helsinki; Riga Station is for the Baltics; Yaroslavsky Station serves the East and North Russia; Kursky Station serves the Caucausus and the Crimea; Paveletsky Station serves Southeastern Russia; Kazansky Station serves the Urals, Central Asia, and Western Siberia.

In St. Petersburg: Finlandsky Station serves trains to Vyborg, Repino, Razliv and to and from Finland; Varshavsky Station is for trains to Tallinn and Riga; Baltiysky Station is for trains to the southern outskirts of the city and Petrodvorets; Moskovsky Station serves Moscow, the North East and South of Russia; Vitebsky Station handles trains to Pushkin, Pavlovsk and Belarus and Ukraine.

TRAVEL BY CAR

It would be a severe understatement to say driving conditions in Russia and the former USSR are rugged. Fuel and service stations are few and far between (and poorly stocked these days) and only major highways are well paved. Bring a heating pad.

Still, should you decide to get about between cities by car, read the section earlier in this chapter on *Car Rental*. Adhere strictly to local driving regulations. If you are bringing a car in, you may be required to sign a statement guaranteeing re-export of the car, or to pay a hefty import duty. This statement is not obviated by damage to a vehicle, by the way.

Russian City Guide

From Angarsk to Yuzhno-Sakhalinsk

What follows is a listing of important addresses and phone numbers in the 78 largest and/or most important cities in Russia (Brest, Belarus and Yalta, Ukraine have also been thrown in for good measure). As such, it may serve as a starting point for arranging business meetings, accommodations and travel to these cities. While there may be other hotels, restaurants and travel agencies in these cities, the existence of those given below was verified just prior to publication and are thus your most reliable contacts. Still, keep in mind that this type of contact information changes frequently. [Editor's note: nearly 50% of this information was found to have changed over the last 12 months.] Corrections and additions are enthusiastically encouraged.

The number listed for information is the local directory information number, which can be called from Moscow, St. Petersburg or other cities which allow direct inter-city dialing. This number can be called to get the number of locally-based enterprises or of individuals living in that city.

KEY

① City's area code

⊕ Local time when 12 noon in Moscow

✈ Air miles to this city from Moscow

⋏ Population

NOTES ON DIALING:

❶ If the number for information for the city is 990-9111 (i.e. as with Omsk),then after dialing 8 and waiting for a second dial tone (see *Long Distance Dialing Within Russia and the CIS*, Chapter 7), dial only the first three numbers of the city code, then 990-9111.

❷ If the number of digits in the phone number you are dialing (city code plus the local phone number) is less than 10, you will likely not be able to place that call without an operator, but you can try filling in the extra digits with 2's or 0's first (dialed between the city code and the local number) to get ten digits. If the number of digits is 11 or 12, try leaving out the final zero(es) or two(s) of the city code when dialing.

ANGARSK   ① 395-18   ✈ 2575   ☆ 275,000

Information: 609-01
Hotel(s): *Sibir*, ul. K. Marksa 52, 89th kvartal, ph. 307-87 • *Sayani*, ul. K. Marksa 19, 59th kvartal, ph. 223-24 • *Hotel for Foreign Specialists* (G.I.S.), ul. K. Marksa 81a, 91st kvartal, ph. 306-18
Restaurant(s): In the hotel *Sibir*, ph. 306-43 • In the hotel *Sayani*, ph. 239-01 • *Modern*, in G.I.S. Hotel, ph. 303-52
Travel agent(s): *Intourist*, ul. Lenina, 78th kvartal, ph. 609-42
Aeroflot: 7A Mikrorayon 10, ph. 595-31, 595-32, 595-34
Central Telegraph/Post: ul. Chaikovskovo 62, ph. 610-50
Bank(s): *Angarsky Commercial Bank*, pl. Lenina 30, ph. 225-66, fax 643-06
City Council/Administration: Mayor's office, pl. Lenina, ph. 226-05, 226-04
Hospital: City Hospital, 22nd Mikrorayon, ph. 975-21
Getting to/from: Angarsk is on the Transsiberian rail line, so there are several E-W trains passing through daily. Angarsk is about 88 hours by train from Moscow, and less than an hour (32 km) by train from Irkutsk.

ARKHANGELSK   ① 818-2   ✈ 621   ☆ 428,000

Information: 300-00
Hotel(s): *Purnavilok*, nab. Severnoy Dviny 88, ph. 432-389 • *Dvina*, pr. Troitsky 52, 495-502 • *Belomorskaya*, ul. Timme 3, ph. 462-504
Restaurant(s): *Yubileiny*, pr. Troitsky 52, ph. 431-880 • *U Alyosha*, Restaurant ship at Pristan pier mooring • *Seabridge* bar and restaurant, also at Pristan pier mooring • *Relax* nightclub, ul. Shubina 9, ph. 494-934
Travel agent(s): *Intourist*, ul. Lomonosova 209, ph. 435-925, 490-000, fax 491-430 • ul. Svobody 6, ph. 439-618 • Lomonosova prosp. 249, ph. 492-155, fax 494-182
Aeroflot: ul. Voskresenia 116, ph. 462-649, 462-508
Central Telegraph/Post: ul. Voskresenia 8, ph. 432-011
Bank(s): Troitsky prospekt 65, ph. 437-593
City Council/Administration: pl. Lenina 5, ph. 438-684
Hospital: ul. Suvorova 1. ph. 475-371
Other useful information: *Train station*, pl. 60-letiya Oktabrya 2, ph. 460-222 • *Port*, Lenina nab. 26, ph. 441-114, 438-081 • *Customs office*, prosp. Vinogradova 61, ph. 373-51
Getting to/from: Daily flights to/from Moscow (2 hrs), Petersburg (3 hrs) and Murmansk (1 hr). Direct trains (20-25 hrs) from Moscow depart daily from Yaroslavl Station. A daily train to Arkhangelsk from Petersburg (35 hrs) transits Vologda, which is the main cross-over point for other indirect train routes. It is about 1100 km by car from Moscow.

ASTRAKHAN   ① 851-2   ✈ 777   ☆ 512,000

Information: 265-21
Hotel(s): *Korvet*, ul. Boyevaya 50a, ph. 340-378 • *Lotos*, ul. Kremlevskaya 4, ph. 229-500 • *Astrakhansky Gostiny Dvor*, ul. Ulyanovykh 6, ph. 222-988 • *Novomoskovskaya*, ul. Sovetskaya 4, ph. 246-389
Restaurant(s): *Secret*, Komsomolskaya nab. (in steamboat, open 19-24) • *Lotos*, ul. Kremlevskaya 4, ph. 249-889 (11-23) • *Restoran Korvet* (in hotel of same name)
Travel agent(s): *Intourist*, ul. Sovetskaya 21, ph. 246-344, fax 229-730
Aeroflot: ul. Pobedy 54, ph. 254-749

Central Telegraph/Post: ul. Chernyshevskovo 10/27, ph. 223-809
Bank(s): ul. R. Lyuksemburga 3, ph. 220-308, fax 246-417 • *Western Union*: IBSB, Krasnaya nab. 30, ph. 228-778
City Council/Administration: ul. Sovetskaya 15, ph. 221-77, 228-519
Hospital: ul. Tatishcheva 2, ph. 256-718
Getting to/from: Daily flights to/from Moscow (2.5 hrs). The daily train to/from Moscow is a long ride: 31 hrs.

BARNAUL ① 385-2 ✈ 1818 ☈ 610,000

Information: 256-683
Hotel(s): *Barnaul*, pl. Pobedy 3, ph. 252-581 • *Tsentralnaya*, ul. Lenina 57, ph. 253-449
Restaurant(s): *Barnaul*, pl. Pobedy 3, ph. 252-435, 252-440
Travel agent(s): *Intourist*, In the *Barnaul* hotel, ph. 229-327
Aeroflot: ph. 252-697
Central Telegraph/Post: ul. Internatsionalnaya 74, ph. 236-688
Bank(s): ul. Gornoaltayskaya 14, ph. 220-946
City Council/Administration: pr. Lenina 18, ph. 233-295
Hospital: ul. Dimitrova 62, ph. 221-466
Other useful information: *Airport*, ph. 252-697 • *Train station*, ph. 292-529
Getting to/from: There are scheduled, daily flights into and out of Barnaul to/from Moscow, Novosibirsk and other points, but, due to Barnaul's climatic conditions, the most reliable way in and out is by train (2 hrs to Novosibirsk) or bus (6 hours). Trains bound for Barnaul from Moscow depart Kazan station (54 hrs).

BELGOROD ① 072-22 ✈ 357 ☈ 311,000

Information: 22-222
Hotel(s): *Tsentralnaya*, ul. Kommunisticheskaya 86, ph. 21-755 • *Belgorod*, pl. Revolyutsii 1, ph. 22-512
Restaurant(s): *Tsentralniy*, ul. Kommunisticheskaya 86, ph. 20-470, 20-596 • *Yuzhniy*, prosp. Vatutina 2A, ph. 59-624
Travel agent(s): *Intourist*, ul. Kommunisticheskaya 82, ph. 78-600, fax 71-370 • *Turburo*, prosp. Vatutina 2A, ph. 74-667 • *Sputnik*, ul. Narodnaya 135, ph. 29-403/26-340
Aeroflot: ul. Lenina 32, ph. 74-951 • *Information*: ul. Bogdana Khmelnitskovo 166, ph. 40-928
Central Telegraph/Post: pl. Revolyutsii 3, ph. 22-054
Bank(s): *Belgorodpromstroibank*, ul. Frunze 72, ph. 21-363/21-517
City Council/Administration: pr. Lenina 38, ph. 77-206
Hospital: ul. Nekrasova 8/9, ph. 60-483 • *Polyclinic #1*, ul. Litvinova 95A, ph. 347-903
Other useful information: *Airport*, ph. 40-205 • *Train station*, 72-117 • *Museum of Local Culture*, ul. Popova 2a, ph. 23-712, 23-382 • *Representation of the Ministry of Foreign Economic Relations*, pr. Lenina 38, Oblispolkom
Getting to/from: As Belgorod is very near to Kharkov (70 km) in Ukraine, there are plenty of trains between Moscow and Belgorod (12 hrs).

BLAGOVESHCHENSK ① 416-22 ✈ 3433 ☈ 214,000

Information: 990-9111
Hotel(s): *Zeya*, ul. Kalinina 8, ph. 421-100 • *Druzhba*, ul. Kuznechnaya 1, ph. 90-540
Restaurant(s): *Druzhba*, ul. Kuznechnaya 1, ph. 490-510

Travel agent(s): *Intourist*, ul. Lenina 108/2, ph. 445-772, 493-326, 477-217 • *Tourist Bureau*, ul. Shevchenko 34, ph. 421-230 • *Sputnik*, ul. Krasnogvardeyskaya 124, ph. 428-391, 421-0720

Aeroflot: ul. Lenina 193, ph. 425-902

Central Telegraph/Post: *Post office*, ul. Pionerskaya 27, ph. 425-660, 425-673, 422-425

Bank(s): *Bashprombank*, ul. Sovetskaya 2, ph. 424-760

City Council/Administration: Administration, ul. Lenina 133, ph. 421-238

Hospital: *Polyclinic #1*, ul. Kalinina 82, ph. 427-538

Other useful information: *Museum of Local Culture*, per. Internatsionalny 6, ph. 422-414

Getting to/from: There are regular trains between Blagoveshchensk and Belogorsk (120 km), which is on the Transsiberian main line. There is also an overnight train to/from Khabarovsk. Belogorsk is a seven day train ride from Moscow and about 25 hours by train from Vladivostok.

BREST (BELARUS)   ☺ 016-22   ✈ 585   ☿ 265,000

Information: 422-222

Hotel(s): *Intourist*, ul. Moskovskaya 15, ph. 52-083 • *Belarus*, Shevchenko bulvar 6, ph. 592-74

Restaurant(s): In the *Belarus* hotel, ph. 59-190 • In the *Intourist* hotel, ph. 52-089 • *Moskva*, ul. Moskovskaya 17, ph. 54-323, 51-023

Travel agent(s): *Intourist*, ul. Sovetskaya 116, ph. 50-510 • *Bureau of Travel and Excursions*, Shevchenko bulvar 6, ph. 67-075 • *Sputnik*, ul. Naganova 10, ph. 32-630, 65-629

Aeroflot: ul. Naberezhnaya 2, ph. 51-031

Central Telegraph/Post: Postoffice, ul. Moskovskaya 32, ph. 51-103

Bank(s): ul. Pushkinskaya 16/1, ph. 66-031, 32-640

City Council/Administration: ul. Engelsa 3, ph. 39-838

Hospital: ul. Lenina 15, ph. 35-838

Other useful information: *Customs office*, Varshavskoye sh. 1, ph. 65-359, fax 226-7371

Getting to/from: As a major train border crossing with the West, Brest can best be reached or departed from by train. Frequent daily trains to/from Moscow take about 12 hours. On the other hand, it is only 5 hours by train to Warsaw. There are, of course, direct flights between Moscow/St. Petersburg and Brest.

BRYANSK   ☺ 083-22   ✈ 202   ☿ 480,200

Information: 748-724

Hotel(s): *Turist*, ul. Duki 62a, ph. 47-711, 47-492 • *Bryansk*, ul. Lenina 100, ph. 66-844

Restaurant(s): in the *Turist* hotel, ph. 47-556

Travel agent(s): *Turist*, ul. Pionerskaya 33, ph. 465-451, 461-792, 465-313

Aeroflot: pr. Lenina 57, ph. 745-430

Central Telegraph/Post: *Main Post Office*, ul. K. Marksa 9, ph. 442-704

Bank(s): *Bryansksotsbank*, ul. Yelyutina 44, ph. 442-012, 463-353

City Council/Administration: Administration, pr. Lenina 35, ph. 443-013

Hospital: *Polyclinic #4*, ul. Fokina 40, ph. 444-852

Other useful information: *Airport*, ph. 745-834 • *Train station*, ph. 21-020 • *Graphic Arts Museum*, ul. Yelyutina 39, ph. 441-503, 60-864 • *Museum of Local Culture*, ul. Partizan 6, ph. 417-053, 410-390

Getting to/from: Bryansk is most reliably accessible by train, as it lies on the direct rail line between Moscow (Kievsky station) and Kiev. Transit time is about 8-10 hours. By car, it is a 325 km drive.

CHEBOKSARY   ① 835-0   ✈ 373   ☀ 440,000

Information: 222-222
Hotel(s): *Druzhba*, ul. Tsivilskaya 11, ph. 234-248 • *Rossiya*, pl. Gagarina 34, ph. 231-176
Restaurant(s): *Moskovsky*, ul. Elgera 11, ph. 248-963 • *Rossiya*, ul. Gagarina 34, ph. 231-176
Travel agent(s): *Intourist*, Egersky bulv. 59, ph. 253-914 • ul. R. Lyuksemburga 16, ph. 245-356
Aeroflot: pr. Lenina 32, ph. 221-471
Central Telegraph/Post: pr. Lenina 2, ph. 222-232, 222-116
Bank(s): ul. K. Marksa 25, ph. 222-290 • *Western Union*: Ayar Bank, ul. Yaroslavskaya 44, ph. 222-062
City Council/Administration: pl. Karla Marksa 36, ph. 223-576
Hospital: Moskovsky pr. 9, ph. 496-208, 249-300
Other useful information: *Airport*, ph. 263-366 • *Train station*, ph. 213-435
Getting to/from: Trains to/from Cheboksari leave from Moscow's Kazansky station. Traveling time is 16 hours.

CHELYABINSK   ① 351-2   ✈ 917   ☀ 1,148,000

Information: 990-9111
Hotel(s): *Malakhit*, ul. Truda 153, ph. 335-478, 330-948 • *Yuzhny Ural*, pr. Lenina 52, ph. 335-382 • *Slavyanka Hotel*, ul. Lenina 20, ph. 771-077 • *Smolino Lodge*, ul. Tsvillinga 27, ph. 348-992
Restaurant(s): *Uralskiye Pelmeni*, ul. Engelsa 28, ph. 653-065, 360-231 • *Yuzhny Ural*, pr. Lenina 52, ph. 335-382
Travel agent(s): *Intourist*, pr. Lenina 52, ph. 334-305, 335-360, 334-411 • *Aeroflot*, pr. Lenina 28, ph. 614-700, 333-638
Aeroflot: pr. Lenina 28, ph. 339-729
Central Telegraph/Post: ul. Kirova 161, ph. 361-533
Bank(s): ul. K. Marksa 80, ph. 652-879, 367-682
City Council/Administration: pl. Revolutsii 2, ph. 333-805
Hospital: *Hospital #1*, ul. Vorovskovo 16, ph. 346-234
Other useful information: *Airport*, ph. 290-325 • *Railway station*, ph. 379-188 • *American Business Center*, Sovetskaya ul. 65, ph. 623-782, fax 623-768, email <abc@ibm.urc.ac.ru>
Getting to/from: Aeroflot has three to five daily flights to/from Moscow (2 1/2 hrs). Urals Air Service has one flight daily to and from Dusseldorf and one flight daily via Yekaterinburg. See also Yekaterinburg for connecting flights through that larger city. There are plenty of trains along this route, going both East and West, every day. Travel time to Moscow is 30 hrs.

CHEREPOVETS   ① 817-36   ✈ 233   ☀ 316,000

Information: 52-222
Hotel(s): *Leningrad*, bulvar Domenschikov 36, ph. 75-616/75-620
Restaurant(s): *Leningrad*, bulvar Domenschikov 36, ph. 71-176
Travel agent(s): *Meridian*, Dvorets Kultury, ph. 24-872
Aeroflot: Pr. Pobedy 78, ph. 57-619
Central Telegraph/Post: *Otdeleniye Svyazi #27*, pr. Stroitelei 6, ph. 79-541
Bank(s): *Cherepovetsky*, pr. Sovetski 57, ph. 53-403, 53-401
City Council/Administration: pr. Stroitelei 2, ph. 72-629
Hospital: *Polyclinic #2*, ul. Belyaeva 24, ph. 36-301

Getting to/from: Just two hours by train from Vologda, Cherepovets is a 6 hour train ride from St. Petersburg and a 10 hour ride from Moscow (Yaroslavsky station).

CHITA   ① 302-22   ✦ 2921   ✦ 377,000

Information: 990-9111
Hotel(s): *Turist*, ul. Babushkina 40a, ph. 65-270
Restaurant(s): *Maran*, ul. Bogomyadgova 23, ph. 33-292
Travel agent(s): *Intourist*, ul. Lenina 56, ph. 31-246 • *Sputnik*, ul. Lermontova 9, kv. 47, ph. 32-985
Aeroflot: ul. Lenina 55, ph. 34-381
Central Telegraph/Post: ul. Chaikovskovo 24, ph. 33-939
Bank(s): *Chitakompromstroibank*, ul. Petrovskovo 37, ph. 32-858
City Council/Administration: ul. Butina 39, ph. 32-407
Hospital: *Polyclinic #8*, ul. Chaikovskovo
Getting to/from: There are daily trains to/from Moscow, as well as to closer cities, such as Khabarovsk, Irkutsk and Vladivostok. Chita is on the Transsiberian rail line, 107 hours from Moscow and 55 hours from Vladivostok.

ELISTA   ① 847-22   ✦ 715   ✦ 95,200

Information: 556-40
Hotel(s): *Elista*, ul. Lenina 237, ph. 54-170 • *Rossiya*, ul. Lenina 241, ph. 54-000
Restaurant(s): *Rossiya* (in hotel of the same name), ph. 54-080
Travel agent(s): *Tourist Bureau*, ul. Lenina 249, ph. 56-498
Aeroflot: ul. Gorkovo 11, ph. 54-296, 53-312
Central Telegraph/Post: ul. Rozy Lyuksemburg 31, ph. 62-903
Bank(s): *Natsionalny Bank*, ul. Krupskoy 3, ph. 57-850, 53-275
City Council/Administration: ul. Lenina 249, ph. 52-314
Hospital: *Republican Hospital*, ul. Pushkina 52, ph. 58-566, 27-897
Other useful information: *Train Station*, ph. 50-926 • *Museum of Local Studies*, Teatralny per., ph. 62-488 • *Art Gallery*, Pervy Mikrorayon 32, ph. 52-953
Getting to/from: By train, via Rostov-on-Don, Krasnodar and Stavropol, the journey to/from Moscow is about 35 hours.

IRKUTSK   ① 395-2   ✦ 2578   ✦ 642,800

Information: 244-311
Hotel(s): *Intourist*, bulvar Gagarina 44, ph. 290-167, 296-338 • *American House B&B*, ul. Ostrovskovo 19, ph. 432-689, email <irkutsk@glas.apc.org> • *Angara*, ul. Sukhe Batora 7, ph. 293-451, 241-631 • *Sibir*, ul. Lenina 8, ph. 937-51 • *Baikal*, (on lake Baikal), ph. 296-234
Restaurant(s): *Angara*, ul. Sukhe-Batora 7, ph. 293-481 • *Chingiz*, ph. 296-297 • *Irkutskiy*, ph. 296-341 • *Pekin* (Chinese cuisine), ph. 296-325 • *Japanese bar*, ph. 296-305 • *Sibir*, ph. 293-861, *Tsentralny*, ul. Litvinova 17, ph. 344-167
Travel agent(s): • *Irkutsk*, bulvar Gagarina 44, ph. 346-965 • ul. Sverdlova 35, ph. 243-888
Aeroflot: ul. Gorkovo 29, ph. 342-535
Central Telegraph/Post: ul. Proletarskaya 12, ph. 344-801
Bank(s): ul. Lenina 16, ph. 336-952 • *Western Union*: Rossiysky Kredit, Rossiyskaya ul. 10, ph. 331-741

City Council/Administration: ul. Lenina 14, ph. 336-504

Hospital: ul. Yubileynaya 100, ph. 466-507

Other useful information: *Airport*, ph. 270-557, 241-590 • *Train station*, ph. 282-284, 294-809 • *Train ticket office*, ul. Dekabristov sobytii 85, ph. 278-538 • *Sprint office*, ul. Bogdanova 8, ph. 336-116 (Access Number: 433-496), fax 335-356 • *Japan-Russia Trade Association*, ul. Gorkovo 31, ph. 245-444 • *Mongolian Consulate*, ul. Lapina 11, ph. 242-370, 342-447 • *Regional Center for Trade and Commerce*, ul. Sukhe-Batora 16, ph. 335-060, fax 272-387

Getting to/from: The flights to/from Moscow are 7 hours • there are 2-3 flights per day. Irkutsk also has daily flights to other RFE cities. Irkutsk lies about halfway along the Transsiberian rail route – it is some 88 hours to Moscow (Yaroslavsky station) and 78 hours to Vladivostok.

IVANOVO   ① 093-2   ✈ 155   ☤ 480,000

Information: 990-9111

Hotel(s): *Intourist*, ul. Naberezhnaya 9, ph. 376-519 • *Sovetskaya*, pr. Lenina 64, ph. 372-547 • *Ivanovo*, ul. Karla Marksa 46, ph. 374-024 • *Tsentralnaya*, prosp. Englesa 1/25, ph. 328-122

Restaurant(s): *Intourist*, in the hotel of same name, ph. 376-590 • *Atlant*, pr. Lenina 64, ph. 342-378

Travel agent(s): *Intourist*, prosp. Lenina 41, k. 120, ph. 320-594 • *Bureau for Travel and Excursions*, ul. Ermaka 20, ph. 320-651 • *Sputnik*, ul. Stepanova 14, ph. 326-048, 328-256

Aeroflot: pr. Stroitelei 24, ph. 361-617

Central Telegraph/Post: Post office, pr. Lenina 17, ph. 325-451

Bank(s): Tekstil, ul. Bagayeva 27, ph. 326-265, 327-603

City Council/Administration: pl. Revolyutsii 6, ph. 327-020

Hospital: *Regional Hospital*, ul. Lyubimova 2, ph. 269-566

Other useful information: *Airport*, ph. 234-104, 374-647 • *Business Center*, ul. 10-ovo Avgusta 1, ph. 381-613 • *Regional History Museum*, ul. Baturina 6/40 • *Representation of the Ministry of Foreign Economic Relations*, pl. Revolyutsii 6, ph. 327-103 • *Customs office*, ul. 9-ovo Yanvarya 7, ph. 374-403

Getting to/from: While only 155 miles away, Ivanovo is about 6-7 hours away by bus or train (Yaroslavsky station). There are flights (1 hr) from Bykovo airport.

IZHEVSK   ① 341-2   ✈ 590   ☤ 647,000

Information: 223-881

Hotel(s): *Kama*, ul. Sovetskaya 3, ph. 781-542 • *Tsentralnaya*, ul. Pushkinslaya 223, ph. 233-090

Restaurant(s): *Otdykh*, ul. Sovetskaya 18, ph. 787-017, 780-574 • *Izhevsk*, in Tsentralnaya Hotel, ul. Pushkinskaya 223, ph. 232-120

Travel agent(s): *Intourist*, ul. Sovetskaya 16, ph. 787-120, 783-513

Aeroflot: At Airport, ph. 641-609

Central Telegraph/Post: ul. Pushkinskaya 278, ph. 228-372, 228-837

Bank(s): ul. Lenina 30, ph. 782-154 • *Western Union*: Rossiysky Kredit, Pushkinskaya ul. 268, ph. 237-145

City Council/Administration: ul. Pushkinskaya 276, ph. 228-487

Hospital: Botkinskoye shosse 17, ph. 265-483

Other useful information:

Getting to/from: Izhevsk is roughly 21 hours by train from Moscow, via Kazan.

KALININGRAD   ① 011-2   ✈ 668   ☀ 408,000   ⊙

Information: 070 or 990-9111
Hotel(s): *Turist*, ul. A. Nevskovo 53, ph. 460-801, 432-332 • *Kaliningrad*, Leninsky pr. 81, ph. 469-440
Restaurant(s): *Olsztin*, ul. Olstinka 1, ph. 444-635 • *Tourist*, ul. A. Nevskovo 53, ph. 431-237
Travel agent(s): *Intourist*, ul. Kirova 7, ph. 228-485 • *Sputnik*, prosp. Mira 5, ph. 210-727
Aeroflot: pl. Kalinina 1, ph. 446-666, 446-757
Central Telegraph/Post: ul. Kosmonavta Leonova 22, ph. 219-270
Bank(s): *Kredobank*, ul. Minskaya 25, ph. 45-3316, fax 45-3624 • *Western Union*: SB RF, Moskovsky prosp. 39, ph. 469-040
City Council/Administration: pl. Pobedy 1, ph. 215-395, 214-898
Hospital: ul. Klinicheskaya 74, ph.461-405
Other useful information: *Representation of the Ministry of Foreign Economic Relations*, ul. Dm. Donskovo 1, Oblispolkom, ph. 467-391 • *Regional Chamber of Trade and Commerce*, pr. Pobedy 55 • *Free Economic Zone Administration*, ul. D. Donskovo, ph. 467-545 • *Customs office*, ul. Portovaya 6, ph. 499-246, 443-460
Getting to/from: There are direct trains betwee Kaliningrad and Moscow, St. Petersburg, the Baltic capitals, Berlin and points West.

KALUGA   ① 084-22   ✈ 93   ☀ 367,000   ⊙

Information: 22-222
Hotel(s): *Kaluga*, ul. Kirova 1, ph. 49-740 • *Zul*, ul. Gogolya 2, ph. 49-649
Restaurant(s): *Kaluga*, ph. 49-677
Travel agent(s): *Intourist*, ul. Kirova 44, ph. 78-763, 76-454, 78-172
Aeroflot: ul. Lenina 35, ph. 23-345
Central Telegraph/Post: Stary Torg 7, ph. 73-996, 74-139
Bank(s): *Promstroibank*, ul. Plekhanovo 20, ph. 74-859, 73-259 • *Western Union*: Orbita Bank, ul. Michurina 38, ph. 97-980
City Council/Administration: ul. Lenina 93, ph. 73-125
Hospital: ul. Vishnevskovo 1, ph. 125-928
Other useful information: *Airport*, ph. 23-345, 74-079 • *Train station*, ph. 62-649, 94-120 • *Museum of the History of the Cosmonauts*, ul. Tsyolkovskovo 79, ph. 45-004, *Tsyolkovskovo Museum*, ph. 46-180 • *Art Museum*, ul. Lenina 104, ph. 73-660, 72-948 • *Tarus Art Gallery*, Tarusa, pl. Lenina, ph. 70-177
Getting to/from: There are regular trains to/from Moscow (Kievsky station). By car, it is 160 km from Moscow, via the M3.

KAZAN   ① 843-2   ✈ 451   ☀ 1,107,000   ⊙

Information: 760-095
Hotel(s): *Tatarstan*, pl. Kuybysheva 2, ph. 326-979 • *Molodyozhny Tsentr* (Youth Center), ul. Dekabristov 1, ph. 327-954 • *Kazan*, ul. Baumana 9/10, ph. 200-91 • *Volga*, ul. Said Galiyeva 1a, ph. 321-894
Restaurant(s): *Kazan*, ul. Baumana 9/10, ph. 327-054 • *Nauruz*, ul. Kuybysheva 7, ph. 324-815
Travel agent(s): *Intourist*, ul. Baumana 9/15, ph. 320-145, 324-195
Aeroflot: Stary Aeroport Kazan-2, ph. 768-035
Central Telegraph/Post: ul. Rakhmatulina 3, ph. 386-137
Bank(s): ul. Baumana 37, ph. 321-522

City Council/Administration: ul. Lenina 1, ph. 327-060, 325-694
Hospital: ul. Chekhova 1a, ph. 384-176
Other useful information: *Airport*, ph. 379-807 • *Train station*, ph. 326-807 • *Sovam Teleport*, ul. Lonzhenskaya 20a, ph. 762-366 (Access number: 763-688)
Getting to/from: There are daily 1 1/2 hour flights between Kazan and Moscow (Domodedovo). Trains to/from Moscow's Kazan station (both day and night trains are available) take some 15 hours.

KEMEROVO   ☾ 384-2   ✈ 1864   ☀ 559,500

Information: 990-9111
Hotel(s): *Kuzbass*, ul. Vesennyaya 20, ph. 250-254 • *Ton*, ul. Pritonskaya nab. 7, ph. 259-902
Restaurant(s): *Kuzbass*, (in hotel of same name) ph. 251-820, 251-598 (in hotel of same name) • *Ton*, (in hotel of same name) ph. 267-209
Travel agent(s): *Intourist*, ul. Dzherzhinskovo 14, ph. 257-821
Aeroflot: 551-788 (airport), booking office, Oktyabrsky pr. 1
Central Telegraph/Post: Oktyabrsky pr. 10, ph. 523-812
Bank(s): *Kuzbassbank*, ul. Lenina 90/4, ph. 539-900
City Council/Administration: Sovetsky pr. 54, ph. 264-610
Hospital: ul. N. Ostrovskovo 22, ph. 264-531
Other useful information: *Airport*, ph. 557-392 • *Train station*, ph. 269-138
Getting to/from: Kemerovo lies on the Transsiberian rail line and is some 52 hours from Moscow. It is a 5-6 hour flight from Moscow to Kemerovo.

KHABAROVSK   ☾ 421-2   ✈ 3790   ☀ 624,000

Information: 216-503
Hotel(s): *Lyudmila*, ul. Muravieva-Amurskovo 33, ph. 388-665 • *Intourist*, Amursky bulvar 2, ph. 399-313 • *Sapporo*, ul. Komsomolskaya 79, ph. 226-745, 332-702, sat. fax 7-509-016-00131 • *Tsentralnaya*, ul. Pushkina 52, ph. 336-731 • *Amur*, ul. Lenina 29, ph. 2224-143 • *Amethyst*, ul. Lev Tostovo 5, ph./fax 334-699 • *Parus*, ul. Shevchenko 5, ph. 334-414, fax 333-930
Restaurant(s): *Hotel Restaurants* • *Sapporo* (Japanese), ul. Komsomolskaya 79, ph. 330-882 • *Niigata* (Japanese), ul. Lenina • *Utes Cafe*, Central Park of Culture, ph. 339-352 • *Harbin*, ul. Volochayevskaya 118, ph. 330-862 • *Rus*, ul. Muravieva-Amurskovo 5, ph. 332-898 • *Unikal* (Japanese), Amursky bulvar 2, ph. 399-315
Travel agent(s): *Intourist*, Amursky bulv. 2, ph. 337-634, 399-351 • *International Travel Associates*, ph. 223-528
Aeroflot: Amursky bulv. 18, ph. 332-280
Central Telegraph/Post: *Main Post Office*, ul. Muravieva-Amurskovo 28, ph. 225-199
Bank(s): ul. Moskovskaya 7, ph. 713-357
City Council/Administration: ul. Karla Marksa 66, ph. 335-346
Hospital: Amursky bulv. 2. Room 125, ph. 399-188
Other useful information: *Airport*, ph. 006, 372-573 • *Train station*, ph. 383-530 • *Sprint office*, ul. Muravieva-Amurskovo 58, ph. 214-937, fax 219-299 (Access Number: 218-799) • *DHL Office*, ul. Muravieva-Amurskovo 4, ph. 336-457, fax 337-249 • *TNT Worldwide Express*, ul. Krasnodarskaya 31/8, ph. 378-033 • *UPS*, Ussuriysky bulvar 2, k. 310, ph. 222-121 • *EMS Garantpost*, ul. Muravyova-Amurskovo 28, ph. 334-786 • *Japan Air Lines* (at airport), ph. 370-686 • *Korean Airways* (at airport), ph. 378-759 • *Daltelecom*, ph. 331-896 • *Regional Chamber of Trade and Commerce*, ul. Shironova 113, ph. 332-610, fax 330-312 • *US Foreign Commercial Service and American Business Center*, ul. Turgeneva 69, ph. 332-800, fax 332-

971, email <abc@abc.khabarovsk.su> • *US Peace Corps*, ul. Leningradskaya 19, ph. 330-522 • *Diplomatic Missions: Chinese Consulate*, Lenin Stadium, ph. 348-537, 399-890, fax 338-390 • *Japanese Consulate*, ul. Pushkina 38a, ph. 338-962, 331-918, fax 331-912
Getting to/from: There are two daily flights between Khabarovsk and Moscow (8 1/2 hours). As the major air hub for the region, Khabarovsk has plenty of flights to and from all cities in the region, as well as to Japan, Korea, Seattle, Anchorage and San Francisco (via Alaska Airlines — at least weekly flights year round).

KOSTROMA   ① 094-2   ✈ 186   ✟ 290,000

Information: 990-9111
Hotel(s): *Volga*, ul. Yunosheskaya 1, ph. 546-262 • *Motel* (Intourist), ul. Magistralnaya 40, ph. 533-661 • *Tsentralnaya*, ul. Sovyetskaya 2, ph. 575-481
Restaurant(s): *Rus*, Yunosheskaya 1, ph. 594-276
Travel agent(s): • *Sputnik*, ul. Lenina 54A, ph. 550-523, 550-521, fax 555-961 • *Tourservice*, prosp. Mira 46, ph. 558-241
Aeroflot: ul. Ivana Susanina 54, ph. 574-213
Central Telegraph/Post: ul. Sovyetskaya 6, ph. 574-953
Bank(s): *Tsentrobank*, ul. Knyazeva 5, ph. 575-112 • *Western Union*: Vokvneshtorgbank, ul. Lenina 20, ph. 576-197
City Council/Administration: ul. Sovyetskaya 1, ph. 576-515
Hospital: *Hospital #1*, ul. Sovyetskaya, ph. 554-832
Other useful information: *Airport*, ph. 553-651 • *Train station*, ph. 543-498 • *EMS Garantpost*, ul. Sovyetskaya 6, ph. 577-841 • *Kostroma Graphic Arts Museum*, pr. Mira 5, ph. 574-678 • *Representation of the Ministry of Foreign Economic Relations*, prosp. Mira 4, ph. 576-602
Getting to/from: By train from Moscow's Yaroslavsky station, it is a 7 hour ride.

KRASNODAR   ① 861-2   ✈ 761   ✟ 630,000

Information: 550-333
Hotel(s): *Intourist*, ul. Krasnaya 109, ph. 558-897 • *Motel Yuzhny*, ul. Moskovskaya 40, ph. 559-336
Restaurant(s): *Burgis*, ul. K. Libknekhta 175, ph. 356-925
Travel agent(s): *Intourist*, ul. Krasnaya 109, ph. 576-697, 558-897
Aeroflot: ul. Krasnaya 129, ph. 576-007, Airport, ph. 572-507
Central Telegraph/Post: ul. Krasnaya 59, ph. 524-811
Bank(s): *Kuban-Bank*, ul. Ordzhonikidze 29, ph. 522-182, 590-608 (Western Union desk)
City Council/Administration: ul. Krasnaya 122, ph. 554-348
Hospital: ul. Krasnaya 103, 577-290
Other useful information: *Regional Center for Trade and Commerce*, ul. Kommunarov 8, ph. 523-754, 522-213
Getting to/from: There are frequent flights to and from Moscow. By train it is a 24 hour ride.

KRASNOYARSK   ① 391-2   ✈ 2066   ✟ 924,000

Information: 275-959
Hotel(s): *Krasnoyarsk*, ul. Uritskovo 94, ph. 273-769 • *Turist*, ul. Matrosova 2, ph. 361-470 • *Oktyabrskaya*, ul. Mira 15, ph. 271-916 • *Ogni Yeniseya*, ul. Dubrovinskovo 80, ph. 273-784, 275-262 • *Sever*, ul. Lenina 121, ph. 224-287, 224-114

Restaurant(s): *Yenisey-Batyushka*, ul. Dubrovinskovo 1a, ph. 265-228 • *Turist*, ul. Matrosova 2, ph. 366-647 • *Krasnoyarsk*, ul. Uritskovo 94, ph. 273-457
Travel agent(s): *Intourist*, ul. Uritskovo 94, ph. 273-643
Aeroflot: ul. Matrosova 4, ph. 222-156
Central Telegraph/Post: ul. Karla Marksa 80, ph. 222-555
Bank(s): ul. Kirova 23, ph. 273-334, fax 239-315 • ul. Dubrovinskovo 70, ph. 271-345
City Council/Administration: ul. Karla Marksa 93, ph. 222-231
Hospital: ul. Mira 35, ph. 270-570
Other useful information: *Airport*, ph. 223-311 • *Train station*, ph. 292-441, 293-439 • *TNT Worldwide Express* (at airport), ph. 236-418 • *Regional Center for Trade and Commerce*, ul. Kirova 26, ph. 239-613
Getting to/from: There are several daily flights (4.5 hrs) to/from Moscow and St. Petersburg (6 hrs) and Khabarovsk (4 hrs). As Krasnoyarsk lies on the Transsiberian rail line, there are also plenty of trains going through East and West. It is 64 hours between Krasnoyarsk and Moscow.

KURGAN   ① 352-22   ✈ 1057   ⋔ 370,000

Information: 24-081
Hotel(s): *Moskva*, ul. Krasina 49, ph. 55-309, 56-663
Restaurant(s): *Moskva*, ul. Krasina 49, ph. 55-333, 55-165
Travel agent(s): *Intourist*, In Hotel Moskva, ph. 55-163
Aeroflot: ul. Lenina 9, ph. 23-965
Central Telegraph/Post: ul. Gogolya 44, ph. 21-666
Bank(s): *Kredobank*, ul. Gogolya 109a, ph. 74-733, 73-398, 73-060
City Council/Administration: pl. Lenina, ph. 22-452
Hospital: *Central Polyclinic*, ul. Gogolya 42, ph. 21-194, 21-545
Other useful information: *Sovam Teleport Office*, ph. 71-637 (Access number: 36-869) • *Art Museum*, ul. M. Gorkovo, ph. 28-865
Getting to/from: Flights from Moscow are about 3 hours in length. By train it is about 36 hours to Moscow.

KURSK   ① 071-22   ✈ 280   ⋔ 433,000

Information: 21-313
Hotel(s): *Kursk*, ul. Lenina 24, ph. 26-980 • *Solovinaya Roshcha* (Intourist), ul. Engelsa 142a, ph. 563-236, 359-236
Restaurant(s): *Kursk*, (in hotel of same name) ph. 21-784 • *Oktyabrskaya*, ul. Lenina 72, ph. 569-220, 569-252
Travel agent(s): *Intourist*, In Solovinaya Roshcha hotel, ph. 359-213 • *Tourist Bureau*, pl. Krasnaya 6, ph. 20-460, 26-055 • *Sputnik*, pl. Krasnaya 6, ph. 21-300, 22-163, fax 22-168
Aeroflot: ul. Karla Marksa 12, ph. 25-682, 20-300
Central Telegraph/Post: ul. Krasnaya ploschad 8, ph. 25-006, 26-295
Bank(s): *Kurskbank*, ul. Gorkovo 34, ph. 568-613, 252-64
City Council/Administration: ul. Lenina 1, ph. 26-363
Hospital: *Hospital #1*, ul. Dimitrova 61, ph. 23-453
Other useful information: *Airport*, ph. 64-120 • *Train station*, ph. 21-798 • *Art Gallery*, ul. Sovetskaya 3, ph. 23-936 • *Museum of Local Culture*, ul. Lunacharskovo 6, ph. 26-474
Getting to/from: There are flights four times a week with Moscow and one per week with St. Petersburg. There are several daily trains to and from Moscow (8 hrs). It is a three hour ride over the border to Kharkov.

KYZYL   ① 394-22   ✈ 2284   ✗ 88,000

Information: 333-05
Hotel(s): *Odugen*, ul. Krasny Partisan 36, ph. 325-18
Restaurant(s): *Uluk-Khen*, ul. Tuvintsev-Dobrovoltsev 18, ph. 358-65
Travel agent(s): *Intourist*, ul. Kochetova 3, ph. 312-81, 301-33 • *Sputnik*, ul. Krasny Partizan 38, ph. 325-29
Aeroflot: ul. Buxtuyeva 3, ph. 341-49
Central Telegraph/Post: ul. Kochetova 53, ph. 246-72
Bank(s): ul. Lenina 23, ph. 349-80, fax 368-10
City Council/Administration: *Mayor's office*, ul. Lenina 32, ph. 323-95
Hospital: ul. A. Kurside 159, ph. 320-22
Other useful information: *Airport*, ph. 300-25, 341-49, Information: 328-70
Getting to/from: Kyzyl's mountain location makes the scheduled daily flights to and from Krasnoyarsk and Novosibirsk uncertain bets. There are buses (9 hrs) three times a day to and from Abakan, a better transportation hub for flights and trains.

LIPETSK   ① 074-2   ✈ 233   ✗ 500,000

Information: 772-222
Hotel(s): *Lipetsk*, ul. Lenina 11, ph. 24-7217 • *Metalurg*, ul. Lenina 36, ph. 24-1311
Restaurant(s): Cafe in the hotel *Metalurg*, ph. 245-125 • *Yakhont*, pr. Pobedy 8, ph. 773-220
Travel agent(s): *Intourist*, ul. Plekhanova 1, Dom Pechati, ph. 246-761, 247-194 • *Sputnik*, ul. Lenina 23, ph. 247-239, 244-900, fax 720-546
Central Telegraph/Post: ul. Plekhanova 1a, ph. 241-307
Bank(s): *Lipetskkombank*, ul. Internatsionalnaya 8, ph. 245-327
City Council/Administration: ul. Sovetskaya 22, ph. 776-524
Hospital: *TOO Meditsina*, ul. Lenina 35, ph. 242-297, 240-164
Other useful information: *Train station*, ph. 260-212 • *Lipetsk Museum of Local Culture*, pr. Lenina 4, ph. 240-478 • *Representation of the Ministry of Foreign Economic Relations*, pl. Lenina 1, Dom Sovetov, ph. 241-571
Getting to/from: Lipetsk is eight hours by train from Moscow (Paveletsky station).

MAGADAN   ① 413-22   ✈ 3791   ✗ 166,800

Information: 209-99
Hotel(s): *Magadan*, ul. Proletarskaya 8, ph. 210-14 • *Biznes-Tsentr*, ul. Proletarskaya 84v, ph. 589-44
Restaurant(s): *Avgust*, pr. Karl Marksa 60a, ph. 517-93 • *U Maksa*, ul. Proletarskaya 84v, ph. 582-55 • *Primorskiy*, ul. Kommuny 14, ph. 272-09, 221-58
Travel agent(s): *Intourist*, ul. Proletarskaya 30A, ph. 210-32
Aeroflot: ul. Naberezhnaya 7, ph. 288-91, 241-43, 243-49
Central Telegraph/Post: ul. Proletarskaya 10, ph. 230-05, 225-72 • Post Office, 205-38
Bank(s): *Western Union*: Rossiysky Kredit, Yakutskaya ul. 48a, ph. 509-62
City Council/Administration: pl. Gorkovo 1, ph. 250-47
Hospital: *Polyclinic*, 2nd proyezd Gorkovo 5, ph. 261-77, 284-28
Other useful information: *Airport*, ph. 933-35 • *Bus station*, pr. Lenina 1, ph. 288-97, 228-97 • *Alaska Airlines* (Airport), ph. 935-39

Getting to/from: If you want to get in or out of Magadan, you need to fly. There are daily flights to and from Moscow and Khabarovsk. Alaska Airlines' flights en route to Khabarovsk and Vladivostok also stop here. There are four flights per week to and from Vladivostok and Novosibirsk.

MAKHACHKALA   ① 872-2   ✈ 980   ✗ 340,000

Information: 70-362
Hotel(s): *Leningrad*, ul. Lenina 57, ph. 681-722
Restaurant(s): *Kavkaz*, ul. Sovetskaya 18, ph. 671-054
Travel agent(s): *Intourist*, prosp. Kalinina 35, ph. 629-398 • *Dagtur*, ul. Kalinina 35, ph. 628-484
Aeroflot: ul. Lenina 119, ph. 675-280
Central Telegraph/Post: pr. Kalinina, ph. 681-940
Bank(s): *Kavkaz-Kredobank*, ul. Chernyshevskovo 115, ph./fax 673-279
City Council/Administration: pl. Lenina 2, ph. 672-157
Hospital: *Zheleznodorozhnaya*, pr. Kalinina 54, ph. 682-709
Other useful information: *Dagestan Historical and Architectural Museum*, pl. Lenina 43, ph. 671-974
Getting to/from: There are daily flights to and from Moscow (3 hrs). The daily train (via Krasnodar) takes about 48 hours.

MURMANSK   ① 815-2   ✈ 917   ✗ 473,000

Information: 514-70
Hotel(s): *Polyarniye Zori*, ul. Knipovicha 17, ph. 550-282, fax 552-422 • *Arktika*, pr. Lenina 82, ph. 557-988
Restaurant(s): *Dary Morya*, pr. Lenina 72, ph. 572-335 • *Polyarniye Zori*, ul. Knipovicha 17 • *Arktika*, pr. Lenina 82, ph. 554-360, 554-355 • *International Seamans' Club*: ul. Karla Marksa 1, ph. 559-126
Travel agent(s): *Intourist*, ul. Knipovicha 17, ph. 554-385, 554-386, fax 552-422 • *Murmansk Lights*, ul. Furmanova 11, ph. 560-273
Aeroflot: pr. Lenina 19, ph. 560-508
Central Telegraph/Post: pr. Lenina 82a, ph. 555-613
Bank(s): ul. Profsoyuzov 11, ph. 550-237
City Council/Administration: pr. Lenina 75, ph. 555-160
Hospital: ul. Pavlova 6, ph. 566-260
Other useful information: *Finnish Consulate*, ul. Karla Marksa 25a, ph. 543-275 • *Norwegian Consulate*, ul. Pushkinskaya 10, ph. 556-337 • *Regional Center for Trade and Commerce*, ul. Papanina 9, ph. 551-286, fax 548-400 • *Customs office*, ul. Gorkovo 15, ph. 586-866
Getting to/from: By train, it is a 39 hour ride from either Moscow (Leningradsky station) or St. Petersburg (Moskovsky station). By plane from Moscow (Sheremetevo I) the flight is 2.5 hrs.

NABEREZHNIYE CHELNY   ① 855-2   ✈ 575   ✗ 513,000

Information: 535-095
Hotel(s): *Tatarstan*, ul. Gidrostroiteley 18a, GES district, ph. 421-028
Restaurant(s): *Druzhba*, Moskovsky pr. 4, ph. 54-1847/542-335
Travel agent(s): *Sputnik*, Novy Gorod 2/07, ph. 535-217/537-036
Aeroflot: pr. Musy Dzhalilya 2/10, ph. 424-491, 421-129
Central Telegraph/Post: pr. Druzhby Narodov, ph. 585-710, 587-600

Bank(s): *Avtogradbank*, ul. Pervomaiskaya 12, ph. 463-191
City Council/Administration: ul. Khasana Tufana 23, ph. 539-227/536-643
Hospital: *Polyclinic #2*, ul. Musy Dzhalilya 19, ph. 421-432
Other useful information: *Post Office*, ul. Gidrostroiteley 1, ph. 424-174 • *DHL Office*, Moskovsky prosp. 52/03a, ph. 594-409
Getting to/from: By train, via Kazan, it is an 18 hour ride to/from Moscow.

NAKHODKA ① OPERATOR ✈ 4039 ☆ 165,000

Information: 550-09 • City code is 423-66 if you are in direct dial range
Hotel(s): *Nakhodka*, Shkolnaya ul. 1a, ph. 471-88 • *Hotel Pyramid*, Vladivostokskaya ul. 2, ph. 598-94, satellite fax 7-504-915-2207, *Yuan Dong*, Nakhodinsky prosp. 51, ph. 499-95
Restaurant(s): in Nakhodka hotel, ph. 453-07
Travel agent(s): *Intourist*, Nakhodinsky pr. 11, 459-68 • *Turburo*, ul. Pogranichnaya, ph. 592-90
Aeroflot: *Morskoy vokzal*, ph. 552-25, 572-25
Central Telegraph/Post: per. Nizmenny, ATS-4, ph. 475-03
Bank(s): *Vneshtorgbank*, ul.Shkolnaya 19, ph. 475-55, fax 458-59
City Council/Administration: Nakhodinsky pr., ph. 553-25
Hospital: *Polyclinic #1*, Pochtovy per. 3, ph. 552-67
Other useful information: *Casino Spartak*, Nakhodkinsky pr., ph. 557-59 • *Sprint office*, ph. 467-20, fax 427-10 (Access Number: 447-72) • *SeaLand Transport*, ph. 915-1101 • *DHL*, Nakhimovskaya ul. 30, ph. 239-13 • **Diplomatic Missions:** *North Korean Consulate*, ul. Sedova 8, ph. 561-99 • *Vietnamese Consulate*, ul. Sportivnaya 41, kv. 34, 265-37 • *Representative of the Ministry of Foreign Economic Relations*, ul. Portovaya 4 • *Customs office (sea port)*, ph. 423-11
Getting to/from: It is about 3-4 hours by train from Nakhodka to Vladivostok. There is a helicoptor shuttle service (30 min) available, and taxis (3-4 hrs) and buses (5 hrs) can be used to get to and from Vladivostok (180 km). There is also an overnight train to Khabarovsk.

NIZHNEVARTOVSK ① 346-6 ✈ 1429 ☆ 247,000

Information: 235-333
Hotel(s): *Venetsiya*, ul. Internationalnaya 39, ph. 220-682, 224-407 • *The Alberta House*, ul. Internatsionalnaya 100, ph. 239-402, 241-420, fax 241-410 • *Dorozhnik*, ul. 60-letiya Oktabrya, ph. 233-704
Restaurant(s): in *Venetsiya* hotel, ph. 220-682 • in *Alberta House*, ph. 241-420
Travel agent(s): *TurBuro*, ul. Mira 54A, ph. 224-314
Aeroflot: ul. Sportivnaya 17, ph. 229-377
Central Telegraph/Post: ul. Lenina 16, ph. 230-809
Bank(s): *Samotlor-Kredobank*, pr. Pobedy 18A ph. 234-976, 223-668 • *Kapitalbank*, ul. Medeleyeva 13, ph. 237-377, 236-303
City Council/Administration: ul. Tayezhnaya 24, ph. 237-347, 242-440
Hospital: *Hospital #1*, ul. Neftyanikov, ph. 231-388, 230-315 • *Polyclinic*, ph. 223-244 • *Canadian Medical Center*, in the Alberta House, ph. 239-402
Other useful information: *American Business Center*, Venetsiya Hotel, ph. 224-407, fax 224-407, email <allan@abcent.vartovsk.tyumen.su>
Getting to/from: Transaero offers flights between Nizhnevartovsk and Moscow. There are also Aeroflot flights between Nizhnevartovsk and Moscow. By train, it is an 1100 km ride (20 hours) to and from Tyumen, which, in turn, is 35 hours from Moscow.

NIZHNY NOVGOROD   ① 831-2   ✈ 249   🏃 1,455,000

Information: 362-222

Hotel(s): *Tsentralnaya*, ul. Sovetskaya 12, ph. 444-270 • *Rossiya*, Verkhne-Volzhskaya nab. 2a, ph. 362-165 • *Oktyabrskaya*, Verkhne-Volzhskaya nab. 9a, ph. 320-670 • *Nizhnegorodskaya*, ul. Zalomova 2, ph. 312-388

Restaurant(s): *U Shakhovskovo*, ul. Piskunova 10, ph. 367-264 • *Okhotnik*, ul. Belinskovo 9, Pushkin garden, ph. 339-324, 372-476 • *Russky Club*, ul. Markina, river station, ph. 313-476 • *Pivnoy*, Nizhne-Volzhskaya nab. 17a, ph. 343-769

Travel agent(s): *Intourist*, ul. Sovetskaya 12, ph. 440-629, ul. Pyatigorskaya 5/4, ph. 656-349

Aeroflot: pr. Lenina 7, ph. 421-561, 420-985

Central Telegraph/Post: pl. Gorkovo 56, Dom Svyazi, ph. 339-815

Bank(s): ul. Sverdlova 26, ph. 335-922, 335-940 • *Western Union: Avtogazbank*, prosp. Lenina 111, ph. 564-158 • *NBD Bank*, pl. Gorkovo 6, ph. 344-035 • *Vikvneshtorgbank*, ul. Maksima Gorkovo 115, ph. 376-531 and at International Airport, ph. 546-591

City Council/Administration: Kremlin, Dom Sovetov, ph. 391-506

Hospital: ul. Rodionova 20, ph. 361-723

Other useful information: Airport, ph. 541-141 • *DHL Office*, Oktyabrskaya pl. 1, office 38-8, ph. 322-599, 327-021 • *American Business Center*, c/o *Institute for Economic Development*, pl. Svoboda 1, ph./fax 372-213, email <abcnn@abc.nnov.su> • *Regional Center for Trade and Commerce*, pl. Oktyabrskaya 1, ph. 366-358, 360-210, fax 364-009 • *Global USA*, Sovnarkhomovskaya ul. 13, ph. 443-746

Getting to/from: There are overnight trains (8 hrs) from Moscow's Kursky and Yaroslavsky stations, plus a new luxury train from Kazansky station. Transaero offers flights to and from the capital and there are several daily flights on Aeroflot airlines (1.5 hrs).

NIZHNY TAGIL   ① 343-5   ✈ 854   🏃 439,000

Information: 223-009

Hotel(s): *Tagil*, ul. Sadovaya 4, ph. 298-219, *Severny Ural*, ul. Lenina 6, ph. 252-265

Restaurant(s): In hotels

Travel agent(s): *Sputnik*, pl. Lenina 28a, ph. 222-942, 221-775, fax 226-868

Aeroflot: pr. Stroiteley 29, ph. 223-723

Central Telegraph/Post: ul. Pervomaiskaya 52, ph. 25-5488

Bank(s): *Nizhnetagilsky Uralkombank*, ul. Karla Marksa 14, ph. 224-970

City Council/Administration: ul. Parkhomenko 1a, ph. 223-643

Hospital: *Polyclinic #2*, ul. Goroshnikova 37, ph. 254-265

Getting to/from: The most common way in and out is via one of the many commuter trains with Yekaterinburg. The trip takes about 3-4 hours. It takes less time on some regular trains that travel through Nizhny Tagil on their way to and from Yekaterinburg.

NOVGOROD   ① 816-00   ✈ 295   🏃 234,000

Information: 93-011

Hotel(s): *Beresta* (Marco Polo), ul. Studencheskaya, ph. 34-747, fax 31-707 • *Sadko*, Fyodorovsky Ruchey 16, ph. 75-366 • *Rossiya*, nab. Aleksandra Nevskovo 19/1, ph. 34-185 • *Intourist*, ul. Velikaya 16, ph. 75-089, fax 75-147

Restaurant(s): *Kafe Posad*, ul. Bolshevikov 14, ph. 94-849

Travel agent(s): *Intourist*, ul. Velikaya 16, ph. 75-089 • *Tourist Bureau*, ul. Suvorovskaya-Nikolskaya 8a, ph. 32-311, 35-332

Aeroflot: ul. Oktyabrskaya 26, ph. 74-002, 75-446, Airport, ph. 74-242

Central Telegraph/Post: ul. Sovetskaya 2, ph. 77-281

Bank(s): *Novobank*, ul. Velikaya 20, ph. 77-279

City Council/Administration: ul. Chernyshevskovo 4, ph. 72-540

Hospital: *Polyclinic #1*, ul. Slavnaya 45, ph. 34-163

Other useful information: *Airport*, ph. 75-156 • *Train station*, Vokzalnaya pl., 70-572 • *Kremlin, Novgorod Museum of History and Architecture*, ph. 73-608, 73-691 • *Vitoslavsky Museum of Wooden Architecture*, Poselok Yurievo, ph. 72-062 • *Representation of the Ministry of Foreign Economic Relations*, pl. Pobedy 174

Getting to/from: Daily trains from Moscow take nine hours, from St. Petersburg four hours. There is also a faster, lux train from St. Petersburg that makes the trip in two hours.

NOVOKUZNETSK   ① 384-3   ⊀ 1864   ✷ 602,000

Information: 409-111

Hotel(s): *Novokuznetskaya*, ul. Kirova 53, 465-155 • *Metallurg*, pr. Metallurgov 19, ph. 446-185

Restaurant(s): *Otel*, ul. Kirova 53, ph. 465-279

Travel agent(s): *Sputnik*, pr. Metallurgov 37, ph. 441-341

Aeroflot: ul. Tsiolkovskovo 57, ph. 472-904, Info: ph. 453-501, 472-935

Central Telegraph/Post: pr. Metallurgov 21, ph. 447-103

Bank(s): ul. Kirova 89a, ph. 463-240, fax 466-091

City Council/Administration: ul. Kirova 71, ph. 462-455

Hospital: pr. Bardina 28, ph. 440-365

Getting to/from: It is a six hour train ride to/from Kemerovo, which is another 52 hours from Moscow. Or 5 hours by plane.

NOVOSIBIRSK   ① 383-2   ⊀ 1740   ✷ 1,476,000

Information: 990-9111

Hotel(s): *Sibir*, ul. Lenina 21, ph. 237-870 • *Tsentralnaya*, ul. Lenina 3, ph. 221-366 • *Novosibirsk*, Vokzalnaya Magistral 1, ph. 201-120 • *Soran*, ul. Ilyicha 10, ph. 356-609

Restaurant(s): *Druzhba*, ul. Lenina 3, ph. 227-244 • *Sibir*, ul. Lenina 21, ph. 231-348, 231-792 • *Okean*, Krasny pr. 92, ph. 251-738 • *Tsentralny*, ul. Lenina 1, ph. 223-445 • *Sobek*, ul. Dostoyevskovo 19, ph. 205-867 • *Sadko*, Krasny prosp. 96, ph. 251-545

Travel agent(s): *Intourist*, ul. Lenina 21, ph. 230-729

Aeroflot: ul. Pyatovo Goda 83, ph. 291-999

Central Telegraph/Post: ul. Sovetskaya 33, ph. 297-959

Bank(s): Krasny prosp. 27, ph. 220-809 • ul. Lenina 12, ph. 222-089 • *Western Union*: Siberian Bank, ul. Lenina 4, ph. 220-572

City Council/Administration: Krasny prosp. 34, ph. 224-932

Hospital: ul. Zalezhskovo 6, ph. 250-719

Other useful information: *Railway station*, ul. Sovetskaya 72, ph. 207-721 • *Bus Station* (intercity), ph. 460-880 • *River Station*, Dobrolyubova ul. 4, ph. 664-204 • *American Business Center*, Hotel Sibir, ul. Lenina 21, ph. 235-569, fax 235-762, email <abc@saic.nsk.su> • *Lufthansa*, Airport, ph. 227-151, 696-958, cargo 696-818 • *Sprint* office, fax 298-861 (Access Number: 227-006) • *DHL Office*, Krasny pr. 28 (Centre of Russia Hotel), ph. 980-203, fax 233-735 • *UPS*, ul. Lavrentyeva 6, ph. 396-400, fax 324-259 • *Regional Center for Trade and Commerce*, pr. Marksa 1, ph. 464-150, 465-401

Getting to/from: Transaero has daily flights to/from Moscow. Lufthansa has direct flights, twice weekly, to/from Frankfurt. Flight time to/from Moscow is 4-5 hours. As a major station on the Transsiberian, Novosibirsk has plenty of trains passing through in both directions each day. It is 51 hours by train to Moscow, 110 hours to Vladivostok.

OMSK   ☽ 381-2   ✈ 1383   ✦ 1,190,000

Information: 990-9111
Hotel(s): *Omsk*, Irtyshskaya nab. 30, ph. 310-721 • *Mayak*, ul. Lermontova 2, ph. 315-431 • *Irtysh*, ul. Krasny Put 155, korpus 1, ph. 232-702
Restaurant(s): *Omsk*, Irtyshskaya nab. 30, ph. 310-731 • *Mayak*, ul. Lermontova 2 (in hotel of same name), ph. 315-800
Travel agent(s): *Intourist*, ul. 10-let Oktabrya 11, ph. 311-490 • *Turist*, ul. Gagarina 2, ph. 250-624
Aeroflot: River terminal, ph. 357-304
Central Telegraph/Post: ul. Gertsena 1, ph. 251-572
Bank(s): Bankovsky per. 1, ph. 242-195 • *Western Union: IBSB*, ul. Yakovleva 181, ph. 250-601 • *Rossiysky Kredit*, ul. B. Khmelnitskovo 226, ph. 679-006
City Council/Administration: ul Gagarina, ph. 34, ph. 243-554, 246-626
Hospital: ul. Berezova 3, ph. 235-285
Getting to/from: There are several daily flights (4 hrs) to/from Moscow. By train it is 42 hours to/from Moscow, 9.5 hrs to Novosibirsk and 120 hours to Vladivostok.

ORENBURG   ☽ 353-2   ✈ 761   ✦ 560,000

Information: 990-9111
Hotel(s): *Fakel*, Parkovy pr. 32, ph. 471-728 • *Orenburg*, ul. Vystavochnaya 30, ph. 418-185
Restaurant(s): *Orenburg*, ul. Vystavochnaya 30, ph. 410-512 • *Fakel*, Parkovy pr. 32, ph. 471-719
Travel agent(s): *Intourist*, ul. Chkalova 16/2, ph./fax 416-181 • Solyanoy proyezd 22, ph. 472-970
Aeroflot: ul. Turkestanskaya 9, ph. 411-555
Central Telegraph/Post: ul. Kirova 16, ph. 478-165
Bank(s): ul. Devyatovo Yanvarya 48, ph. 473-150
City Council/Administration: ul. Sovetskaya 60, ph. 475-055
Hospital: ul. Aksakova 23, ph. 414-722
Getting to/from: By train to/from Moscow, 40 hours.

ORYOL   ☽ 086-22   ✈ 202   ✦ 345,000

Information: 62-523
Hotel(s): *Oryol*, pl. Mira 4, ph. 51-560 • *Rossiya*, ul. Gorkovo 37, ph. 67-550
Restaurant(s): *Orlik*, ul. Avtovokzalnaya 3, ph. 23-152 • *Oka*, ul. Lenina 16, ph. 64-291, 62-096
Travel agent(s): *Intourist*, ul. Gorkovo 39, ph. 95-909, 31-520, fax 95-683 • *Sputnik*, ul. Saltykova-Schedrina 19/21, ph. 63-634, 65-635, fax 63-215
Aeroflot: ul. Moskovskaya 14, ph. 53-412
Central Telegraph/Post: ul. Lenina 43, ph. 63-934
Bank(s): *Sotef*, ul. Gurtyeva 2, ph. 95-060/93-923, fax 9-57-71
City Council/Administration: Proletarskaya Gorka 1, ph. 62-212

Expanding your business outside Moscow?

.... Now it's as easy as *ABC*!

Our American Business Centers have the professional office and business support services you need to succeed!

Contact one of the American Business Centers today in:

ALMATY, KAZAKSTAN
Phone: 7 (3272) 636-618
Fax: 7 (327) 581-1578

CHELYABINSK, RUSSIA
Phone: 7 (3512) 189-828
Fax: 7 (3512) 189-829

KHABAROVSK, RUSSIA
Phone: 7 (4212) 336-717
Fax: 7 (4212) 334-012

KIEV, UKRAINE
Phone: (380–44) 219-1168
Fax: (380–44) 417-1419

NIZHNEVARTOVSK, RUSSIA
Phone: 7 (3466) 224-407
Fax: 7 (3466) 224-407

NIZHNY NOVGOROD, RUSSIA
Phone: 7 (8312) 372-213
Fax: 7 (8312) 372-213

NOVOSIBIRSK, RUSSIA
Phone: 7 (3832) 235-569
Fax: 7 (3832) 235-762

ST. PETERSBURG, RUSSIA
Phone: 7 (812) 110-6042
Fax: 7 (812) 311-0794

TASHKENT, UZBEKISTAN
Phone: 7 (3712) 332-880
Fax: 7 (3712) 406-676

VLADIVOSTOK, RUSSIA
Phone: 7 (4232) 300-093
Fax: 7 (4232) 300-092

VOLGOGRAD, RUSSIA
Phone: 7 (8442) 335-946
Fax: 7 (8442) 362-732

YEKATERINBURG, RUSSIA
Phone: 7 (3432) 564-623
Fax: 7 (3432) 564-524

YUZHNO-SAKHALINSK, RUSSIA
Phone: 7 (4242) 223-142
Fax: 7 (4242) 223-142

For more information in the U.S., call 202/482–4655, option 21.
The ABC Program is funded by USAID and administered by the U.S. Department of Commerce

THE WORLD'S NUMBER ONE
INTERNATIONAL AIR EXPRESS CARRIER

**Your parcels and documents delivered
internationally and within the CIS**

Please call us at DHL–CIS Country Office:
(095) 956-1000 (information and free pick-up orders)
(095) 956-1001 (administration)

DHL offices in Russia:
Moscow • St. Petersburg • Archangelsk
Nizhny Novgorod • Samara • Togliatti
Novosibirsk Vladivostok • Khabarovsk
Nakhodka • Yuzhno-Sakhalinsk • Kazan
Tomsk • Krasnodar • Yekaterinburg
Rostov-on-Don • Naberezhny Chelny

Hospital: Bulvar Pobedy 10, ph. 93-852

Other useful information: *Airport*, ph. 22-056, 53-127 • *Train station*, ph. 92-280 • *State Literature Museum named for I. S. Turgeneva*, ul. Turgeneva 11, ph. 65-500, 65-574 • *Orlov Museum of Local Culture*, ul. Gostinichnaya 2, ph. 56-797, 56-793 • *Orlov Oblast Art Gallery*, ul. Saltykova-Schedrina 33, ph. 60-587, 63-870

Getting to/from: There are infrequent flights to and from Moscow and St. Petersburg (1 1/2 hours). There are, however, many daily trains (8 hrs), as the city lies on the main route between Moscow and Kharkov.

PENZA   ① 841-2   ✦ 342   ⫟ 551,000

Information: 664-895

Hotel(s): *Penza*, ul. Slavy 10, ph. 668-209 • *Lastochka*, ul. Mira 35, ph. 634-396

Restaurant(s): *Penza*, ul. Slavy 10 • *Lastochka*, ul. Mira 35, ph. 637-350

Travel agent(s): ul. Lermontova 34, ph. 331-256

Aeroflot: ul. Bakunina 25, ph. 663-762

Central Telegraph/Post: Teatralny proyezd 5, ph. 665-828

Bank(s): ul. Moskovskaya 62, ph. 662-210 • *Western Union*: Orbita Bank, Sovetskaya ul. 9, ph. 664-443

City Council/Administration: pl. Marshala Zhukova 4, ph. 631-463

Hospital: ul. Lermontova 28, ph. 664-820

Other useful information: *Airport*, ph. 349-207 • *Train station*, ph. 638-030

Getting to/from: Penza lies about 10 hours SE of Moscow by car and about 12 hours by train (Kazansky station).

PERM   ① 342-2   ✦ 700   ⫟ 1,110,000

Information: 990-9111, 333-420

Hotel(s): *Ural*, ul. Lenina 58, ph. 344-417 • *Turist*, ul. Ordzhonikidze 43, ph. 342-494 • *Prikamiye*, Komsomolsky prosp. 27, ph. 348-662, 349-428

Restaurant(s): *Yevropeisky*, ul. Lenina 72B, ph. 338-716, 332-891

Travel agent(s): *Intourist*, ul. Lunacharskovo 90, ph. 335-585, 330-907, 338-714, fax 333-843 • ul. Gorkovo 14a, ph. 325-028, fax 326-742

Aeroflot: ul. Krisanova 19, ph. 334-668, 333-547, information: 272-244

Central Telegraph/Post: ul. Dvadtsat Pyatovo Oktyabrya 9, ph. 328-418

Bank(s): *Permkombank*, bulv. Gagarina 65, 481-348, 481-622 • *Sota store*, ul. Popova 25, ph. 343-630

City Council/Administration: ul. Lenina 23, ph. 324-084

Hospital: ul. Sovetskoy Armii 17, ph. 272-593

Other useful information: *Sovam Teleport office*, ph. 391-500 (Access number: 391-259) • *Sprint office*, ph. 488-341 (Access number: 659-636) • *Regional Center for Trade and Commerce*, ul. Popova 9, ph. 333-170, fax 333-840

Getting to/from: There are scheduled daily flights with Moscow (3 hrs). By train, Perm is 22 hours by train to/from Moscow on the Transsiberian rail line, and about 6-7 hours from Yekaterinburg.

PETROPAVLOVSK-KAMCHATSKY ① 415-00 ✈ 4288 ☗ 280,000

Information: 91-909
Hotel(s): *Petropavlovsk*, pr. Karla Marksa 31, ph. 50-374, 50-911 • *Avacha*, ul. Leningradskaya 61, ph. 27-331
Restaurant(s): *Geyzer*, ul. Toporkova 10, ph. 56-393
Travel agent(s): *Intourist*, ul. Leninskaya 18, ph. 23-200, 28-442 • *Putnik*, ul. Leninskaya 18, ph. 24-991
Aeroflot: pr. Karla Marksa 31, ph. 54-950, fax 91-537, kassa: 55-916
Central Telegraph/Post: ul. Sovetskaya 65, ph. 24-485
Bank(s): *Kamchatbiznesbank*, ul. Leninskaya 24, ph. 33-305, 32-503, fax 22-482 • *Western Union*: IBSB, Dalnaya ul. 28/1, ph. 273-586
City Council/Administration: ul. Leninskaya 14, ph. 21-000
Hospital: *Polyclinic #3*, ul. Polyanka 2, ph. 55-381 • *Polyclinic #5*, ul. Leningradskaya 114, ph. 23-745
Other useful information: *Airport*, ph. 56-119, 56-719 • *Sprint office*, 24-364 (Access number: 70-031) • *Tourist Center Taratunka*, ul. Tushkanova 3 • *Oblast Museum for Local Culture*, ul. Leninskaya 20, ph. 22-244, 25-411, 25-417 • *Representation of Ministry of Foreign Economic Relations*, ul. Leninskaya 14
Getting to/from: There are two daily flights to/from Moscow (9 hrs). There are daily flights to Khabarovsk (3 hrs) and Vladivostok (3 hrs).

PETROZAVODSK ① 814-22 ✈ 435 ☗ 278,000

Information: 51-201
Hotel(s): *Severnaya*, pr. Lenina 21, ph. 71-258, 71-958 • *Karelia*, nab. Gyullinga 2, ph. 58-897, 52-306 • *Pyotr/Pietari*, Shuyskoe sh. 16, ph. 45-397 • *Karelian Government Hotel*, ul. Sverdlova 10, ph. 75-661
Restaurant(s): *Severnaya*, in hotel of same name, ph. 73-691 • *Petrovskiy*, ul. Andropova 1, ph. 70-992, *Restoran Maxim*, prosp. Lenina 23, ph. 75-038, *Restoran Tok*, in Hotel Karelia, ph. 55-700
Travel agent(s): *Intourist*, ul. Lenina 21, ph. 76-306 • *Sputnik*, ul. Engelsa 5, ph. 75-861, 71-281, fax 75-660
Aeroflot: ul. Antikainena 20, ph. 70-503
Central Telegraph/Post: ul. Maksima Gorkovo 4, ph. 72-091
Bank(s): *Tekobank*, ul. Sovetskaya 22, ph. 49-352
City Council/Administration: pr. Lenina 2, ph. 74-941
Hospital: *Republic Hospital*, ul. Pirogova 3, ph. 74-035
Other useful information: *Train station*, pl. Gagarina, ph. 74-159 • *Airport*, ul. Anekaynena 20, ph. 79-674 • *Graphic Arts Museum*, pr. K. Marksa 8 • *Museum of Local Culture*, pl. Lenina 1 • *Representation of the Ministry of Foreign Economic Relations*, ul. Gertsena 13, ph./fax 72-734 • *Sovam Teleport office*, ph. 52-250 (Access number: 72-071) • *Ben & Jerry's Ice Cream Shop*, Pioneer Palace, ul. Gertsena.
Getting to/from: Daily flights to and from St. Petersburg (2 hrs) and Moscow (2 hrs) • Three flights weekly from Arkhangelsk & Murmansk • MWF flights from Helsinki via Finnair • Six trains daily to/from Moscow (Leningradsky station) or St. Petersburg (Moskovsky station) with passage times of 16 and 7-17 hours, respectively, depending on the train.

PSKOV   ① 811-22   ✈ 373   ✦ 208,000

Information: 22-145
Hotel(s): *Oktyabrskaya*, Oktyabrsky pr. 36, ph. 39-912 • *Rizhskaya*, Rizhskoye shosse 2-6, ph. 62-223
Restaurant(s): *Kavkaz*, Oktyabrsky pr. 10, ph. 24-637 • *Pskov*, ul. Yana Fabritsiusa 5a, ph. 28-758
Travel agent(s): *Intourist*, pr. Rizhski 25, Hotel Rizhskaya, k. 214, ph. 62-254 • *Sputnik*, Oktyabrsky pr. 36, Hotel Oktyabrskaya, room 201, ph. 38-581, 22-119, fax 165-414
Aeroflot: ul. Narodnaya 25, ph. 43-330
Central Telegraph/Post: ul. Nekrasova 17, ph. 25-454
Bank(s): *Pskovbank*, pr. Ryzhsky 40B, ph. 63-743
City Council/Administration: ul. Nekrasova 22, ph. 22-667
Hospital: *Polyclinic #1*, ul. N. Ostrovskovo 19, ph. 25-357/25-352
Other useful information: *Airport*, ul. Germana 34, ph. 22-215 • *Train station*, Vokzalnaya ul. 22, ph. 35-002 • *Pskov State Museum for History, Architecture and Art*, ul. Nekrasova 7, ph. 22-518 • *Mirozhsky Monastyr*, ph. 33-340 • *Representation of the Ministry of Foreign Economic Relations*, ul. Nekrasova 23, ph. 34-067.
Getting to/from: There are two overnight trains to Pskov from Moscow's Leningradsky station (9 hrs). It is about a 5 hour train ride from St. Petersburg.

ROSTOV   ① 085-36   ✈ 109   ✦ 36,400

Information: 30-780
Hotel(s): *Mezhdunarodny Turistichesky Tsentr* (Dom na Pogrebakh), Rostov Kremlin, ph. 31-259, 31-244, ph./fax 30-728 • *Romz*, ph. 95-831
Restaurant(s): *Pogrebok Alyoshi Popovicha*, Kremlin
Travel agent(s): *Intourist*, Kremlin, ph. 32-571 • ul. Okruzhnaya 64, ph. 31-947
Aeroflot: ul. Karla Marksa 17, ph. 31-743
Central Telegraph/Post: ul. Severnaya 44/2A, ph. 32-578
Bank(s): ul. Fevralskaya 10, ph. 30-454
City Council/Administration: Sovetskaya pl. 15, ph. 33-485
Hospital: ul. Leninskaya 37, ph. 33-636
Getting to/from: By train it is some 4 hours from Moscow's Yaroslavsky station, 5 hours by commuter train (changing in Aleksandrov). You can also make the trip by bus (5 hrs) from Moscow's Shcholkovsky bus station.

ROSTOV-ON-DON   ① 863-2   ✈ 590   ✦ 1,028,000

Information: 326-609
Hotel(s): *Intourist*, Bolshaya Sadovaya 115, ph. 659-065 • *Rostov*, Budyonnovsky pr. 59, ph. 391-666 • *Turist*, pr. Oktyabrya 19, ph. 325-427
Restaurant(s): *Intourist*, B. Sadovaya 115, ph. 659-080 • *Kazachiy Khutor*, left bank of the Don, ph. 631-822 • *Petrovsky Prichal*, left bank of the Don, ph. 631-354
Travel agent(s): *Intourist*, B. Sadovaya 115, ph. 655-049 • Voroshilovsky pr. 66, ph. 329-315
Aeroflot: Sotsialisticheskaya ul. 144-146, ph. 659-112
Central Telegraph/Post: Budyonovsky prosp. 50, ph. 662-584
Bank(s): B. Sadovaya 70, ph. 666-777 • pr. Sholokhova 31a, ph. 539-656 • *Western Union*: Doninvest, Khalturinsky per. 99, ph. 679-077 • *IBSB*, ul. Maksima Gorkovo 143, ph. 385-543 • *Promstroybank*, Voroshilovsky prosp. 43, ph. 625-249

City Council/Administration: Bolshaya Sadovaya 47, ph. 666-263
Hospital: ul. Pushkinskaya 127, ph. 662-231
Other useful information: *Airport*, ph. 520-742 • *Train station*, ph. 662-103 • *Sprint office*, ph. 657-420 (Access number: 640-110)
Getting to/from: There are daily flights to/from Moscow (Vnukovo). It is a 20 hour train ride to/from Moscow (Kazansky station) traveling via Voronezh.

RYAZAN   ① 091-2   ✈ 110   🏃 531,000

Information: 990-9111
Hotel(s): *Lovich*, pl. Dimitrova 4, ph. 726-920 • *Priokskaya*, ul. Kalyaeva 13E, ph. 771-257
Restaurant(s): *Lovich*, pl. Dimitrova 4, ph. 726-114
Travel agent(s): *Sputnik*: ul. Sadovaya 44, ph. 773-925 • pl. Dimitrova 4, office 223, ph. 726-309
Aeroflot: ul. Dzerzhinskovo 69, ph. 764-110
Central Telegraph/Post: ul. Astrakhanskaya 61, ph. 772-517, 775-401
Bank(s): ul. Griboyedova 24/5, ph. 444-625 • ul. Podbelskovo 43, ph. 447-769 • *Western Union*: Orbita Bank, Kuybyshevskoye sh., AO Teplopribor, ph. 446-553
City Council/Administration: ul. Radishcheva 28, ph. 772-741
Hospital: ul. Internatsionalnaya 3A, ph. 533-101
Getting to/from: There are frequent trains (4 hrs) between Moscow and Ryazan, leaving and arriving at Moscow's Kazansky station. By car, it is about a 200 km drive down the M6.

SALEKHARD   ① 345-91   ✈ 1165   🏃 32,000

Information: 460-30
Hotel(s): *Yashaya*, ul. Respubliki 100, ph. 415-50
Restaurant(s): *Polyarny krut*, ul. Bogdana Klunyantsa 55, ph. 435-32
Travel agent(s): *Intourist*, ul. Respubliki 72, ph. 454-13
Aeroflot: ul. Gubynina 12, ph. 482-15
Central Telegraph/Post: ul. Matrosova 2, ph. 452-58
Bank(s): ul. Mura 13a, ph. 452-73, fax 474-85
City Council/Administration: ul. Respubliki 72, ph. 451-35
Hospital: *City polyclinic*, ul. Mira 39, ph. 403-62
Getting to/from: You can fly, take the train to Labytnangi (via Pechora) or, in warm seasons, ride a boat up the Ob river from Khanti-Mansiysk.

SAMARA   ① 846-2   ✈ 528   🏃 1,258,000

Information: 334-583
Hotel(s): *Rossiya*, ul. Maksima Gorkovo 82, ph. 390-311 • *Volga*, Volzhsky pr. 29, ph. 338-796 • *Oktyabrskaya*, ul. Avrory 209, ph. 222-985
Restaurant(s): *Parus*, ul. Krasnoarmeyskaya 1A, ph. 324-768 • *Tsentralny*, ul. Frunze 91, ph. 330-744
Travel agent(s): *Intourist*, ul. Kuybysheva 103, ph. 333-411, fax 336-392 • ul. Kuybysheva 44, ph. 332-778, 332-561
Aeroflot: ul. Molodogvardeyskaya 223, ph. 330-386
Central Telegraph/Post: ul. Krasnoarmeyskaya 17, ph. 333-760
Bank(s): ul. Kuybysheva 112, ph. 320-325
City Council/Administration: ul. Kuybysheva 135, ph. 323-044

Hospital: Moskovskoye sh. 2a, ph. 663-814

Other useful information: *Sprint office*, ul. Krasnoarmeyskaya 17, ph. 330-021 (Access Number: 332-690) • *Regional Center for Trade and Commerce*, ul. A. Tolstovo 6, ph. 321-159, fax 327-662 • *Peace Corps Business Center*, Moskovskoye sh. 34, k. 5, ph. 357-403, fax 345-722 • *Aviakompania Samara*, ph. 227-530 • *Airline Ticket and Reservation office*, 520-445 • *Customs office*, ul. Sklarenko 20, ph. 355-757

Getting to/from: There are frequent flights to and from Moscow (3 hrs). There is 26 hours traveling time by train between Moscow and Samara.

SARANSK   ☾ 834-22   ✦ 311   ☆ 347,000

Information: 422-22

Hotel(s): *Saransk*, ul. Kommunisticheskaya 35, ph. 178-882 • *Tsentralnaya*, ul. Sovetskaya 49, ph. 170-671

Restaurant(s): *Saransk*, in the hotel of same name, ph. 178-846 • *Natsionalny*, ul. Sovetskaya 47, ph. 175-438

Travel agent(s): • *Mordov Turist*, ul. Polezhaeva 155, ph. 437-35, 413-56, 178-901

Aeroflot: ul. Razina 42, ph. 176-223

Central Telegraph/Post: ul. Bolshevitskaya 31, ph. 173-026, 174-463

Bank(s): *Mordovsky Finist-bank*, ul. Sovetskaya 52, ph. 176-394

City Council/Administration: ul. Sovetskaya 30, ph. 176-836

Hospital: *Hospital #3*, ul. Kommunisticheskaya 86, ph. 176-493, 174-778

Other useful information: *Airport*, ph. 176-688 • *Train station*, ph. 435-40 • *Mordovsky Museum of Local Culture*, ul. Moskovskaya 48 • *Graphic Arts Museum*, ul. Sovetskaya 29 • *Representation of the Ministry of Foreign Economic Relations*, ul. Sovetskaya 26, Dom Sovetov, room 501, ph. 419-21, 436-50 and ul. Kommunisticheskaya 33, kab. 509, ph. 172-775

Getting to/from: Ten hours from Moscow by train.

SARATOV   ☾ 845-2   ✦ 435   ☆ 912,000

Information: 245-300

Hotel(s): *Slovakia*, ul. Lermontova 30, ph. 267-618 • *Olympia*, ul. Chernyshevskovo 57, ph. 251-441

Restaurant(s): *Slovakia*, ul. Lermontova 30, 269-124

Travel agent(s): *Sputnik*, Nemetskaya ul. 19, ph. 242-225

Aeroflot: per. Mirny 17, ph. 245-058, info: 696-243, kassa: 240-070

Central Telegraph/Post: ul. Pervomayskaya 124, ph. 240-452

Bank(s): ul. Sovetskaya 2, ph. 267-652, 269-640

City Council/Administration: ul. Pervomayskaya 78, ph. 240-249

Hospital: ul. Lizunova 19, ph. 259-148, 250-263

Other useful information: *TNT Worldwide Express*, ul. Vysokaya 12, ph. 640-498 • *Regional Chamber of Trade and Commerce*, ul. Radishcheva 13, ph. 247-610, fax 267-700

Getting to/from: There are daily flights (2 hrs) and daily trains (26 hrs) to/from Moscow.

SMOLENSK   ☾ 081-22   ✦ 217   ☆ 350,000

Information: 052-881

Hotel(s): *Rossiya*, ul. Dzerzhinskovo 23/2, ph. 33-610 • *Tsentralnaya*, pl. Lenina 2/1, ph. 31-754/33-604 • *Smolensk*, ul. Glinki 11/30, ph. 30-397

Restaurant(s): In the *Rossiya*, ph. 96-472, 96-530 • *Cafe Sputnik*, ul. Nikolaeva 7, ph. 69-992

Travel agent(s): *Intourist*, ul. Konenkova 3, ph. 36-980
Aeroflot: ul. Oktyabrskoy Revolyutsii 13, ph. 36-063
Central Telegraph/Post: ul. Oktyabrskoy Revolyutsii 6, ph. 31-201/30-221
Bank(s): *Dnepr*, ul. Bolshaya Sovetskaya 41/18, ph. 36-255
City Council/Administration: *Meriya*, ul. Oktyabrskoy Revolyutsii 1/2, ph. 30-602/31-508
Hospital: *Regional Hospital*, pr. Gagarina 27, ph. 55-3205
Other useful information: *Train station*, ph. 22-250 • *Art Gallery*, ul. Krupskoy 7, ph. 32-709
Getting to/from: From Moscow's Belorussky station, the train ride is 7 1/2 hours long. There are also daily flights to and from Moscow (1 1/2 hrs). By car it is 390 km.

SOCHI   ① 862-2   ✈ 839   ⚡ 345,000

Information: 924-455
Hotel(s): *Lazurnaya*, pr. Kurortny 103, ph./fax 975-974 • *Zhemchuzhina*, ul. Chernomorskaya 3, ph. 992-299
Restaurant(s): *Kavkazsky Aul*, Agura, ph. 979-084 • Kavkaz, ph. 921-437
Travel agent(s): *Intourist*, Kurortniy pr. 91, ph. 990-735, fax/ph.928-681 • *O.K. Travel*, pr. Kurortny 89, room 411, ph. 990-215, telex 191-111
Aeroflot: ul. Navaginskaya 16, ph. 922-936
Central Telegraph/Post: ul. Vorovskovo 1/2, ph. 922-320
Bank(s): *Menatep*, ul. Konstitutsii 16, ph. 999-655 • *Western Union*: Kubanbank, ul. Vorovskovo 56, ph. 686-019
City Council/Administration: ul. Sovetskaya 26, ph. 922-251
Hospital: *Gorodskaya (City Hospital)*, ph. 914-230
Other useful information: *Museum of the Tourist City Sochi*, ul. Ordzhonikidze 29, ph. 923-157
Getting to/from: There are daily flights year round from Moscow (2 hrs) and St. Petersburg (3 hrs), several daily flights in summer. It is 38 hours to/from Moscow by train.

STAVROPOL   ① 865-2   ✈ 760   ⚡ 330,000

Information: 225-252
Hotel(s): *Hotel Complex Intourist*, ul. K. Marksa 42, ph. 231-319
Restaurant(s): *Intourist*, in hotel of same name, ph. 237-275
Travel agent(s): *Travel Bureau*, ul. Dobrolyubova 18, ph. 252-683, fax 250-713 • *Sputnik*, pr. Marksa 76, ph. 230-622, 326-387, fax 260-439
Aeroflot: per. Zootekhnichesky 13, ph. 345-926, 223-050
Central Telegraph/Post: ph. 230-587, 230-608
Bank(s): *Stavropolpromstroibank*, ul. Pushkina 4A, ph. 327-730, fax 227-230
City Council/Administration: pr. Karla Marksa 94, ph. 230-310
Hospital: *Regional Hospital*, ul. Semashko 1, ph. 297-231
Other useful information: *Airport*, ph. 223-050 • *Train station*, ph. 59-297 • *Graphic Arts Museum*, ul. Dzerzhinskovo 115, ph. 230-052 • *Regional Center for Trade and Commerce*, ul. Lenina (in Dom Sovetov), ph. 225-831
Getting to/from: There are daily flights to/from Stavropol from Moscow, from Vnukovo Airport.

SYKTYVKAR   ① 821-22   ✈ 621   ⚡ 225,000

Information: 423-609
Hotel(s): *Syktyvkar*, ul. Kommunisticheskaya 67, ph. 430-143 • *Tsentralnaya*, ul. Pervomayskaya 83, ph. 424-280

Restaurant(s): *Fortuna* (restaurant, bar, casino), ul. Gorkovo 2 • *Syktyvkar*, ul. Kommunisticheskaya 67 • *Tsentralny* (hotel), ul. Pervomaiskaya 83
Travel agent(s): *Intourist*, ul. Pushkina 28, ph. 421-165, 420-124
Aeroflot: ul. Sovetskaya 68, ph. 422-222
Central Telegraph/Post: ul. Lenina 60, ph. 421-150, 420-306
Bank(s): ul. Lenina 45, ph. 421-548
City Council/Administration: ul. Babushkina 22, ph. 421-004
Hospital: *Polyclinic #3*, ul. Kommunisticheskaya 41, ph. 435-837
Other useful information: *Airport*, ul. Pervomaiskaya 53, ph. 494-595 • *Bulgarian Consulate*, ul. Babushkina 10, ph. 420-768
Getting to/from: Syktyvkar is nearly a 2 hour flight from Moscow (Sheremetevo-1), and 24 hours by train from Moscow's Yaroslavsky station.

TAMBOV   ⊙ 075-2   ✈ 249   🏃 335,000

Information: 990-9111
Hotel(s): *Tolna*, pl. Tolstovo 2, ph. 222-013, 210-100 • *Tambov*, ul. Maksima Gorkovo 2/90, ph. 227-502
Restaurant(s): *Tsentralny*, ul. Internatsionalnaya 14, ph. 227-106 • *Tolna*, in the hotel of same name, ph. 210-140
Travel agent(s): *Intourist*, pl. Tolstovo 2, ph. 210-164 • *Sputnik*, ul. Internatsionalnaya 30G, ph. 222-017, 226-691, fax 222-017
Aeroflot: ul. Kooperativnaya 10, ph. 370-770
Central Telegraph/Post: ul. Oktyabrskaya 1, ph. 220-440
Bank(s): *Tambovkreditprombank*, ul. Sovetskaya 118, ph. 220-508, 224-359, fax 222-664
City Council/Administration: ul. Kommunalnaya 6, ph. 222-030
Hospital: *Regional Hospital*, ul. Moskovskaya 29, ph. 222-606
Other useful information: *Airport*, ph. 332-108 • *Train station*, ph. 223-140 • *Tambov Travel Bureau*, ul. Internatsionalnaya 29, ph. 225-680 • *Art Gallery*, ul. Sovetskaya 97, ph. 224-627 • *Tambov Museum of Local Culture*, ul. Derzhavinskaya 3, ph. 227-072, 226-313
Getting to/from: Tambov is a 6 hr. train ride from Moscow's Paveletsky train station.

TOLYATTI   ⊙ OPERATOR   ✈ 513   🏃 654,700

Information: 372-010
Hotel(s): *Zhiguli*, ul. Mira, ph. 223-311
Restaurant(s): *Zhiguli*, in the hotel of same name, ph. 296-245
Travel agent(s): *Intourist*, ul. Zhilina 24, ph. 235-292 • *Sputnik*, ul. K. Marksa 38, ph. 260-026, 260-126, 224-549, 269-361
Aeroflot: Bulvar Lenina, ph. 284-215, 484-215
Central Telegraph/Post: Post office of Central region, ul. Mira 67, ph. 232-058
Bank(s): *Avtovazbank*, ul. Voroshilova 33, ph. 30-3518, 263-395, 245-201, 303-563 • *Western Union*: Doninvest, ul. Sverdlova 22, ph. 337-624
City Council/Administration: *Mayor's office*, pl. Tsentralnaya 4, ph. 235-363
Hospital: ul. Banykina, ph. 280-222, 484-107
Other useful information: *DHL Office*, ul. Karla Marksa 46, ph. 234-354, 225-473
Getting to/from: By car or train, Tolyatti is just 50 km from Samara. See the information on getting to and from Samara, above.

TOMSK   ☽ 382-2   ✈ 1771   ⚔ 507,000   🕐

Information: 223-894
Hotel(s): *Rubin*, pr. Akademichesky 16, ph. 259-689 • *Oktyabrskaya*, ul. Karla Marksa 12, ph. 222-151
Restaurant(s): *Rubin Hotel*, 259-177 • *Beryozka* (bar), ul. Krasnoarmeyskaya 122, ph. 444-414
Travel agent(s): *Intourist*, ul. Belinskovo 15, ph. 232-537, fax 756-821
Aeroflot: ul. Nakhimova 13, ph. 412-466
Central Telegraph/Post: ul. Lenina 93, ph. 223-715
Bank(s): ul. Belinskovo 54, ph. 445-570
City Council/Administration: pr. Lenina 73, ph. 233-450
Hospital: *Medical Univerisity Hospital*, pr. Lenina 38, ph. 230-581, 234-316
Other useful information: *Airport*, ph. 443-575 • *Train station*, ph. 443-780
Getting to/from: Tomsk is located 80 km north of Novosibirsk on the Transsiberian main line (and a 53 hr trip to/from Moscow). There are many trains to and from Moscow. There are also regular flights from Moscow.

TULA   ☽ 087-2   ✈ 109   ⚔ 545,000

Information: 257-403
Hotel(s): *Moskva*, pl. Moskovskovo vokzala, ph. 208-952
Restaurant(s): *Moskva*, pl. Moskovskovo vokzala, ph. 208-963 • *Druzhba*, pr. Lenina 78, ph. 256-407
Travel agent(s): *Intourist*, ul. Sovetskaya 52, ph. 272-774, fax 273-369
Aeroflot: Krasnoarmeysky pr. 9, ph. 205-457
Central Telegraph/Post: pr. Lenina 22, ph. 314-978
Bank(s): ul. Sovetskaya 88, ph. 313-089 • *Western Union*: Orbita Bank, Komsomolskaya ul. 54, ph. 774-350
City Council/Administration: pl. Lenina 2, ph. 278-085
Hospital: ul. Pervomayskaya 13, ph. 318-540
Other useful information: *Airport*, ph. 774-130
Getting to/from: There are frequent trains (4-5 hrs) to Tula from Moscow's Kursky station. By car, it is a 195 km drive.

TVER   ☽ 082-2   ✈ 93   ⚔ 460,000

Information: 337-474
Hotel(s): *Motel Tver*, Sankt-Peterburgskoye sh. 130, ph. 355-692, 426-210 • *Volga*, ul. Zhelyabova 1, ph. 338-100
Restaurant(s): *Tsentralny*, Novotorzhskaya ul. 3/8, ph. 330-391, 338-082 • *Motel Tver*, Sankt-Peterburgskoye sh. 130, ph. 596-98 • *Novy Torzhok*, ph. 380-60 • *Globus*, nab. Afanasiya Nikitina 144, ph. 315-714
Travel agent(s): *Intourist*, Sankt-Peterburgskoye shosse 130, ph. 355-768, fax 554-566 • *RusSoftTour*, ul. Triokhsvyatskaya 10, ph. 425-419
Aeroflot: pr. Chaykovskovo 17, ph.327-716, 427-716
Central Telegraph/Post: ul. Novotorzhskaya 23/35, ph. 334-332, 336-507, 338-532
Bank(s): ul. Volodarskovo 34, ph. 327-217, 331-243 • *Western Union* (*Orbita Bank*), ul. Mussorgskovo 12, ph. 310-092
City Council/Administration: ul. Sovetskaya 11, ph. 330-131

Hospital: Sankt-Peterburgskoye sh. 105, ph. 555-878

Other useful information: *Train station*, ph. 333-221, 336-011 • *Tver InterContact Group* (Business Services, courier, homestays), ul. Triokhsvyatskaya 10, ph. 425-419 • *Tver Local Culture Museum*, ph. 318-404

Getting to/from: By commuter train, a 2 hour ride from Moscow's Leningradsky station. By car, 200 km on the M10.

TYUMEN   ☾ 345-2   ✈ 1041   ✻ 500,000

Information: 252-096

Hotel(s): *Quality Hotel*, ul. Ordzhonikidze 46, ph. 394-040, fax 394-050 • *Tourist*, ul. Respubliki 162, ph. 323-546 • *Prometei*, ul. Sovetskaya 61, ph. 251-423

Restaurant(s): *Four Seasons Restaurant and Cafe Vienna*, in *Quality Hotel* • *Prometei*, ul. Sovetskaya 20, ph. 250-027

Travel agent(s): *Intourist*, ul. Melnikaite 93, ph. 242-371 • *Sodruzhestvo*, ul. Geologorazvedchikov 2, ph. 228-777, fax/ph. 226-250 • *Sputnik*, ul. Respubliki 19, kom. 201, ph. 240-713, fax 240-480

Aeroflot: ul. Respubliki 156. ph. 223-252, 262-946

Central Telegraph/Post: ul. Respubliki 12, ph. 261-398, 250-991

Bank(s): Zapsibkombank, ul. 8-ovo Marta 2/57, ph. 246-780

City Council/Administration: ul. Pervomaiskaya 20, ph. 246-526

Hospital: *Regional Hospital*, ul. Kotovskovo 55, ph. 226-258

Other useful information: *Airport*, ph. 239-747, 239-590 • *Train station*, ph. 292-253 • *Museum for Local Culture*, ul. Respubliki 2, ph. 261-159, 268-071

Getting to/from: There are many daily flights to and from Moscow and St. Petersburg (4 hrs). Moscow is 35 hours away by train. Yekaterinburg is 5 hours away by train.

UFA   ☾ 347-2   ✈ 715   ✻ 1,100,000

Information: 225-720

Hotel(s): *Bashkiria*, ul. Lenina 25/29, ph. 223-347 • *Rossiya*, pr. Oktyabrya 81, ph. 358-907

Restaurant(s): *Sakmar* (restaurant & casino), ul. Pervomayskaya 46, ph. 421-412

Travel agent(s): *Intourist*, ul. Lenina 25, ph. 231-204, 221-111

Aeroflot: ul. K. Marksa 26, ph. 233-656

Central Telegraph/Post: ul. Chernyshevskovo 6, ph. 236-287

Bank(s): ul. Tsuryupy 5, 236-426

City Council/Administration: pr. Oktyabrya 120, ph. 312-816

Hospital: Lesnoy proyezd 3, ph. 323-033

Other useful information: *Central Post Office*, ul. Lenina 28, ph. 232-612

Getting to/from: There are daily flights to and from Moscow (Domodedovo) and it is a 24-26 hour train ride between Moscow and Ufa.

ULAN-UDE   ☾ 301-22   ✈ 2719   ✻ 365,000

Information: 990-9111

Hotel(s): *Barbuzin*, ul. Sovetskaya 28, ph. 21-958, 25-746

Restaurant(s): *Barbuzin*, in the hotel of same name, ph. 26-823

Travel agent(s): *Intourist*, ul. Ranzhurova 12, ph. 29-267, teletype 219268 • *Sputnik*, pr. Pobedy 9, ph. 25-722, 20-834, 21-862

Aeroflot: ul. Yerbanova 14, ph. 22-248, 32-110, 22-248
Central Telegraph/Post: ul. Lenina 61, ph. 23-520/22-703
Bank(s): *Mosbiznesbank*, ul. Lenina 27, ph. 25-401
City Council/Administration: ul. Lenina 54, ph. 25-544, 224-455
Hospital: *Urgent Medical Aid*, 47th kvartal, Oktyabrsky rayon, ph. 71-566
Other useful information: *Museum of Eastern Art*, ul. Profsoyuznaya 29, ph. 21-001 • *Ethnographic Museum of Baikal Peoples*, ul. Kuibysheva 29, ph. 22-909
Getting to/from: There is a daily flight to/from Moscow and to/from Vladivostok. Ulan-Ude is on the Transsiberian main line, some 65 hours ride from Vladivostok (and nearly 100 hours to Moscow).

ULYANOVSK   ① 842-2   ✈ 435   ☀ 668,000

Information: 322-222
Hotel(s): *Venets*, ul. Sovetskaya 19, ph. 394-880, 394-870 • *Oktyabrskaya*, ul. Plekhanova 1, ph. 314-282
Restaurant(s): *Venets*, ul. Sovetskaya 19, ph. 394-897
Travel agent(s): *Intourist*, ul. Sovetskaya 19, ph. 319-735
Aeroflot: ul. K. Libknekhta 28A, ph. 314-442
Central Telegraph/Post: ul. Lva Tolstovo 60, ph. 312-072
Bank(s): ul. Goncharova 26, ph. 325-254
City Council/Administration: ul. Kuznetsova 7, ph. 313-080
Hospital: ul. Orenburgskaya 3, ph. 251-611
Getting to/from: There are daily flights to/from Moscow (2 hrs). By train, the commute is 18 hours.

VLADIMIR   ① 092-22   ✈ 110   ☀ 360,000

Information: 32-222
Hotel(s): *Zolotoye Koltso*, ul. Chaikovskaya 27, ph. 48-807, 48-819 • *Klyazma*, ul. Sudokhodskoye shosse 15, ph. 22-310, 24-237 • *Zarya*, ul. Pushkina, ph 36a. 91-441 • *Vladimir*, ul. Tretyevo Internatsionala 74, ph. 23-042
Restaurant(s): *Zolotoye Koltso*, ul. Tretyevo Internatsionala 74, ph. 47-583, 48-807 • *Vladimir*, ul. Tretyevo Internatsionala 74, ph. 27-325 • *Lada*, ul. pr. Lenina 23, ph. 23-274
Travel agent(s): *Intourist*, ul. Tretyevo Internatsionala 74, ph. 24-262, fax 27-514 • *Bureau for Travel and Excursions*, ul. Kremlevskaya 5A, ph. 26-414, 22-322, fax 22-428
Aeroflot: pr. Lenina 47a, ph. 43-345, 42-927
Central Telegraph/Post: ul. Gorokhovaya 20, ph. 31-859
Bank(s): *Menatep*, ul. Tretyevo Internatsionala 49, ph. 24-138
City Council/Administration: ul. Gorkovo, ph. 32-817
Hospital: *Regional Polyclinic*, Sudogodskoye shosse 41, ph. 29-508
Other useful information: *Airport*, ph. 40-288 • *Train station*, 92-253 • *EMS Garantpost*, Podbelskaya pl. 22/28, ph. 329-279 • *Museum of Crystal and Lacquer Miniatures*, ul. Moskovskaya, ph. 24-872 • *Vladimir-Suzdal Museum of History, Architecture and Art*, ul. III Internatsionala 43, ph. 22-515 • *Representation of the Ministry of Foreign Economic Relations*, ul. Mira 20, ph. 30-388
Getting to/from: By normal or commuter train from Kursky station, it is a 3-4 hour train ride to Vladimir.

VLADIVOSTOK ☎ 423-2   ✈ 4008   ✦ 675,000

Information: 250-269
Hotel(s): *Gavan*, ul. Krigina 3, ph. 219-873, fax 226-848 • *Hotel Versailles*, Svetlanskaya 10, ph.
264-201, fax 265-124 • *Hotel Acfes Seiyo*, pr. 100-letiya Vladivostoka 103, ph. 318-760, sat.
fax 7-509-851-2345 • *Vladivostok*, ul. Naberezhnaya 10, ph. 222-208 • *Ekvator*, ul.
Naberezhnaya 20, ph. 212-860 • *Amursky Zaliv*, ul. Naberezhnaya 9, ph. 225-520 • *Vlad
Motor Inn*, kilometer 19 (on way to airport), 215-829, satellite fax, 7-509-851-5116
Restaurant(s): *Okean*, ul. Naberezhnaya 3, ph. 268-186 • *Vladivostok-Sakura* (Japanese, in
Hotel Vladivostok), ul. Naberezhnaya 10, ph. 260-305 • *Nagasaki*, ul. Svetlanskaya 115, ph.
265-043 • *Ekvator*, ul. Naberezhnaya 20, ph. 212-873 • *Captain Cook's*, Devyataya ul. 14, ph.
215-341 • *Oasis*, Batareynaya ul. 4, ph. 251-970
Travel agent(s): *Intourist*, Okeansky pr. 90, ph. 256-210, fax 258-839 • *Primorsky Club*, ul.
Russkaya 17, ph. 318-037
Aeroflot: ul. Posyetskaya 14, ph. 226-411, International dept., ph. 222-581
Central Telegraph/Post: Okeansky pr. 24/2, ph. 222-806
Bank(s): *ATR-Credobank* (exchange buro), ul. Aleutskaya 16, ph. 222-885, fax 222-264 • ul.
Svetlanskaya 71, ph. 228-791 • *Zhilsotsbank*, Okeansky pr. 19, ph. 222-005 • *Western Union*:
Evrobank, Tigrovaya ul. 29, ph. 211-889 • *IBSB*, Melnikovskaya ul. 101, ph. 251-792
City Council/Administration: Okeansky pr. 20, ph. 223-016
Hospital: ul. 25 Oktyabrya 57, ph. 257-553 • *Health Asia Clinic*, contact via *Vlad Motor Inn* (see
above), ph. 215-829
Other useful information: *Airport*, ph. 006, 237-975-75 • *Train station*, ph. 210-440 • *American
Business Center*, ul. Pushkinskaya 32, ph. 300-093, fax 300-092, email <abcvlad@sovam.com>
• *Vlad Taxi Service*, ph. 250-309 • *Regional Chamber of Commerce and Trade*, Okeansky pr.
13A, ph. 268-423, fax 227-226 • *Sovam Teleport*, ul. Krasnovo Znameni 10, ph. 252-731, fax
259-711 • *DHL Office*, Khabarovskaya ul. 27B, ph. 255-252, ph./fax 255-226 • *TNT Worldwide
Express*, ul. Uborevicha 24/1, ph. 225-4552 • *Alaska Airlines* (at airport), ph. 318-037, 320-
632, fax 320-710 • *Customs office* (sea port), ph. 220-229 • **Diplomatic Missions**: *US
Consulate*, ul. Pushkinskaya 32, ph. 268-458, 300-070, fax 300-072, 300-091, tlx 213206,
Foreign Commercial Service, ph. 300-093, fax 300-092 • *Indian Consulate*, ul. Aleutskaya 14,
ph. 228-110, fax 228-666 • *South Korean Consulate*, ul. Aleutvskaya 45, 5th floor, ph. 228-
133, 228-115, fax 229-471 • *Australian Consulate*, ul. Uborevicha 17, ph. 228-628, fax 228-
778 • *Japanese Consulate*, ul. Mordovtseva 12, ph. 267-502, fax 267-541 • *Phillipine
Consulate*, ul. Aleutskaya 14, ph. 221-351, fax 220-906, 225-198
Getting to/from: Alaska Airlines has two weekly flights in the summer and one weekly flight in
winter to/from Seattle and Anchorage. Transaero has direct flights to/from Moscow on MWF
and Su. Aeroflot has daily flights to/from Moscow and one flight per week from Niigata. Korean
Air has two weekly flights to/from Seoul. Since Vladivostok is at the terminus of the
Transsiberian railway, it is some 9289 km and 160 hours away from Moscow by train.

VOLGOGRAD   ☎ 844-2   ✈ 559   ✦ 1,007,000

Information: 330-301
Hotel(s): *Actyor*, Krasnoznamenskaya ul. 15, ph. 365-338 • *Intourist*, ul. Mira 14, ph. 364-553
• *Volgograd*, ul. Mira 12, ph. 361-772 • *Oktyabrskaya*, ul. Kommunisticheskaya 5A, ph. 338-
120 • *Krugozor*, ul. Zemlyachki 11, ph. 390-269
Restaurant(s): *Volgograd*, ph. 336-324 (in hotel of same name) • *Intourist*, 361-117 (in hotel of
same name) • *Drakon* (Chinese), pr. Lenina 10, ph. 367-651 • *Carribean Columbian
Restaurant* in Aktyor hotel

Travel agent(s): *Intourist*, ul. Mira 14, ph. 361-468, 364-552, 337-512, fax 361-648 • *Sputnik*, ul. Chuykova 65, ph. 347-242
Aeroflot: Alleya Geroyev 5, ph. 335-305
Central Telegraph/Post: ul. Mira 9, ph. 336-743, 336-152
Bank(s): ul. Mira 19a, ph. 335-022 • *Western Union*: Sberbank, ul. Metallurgov 33, ph. 783-429
City Council/Administration: ul. Volodarskovo 5, ph. 335-010
Hospital: *Hospital #3*, ul. Chaikovskovo 1, ph. 342-056
Other useful information: *American Business Center*, ul. Lenina 9, #30, ph. 335-946, fax 362-732, email <abcv@abc.tsaritsyn.su> • *Railway station*, ph. 330-331 • *River station*, ph. 448-209 • *Airport*, ph. 321-060, 317-355
Getting to/from: Aeroflot has daily flights to/from Moscow's Domodedovo airport (1 1/2 hrs). There are frequent daily trains to/from Moscow's Paveletsky station—travel time is 22 hours.

VOLOGDA   ☾ 817-22   ✈ 249   ☆ 300,000

Information: 22-222
Hotel(s): *Spasskaya*, ul. Oktyabrskaya 25, ph. 20-145 • *Vologda*, ul. Mira 92, ph. 23-079
Restaurant(s): *Spassky*, ul. Oktyabrskaya 25, ph. 63-138
Travel agent(s): *Intourist*, ul. Blagoveshchenskaya 26, ph. 24-281, 26-063 • *Travel Bureau*, Kremlevskaya pl. 8, ph. 26-090, 24-389, fax 22-593 • *Vologdaturist*, Sovetsky prosp. 70, ph. 23-544
Aeroflot: ul. Gertsena 45, ph. 23-302, 90-799
Central Telegraph/Post: ul. Kalinina 103, ph. 22-340
Bank(s): *Skombank*, ul. Kremlyovskaya pl. 12, ph. 24-783, 23-141
City Council/Administration: ul. Kamenny Most 4, ph. 20-042
Hospital: *Polyclinic #3*, ul. Blagoveschenskaya 39, ph. 23-137
Other useful information: *Train station*, pl. Babushkina, ph. 20-673 • *Oblast Museum of Local Studies*, ul. S. Orlova 15 • *House-Museum of Peter I*, pr. Sovetsky 47 • *Representative of the Ministry of Foreign Economic Relations*, ul. Gertsena 2, ph. 29-141, 51-322
Getting to/from: From Moscow's Yaroslavsky station, 8 hours by train. By car, 500 km along M8.

VORONEZH   ☾ 073-2   ✈ 280   ☆ 955,000

Information: 522-222
Hotel(s): *Brno*, ul. Plekhanovskaya 9, ph. 509-249 • *Tsentralnaya*, pr. Revolutsii 43, ph. 550-418 • *Rossiya*, Teatralnaya ul. 23, ph. 555-898
Restaurant(s): In hotels of same name: *Brno*, 509-249 • *Rossiya*, 565-037 • *Tsentralny*, 554-631
Travel agent(s): *Intourist*, ul. 9 Yanvarya 12, ph. 553-746 • ul. Plekhanovskaya 2, ph. 556-884
Aeroflot: ul. Plekhanovskaya 22a, ph. 520-447
Central Telegraph/Post: pr. Revolutsii 35, ph. 553-790
Bank(s): ul. Ordzhonikidze 25, ph. 555-374 • *Western Union*: *Pervy Russky Bank*, ull Kukolkina 11, ph. 777-574
City Council/Administration: ul. Plekhanovskaya 10, ph. 550-844
Hospital: pr. Patriotov 23, ph. 336-960
Other useful information: *Airport*, ph. 169-428 • *Train station*, ph. 502-113 • *Regional Center for Trade and Commerce*, ul. Plekhanovskaya 53, ph. 521-374, fax 521-326 • *Contact Voronezh*, ul. Kommissarskoy 7, 3rd flr, ph. 550-600
Getting to/from: There are several daily flights to/from Moscow (1.5 hrs). By train it is 12 hrs to/from Moscow.

VYATKA   ① 833-2   ✈ 482   ⚲ 523,500

Information: 990-9111
Hotel(s): *Administratsii Oblasti*, ul. Gertsena 49, ph. 691-018 • *Vyatka*, Oktyabrsky pr. 145, ph. 648-396
Restaurant(s): *Vyatka*, in the hotel Vyatka, ph. 648-304 • *Rossiya*, ul. Moskovskaya 5, ph. 627-827
Travel agent(s): *Intourist*, ul. Volodarskovo 127, ph. 690-949 • *Lyukon*, ul. R. Lyuksemburg 30, ph. 624-134 • *Tourist Council*, ul. K. Marksa 79, ph. 625-748, 622-538
Aeroflot: ul. Gorkovo 56, ph. 644-472, 625-281
Central Telegraph/Post: ul. Drelevskovo 39, ph. 625-565
Bank(s): *Mezhkombank*, ul. Komsomolskaya 43, ph. 645-232, 641-911
City Council/Administration: *Mayor's office*, ul. Vorovskovo 39, ph. 628-940
Hospital: *Polyclinic #1*, ul. K. Marksa, ph. 691-780
Other useful information: *Museum of Local Culture*, ul. Lenina 82, ph. 627-896 • *Representation of the Ministry of Foreign Economic Relations*, ul. K. Libknekhta 69, Oblispolkom, room 69, 691-793
Getting to/from: Trains to/from Moscow's Kazan station take about 18 hours.

VYBORG   ① 812-78   ✈ 466   ⚲ 81,000

Information: 225-02
Hotel(s): *Druzhba*, ul. Zheleznodorozhnaya 5, ph. 257-44
Restaurant(s): *Druzhba*, ph. 221-00 (in hotel of same name) • *Kruglaya Bashnya*, Rynochnaya pl. 306-00 • *Sever*, pr. Lenina, ph. 218-37
Travel agent(s): *Saimaa Lines Tours*, ul. Zheleznodorozhnaya 5, ph. 247-60
Central Telegraph/Post: Moskovsky pr. 26, ph. 225-40
Bank(s): Zheleznodorozhnaya 5 (in *Druzhba* hotel), ph. 943-51
City Council/Administration: ul. Sovetskaya 12, ph. 221-75
Hospital: ul. Onezhskaya 8, ph. 223-75
Other useful information: *Customs office*, ul. Zheleznodorozhnaya 9/5, ph. 288-59, 266-97
Getting to/from: Given Vyborg's location near the border with Finland, all trains and buses between Helsinki and Russia stop here. It is a four hour bus ride between St. Petersburg and Vyborg and 2 1/2 hours by train from Finlyandsky station.

YAKUTSK   ① 411-22   ✈ 3075   ⚲ 225,000

Information: 22-141
Hotel(s): *Hotel Ontario*, Viliuskaya ul., ph./fax 22-046, 65-058 • *Lainer*, ul. Bykovskovo 1, ph. 95-227 • *Sterkh* (*Lena*), pr. Lenina 8, ph. 44-890, 42-701, sat. fax 7-509-854-5001 • *Presidential Administration Hotel*, ul. Ammosvova, ph. 40-300, 40-106
Restaurant(s): *Volna*, pr. Lenina 7, ph. 24-875
Travel agent(s): *Intourist*, ul. Lomonosova 45, ph. 60-740, 42-090 • *Sputnik*, pr. Lenina 30, ph. 40-827
Aeroflot: ul. Ordzhonikidze 8, ph. 20-203, 22-460, 20-265, 95-554
Central Telegraph/Post: pl. Ordzhonikidze 4, ph. 23-846, 20-352
Bank(s): *Aeroflotbank*, ul. Ordzhonikidze 23, ph. 25-831
City Council/Administration: pr. Lenina 15, ph. 23-020
Hospital: *Healing Center* (*Lechebny Tsentr*), ph. 64-686 (in suburbs)

Other useful information: *Airport*, ph. 95-427 • *Yakutsk State Museum of History and Culture of the Northern Peoples*, pr. Lenina 5/2, ph. 23-753

Getting to/from: You have to fly to Yakutsk. There are daily (6 hr) flights to/from Moscow and less frequent flights with other RFE cities.

YALTA   ☽ 60-0   ✈ 777   ☨ 110,000

Information: 322-222

Hotel(s): *Yalta*, ul. Drozhinskovo 50, ph. 350-150 • *Orianda*, ul. Lenina 35/2, ph. 328-286

Restaurant(s): *Mramorny* (in the *Yalta Hotel*), ph. 350-130 • In the *Orianda Hotel*, ph. 328-324

Travel agent(s): In the *Yalta Hotel*, ph. 352-240, 350-297

Aeroflot: ul. Moskovskaya 37, ph. 325-741, 323-732

Central Telegraph/Post: ul. Moskovskaya 9, ph. 329-713

Bank(s): ul. Chekhova 26, ph. 326-948 • *Western Union: Transbank*, Rusvelt ul. 5, ph. 321-502

City Council/Administration: ul. Sovetskaya 1, ph. 324-202

Hospital: Livadiya village, Sevastopolskoye sh. 22, ph. 314-534

Getting to/from: There are daily flights between Moscow and Simferopol airport. Between Yalta and Simferopol, you can easily take a trolley or taxi.

YAROSLAVL   ☽ 085-2   ✈ 155   ☨ 638,000

Information: 225-766

Hotel(s): *Yubileynaya*, Kotoroslennaya nab. 11A, ph. 297-435 • *Yaroslavl*, ul. Ushinskovo 40/2, ph. 221-275 • Kotorosl, ul. B. Oktyabrskaya 87, ph. 212-415

Restaurant(s): *Kotorosl*, 211-536 • *Medved*, ul. Svobody 40/2, ph. 221-715

Travel agent(s): *Intourist*, Kotoroslennaya nab. 11A, office 230A, ph. 221-613, 229-306 • *Tourist Bureau*, ul. Nekrasova 3, ph. 225-271

Aeroflot: ul. Svobody 20, ph. 222-420

Central Telegraph/Post: ul. Pobedy 36, ph. 253-584

Bank(s): ul. Sverdlova 34, ph. 220-216

City Council/Administration: *Mayor's office*, Sovetskaya pl. 3, ph. 222-328

Hospital: ul. Zagorodny Sad 11, ph. 231-993

Other useful information: *Airport*, ph. 113-916, 666-569 • *Train station*, ph. 272-111

Getting to/from: Almost all trains from Yaroslavsky station stop here five hours out from Moscow. You can also get to Yaroslavl by bus from Shcholkovsky bus station in 6 hours.

YEKATERINBURG   ☽ 343-2   ✈ 870   ☨ 1,375,000

Information: 990-9111

Hotel(s): *Yubileynaya*, pr. Lenina 40, ph. 515-758 • *Oktyabrskaya*, ul. Sofii Kovalevskoy 17, ph. 445-146 • *Sverdlovsk*, ul. Chelyuskintsev 106, ph. 536-261

Restaurant(s): *Kharbin* (Chinese), ul. Kuybysheva 38, ph. 226-325 • *Kosmos* (with casino), ul. Dzerzhinskovo 2, ph. 512-195 • *Sverdlovsk*, ul. Chelyuskintsev 106, ph. 536-461 • *Staraya Krepost*, ul. Chelyuskintsev 102, ph. 530-575 • *Okean*, ul. Lenina 40, ph. 578-042 • *Centrally*, ul. Malysheva 74, ph. 550-741 • *Russian Club*, ul. Festivalnaya 12, ph. 373-591

Travel agent(s): *Intourist*, ul. Lenina 40, ph. 519-102 • ul. K. Marksa 43, ph. 240-098

Aeroflot: ul. Bolshakova 99A, ph. 299-051

Central Telegraph/Post: pr. Lenina 39, ph. 517-222

Bank(s): *Uralvneshtorgbank*, ul. Generalskaya 7, ph. 573-869 • ul. Mamina-Sibiryaka 58, ph. 558-370 • *Western Union: IBSB*, Moskovskaya ul. 56/2, ph. 439-255 • *Mezhekonomsberbank*, ul. Moskovskaya 66/2, ph. 439-255

City Council/Administration: *Mayor's office*, prosp. Lenina 24A, ph. 589-401

Hospital: ul. Volgogradskaya 185, ph. 283-459

Other useful information: *US Consulate*, PO Box 400, ph. 601-143, fax 601-181 • *American Business Center*, ul. Gogolya 15a, 3rd flr., ph. 564-623, fax 564-524, email <abc_yekat@msn. com> • *Lufthansa*, Koltsovo Airport, ph. 268-915, fax 242-741, info: 266-164 • *Sprint office*, ph. 495-356 (Access Number: 414-368) • *Regional Center for Trade and Commerce*, ul. Vostochnaya 6, ph. 530-449, fax 557-351 • *Sverdlovsk Regional Administration*, Oktyabrskaya pl. 1, ph. 511-365 • *Railway tickets home delivery service*, ph. 519-915, 519-916

Getting to/from: There are at least four daily flights from Moscow, one of which is on Transaero; there is one daily flight from St. Petersburg and there are direct flights from Frankfurt on Lufthansa on Thursdays and Sundays. Yekaterinburg is 30 hours by train from Moscow.

YOSHKAR-OLA   ① 836-25   ✈ 388   ♀ 275,000

Information: 62-222

Hotel(s): *Yubileynaya*, Leninsky pr. 26, ph. 62-223

Restaurant(s): *Yubileyny*, in the hotel of same name, ph. 92-557

Travel agent(s): *Intourist*, Leninsky pr. 29, ph. 56-272 • *Sputnik*, ul. Palatnaya 77, ph. 56-217 • *Tourist Bureau*, ul. K. Marksa 109, ph. 56-519, fax 112-151

Aeroflot: ul. Volkova 164, ph. 55-967

Central Telegraph/Post: ul. Sovetskaya 138, ph. 56-118

Bank(s): *Marprombank*, ul. Pushkina 30, ph. 11-5251, fax 11-1021 • *Western Union: Ayar Bank*, ul. Volkova 149, ph. 56-635

City Council/Administration: Leninsky pr. 27, ph. 56-434/56-401

Hospital: *Polyclinic #1*, pr. Gagarina 15, ph. 53-577

Other useful information: *Airport*, ph. 53-370 • *Train station*, ph. 53-303 • *Art Gallery*, ul. Sovetskaya 153, ph. 56-001

Getting to/from: Trains to/from Moscow's Kazan station take about 17 hours.

YUZHNO-SAKHALINSK   ① 424-22   ✈ 4178   ♀ 172,900

Information: 561-21

Hotel(s): *Sakhalin-Sapporo*, ul. Lenina 181, ph. 366-29, sat. fax 7-504-416-2001 • *Natalia*, ul. Antona Byukli 38, ph. 36-683, sat. fax 7-504-416-2007 • *Lada*, ul. Komsomolskaya 154, ph. 331-45

Restaurant(s): In *Sakhalin-Sapporo*, ph. 327-90 • *Lada*, ul. Komsomolskaya 154, ph. 316-39

Travel agent(s): *Sakhalin-Tourist*, ul. Sakhalinskaya 2, ph. 361-05

Aeroflot: ul. Lenina 198, ph. 519-22, kassa 340-90

Central Telegraph/Post: ul. Lenina 220, ph. 221-06

Bank(s): Kommunistichesky pr. 47, ph. 226-66, 224-96

City Council/Administration: ul. Lenina 173, ph. 233-13

Hospital: ul. Mira 430, ph. 553-41

Other useful information: *Airport*, ph. 554-46, 953-21 • *Train station*, ph. 121-34 • *American Business Center*, Kommunistichesky pr. 32, #517A, ph. 223-142, email <abc@abc.sakhalin.su> • *Kholmsk Sea Port*, ph. 229-83 • *Korsakov Sea Port*, ph. 223-52 • *Sprint office*, ph. 298-223 • *DHL Office*, Sakhincenter, office 228, Kommunistichesky pr. 32, ph. 226-97, 34-273

Getting to/from: There are two daily flights to/from Khabarovsk (1 1/2 hrs) and one daily flight to/from Vladivostok (2 hrs) and one daily flight to/from Moscow (9 hrs).

5 Money & Crime

The Ruble

For decades the Soviet/Russian ruble was a wholly-non-convertible currency. It had no value beyond Soviet borders and had a fairly warped value within those borders. Since the ruble was not directly convertible to foreign currencies, the Soviet government had to, for the purposes of international trade and tourism, create artificial rates (i.e. the commercial ruble, the gold ruble, the tourist ruble), which were nothing more than accounting tools for changing between different foreign currencies at world market rates. It was impossible to turn an everyday ruble into, say, a gold ruble.

Actions taken by the Russian government since the collapse of the Soviet Union have fundamentally altered this situation. As a result, the nature and value of the Russian ruble have been changed irretrievably, and with them the Russian economy.

First, in December 1991, by Presidential decree, virtually all bureaucratic barriers to the conduct of foreign trade through private channels were abolished. The centralized system of foreign trade, necessitated by the Soviet planned economy and artificial internal pricing, had, since the late 1980s, been increasingly challenged by the growing private sector and joint ventures. The Soviet government had attempted to exercise control at various times through the use of licensing, quotas and other customs controls. But now all bets are off. Any legally-registered company could trade in any legal commodity (with the exception of certain "strategic" goods, such as petroleum and precious metals).

Second, in January 1992, the Russian government freed prices on nearly all goods. Prices soared. And, as expected, the shops began to fill with goods (mainly imported). Wages and pensions were also unleashed, setting in motion an inflationary spiral.

Third, in July 1992, the government eliminated all artificially-created exchange rates for the ruble (see effects in chart, opposite). This forty-year-old practice (begun by Stalin) had contributed to the ruble's "soft," or inconvertible, status by grossly overvaluing it for foreign trade operations. At the time of this change, at least four different artificial ruble rates were used for trade, tourist and banking operations. Now there was to be just one "official" ruble exchange rate, and this would be set through a currency auction mechanism (the Moscow Interbank Currency Exchange – MICE). Commercial banks would, further, be allowed to set exchange rates for individuals independent of this official rate. But, since MICE was the major mechanism for large-scale currency conversion, banks would become very attentive to activity on this exchange. Before this move, the ruble was valued at 125R to the dollar. By early 1993, commercial banks were buying dollars for in excess of 700 rubles, by early 1994, the rate had slid to over 1500R/$1, by early 1995, to over 4000R/$1, and approaching 5000R/$1 in early 1996 (see chart below).

Also in mid-1992, the Russian government began to take steps to stem the "dollarization" of the Russian economy. All stores selling goods for cash hard currency were required to offer their goods at ruble prices as well, which meant goods would be (and still are) tagged with dollar prices and the store would set a "house rate" of exchange into rubles at which goods could be bought, usually set well above the current average dollar sell rate.

A year and a half later, in January 1994, the government brought into force a ban on the use of foreign cash currency for the purchase and sale of goods and services in Russia. *All commercial transactions for cash must now be in rubles.* Credit card purchases are still valued in dollars or DM, as are foreign trade contracts. But, inside Russia, the ruble is the only legal tender that may be used in cash operations.

Then, in 1995, the government closed the final door. All wages and benefits paid to employees had to be paid in rubles. Previously, foreign companies and joint ventures had been allowed, at the least, to wire salary payments to employees' bank accounts. At the same time, the government reinstated soviet-era controls on companies' withdrawals from hard currency bank accounts.

One result of these four measures is an abundance of consumer goods. Almost any good is available in Russia, and certainly in Moscow. And all

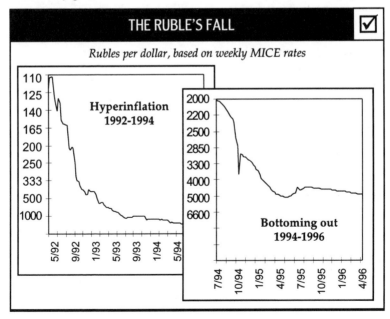

THE RUBLE'S FALL ☑

Rubles per dollar, based on weekly MICE rates

Hyperinflation 1992-1994

Bottoming out 1994-1996

goods are available for rubles, usually lots of them. This includes a wide assortment of imported Western goods, from Snickers to Reebok sneakers. Thus, whereas a couple of years ago, the Russian consumer market was typified by crippling shortages and excess liquidity, now it is characterized by a wealth of consumer goods and high inflation.

In mid-1995, the Russian government took aim at inflation by putting in place a "ruble corridor," vowing to intervene in the MICE to keep the ruble-dollar exchange rate within normative levels (4500-4700 from July-Dec. 1995 and 4700-4900 from Jan-July 1996). This policy has greatly contributed to a more stable ruble; whether it will continue is uncertain.

Internal convertibility and inflation: The ruble is now, for all intents and purposes, internally convertible. The trade-off is that the ruble is also seriously devalued, because the Russian Central Bank has continued printing money to support state enterprises and fund inter-enterprise debt, rather than let them fail. What is more, the government has yet to propose and parliament has yet to pass a budget prior to the calendar year which it must affect. This complete lack of fiscal and monetary controls only destabilizes the economy, contributes to hyper-inflation and continued depression. The only upside is that privatization, first by voucher and now via cash auctions, has remained on track and the vast majority of Russian industry is now in private hands (albeit much of it still dependent on government handouts in this "transitional period").

The implication of all this for travelers is that the ruble corridor has stabilized a previously volatile situation at bureaus de change. As long as the corridor is in effect, visitors will not need to pay as close attention to exchange rate trends (which is not to say that all exchange points profer the same rate, by no means is this true). Inflation in the consumer sector has slowed in 1995 and 1996 and now tends to outpace declines in market exchange rates to the dollar, which results in rising real prices.

For Western traders, the obvious implication is to avoid the inflationary and convertibility problems of the domestic economy by selling to Russian companies for hard currency on irrevocable letters of credit, rather than through consignment or installments (unless such consignments are valued in dollars). Russian law also allows barter operations, and many Western firms have succeeded in overcoming payment problems by taking it in-kind. New tax laws, however, make certain of these operations less or more favorable – see Chapter 9.

WHAT THE RUBLE IS WORTH

What the ruble is actually worth is a somewhat difficult question to answer. As an individual unit, a single ruble is worth very little in relation to other currencies (i.e. 0.0002 cents at time of publication). But, as a currency, the ruble is stronger than it was five or ten years ago, in the sense of guaranteeing access to goods and services. Certainly hyperinflation has meant a swift devaluation of the ruble's buying power. But it is significant that, if one has the requisite number of rubles to pay the stated price of a

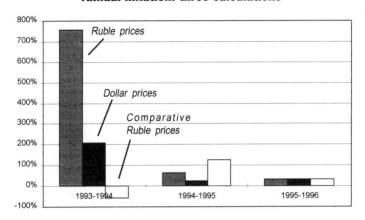

good, that good is more readily available than it was a few years ago, and without having to tack on additional costs, such as bribery, *blat* or barter. Of course, if inflation is not slowed permanently, the ruble will become so utterly devalued that it will be simpler to engage in barter operations (it would also be naive to assert that *blat*, or influence, has lost sway – particularly in the provinces – but it certainly has lessened greatly).

Equivalent dollars: An instructive demonstration of the ruble's value is shown in the chart above, which is based on a methodology published in 1992 by the Institute of World Affairs. Equivalent dollars are calculated by first representing ruble prices in terms of the share of average Russian monthly income required to purchase certain goods, then multiplying this share (percent) by the average monthly US income. Thus, if the average Russian is spending 80% of an average monthly income on food, and the average US monthly income is $2000, then the Russian is spending the equivalent of $1600 per month on food (80% x $2000).

A small basket of goods, mainly food items, was selected by way of demonstration. From 1993-1994 inflation on these goods topped 700% in nominal ruble terms. In 1994-1995, that inflation rated dropped to around 50%, in 1995-1996 it had dropped further to **32%**. Over the same period, the real rate of inflation, measured in dollars required to purchase the rubles needed to buy this basket of goods, was considerably less (see chart). Interestingly enough, the equivalent dollar rate of inflation is negative between 1993 and 1994, and highest of the three indices between 1994 and 1995. By 1996 is was in sync with the other two indices.

Finally, looking at the "equivalent dollar" rate, vs. simple dollar and ruble exchange rates, highlights the gradual normalization of the ruble's value over the past 3-4 years. This is most evident by the fact that the inflation rate for all three forms of measurement are exactly the same, 32%, for 1996-1996.

Ruble flight: As one might expect, this economic reality has led entrepreneurs and private citizens to hedge inflation by turning rubles into dollars or stable-valued commodities, converting them back to rubles only as necessary. The net effect is further devaluation of the ruble.

The government has responded to this (and to its need to service its foreign debt), by imposing stiff taxes on currency earnings and restricting some dollar operations. This has resulted mostly in the flight of currency to hidden (i.e. non-taxable) foreign bank accounts.

Denominations

The ruble (at the time of publication) comes in denominations of 100, 200, 500, 1000, 5,000, 10,000, 50,000 and 100,000 rubles.

Inflation has led the Soviet, and now Russian government to introduce higher and higher ruble notes. In 1991, 200 and 500 ruble notes were introduced. In 1992, notes of 5,000 and 10,000 denominations were printed. In 1993, the 50,000R and 100,000R notes began circulating, while lower denomination notes (1, 3, 5, 10, 25, 50) began being taken out of circulation. In 1994 and 1995, the government introduced all new notes with greater protections against counterfeiting, which means there are two varieties of such notes in circulation, all valid.

The ruble consists of 100 kopeks. Yet, due to the steep and steady devaluation of the ruble, kopeks are obsolete. There are 1, 5, 10, 20, and 50 ruble coins. Both telephones and metros have been or are being shifted over to accept only tokens (жетони – *zhetoni*), so that prices can be changed more easily. In some cities (including Moscow and St. Petersburg), a 1R coin (and sometimes the similarly-sized 15k pieces) still works on phones that have not yet been converted to zhetoni. In still other cities, the absence of kopeks, combined with budget shortages has led municipal authorities to make outdoor payphone use free of charge.

WARNING: In 1993 the Russian government banned use of all bills and coins printed or minted prior to 1993. *Do not accept as change any bills that are not dated 1993 or later. (This includes all USSR rubles.)*

Currency Questions

CHANGING MONEY

The loosening of controls on the ruble's exchange rate has been accompanied by a loosening of exchange restrictions for individuals. While you must fill out a customs declaration upon entering and exiting the country (in which you note the amount of currency in your possession), this has become something of a pointless formality. You may legally change dollars into rubles and rubles into dollars at any licensed commercial bank or exchange point, and are not required to show any identification for either transaction, nor to have either type of operation noted on your declaration (as was the case a few years ago). *Caveat:* A 1995 law requires presentation of photo identification and notation of same for exchanges over $500. In practice, this is being loosely enforced at best. Some banks will always request an ID for any exchange operatoin; others never do; still others do when you request a receipt.

It is now possible, as well, to buy most major Western currencies at major hotels and banks.

Banks change their rates of exchange daily and there are some significant differences in exchange rates among banks, so it does bear shopping around a bit if you are exchanging large sums of money. Some banks charge a fee (usually a percentage of the amount being exchanged) for exchange transactions and thus "hide" a less advantageous rate of exchange in such fees. Be sure to find out all fees before handing over your cash.

You should only exchange money through officially licensed banks, not at kiosks and not on the street (see section below on Crime).

PURCHASING

Effective January 1, 1994, all cash transactions in Russia must be effected in Russian rubles. It is illegal to pay in cash foreign currency for goods or services in stores, restaurants, or on the street. This, of course, does not mean this is not regularly done, just that it is technically illegal (except in selected establishments which still retain a license to accept payment in cash foreign currency).

It is legal, however, to pay for transactions with a credit card (VISA, MC and AMEX are all widely accepted). In this instance, your credit card will be debited in dollars or deutschemarks, or whatever currency the establishment is using as its currency for pricing.

Beware the house rate: It is a widely-used practice for foreign-produced goods to be tagged in stores with dollar or DM prices, and for the ruble total of the purchase (if done in cash, vs. a credit card) to be calculated according to a "house rate" of exchange, which is usually changed daily. These house rates can be quite usurious – find out what they are before you buy. House rates are usually pegged just above the rate at which the store must purchase dollars (the commercial bank *dollar selling rate*). And since you likely obtained rubles at the lower (usually by 5-10%) *dollar buying rate*, it usually makes more sense to purchase goods with a credit card in these stores. *If you have exchanged foreign currency for rubles at a rate lower than the store's house rate, use your credit card.* You will save at least 5-10% on your purchase.

Leave home without them: In general, travelers checks are a hassle in Russia and are only readily accepted without objections when exchanging money in better-established banks. Cash and credit cards are the best form of hard currency to carry – in fact credit cards rank above cash in terms of their ease and safety of use. It is now even possible at several venues to obtain cash (dollars or rubles) with your VISA or AMEX card (look for MC, Eurocard or VISA stickers prominently displayed at exchange points; for AMEX, start at the local American Express office in Moscow and St. Petersburg). If you bring cash, small bills (e.g. $20 or less) are preferable to large ones because making change will be easier and it will be more convenient for tipping, cab rides, etc. Non-American visitors would be wise to change their intended hard currency spending money into dollars, as the relative value of pounds, deutschemarks, yens or francs is not widely known in this 'dollarized' economy.

 IF YOU LOSE YOUR CREDIT CARD

...here are the numbers to call

AMEX, Moscow ph. 956-9000, St. Petersburg ph. 311-5215 (or via AT&T USA Direct to the US, call 919-333-3211 collect)
Other cards: Moscow ph. 284-4873 or 284-4802, St. Petersburg, ph. 312-6015

DEALING WITH A CASH CRUNCH

Time was, if you ran out of cash while traveling in Russia, you were in something of a quandary. But, thanks to some advances in consumer services in this area, travelers and business people in Russia now have quite a few options for dealing with a cash crunch.

Wire transfers

Electronic wire transfers have long been the preferred mode of getting money into and out of accounts in Russia. And it is now possible to use this means to send cash to (Western) contacts in Russia or to receive it when sent by the home office.

The easiest channel is through DialogBank, which has a very service-oriented office on the ground floor of Moscow's Slavyanskaya-Radisson hotel. From the US or any other Western country you can transfer any amount of money to DialogBank's correspondent account in New York

(Bank of New York at the time of publication). In the transfer, you designate the full name of the individual who is to receive the money in Moscow and his/her passport number (a Russian citizen cannot be the recipient). The wire takes about 2-3 days to arrive after it is sent, and can be picked up in cash at the DialogBank office.

The minimum acceptable transfer amount is $1000. There is a 3% service charge on the receiving end for the transfer, plus a $15 fee. The bank you send the wire from will also likely take a $10-30 fee. You will want to add the full amount of any anticipated fees to the total amount you would like to have received in Moscow. You must indicate that the beneficiary is DialogBank. Contact DialogBank (see below) for account information prior to effecting a transfer.

Immediate cash with plastic

You may use your American Express (Amex) card to obtain a small amount of cash at the ATM machines in the Amex Moscow office (see below) or in the lobby of Moscow's Hotel Mezhdunarodnaya. But this, of course, requires that you have registered a PIN for your card. You can also obtain larger cash advances off your Amex card at any Amex office. The commission is 4%.

DialogBank offers a slightly better commission on a different type of transaction. You, in effect, carry out a remote-transfer from your bank account in the West, using your Amex card to secure a check written off that account (i.e., if the check bounces, you'll see the charge show up on your next Amex statement). *This is a good reason to bring along your personal and/or business checkbook when you travel to Moscow.* You can undertake this operation once every 21 days. If you have a regular Amex card (green), the limit during this period is $1000, with a gold card $5000, and with a platinum card $10,000. The cost of conducting such a remote-transfer is 3% of the total amount or $30, whichever is greater.

Cash advances off VISA, MC and Eurocard cards are also available. Normal cash advance interest charges apply, plus banks usually charge a 3-4% commission. Many banks and exchange points in Moscow and St. Petersburg (particularly those in hotels) offer this service – look for credit card stickers prominently displayed at exchange points. For other cities see the Russia City Guide (Chapter 4).

Western Union

This is essentially a wire transfer without the bank. Cash may be directly transferred from a Western Union (WU) office outside Russia (most US and

AMERICAN EXPRESS OFFICES

American Express: *Moscow*, ul. Sadovaya-Kudrinskaya 21a, ph. 956-9000, 956-9004; *St. Petersburg*: Grand Hotel Europe, ph. 315-7487

major European cities have one) or by having your home office call WU (800-325-6000) and drawing the money off your VISA or MC. There is no limit on the amount you may transfer. There is a commission on the sending end which decreases proportionally, the more money you send.

The money is available within minutes in Russia, and can be sent to persons of any nationality. WU serves many large Russian cities, including Moscow, St. Petersburg, Novosibirsk, Omsk, Rostov-on-Don, Saratov, St. Petersburg and Volgograd. Other cities are steadily being added. These offices are listed in the Russia City Guide (Chapter 4). To get the most current lists of cities and banks where money can be received, call either the WU Moscow office (*Sberbank*, ul. Yunosti 5/1, ph. 119-8250 or 119-8266, fax 310-4709) or WU in the US, at 800-325-6000. Tell them the city you want to send to, and they will let you know if there is a WU office there yet.

Money can be picked up in dollars or rubles at the current WU rate (which is near the MICE rate). The receiving party can be notified by phone or telegram upon the money's arrival (not the most reliable of alternatives), or may call the WU number in Moscow (see above) to find out where to pick the money up (better). When you send the money, you can also find out from the WU agent the address of banks in the city where the money can be picked up.

Crime

The 'golden days' when Russia was about the safest place in the world to travel to (with respect to crime) are gone. As a foreigner in Moscow or St. Petersburg (more so in Moscow), you stand out as a person with hard currency, by both the way you dress and act, and by the places you frequent. While there is no significant dislike for foreigners (in fact the opposite is usually true), some foreigners have experienced local resentment for reminding Russians "of all they do not have." And in times of heightened unemployment, inflation and desperation, foreigners are an obvious target for crime. This is not to say that Moscow and St. Petersburg have become dangerous, just that they are no longer as safe as they used to be and some precautions are in order. With this in mind, here is a compilation (with thanks to many fellow travelers, the US Department of State and the Russian Interior Ministry) of some of the most useful tips for avoiding becoming a victim (see also the box on the page opposite).

PROTECT VALUABLES. Don't bring valuables with you to Russia that you don't really need. Do not leave money in your hotel room or apartment, and carry it with you in a secure place. There has been an increased incidence of burglary of hotel rooms, seemingly with the collusion of staff. Use hotel safes for highly valuable items or, better yet, leave them at home.

TRAIN WISELY. When you travel by train, always buy tickets for the entire cabin, even if you are traveling alone. Do not let the conductor put other passengers in your cabin, even if he insists that this is "the required procedure." Pay the conductor a modest "fee," if you must, to quiet him.

☑ ADDITIONAL TIPS FOR SAFE TRAVEL

- Learn some key Russian phrases, like "help" and "fire." Learn to use Russian phones.
- Reduce your vulnerability by lowering your visibility. Don't stand about with cameras. Don't talk loudly in public. Dress conservatively.
- Pay attention. Street thieves in Moscow, as anywhere, usually seek distracted people, whether they be making a purchase or enjoying the sights. Most all crimes are opportunistic, not planned. Keep your guard up in unfamiliar areas.
- Travel light. Carry with you just the money you need. To deter a pickpocket, keep your money in a front pants pocket.
- Get to know Moscow and the neighborhood you are living in. Avoid remote newly-built districts (*novostroyka*). Maryino, Orekhovo-Borisovo, Belyaevo and other remote areas are overcrowded with unemployed *limitchiks* – persons with limited residence permits, and other transient populations which have higher levels of crime incidence.
- Don't leave your purse, briefcase or suitcase unattended. Ever.
- Always walk confidently and at a steady pace. Criminals tend to prey on those who seem to feel unsure of themselves.
- Be alert while crossing the street. Moscow's motorbikers have become particularly adept at robbing pedestrians of their handbags when crossing the street.
- Be wary of talking with strangers in the street. When approached by suspicious people, enter a public place (i.e. a restaurant or store).
- Fast food restaurants in Moscow have proven a dangerous place at times – i.e. when walking out of a McDonald's with hamburgers, don't be flashy with money.
- Crime in the subway has been on the rise. Gangs of gypsies have been especially active in this respect, using a razor blade to cut handbags while the children distract the victim and cling on him or her. Do not be soft on these kids. The best proven tactic is to be very physical and loud. Do not let them grab you. Swing your arms and/or umbrella. Do not be passive.
- Also avoid isolated cars in the metro. Try to stand close to the exit in the car. Avoid standing at the far end of the platform while waiting for the train. Do not let anyone stand behind you in the metro or on the platform. If you feel uncomfortable, try to find a support. Lean against the marble wall.
- Do not stare at drunks. At best, a Moscow drunkard will try to open a protracted conversation with you and you risk missing your stop on the metro. At worst, he may react angrily, taking your glance as a provocation.
- Stick to taxis clearly marked as such (with the green light glowing in the windshield). Do not ever get in a car that already has a passenger. Avoid taxis which suddenly pull out from the curb or from around the corner when you stand down in the street. Do not ride with *chastniki* (private drivers).
- Unless you are prepared (physically and psychologically) to retaliate immediately in kind to attacks on your person, stay passive. Unless you are properly licensed and trained to use a firearm, it could be your worst defense. A gas pistol requires permission from a local militia post.
- Don't be afraid to show your fear, scream, whistle, or do anything to attract attention. Yet, if someone grabs your purse or bag, let them have it: your purse can be replaced, your life cannot.

There have been cases of theft from sleeping cars on overnight trains (particularly between Moscow and St. Petersburg). Always lock your train cabin door and use the little flip-out *sekretka*, and secure the door with a rope or belt when you sleep.

MIND THE COMPANY YOU KEEP. Avoid beggars, prostitutes, black market dealers, and groups (especially bands of gypsies). These people are often pickpockets as well. Do not give donations to "suspicious looking" beggars and avoid making eye contact with gypsies. There also have been incidents where a deaf-mute approaches a foreigner for assistance, distracting him while cohorts pick their pockets or worse. Gangs of adolescent thieves are also on the rise. *Do not be afraid to defend yourself aggressively if you are accosted openly. Swing your bags and yell.* Wrapping rubber bands around your wallet is a good way to make it harder to pick from your pocket.

AVOID BAD SECTIONS. Be wary of black marketeers, street urchins and gypsies in front of tourist hotels, around major tourist sites and in large crowds. Other areas of heightened criminal activity are: train stations, flea markets, food markets, airports, large public gatherings, cheap hotels or hostels, casinos and nightclubs, parking lots where cars are sold and areas with lots of "unofficial" commercial activity or kiosks.

BE CAREFUL WHERE AND HOW YOU BUY. It is easy to be distracted during the purchase of souvenirs and to be ripped off in the process. Be sure that the goods you buy are the ones you get. If you think you are getting a deal that is too good to be true, you probably aren't – look for a set up. Don't flash a lot of cash around during a purchase – you can bet your actions will be under some scrutiny during this part of a transaction, and it is wise not to openly display the location of your money, passport or other valuables. Don't place convenience over personal safety. And don't allow yourself to be rushed. Always be sure to get your credit card back after each transaction. *Exchange money only at officially-registered exchange points.*

DRINK WISELY. The incidence of foreigners being slipped a "mickey" has reached anecdotal levels, but is not widespread. Still, it is wise to drink only with a trusted friend, and for one of you to remain sober. Even slight intoxication alters your judgement and responses significantly, a fact professional thieves prey on. Do NOT purchase drinks from opened bottles except in a reputable bar.

KEEP YOUR OWN COUNSEL. Do not tell strangers where you are staying or what your travel or evening entertainment plans are. Do not open your door to unknown individuals. Be cautious about accepting invitations to first-time acquaintances' apartments. Be careful who you visit and what cars you get into. There have been cases of harassment of foreign motorists by militia officers, but this is very rare and declining. If you suspect this is about to happen to you, be polite, do not speak Russian, and be "accommodating." Look for a badge number.

TAXI RULES. Use only an official "limo" service from the airport. And at night, stick to official taxis, versus gypsy cab rides, which are not recommended in any case. *Never, never get in a cab that already has a rider.*

If your luggage is put in the trunk, do not exit the car until the driver gets out and proceeds to open the trunk, and leave the passenger door open until all your luggage is removed from the vehicle.

DON'T BE FLASHY. Keep a low profile. Dress and act conservatively. Be polite and low-key. Avoid loud conversations and arguments. Showing lots of dollars around in restaurants and other semi- or fully-public places is not advisable. Don't keep all of your money in one place – put smaller amounts in different pockets and recall what is where, and take out only the money you need. Keep your wallet pocketed (in your front pocket, preferably) in public places.

USE THE BUDDY SYSTEM. If you want to walk the streets at night, stick to main avenues and, when possible, take along a friend. Do not use short cuts or poorly-lit streets. Do not stop at night for strangers or people who need a cigarette lit. Before going into a pedestrian underpass, be alert to who is already in or going into the underpass. *Stay away from parks at night.*

WHAT TO YELL. If you are in trouble, and there are people near who may help, yell 'pozhar' (fire) to attract attention.

IF YOU ARE MUGGED OR ASSAULTED. While this is unlikely if you heed the tips above, it is always a possibility. If you are victimized, get in touch with the militia or service bureau in your hotel, and/or with your embassy. It will only serve to help others. Never resist giving up valuables to armed attackers. Never carry items around with you that you cannot do without.

6 | Food & Health

Food

OPTIONS

The restaurant business was at the forefront of the Soviet Union's first tentative steps toward the market in the late 1980s. Cooperative restaurants sprang up in sidestreets around Moscow, St. Petersburg and larger cities, offering a welcome alternative to the sluggish service and mediocre meals of state-owned restaurants. Now, after ten years, the number of privately-owned restaurants and cafes in larger cities of Russia is rivaled only by the explosive growth of stores selling imported Western goods.

From the beginning, dining out at private restaurants has been a luxury reserved for those with an abundance of rubles: Russia's *nouveau riche* and foreigners. Indeed, a recent poll in Moscow showed that just 1% of average Muscovites went out for an evening meal at a restaurant during the course of a year.

Yet, even for those with means, dining out in Moscow and St. Petersburg is getting more and more expensive. The arrival of an internally convertible ruble and a wide variety of imported foodstuffs (to replace domestic food products, which are difficult to procure in a reliable manner) has meant radical increases in both nominal and real prices. Translation: the time is past when you can dine out on the cheap and get a really good meal.

Of course, the upside is that there are now a wide variety of restaurants offering tasty food and good service. It is no longer as difficult as it once was to find a good meal in either of the Russian capitals. New pizzerias, bistros and cafes are opening daily. Choice, rather than necessity, now drives the market.

Prices for a good dinner, as in any city, range all over the map, with a distinct lean to the pricey end of the scale (for the reasons noted above). It is fairly difficult to find a good dinner out for less than $20-25 per head (before drinks), and it can be quite easy to stumble into a $100+ per head meal. The arrival of fast-food restaurants and delis means that good lunches can be had for considerably less, often in the $5-10 range.

You will tend to get more *borscht* for your buck (and more local flavor) by frequenting locally-owned restaurants, vs. hotel restaurants or joint venture restaurants (which, admittedly, can be much more convenient). But, irregardless of ownership type, popular restaurants get swamped in evenings on a scale rarely seen elsewhere. Always call ahead for reservations if you are intent on eating at a particular spot. Hotel restaurants tend to be the easiest to get into on the shortest notice.

SOME GENERAL TIPS FOR DINING OUT

❶ **Do not drink the water.** Moscow tap water is fairly harmless in small doses, but not if your system is not used to it. St. Petersburg water should not be drunk on any condition, unless it is boiled; it harbors the *giardia lamblia* bacterium, which is harmless if your system is used to it, debilitating if not (see the *Health* section below). Tea and coffee are safe if the water has been adequately boiled. Water in the provinces is generally unpredictable. Bring bottled water.

If you get desperate, the safest tap water is probably that in the newest hotels, some of which have installed filtration systems. Bottled water, colas and other canned beverages are available in most major hotels and grocery stores (avoid bottled water from St. Petersburg). Be careful of melons which may have been injected with water to increase their size.

❷ **Always make reservations** if you are determined to eat at a particular restaurant. Otherwise, the choices are legion in Moscow and St. Petersburg.

❸ **Tipping** is increasingly expected. 10-15% is adequate.

❹ **Take your time.** When you go out for lunch in a Russian restaurant (vs. a cafe or fast-food spot), expect it to take at least an hour to hour and a half. When you go out to dinner, it is a night-long engagement. Most Russian restaurants do not try to turn tables every 45 minutes as Western restaurants do. You will not be hurried along; sit back and relax. When a Russian goes out to dinner, it is for a night of entertainment. Eating and running, particularly at someone's home, is considered rude.

❺ **Share the costs.** When dining with Russian guests or hosts, the rule is usually that the host pays for the meal. If you are eating out with persons whose organization will probably not pay for the meal, insist on paying or at least going dutch. While you can joke about the low value of the ruble over dinner, do not ever be ostentatious or throw a lot of money around when it comes time to pay the check. Remember, most Russians do not eat out that often. The prices have just gotten too high.

❻ **Always carry a cotton handkerchief** for dining out, as Russian cities are dirty, and you will probably want to wash your hands before eating, and often restaurant restrooms lack clean towels (although hot air dryers are sometimes available). The handkerchief will also come in handy for wiping off silverware in some of the greasier of greasy spoons.

Health

For the uninitiated, travel in Russia can be physically taxing at the least and exhausting at the worst. This is particularly true for elderly persons and persons with special health concerns or problems. The air quality in major cities, while tolerable, can cause problems for people with asthma or other lung problems. Pharmacies which stock basic cold and influenza medicines or other over-the-counter drugs are few and far between.

Balanced meals, i.e. with healthy portions of fruits and vegetables, are readily available only in Moscow and St. Petersburg, so vegetarians or persons with special dietary needs may find satisfying their requirements quite difficult. On top of this, the general situation with health care, be it emergency medical services, hospitals, or the supply of medicines and disposable needles, is well below the accepted standards in most Western nations. Even basic health care services may be totally unavailable outside major metropolitan areas (see the *Russian City Guide*, Chapter 4).

This said, most or all of these and other potential health-related problems can be avoided by gaining a proper understanding of the environment one is traveling into and by taking proper precautions.

PRECAUTIONS

Business and independent travelers will ensure a more enjoyable and successful trip by checking/updating their health insurance status, getting necessary inoculations, bringing required medicines and taking certain precautions before and during travels.

Health Insurance

Before you depart for Russia for travel or residency, check with your health insurance carrier or overseer (whether private or state, as in the case of the UK or Canada) to understand the nature and extent of coverage they extend to a policyholder traveling to Russia or the former Soviet Union. If your provider does not cover you for travel to this region, you are strongly advised to either purchase a rider to your policy expressly granting this coverage or seek a temporary insurance provider which specializes in travel insurance (see below or ask your travel agent).

You may also wish to consider insurance covering the eventuality of medical evacuation from Moscow to Finland, New York or Germany. The minimum cost for such an evacuation by normal air carrier can be over $10,000, or nearly $100,000 if by special hospital aircraft. A few US companies that insure against this eventuality are listed below.

Third, study up ahead of time on the health care facilities available in the cities/regions you will be visiting. Recommended facilities for Moscow and St. Petersburg are listed below. Also find out where your country's nearest embassy or consulate is located. They are there to serve you in the event of emergencies, including medical emergencies.

SPECIALIZED TRAVEL INSURANCE PROVIDERS

American Medical Center, 5200 Blue Lagoon Dr., Miami, FL 33128, ph. 305-262-8489, fax 305-262-5348. Offers a Traveler's Medical Access Plan that guarantees full access to American-staffed and run medical centers in Moscow and St. Petersburg.

Traveler's Emergency Network, 103 West Main St., Durham, NC 27702, ph. 800-275-4836. Offers a $30 traveler's insurance policy covering evacuation, physician referral, prescription delivery and more.

Travmed, PO Box 5375, Baltimore, MD 21094-5375, ph. 800-732-5309. Offers, for about $3.50 per day, physician referral, evacuation, $100,000 in emergency medical coverage and more. Longer term plans also available.

EVACUATION SERVICES

American Aero-Med, 1575 West Commercial blvd., Hanger 36B, Fort Lauderdale, FL 33309, ph. 800-443-8042, 305-776-6800.

Euro-Flite, 3000 Wesleyan, Ste 200, Houston, TX 77027, ph. 713-961-5200, fax 713-961-4088; Head office: Box 187, 01531 Vantaa, Finland, ph. (358-0) 174-644, fax (358-0) 870-2507. Offers quick bedside-to-bedside evacuation with certified medical staff from anywhere in Russia to Finland (also cargo and charter services).

International SOS Assistance, as well as air evacuation, have various health insurance and trip cancellation policies, ph. 800-523-8930.

Medicines

Bring your own. This includes not just any prescription medicines you would need for your trip (including the eventuality that it might be extended), but also non-prescription, over the counter items which you might consider necessary. While Western-style pharmacies have been opening up in Moscow and St. Petersburg, it is best not to count on the availability of something easily obtainable in your home country. Chapter 2 lists the bare essentials any traveler or short-term resident should take: disposable syringes, Pepto-Bismol or medicine containing bismuth, antacids, ibuprofen, prescription drugs, and iodine tablets for disinfecting water. In addition, you may wish to consider taking some or all of the following: flu or influenza medicine, cold medicine, cough drops, antibiotics, bandages and antibiotic creme. Carry wash-n-dry towelettes for when you can't wash up.

Immunizations

Check with your physician and consider updating your immunizations, particularly for the "childhood diseases": diphtheria, measles, mumps, rubella and polio. An alarming trend has been the rise of diphtheria in Russia in recent years, due to vaccine shortages. Over 2000 cases were reported in Russia last year. You need three boosters over a period of 6-12 months to have adequate protection, so get started as soon as possible. A tetanus update can't hurt while you are at it.

If you are planning on traveling to the provinces, you should be immunized against hepatitis A and typhoid, and receive immunoglobulin injections. Tick-borne encephalitis (which can also be transmitted via unpasteurized milk) and lyme disease (transmitted by tick bites) have also been reported in Siberia. You can, and should, get a vaccination against the former. This can be done in Europe or upon arrival in Moscow.

If you decide belatedly (i.e. after you arrive in Moscow or St. Petersburg) to travel East or North in Russia, almost all of these immunizations can be obtained at the American Medical Center or European Medical Center (see addresses below) and from some embassy medical services.

Finally, the US Center for Disease Control operates a special International Travelers Hotline that summarizes the most prevalent diseases and health risks of different regions. Call (404) 332-4559 – includes a Fax-back service where you can order printed medical reports of travel destinations.

HIV (AIDS) Law

After much deliberation and despite wide censure from domestic and international sources, Russia passed a law, effective August 1, 1995, requiring all persons entering Russia for a period of three months or greater (on a single-entry visa or for residency) to present a certificate attesting that they are free of the HIV virus. This certificate is reportedly to be submitted prior to visa application, though, at press time, this measure was not being implemented at Russian consulates in the US.

Persons currently in Russia and wishing to extend a visa for beyond a three month period may be required to present such a certificate to UVIR prior to visa extension. In this case, testing is available at the medical providers listed below.

A pound of cure

Prevention is your most reliable means to ensuring a problem-free trip. Here is a list of some tips from seasoned travelers and doctors:

❶ **Drink on the plane.** Take in lots of water or fluids (alcohol doesn't count) during the flight over, if it is over 5-6 hours in length. Otherwise you will find yourself dehydrated for several days. Caffeinated drinks and alcohol will also dry you out.

❷ **Don't drink the water.** To repeat, St. Petersburg water carries the *giardia lamblia* parasite, the cure for which is unsure. While Moscow water is usually safe, the city water in Siberian cities is notoriously polluted from industrial wastes. Don't take risks. Bottled water is now available in most Western hotels and almost all hard currency food stores. For a complete listing, see our *Where in Moscow* or *Where in St. Petersburg*. If traveling beyond these cities, take along what you will need and boil any water for five minutes before drinking. Avoid ice cubes, use bottled water for brushing your teeth, and avoid uncooked fruits and vegetables that cannot be peeled.

❸ **No sushi.** With price rises, food is sitting on the shelves longer than it used to in Russia. And refrigeration is not widespread or dependable. Salmonella can be found in chicken, eggs and cheese that is insufficiently cooked. Pork and game meat should also be cooked thor-

Your East-West–Express Connection.

Reliable express-service for

documents and packages.

Fed**Ex**
Federal Express

The World On Time

Just give us a call: 7 (095) 262-7480.

oughly to avoid trichanosis. Raw fish, a delicacy in some regions (particularly in the Far East, where cold fish soup is common) can be dangerous. Many fish have been contaminated with opisthorchiasis which affects the liver and other vital organs. So abstain from raw fish and make sure all fish is thoroughly cooked.

❹ **Fruits too.** Bigger has always been better in Russia/the USSR. This goes too for fruits. One way to achieve this is to inject fruit (i.e. watermelon, melons) with water while it is growing. The sensitive traveler will want to avoid such fruits (see above on drinking water). Also, when possible, peel fresh fruit or wash it off *very* well.

❺ **Problem salt.** Long term residents will want to buy Western-made salt, fortified with iodine. Russian salt is not and this has caused some problems for expatriates.

❻ **Get documented.** If you have a preexisting medical condition, you should carry a letter from your physician describing the condition and

---

HEALTH PRECAUTIONS CHECKLIST ☑

ITEMS TO BRING:

- ❑ Aspirin, *Tylenol*, acetaminophen *(for fevers, pain, headaches and flu)*
- ❑ Cold medicine, cough drops, flu medicine
- ❑ Pepto-Bismol and/or Immodium, antacids *(for diarrhea, food poisoning and indigestion)*
- ❑ Disposable syringes, general antibiotic *(in the event of an accident)*
- ❑ Iodine tablets or chemical water purifier *(to purify water, kill giardia and prevent diarrhea and other drinking-water-related problems – conventional water filters may also do the job)*
- ❑ Condoms, tampons and sanitary pads
- ❑ Benadryl, cortisone creme *(for allergic reactions and rashes)*
- ❑ Prescription medicines and a copy of eyeglass/contact lens prescriptions

TO GET BEFORE DEPARTURE:

- ❑ A full medical check-up if going for a long stay.
- ❑ Immunization updates for diphtheria, tetanus and polio – DTP *(the US Center for Disease Control says that diphtheria boosters must be recieved three times to be effective, and spread out over 6-12 months, so get started early)*
- ❑ Immunization against Hepatitis B
- ❑ A gamma globulin injection or *Havrix (to prevent contracting Hepatitis A)*
- ❑ Update of any immunizations for "childhood diseases"
- ❑ A health insurance rider or separate policy covering evacuation and emergency medical services
- ❑ The latest health report on the region from the CDC, phone (404) 332-4559.

including any information on prescription drugs, including the generic name for them, that you may need to take. Any prescription drugs you bring in should be kept in their original containers, to avoid customs problems.

❼ **Just to be safe.** Diarrhea does not just come from what you may eat or drink. Avoid use of reusable towel machines in public restrooms. Use only disposable paper towels or wipes to dry off your hands.

WHEN PRECAUTIONS FAIL

If you do come down with something serious that you do not have medicine for and/or need to seek medical attention, consult the list of facilities and services listed below.

Diarrhea: This is the most common traveler's ailment and can be debilitating in extreme cases. If you develop diarrhea that is bloody or lasts longer than five days, consult a physician immediately. If you run out or forgot to bring your Pepto Bismol or Immodium, here is an alternative cure that may work (if you can find the ingredients):

Medical Services: Below is a list of medical service providers in Moscow and St. Petersburg. Also contact your consulate or embassy for any other facilities they may recommend or have experience with. Medical facilities in the 78 largest Russian cities are listed by city in Chapter 4.

MOSCOW

Ambulance: 03
American Medical Center, 2nd Tverskoy-Yamskoy p. 10, ph. 956-3366
Diplomatic Polyclinic, 4th Dobryninskiy per. 4, ph. 237-8338
European Medical Center, Gruzinskiy per. 3, ph. 251-6009
French Embassy Doctor, ph. 230-2343
Tourist's Clinic, Gruzinskiy per. 2, ph. 254-4396

ST. PETERSBURG

Ambulance: 03
American Medical Center, nab. Reki Fontanka 77, ph. 119-6101
Emergency Medical Assistance: 278-0055
Polyclinic #2, Moskovskiy pr. 22, ph. 316-6272

 TRAVELER'S DIARRHEA HOME REMEDY

Prepare in one glass 8 ounces of orange, apple or other fruit juice, a half teaspoon of honey or corn syrup, and a pinch of salt. In a second glass, prepare 8 ounces of boiled or bottled water and a quarter teaspoon of baking soda. Drink alternately from each glass until your thirst is quenched. Supplement this as desired with carbonated beverages, water or tea made with boiled or carbonated water. Avoid solid foods and dairy products until recovery occurs.

Courtesy of the US National Institutes of Health

Communication & Shipping 7

Telecommunications

The Russian phone system is still arguably the worst in any industrialized country. Line quality is poor to abysmal. Cutoffs and crossed-lines are frequent. International phone lines are difficult if not impossible to access. In general, be prepared to be frustrated by the Russian phone system.

PHONES

This said, it bears noting that some huge strides have been made by Russo-Western joint ventures to, in effect, leapfrog the limitations of the antiquated Russian phone system, parts of which date to before the 1917 revolution. Cellular overlays, microwave transmitters and innovative satellite patches are providing some temporary and valuable solutions for direct international dialing. Mobile phones can be leased for car or home. AT&T and Sprint have both introduced direct-dial (USA Direct and World Connect) services from Moscow. There are now more lines into and out of Russia; whereas just a few years ago there were a total of twelve circuits, there are now a couple thousand.

Still, the domestic phone system remains founded on a decaying copper wire system (some Moscow phone lines laid in 1905 are still in use) which, along with mechanical switching is noisy and enervating. The aim of this section, therefore, is to help you make the best of this situation and to take advantage of the new high-tech solutions.

Placing a Call

Phoning from a phone booth on the street in Moscow or St. Petersburg requires use of a token (жетон – *zheton*). A token, at the time of publication costs 1500 rubles. Tokens are available at newspaper stands, metro stations in some stores and many kiosks. This zheton system is still being phased in and you can still find booths requiring a one ruble coin (15k coins will also work on these phones, as the 15k and 1R coins are similar in size and weight). In other cities, the cost of a phone call from the street varies widely, since phone booths belong to the city and each city is implementing price hikes in its own way.

For directory assistance in getting a local phone number, dial 09.

Long Distance Dialing within Russia and the CIS

To dial long distance direct within Russia and the Commonwealth, you must first dial 8, wait for the dial tone, then dial the city code (see the table on page 5), then the local phone number. For example, if you needed to dial the Nizhny Novgorod number 78652, you would dial 8-8312-78652.

From some cities, you will need to order intercity calls with the operator, depending upon the capabilities of the local network. But in major cities you can direct dial to most other major cities. From Moscow you can dial most anywhere (Nakhodka and Tolyatti being notable exceptions). From some provincial cities, however, you cannot direct dial Moscow.

Connection times can be very long, due to the fact that Russia still relies on mechanical telephone switching systems. If your call has not connected within one minute, hang up and try again.

Other problems: You will often need to add zeroes or twos between the city code and the local portion of a phone number. *There must be ten digits for you to complete an intercity call by direct dialing.* If adding 2's or 0's does not work, you will need an operator to put the call through.

From some phones, you must dial the number of the phone you are calling from after dialing the number you are calling. In Moscow, to find out your line's ability to dial intercity calls and what extra numbers you may need to add, call 271-9118; in St. Petersburg, you dial 07. These are also the numbers to dial if you have any problems with intercity dialing.

To get the city codes for cities not listed in the table on page 5, find out the local directory assistance phone number from your hotel desk (or call the information number listed for the city in Chapter 4). It differs from city to city; in Moscow or St. Petersburg it is 07.

Dialing Internationally from Russia

To dial internationally, you must dial 8, wait for the dial tone, then 10, then the country code, then the city or area code (without the zero which may often precede it), then the number within the country you are dialing. See the table on page 6 for a listing of international country and city codes.

Since 1993, it has been possible to dial international calls directly any time of the day from Moscow and St. Petersburg, subject to the amount of other traffic on the lines (which is steadily declining with continual hikes in the cost of making international calls). Most, but not all, apartment phones in these cities have this capability. If your phone does not have a direct dial capability, or if you cannot get through, you have at least four options.

Operator assisted calls: You can book a call with an international operator any time of the day or night. To book an international call while in Moscow or St. Petersburg, dial 8, wait for a dial tone, then dial 194 or 196. From a hotel in Moscow dial 333-4101, in St. Petersburg 315-0012. There are operators who speak English; when the operator answers the phone, say clearly and slowly: "Pah angleesky." They ought to understand and hook you up with the right operator. Tell the operator what you want. If you want the next possible available line, be prepared to wait several hours to get a call back from the operator. You can set a specific time for the operator to call you back with the call connected, but do not be surprised if you do not get called back or get called back later than requested. It happens.

With inflation, international call rates are being increased every month or two. Still, the cost for calling Europe is holding at about $1-1.50 per

CALLING WITH YOUR CARD

AT&T USA Direct (Moscow): **155-5042**
Sprint Express (Moscow): **155-6133**
MCI World Phone (Moscow): **960-2222**

minute in rubles (depending on the time of day). For calls to the US, the price is a bit higher (around $2 per minute), for Australia and Japan higher still. If you are staying in a hotel, be sure to ask ahead of time what the per minute rates are. If you are quoted a ruble price, be sure to get the exchange rate at which you will be paying. If you wish, you can connect up and have your party call you back (find out your hotel's switchboard number, or your room's direct number – the caller may also have to give your hotel room number).

Put it on your card: If you have an AT&T or Sprint calling card, you can now call an AT&T USA Direct (which also has Russia-speaking operators) or Sprint Express number in Moscow (see above) and be immediately connected with a US operator. The connect charges are not cheap. You pay $3.25 for the first minute and $2.50 for each additional minute, plus a $2-2.50 service charge per call. If you have an MCI card, you can call the MCI Call USA number in Helsinki and pay about the same charges, plus the cost of the call to Helsinki. All three services also allow you to call non-US numbers through the US operator. *You may now also dial 800 numbers via USA Direct, MCI or Sprint international access numbers, although the call will not be toll-free.*

Call collect: You can use the AT&T, Sprint and MCI numbers above to place a collect call. For this you don't need a card (the call recipient will be billed the above charges, plus a hefty fee, about $5).

Call-back services: These services have just made their appearance in Russia. After setting up an account, you are able to dial a number outside the country, usually in the US. You are then automatically phoned back at the number you are calling from, whereupon you are given access to a dial-tone which allows you to make calls anywhere in the world. These services take advantage of market differentials and are usually able to provide a lower cost service (usually less than a dollar a minute between the US and Russia) at the same quality level. Still, check carefully into the background and vitae of any company offering call-back services. Several that come recommended are: AAA, Phoenix Network, Cyberlink, Kallback.

Leap-frogging: For persons setting up offices or staying in Russia longer term, there are a number of companies offering different techno-logical fixes to leapfrog the bottleneck in international dialing: everything from installation of local and international direct lines, to cellular phones, to independent Inmarsat direct links via satellite from any location in Russia. A common solution is to have a "satellite phone" or fax number, which allows one to bypass the Russian phone system altogether. In such instances, this satellite number has a different city code from "local" phones (i.e. 501, 502, 509). For a complete city-specific listing of telecommunications service companies, see the Yellow Pages in our *Where in Moscow* or *Where in St. Petersburg*. The only service which is not city-specific is that provided by the US company BelCom. They provide portable single and multichannel satellite telephone systems that allow direct communication (voice, fax, telex and data) from remote locations in the CIS. Contact (in the US): BelCom Communications, 515 Madison Ave., New York, NY 10022, ph. (212) 371-2335, fax (212) 755-0864.

Communicating with Russia from Abroad

Since the fall of 1989, it has been possible to direct dial Moscow from the United States. It has long been possible to do this from most European countries. It is now theoretically possible to dial direct to most any Russian city which you can direct dial from Moscow, but you must contend with low capacity lines. In practice, poor line quality and congestion make calling direct to anywhere but Moscow something of a trial. Often, the costlier variant of dialing via an operator can help speed the call and secure better line quality.

To dial Russia from the US, dial 011-7, then the city code (see table page 5), then the local number.

The best time to call Moscow from the US is during US non-business hours (i.e. nights and weekends). At any time, your ability to dial successfully will depend upon where in the US you are calling from. New York and Washington are best placed on the US network and Western cities like Houston and San Diego are much farther down on the electronic totem pole and will, regardless of the time, find direct dialing much more difficult. Calling from Europe is usually much easier than from the US.

The cost of a call from the United States to Russia, with any of the major carriers, is about $2 a minute (less on weekends). From the US, Sprint offers the greatest number of lines into Russia, as it has its own circuits, plus it uses AT&T circuits for overflow traffic, whereas the reverse is not true. You can access Sprint, regardless of your carrier, by dialing 10333, then the complete number (beginning with 011, as above). You can access AT&T, regardless of your carrier, by dialing 1028801, then the country code and number. MCI can be accessed from any phone by dialing 10222.

FAX

Sending faxes to and from Russia is much easier than it used to be. Still, line quality is not consistently sufficient to sustain a good transmission, and business hours are the most difficult time to get through. And at $2-3 per minute, the costs can be astronomical. From Europe, the situation is, of course, somewhat better.

Most all Russian businesses now have fax machines (vs. the old telex standby), and it is becoming as much a mainstay of business activity there as in the West. A fact is worth noting in this context. A fax machine (or modem) in Russia must technically be registered with the local authorities (in this instance the local telephone network), and its hookup inspected by them (to make sure it complies with Russian standards). There is an initial hookup fee and an annual "service charge." Of late, there have been campaigns to "catch" unregistered fax machines, with "offenders" paying fines which basically amount to the hookup and annual fees, plus a factoring.

For fax bureaus in Moscow or St. Petersburg, see the Yellow Pages in our *Where in Moscow* or *Where in St. Petersburg*.

FAX FORWARDING

Through the use of electronic mail services (see below) and satellite technology, fax forwarding services are available to Russia and the CIS. The procedure involves either sending an electronic mail message for conversion into a fax and transmission within Russia, or faxing a message to a Western fax relayer, who stores the fax and sends it on electronically, for retransmission within Russia. In either case, the sender's hassle is greatly reduced and, in most cases, the quality of transmission is greatly improved. The current providers of this service are:

Global SprintFax: US Sprint offers a service called Global SprintFax. When you subscribe to this service (start-up fees of about $500, plus a $100 monthly minimum), you can send a fax to a local number in the West or Russia; it is digitized and sent electronically over dedicated lines to or from Russia, and then faxed out from the location closest to your fax's destination. This means no hassle with direct-dialing to Moscow, and greatly improved transmission quality. The cost between Europe and Russia is about $1.50, between the US and Russia, about $3 a page. Contact your local Sprint sales representative, or Sprint in Moscow (see *Electronic Mail*). Since Sprint has set up fax servers throughout Russia and the former USSR, your fax will often be un-digitized and sent from a server quite close to your recipient's number. Sprint's Email service (see below) uses these same servers to turn text Email messages into faxes at the user's request.

Email carriers: All other major Email carriers (i.e. Compuserve, Glasnet, Prodigy, MCI Mail, Sprint, AmericaOnline) also allow you to send electronic mail messages to a fax machine, including faxes in Moscow. This tends to be a bit more expensive than sending it yourself, but it does take the task off you hands; typically the number is tried repeatedly by the service until it gets through. These services will send your fax from a US-based server (except Glasnet, which uses a Moscow-based one) and use direct dial international phone lines, which means the quality will be a bit less reliable. In any case, the main limitation of most Email-based fax systems is that you can only send text messages (with the caveat that some allow you to store letterhead graphics on-line for inclusion in cover sheets). If you are already on an Internet Email system you may want to investigate the FaxGate service offered by a Moscow-based email service called Elvis+. You set up a deposit account and then can transmit on messages via their fax server. For more info, use WWW and jump over to http://www.elvis.ru/ or send an email message to <gatemast@elvis.sovusa.com>

ELECTRONIC MAIL

One way any business or individual can circumvent communications difficulties (i.e. relying on phone and fax communications with Moscow or outlying areas) is to tap into an electronic mail (Email) service. Because this requires only local calls at either end of a communication channel and not a direct link between communicating parties, it is a much simpler, more flexible, and a much less expensive means of communication.

What you need. To use Email, aside from a computer, you need communications software, a modem and an account on an Email system, which together should not cost more than $100.

To use Email in Russia, the user must have either a modem with error correction capability (to compensate for the bad lines), often known as **MNP5 or V.42 bis Error Correction**, or telecommunications software which can effect the same type of correction. Such error correction is pretty much standard on new modems, but check to make certain in any case.

To connect your modem (or fax) to Russian phone lines, you will also need an adaptor that converts a US RJ-11 phone plug to the flat, four-pronged Russian phone plug. To get one in the US, call 800-639-4301 and ask for item A710. They are also available at selected stores in Moscow. To convert from European plugs to Russian plugs, call TeleAdapt in the UK at 44-81-421-4444, fax 44-81-421-5308.

What Email is. Email is an electronic, often instantaneous, postal service. You write your mail in a word processing program on your computer (or directly in an email program), then save it as a text file (which strips out text formatting codes like bold, italic and font sizes). You then use your communications software to connect (log-on) to your Email service by modem and transmit (upload) your text message onto the system, providing an address of the recipient that the system understands (i.e. <ris@sover.net>). The Email system then forwards your message intact through a network of servers (X.25 pads) and satellite connections, to land in your intended recipient's mailbox and await her next log-on to the service at that end. Mail sent to you from colleagues and friends also sits in your Email "in-box" until you log-on to retrieve (download) it.

The beauty of using Email to communicate with Russian partners is that, like faxes, it lets you communicate freely regardless of wide differences in time zones. But, unlike faxes, Email requires only local phone calls on both ends and, thanks to error-correcting technology, communications rarely get garbled the way a fax bouncing off satellites can.

But the value of Email only begins with the ability to send text messages in and out of Russia effortlessly. Because Email systems also allow you to send and receive *binary* files (formatted word processing files – including documents in Russian, spreadsheets, graphics files, etc.), you can easily exchange complex reports, publications and files. And it can be done quite inexpensively, particularly if you use compression software to decrease the size of your binary files (often to 10-25% of their original size) – needless to say, both the sender and the receiver must be using the same software. Software called PKZIP/PKUNZIP is the standard and can be obtained on most any Email/bulletin board network, such as Compuserve.

Another advantage of Email is that you can very easily send and receive telexes right from your computer. This is particularly important since many larger Russian enterprises and factories still use telex as a primary means of communication. This puts you in easy touch with all points of Russia and the Commonwealth with a simple keystroke.

If you have a fax modem instead of an ordinary modem (indeed, most all modems these days are fax modems), you can use the fax modem to receive faxes (even those sent to yourself, if you have two lines), then save the file as a bitmapped image (which can be viewed or printed by most any graphics or word processing software), compress it, and send it as a binary file to or from Russia.

How to get started. You can't buy a modem or communications software these days without getting a free signup package for one of the major services. Compuserve, America OnLine, MCI Mail and Sprint are the large services easiest to access from Russia. In addition, several companies operate Email services which are primarily Russian-Western services.

Most Email systems are inexpensive to use on the Western side (i.e. sending from the US to Russia or receiving in the US from Russia). The most expensive part of the equation in any case is sending and receiving on the Russian end. Prices between services vary, as do the services and features each provides.

To get started in the West, you can contact any of the offices below to set up an Email account. If you are already using an Email service, chances are, if a Russian partner can get hooked up on a system there (i.e. Relcom), they can communicate with you via Internet addressing (ask your Email service's customer service department about this).

If you and your Russian partner plan to transmit binary files back and forth, you will make your task considerably easier if you both have accounts on the same host system, e.g. Compuserve or Glasnet. You can send binary files over the internet, say between Relcom and Compuserve, but this requires some translation software and a bit of technical prowess at either end of the transaction.

Electronic Mail Services

America OnLine, ph. 800-827-6364

Compuserve, PO Box 20212, Columbus, OH 43220, ph. 800-848-8990

The two largest US-based services each now offer direct access to accounts from Moscow, St. Petersburg and other cities. A surcharge of $6-15 usually applies and often you will have to go through other hosts (esp. the Sprint host in other cities), like Scitor, Infonet or others. Compuserve offers up to 9600 baud access in Moscow; America OnLine has 28800 baud access in St. Petersburg and 9600 baud in Moscow.

Geonet, Izmailovskoye sh. 71, Moscow, ph. 166-2339, fax 166-2338, email <n.romanov@mos1.geonet.de>

Geonet is a somewhat no-frills on-line service provider, compared to some of the other systems, but it is quite cost competitive, and offers email, fax and telex capability. In the US, call 415-434-3221.

Glasnet, 437 Mundel Way, Los Altos, CA 95072, phone 415-948-5753; fax 948-5753, email: <glasadmin@igc.apc.org>.

This system is low cost and has one of the most powerful Moscow servers. In addition to true, high speed (14.4k) Internet access, GlasNet has a new, easy-to-use graphic interface called InterACT, that allows users to easily move between Email, news groups, WWW, Gopher, FTP and Telnet. GlasNet also features GlasMail, which allows you to send email messages from the West, for delivery in Russia by fax or surface mail. GlasNet is a non-profit organization, connected with IGC in the US (on the US side, you get an account on IGC computers, but it will also get you connected when you are in Moscow). You can set up Russian contacts with 'sponsored' accounts that allow almost unlimited access for $25 a month. You can also pay in rubles. There is low-cost access nationwide in the US (via 800 number) and worldwide via other non-profit servers. For a Russian account, contact Glasnet in Moscow at 207-0704, fax 207-0889.

Infocom, in the US, phone Infonet at 800-766-8737

This Russo-Finnish joint venture has been much lower profile than Sprint or Sovam and is a bit pricier as well. It links you into the large Infonet network (and to Compuserve, see above). Not as widespread a service in North America; in Europe, call directory assistance for the local affiliate company. For a Russian account, contact Infocom JV at Kamergersky per. 4, ph. 925-1235, fax 200-3219.

☑ TELEX/EMAIL

TRANSLITERATION KEY

А	A
Б	B
В	V
Г	G
Д	D
Е	YE
Ё	YO
Ж	ZH
З	Z
И	I
К	K
Л	L
М	M
Н	N
О	O
П	P
Р	R
С	S
Т	T
У	U
Ф	F
Х	KH
Ц	TS
Ч	CH
Ш	SH
Щ	SHCH
У	Y
Э	E
Ю	YU
Я	YA

Relcom, In Moscow, Ovchinnikovskaya nab. 6, ph. 231-2129, 231-6395, fax 198-9510, email: postmaster@ kiae.su.

This is the largest domestic Russian/CIS telecommunications network, founded originally, as was the case with Internet in the US, for academic purposes. It has since gone commercial and has more nodes in Russia than any other access provider. They can offer full internet access, as well as access to major on-line services, all at competitive rates.

Sovam Teleport, ul Nezhdanovoi 2a, ph. 229-3466, fax 229-4121

Another very strong local provider, Sovam offers full internet access, access to major on-line services, and an increasingly rich WWW content on its host server.

SprintNet, 12490 Sunrise Valley Drive, Reston, VA 22096, ph. (800) 736-1130; in Northern Europe: Norton House, Kingsland Business Park, Basingstoke RG24 OPL, England; in France: Z.A. De Courtaboeuf, Miniparc Du Verger, 1 Rue De Terre Neuve, 91967 Les Ulis Cedex B

Sprint's prices are reasonable on the US and European end, but high on the Russian end ($45 per hr.), which is reflective of the company's focus on higher-end telecom services. The best selling point is that this system, which has the usual fax, telex and database/news service access capabilities, sits on the world's largest data network, making international access easier. It also offers the largest number of nodes in Russia. For a Russian account (access numbers in dozens of cities of the former USSR) contact Sprint in Moscow at (095) 201-6890.

TELEX

As noted above, one of the main ways to communicate from all points of Russia and the Commonwealth is by telex. Sending telexes can be inexpensive and simple. You can send telexes from almost any post office in any city or town in Russia. And if you have Email back at your home office, this may be a viable way to communicate quickly. Use the table on the previous page for sending Russian language telexes from the West. A US company, ANSAT, installs bi-lingual telex terminals, ph. 202-483-0400.

VIDEO-CONFERENCING

You can now meet your Russian partners face-to-face, without ever leaving the home office. The following service providers offer video-conferencing services between some US cities and Moscow.

Americom Business Center, 2010 Main Street, Ste 1260, Irvine, CA 92714, ph. 714-752-6577, fax 714-752-6564.

Brown University, Providence, RI 02912, ph. 401-863-7304.

Video Bridge, 1 Kendall Sq., Ste 2000, Cambridge, MA 02135, ph. 617-621-7147, fax 617-621-7069.

Shipping to/from Russia
AIR MAIL

The Russian mail system is slow, unreliable and not very safe. It's fine for personal letters, but don't send anything of value by the post. Use one of the alternatives listed under Express Mail below (indeed, it is still technically illegal to send certain items of value, like stamps, lottery tickets, checks, cash, stock certificates and photographic negatives by mail into Russia). You may send, by airmail, goods as gifts to Russians that are valued at <$200, although, as noted above, it is not recommended to send anything of value by mail.

The cost of a domestic letter is low by international standards (R250 at the time of publication). An international letter cost R2000 ($0.40) at the time of publication, an international parcel (<10 kg) cost R300,000 ($58).

EXPRESS MAIL & COURIER SERVICES

A number of Western companies, either independently or through joint ventures, now provide express letter and package service to and from Russia. Typical delivery time (to Moscow or St. Petersburg) is 2-4 days to and from the US and 1-3 days to and from Europe. Delivery to outlying cities takes somewhat longer. For pick up or contact numbers, see the Yellow Pages in our *Where in Moscow* or *Where in St. Petersburg*. DHL and TNT deliver to the largest number of cities in the CIS, followed by Annandale, and then Fedex.

The following companies are currently serving the major CIS and Baltic cities (subject to change without notice, this information is correct at the time of printing). Prices fluctuate greatly according to the city being delivered to. The basic price for a one pound package of documents to Moscow (from the US) is indicated as a benchmark. Other cities often carry a surcharge. Call the carrier for more information. For an excellent summary of express mail services to the Russian Far East, contact the publishers of *Russian Far East Update* at ph. 206-447-2668. Prices below do not include duties or taxes.

Express Mail Services

Airborne Express, ph. 703-802-3812; $69
Alaska Airlines (to/from Russian Far East), ph. 800-426-0333; $40
US Postal Service's EMS Service (check local phone directory), $38
Federal Express, ph. 800-247-4747; $68
DHL, ph. 800-225-5345; UK: 81-890-9393; $71
Emery Worldwide, ph. 800-323-4685; $65
TNT Express Worldwide, ph. 800-558-5555; UK: 81-561-1133; $78.50
UPS, see local phone directories for 800 numbers; $65

National mail services, such as US Postal Service (noted above) and Royal Mail also provide express mail services to Moscow and some major cities, usually using the Russian mail service for outlying cities. Most all air carriers serving Russia also offer air cargo or air freight services. You may need to use a freight forwarder for such services, however (see section following).

For express mail services *within* Russia, in addition to the companies listed above, a less-expensive, though widely-employed alternative is to pay a train car conductor to put your package in their compartment, for pick up at the other end of the line by a colleague who meets the train (you call your friend and tell them the train car and train that the packet is arriving on). This used to be safer than it currently is, with crime on the trains increasing, but is still a good alternative for non-valuable items.

Courier Services

Post International: Twice-weekly courier service between New York and Moscow. For $50-70 per month, clients may send up to a pound of printed matter into and out of Moscow each week. Additional material costs $10/lb. Non-members can send a letter to the US or Europe for about $2. Contact Post International in Moscow at 200-0927 or 200-2848. In the US, call 212-315-2408.

PX Post: This British-run venture offers a daily, private mail service between Moscow and the West. Mail and parcels can be sent overseas (2-5 day delivery time) from Moscow for as little as $0.50 to Europe and $0.70 to the US. International mail and parcels are received in Moscow for $0.50 per ounce. You can also get a monthly account that gives you discounts on higher volumes of mail, plus free pick up and delivery of your mail in Moscow. The main office is open 9 am to 8 pm M-F and 10 am to 5 pm on Saturdays, and there are other mail counters for drop-of around Moscow. PX Post in Moscow at 956-2230, fax 956-2231.

Russia House, Ltd.: Operates a weekly courier between Moscow and London, on a pay as you go basis. Cost is £40 for up to three kilos, in the UK, call 71-439-1271.

AIR/SEA CARGO

For heavier shipments, it is more cost effective to send via air or sea freight. Air freight can be as quick as an express courier (after documentation and upon delivery to the point of departure), and becomes cost effective at weights of 20-25 pounds. Sea freight will take 3-4 weeks and can be subject to significant unloading delays at destination points, and is only suitable for containerloads. Most any freight forwarder can arrange all documentation and shipping services for you, by air or land. And there are thousands of freight forwarders. Be sure to check forwarders out thoroughly before committing your shipments to their care.

You will need to have an Air Waybill for air express or air freight shipments, plus a pro forma commercial invoice listing the contents of the shipment, their weight and the number of pieces. The latter should also state the total value of the shipment, and you may need to state the cost of shipping. There is, at the time of publication, a 15% duty on the total value of most all shipments into Russia, including on the cost of shipping.

Below is a list of just a few freight forwarding and shipping companies who are known to have a good deal of experience shipping to Russia. It is worth comparing their prices on mid-sized shipments (50-2000 lbs.) with those offered by regular express carriers, especially DHL.

US Shippers and Freight Forwarders

Air-Sea Forwarders, PO Box 90637, Los Angeles, CA 90009, phone 213-776-1611, fax 310-216-2625

Baltic Shipping Company, c/o Rice, Unruh, Reynolds Co., 29 Broadway, Room 1315, New York, NY 10006, ph. 212-943-2350, fax 212-363-5032

Danzas Corp., 3650 – 131st Ave, SE, Newport Towers, Suite 700, Bellevue, WA 98006, ph. 800-426-5962, 206-649-9339, fax 206-649-4940 (call this office for the office closest to you)

Finn Container Cargo Services, Inc., 3000 Weslayn, Suite 200, Houston, TX 77027, ph. 713-961-5200, fax 713-961-4088

Hecny Transport, 147-39 175th Street, Jamaica, NY 11434, ph. 718-656-5537, fax 718-632-8491

Kintetsu World Express, 66 Powerhouse Rd., Roslyn Heights, NY 11577, ph. 516-625-8700, fax 516-625-8724

Radix Group, Intl., Building 75, North Hangar Road, JFK Int'l Airport, Jamaica, NY 11430, ph. 718-917-4800, fax 718-917-6509

Schenkers, 150 Albany Ave., Freeport, NY 11520, for air freight: ph. 516-377-3006, fax 516-377-3076, for sea freight: phone 201-434-5500

Sea-Land Service, Inc., 379 Thornall St., 5th Floor, Edison, NJ 08837, ph. 800-753-2500

Stalco Forwarding Services, 254 W. 35th St., 16th floor, New York, NY 10001, ph. 212-736-1960, fax 212-594-9588

Vinlund, PO Box 261, Hanover, NH 03755; in Moscow: ul. Tverskaya 17, ph. 229-6380/1393, fax 230-2101

Shippers Outside the US

John Nurminen Oy, Pasilankatu 2, SF 00240, Helsinki, Finland, ph. (0) 015-071, fax (0) 0145-614

Scan Cargo Transport a/s, 44 Fabriksparken, Dk 2600 Glostrop, Denmark, ph. (424) 535-11, telex 331-63

Sovfracht, ul. Rozhdestvenka 1/4, Moscow, Russia 103759, ph. (095) 926-1118, fax (095) 230-2640, telex 411168

Sovtransservice GmbH, Wendenstrasse 151, 2000 Hamburg 26, Germany, ph. (40) 251-3126, fax (40) 258-065, telex 211-294

Doing Business 8

This new period in Russian history offers unique opportunities and certain risks for investors. The Russian investment frontier has been open for ten years. Thousands of firms and individuals have ventured East (or West, as the case may be) in that time. Some have been wildly successful. Most have been sobered. Many have failed. This section considers some of the lessons of the past decade and, at the same time, summarizes some of the unique aspects of the Russian market.

The Russian Style of Business

When it comes to understanding the Russian business culture, it is prudent to remember that the imprint of over 70 years of communist administrative style and practice lays heavy on Russian industry and trade. It is also worth remembering that, while Russia lived some 74 years under communist rule, it has lived over a thousand years under authoritarian and autocratic rule. There are only remote pockets of democratic or free market experience in the whole of Russian and Soviet history.

At times it may be difficult to discern which elements of the present Russian style of business are Russian and which are Soviet. Regardless, there are certainly some distinctive characteristics of the Russian business "style" which are unique.

It should be noted that this is a necessarily cursory review of some of the characteristics of Russian business culture. While there are certainly risks in such generalization, there must be a starting point for understanding potential cultural differences which are bound to arise when doing business in Russia.

RED TAPE

In 1839, the Marquis de Custine, while waiting to enter Russia through St. Petersburg, unnerved by the customs bureaucracy, was consoled by a Russian customs agent who commented that "Russia is the land of useless formalities." In this respect at least, Russia has not changed much in 150 years.

Doing business in Russia means daily taking on a bureaucracy with few equals. Be it in customs clearing, taxation or enterprise registration, red tape binds the economy and society to the point of strangulation. Notaries, auditors, bookkeepers and inspectors hold the business person hostage to an endless procession of stamps, forms and signatures.

But, as in Custine's case, the bureaucrat himself is also long-suffering and will often beat you to the punch in decrying the bureaucracy's injustices and intractability. This rebellion against the system, while working complacently within it, often leads to a frustrated bureaucrat finding himself able to overlook minor infractions for personal gain (in fact, one could argue the system is supported by such outlets for personal gain). But, short of bribery, there is the opportunity to use the latent sympathy of individual bureaucrats to ease a difficult situation. This should not be taken to the extreme, however. Crying outrage most often begets stonewalling.

FORMALISM

The bureaucracy's useless formalities belie a more general formalism in the business sphere which is in stark contrast to the more casual Western business style, in particular the American.

Paper communications are very formulaic and formal (see our *Business Russian*, reviewed in Chapter 1, for samples).

Business is rarely conducted over the phone, and face to face negotiations are the only real forum for decision-making. For this, the Soviet KGB carries much of the blame. But it is also that Russians very much feel that any matter of import should be discussed by looking one another in the eyes.

Even the simplest meetings are termed negotiations (переговоры–*peregovori*) and include a certain protocol all their own. There is the ceremonial exchange of business cards, the rambling speeches, the tea and cookies, and the ever-serious tone implying that issues of great import are being negotiated.

The problem with such meetings, which certainly harken back to the pre-1987 period, is that they take time, too much time. They are rarely productive in a practical sense. But certainly the older management personnel, raised in the communist form of economic management, are more prone to this type of formalism. The younger and newer entrepreneurs tend to eschew such formalities and rightly place a higher value on their time and energies.

SENSE OF TIME

Even the younger, more impatient Russians, however, share with their counterparts among the older management a sense of time and timeliness which differs somewhat from Western business practice.

Being late for business meetings is far from taboo in Russia. In fact it is almost the rule. Punctuality is very rare. Given that, expect meetings to drag on into overtime.

The flip side of this more casual relationship to time is that Russian business people generally have a greater reserve of patience than their Western counterparts. They are likewise more conservative (pessimistic?) about change and schedules for change. Therefore, expect new ideas to be met with a brick wall of skepticism. Expect change to meet with great delays. Conversely, expect decisions made and commitments believed in to be pursued with incomparable vigor and effort.

MANEUVERING

Every negotiation is an occasion for Machiavellian intrigues, maneuvering and posturing. Rest assured that there is nothing personal in this and great malice is not usually intended. This is just part of the game of business as Russians see it. Not unlike a round of chess.

Whereas Americans and other Western business persons tend to work from the assumption that the result of any negotiation should be a win-win situation, all too often Russian business people are zero-sum thinkers: our side cannot win without putting the other side at a disadvantage.

This is reinforced by a general political and business ethos that implies that, in order to get by, you must deceive the authorities and find loopholes in laws. So far there has been little in Russian business legislation to show such behavior to be unjustified. For now, the sphere of business is one of intrigues and mirrors.(Two books, referenced in Chapter 1, are highly recommended reading in this realm: *From Nyet to Da*, and *Negotiating with the Soviets*.)

"SVYAZI"

For seven decades, the binding force which held the Soviet economy together was the Communist Party. It was an institutionalized "old boy" network. Doing anything of consequence under the old system required Party approval and patronage. If you didn't have connections (связы-*svyazi*), you stood little chance of getting anywhere or getting anything done.

While the edifice of both the Soviet Union and the Party has crumbled, the importance of connections in this highly bureaucratic society has not waned. It has just become less institutionalized.

Rare is the occasion when a business meeting will not be a venue for name dropping and claims of uncommon influence (at the highest levels). It is often difficult, if not impossible, to test the veracity of these claims, but the importance of "friends in high places" is not to be overlooked.

The importance of connections and access is heightened by deeply ingrained traditions of patronage and co-optation. Connections and the ability to take care of your friends are real indicators of status, still even more so than the new status symbols of incipient capitalism. But this is not surprising in a society where the economy has always been highly politicized and statist (and founded on scarcity).

CULT OF LARGESSE

Russians are lovers of grand designs and largesse. It is often said that, much as with Texans, this has to do with their geographic disposition, that huge open spaces give rise to expansive thinking. Regardless of the reasons, Russians, like Americans, love to do things in a big way. You only need to look at the Stalinist architecture of Moscow or the feat of St. Petersburg for examples.

The positive connotations of this are ambition and vision (i.e. the Virgin Lands program and the Soviet Space Program). The negative connotations are hastiness and inability to build a proper foundation (Stalin's sinking Palace of Soviets and the poor quality of St. Petersburg water come to mind). And unfortunately, too many of the "first wave" of Russian entrepreneurs are after the fast buck and the big score, erecting empires on sand, trying to be the biggest, rather than the best, trying to do all things, rather than one thing very well. Too few recognize the worth of building lasting value and doing one thing and doing it very well. The solution is merely a matter of channeling innate ambition and vision, which, some have postulated, will be the manner of the coming "second wave" of Russian entrepreneurs.

EGALITARIANISM

Any Western investor who begins an enterprise in Russia and takes on a significant number of employees will soon notice some real differences between Russian workplace mentality and that in the West. Russian workers (particularly the older ones) typically expect a much higher level of support and non-wage compensation. This is very much a result of a scarcity economy and of uncertainty (and of course of the big-brother socialism which gave birth to such an economy).

As well, Russian workers seek higher levels of workplace democracy. This is a legacy of socialist trade unions (which are yet a force to be reckoned with in Russia) and of the Russian *mir* (мир) or village, where decisions were made consensually and supported unanimously.

Stretching from these same roots, Russian workers are much more sensitive than their Western counterparts to wage differentials. From childhood, collectivism has been stressed over individualism and even individual bonuses for individual achievement are much less preferred than group bonuses based on group efforts. Certainly some aspects of this are softening up as "marketization" rocks the society to its core. But old habits die hard.

Choosing a Partner

The present somewhat uncertain times, along with the lessons of the last seven years, recommend a more circumspect and cautious approach to the selection of a partner and the cementing of business relationships.

The process of choosing a partner can be either passive or proactive. The passive approach means working with the first person who comes along who claims expertise and capabilities in your area of interest. A proactive stance means you and the goals and needs you identify drive your search. Only a proactive stance is in your best interests.

If you think that there is an opportunity for your business in Russia, try to step back far enough from the project idea to identify all of the components. What needs to be put in place – from your point of view – for the project to succeed? Identify what you need for real estate, equipment, supplies, personnel and so forth. Ask yourself, when considering a partner, how effectively the Russian organization can provide what is necessary.

Do not choose a partner before you know exactly what your needs are. Do not choose a partner unless they have a proven ability to satisfy those precise needs. Beware the prospective partner who claims to be capable of everything. Doing any *one* thing in Russia is difficult.

Keeping these points in mind, there are some questions you should ask yourself before getting too closely tied with any partner.

WHAT TO ASK ABOUT A PARTNER

- Do your potential partners have any experience in foreign trade or business management?
- Does your potential partner have any valuable political affiliation? And in these uncertain times, is this a help or a hindrance?
- In these times of rising organized crime, you may want to get a good handle on what your partner's relationship is with his *krisha* (literally their 'roof' or protector). Everyone has one, it seems, and if your partner doesn't, find out why. In either event, make sure you feel comfortable with your partner's decision and, of course, with their *krisha*.
- Does your prospective partner want to build General Motors overnight or are they willing to focus, to start slowly and carefully?
- Does your partner measure business/organizational success in the number of bodies employed or by the bottom line? Can they construct a realistic business plan?
- Do the people that work with your prospective partner have good educational backgrounds? Did they achieve their current position by virtue of skill and intelligence or was there some other, less valuable reason? How do they go about selecting and hiring personnel?
- Does your prospective partner have an abundance of young, energetic personnel?
- Does your partner have access to a valuable section of the market you are targeting, or the supplies you will need to provide your service or product?
- Will your partner have a real ownership interest? That is, will the partner be making a commitment or investment and getting a return in a fashion that will motivate people – will there be individual motivation as opposed to merely institutional motivation?
- How is privatization affecting this partner?

- How is this partner coping with the difficult issues currently thwarting honest Russian business: crime, inflation and unclear legal jurisdictions?
- How would you evaluate this partner's respect for important legal issues, such as intellectual property rights, taxation, registration?
- Would you be working with this partner because you like him/her or because you have so far found no one else to work with? Too many people have been unwilling to admit the latter when it is the case and have thus contributed to the high failure rate of joint ventures. Would you work with these people in your home country?

GETTING STARTED

If you have found a partner you feel you can work with, it is most advisable to begin working with your partner on a contract basis, if your type of venture would allow this. You need to develop a framework within which you can test one another's abilities, strengths and weaknesses, while not committing blindly to a long term engagement. If the Western partner is contributing technology, it can be provided on a lease or license basis, as opposed to contributing to the equity or authorized capital or a new joint venture.

Such an arrangement also allows you to get to know the market, the environment, your partner and the problems you will face. When you are fully informed, you can always form a more lasting structure.

The key is to go slowly and not commit more resources than your familiarity with the Russian market can bear. The Russian market is significantly different from any other that it is worth emphasizing the importance of this. The thousands of unexecuted Letters of Intent, and the hundreds of inactive joint ventures are a testimony to the unrealistic expectations and misplaced efforts of thousands of Western and Russian firms.

Recruiting Personnel

Like your search for the right partner, your search for management and other personnel should be proactive: driven by your venture's short and long term goals, not by who you happen to meet, and when. It is easy to be drawn into Russia's ubiquitous old-boy network, hiring friends of friends (which, in and of itself, can create managerial nightmares). While in some cases this may be a desirable alternative, more often than not it leads to "satisficing" in the job search, not going out and looking for the ideal candidate.

Any new venture in Russia has two distinguishable stages as concerns hiring: short-term start-up and long-term sustained activity. The personnel needed for each stage may or may not be the same, depending upon the type and scope of your endeavor. The first task is therefore to identify your needs in each stage and let this frame your recruitment efforts. The most

successful ventures have limited strong Western management involvement to the first stage of activity, seeking to train qualified Russian
managers to lead for growth in the second stage.

Among Russians, Western companies and joint ventures are seen as
highly-preferred work situations by virtue of the higher compensation,
better working conditions and potential access to foreign travel that they
offer. On the surface, this would seem to offer prospects of hiring Russia's
"best and brightest." But the reality is that finding good employees is a
difficult task in any environment.

Advertising: Many foreign firms have found advertisement in local
Russian papers an efficient way to find prospective employees. It is
relatively inexpensive and effective, since there tend to be single, dominant
newspapers in a municipality. Be warned, however, that if you are not
careful in using highly-specific job descriptions, you could be inundated
with responses. If you are seeking personnel without foreign language
skills, these media may be your best bet. But if language skills are a must,
you will want to focus advertising efforts on the locally-published media
for expatriates and English language speakers (if such exists), such as the
Moscow Times or Moscow *Tribune* in Moscow or the *St. Petersburg Times* in
that city.

Executive search firms: Local and internationally-based executive
search services (see the list in Chapter 1) are also beginning to operate in
Russia. Some can offer background checks, which one would be hard-
pressed to conduct independently. All can undertake the time-consuming
task of pre-screening. *A caveat:* Locally-based firms are relatively new to
this line of work. Thus, you must consider how to check the record of those
you seek to have doing background checks for you.

The resume and job interview, as employed in the US, are not yet the
general norm in Russia, although applicants for work in foreign firms do
now regularly submit resumes. Consider that, until just a few years ago,
in the absence of a private sector, jobs were "filled" and employees
"placed" by government bodies and institutes. Little recruiting *per se* took
place. Job expertise was generally assumed based on one's passage through
an institute. The resume was the individual's labor book (*trudovaya
knizhka*), which followed him or her from job to job and which recorded
demerits and promotions. Most importantly, since no one was spending
his or her own money and since labor was relatively cheap, hiring was not
seen as a critical procedure to spend time on (vs., say, acquiring production
supplies).

What all this means is that Russia has long lacked a sophisticated,
competitive labor market. The norms in place are not likely those that will
provide you with any guidance in making hiring decisions. If you want
resumes, you may have to inform applicants of how you would like them
formulated. Some firms have found therefore, that, even for senior positions, having applicants fill in a form is the most effective means of
generating the right types of information. Likewise, effective, challenging
interviews need to be built up to through a series of screening interviews.

Pay scales: In deciding what to pay management and employees, be careful to use local standards for your benchmark, not your company's standards at home or in other countries. Talk to other locally-active Western and Russian business people to become educated on generalized expectations and what the market is demanding (Ernst and Young publishes for its clients perhaps the best salary survey, complete with cost of living adjustments). Finally, look to ways to build in protections for employees against inflation and social welfare concerns that are mounting with the breakdown of Russian institutions. Become familiar with Russian labor law and the expectations it has bred (see Chapter 9).

Russian vs. Western managers: Eventually you will run up against the issue of whether to hire Russian or expatriate personnel for management positions. The fact is that finding the best qualified candidate is less and less a case of finding the right nationality. In a recent study published by the Harvard Business School, researchers found that the most successful joint ventures in Russia have "put local managers in charge and delegated radically." There is a limitless supply of qualified Russian managers who seek a productive work environment, something the Soviet system rarely allowed. As the Harvard interviews showed, Russian managers are more able to quickly adapt to Russia's fast-changing legal and regulatory environment; they have no cultural or linguistic barriers to overcome; they are better at turning seemingly intractable problems to the venture's advantage; and, if given the material wherewithal, have demonstrated commitments to quality and service matching any Western counterpart.

This said, successful joint ventures and foreign companies have found it prudent to invest in the management or technical experience of expatriates in the earliest stages of a venture's start-up. Here the focus is on getting the enterprise off on the right foot, in accordance with the foreign company's expectations, and beginning a process of the transfer of know-how. Experience has also shown that foreign companies are wise to construct water-tight systems of financial control from the outset, based on Western accounting standards and norms.

Crime and Business

The predominant outsider impression of what it means to do business in Russia these days seems to be: thick-necked "mafia" hoods shaking down helpless businessmen in an age-old protection racket. Or camoflauge-bedecked security guards, with automatic weapons at the ready, guarding the entrances to bureaus de change. Or suave, monied "new Russians" taking over a newly-privatized enterprise by buying significant stock holdings, exterminating a recalcitrant general director, and placing their own candidate in the job.

Yes, these things do happen in Russia. And, yes, the Western business person in Russia needs to worry about such things. Within reason.

In the absence of effective (read well-paid) police forces and abetted by less than efficient civil and criminal legal systems, organized groups in

Russia do take the law into their own hands. Often. But this does not mean that thugs are running wild on the streets, shooting up store fronts (say, like in Los Angeles). Or that sleazy hoods hang out on street corners looking to prey on unsuspecting foreigners (like, perhaps, in Miami). For the average business person, Russia remains a safe place to do business, if a financially risky and a bureaucratically-entangled place.

Where the dangers are greatest. The greatest susceptibility to crime groups lies in those business sectors where there are large daily cash turnovers and high margins of profit. Not surprisingly, these are the same places where you will encounter the armed, camoflauged security guards. For example: banks, exchange points, heavily-trafficked mini-marts and grocery stores, elite restaurants, casinos, bars and nightclubs.

What is more, any type of high-profile retail outlet, Western or Russian-owned, is in high risk of being subject to protection schemes and, less harmlessly, bribery. As is any trading operation which deals with transportation and shipping. Typically, any such enterprise engages (or is engaged by) a *krisha* (literally a "roof," or protector) against other, hopefully less powerful organizations. Savvy business people go in search of a krisha before the wrong one comes in search of them.

There seems to be greater danger of this sort of business crime in larger cities, like Moscow and St. Petersburg, where there are competing criminal groups. Smaller cities and towns tend to be "run" by those in power politically, so making deals with their involvement or consent tends to insure a higher level of safety. Add to this the fact that some of the greatest current investment opportunities in Russia are outside the two capitals and you have two compelling reasons for doing business in the provinces.

Security companies. It is adviseable to engage a local security company for protection in the types of businesses enumerated above, and for the foreseeable future.

Interestingly enough, in a recent interview in the local press, the head of the Moscow Militia revealed that former employees that have gone on to work as security forces for local foreign businesses have a record of reporting back to the militia about crimes their new employers commit. Apparently there is security, and then there is security with discretion.

Protection money and bribes. Again, as regards protection money, it depends on the type of business you are in and the region/city you choose to operate in. Bribes are a much more widespread phenomenon. Any person doing business in Russia is likely to be subjected to bribe requests at some point. They may be blatant and open, or they may be hidden in barter or "consulting" deals. In any case, the person doing business in Russia needs to accept that the costs of doing business there are high and rising (only superceded by the cost of not doing business there). And many of these costs are "highly discretionary." In point of fact, some American business people are finding the Foreign Corrupt Practices Act (which forbids payment of bribes to obtain business, but apprently not payments to "grease bureaucratic wheels") useful. It can offer a justification for not giving in to certain types of bribe demands.

Vetting prospective business partners. Your approach on this score depends on the scale of your operation and investment. If you are going in big, start with the due diligence services offered by one of the Big Six accounting firms or major legal firms resident in Moscow. What they can't do themselves, they will know how to get done elsewhere. Others have been down this road before you.

If this is beyond your means, look up Security Firms (many of them founded by KGB or Internal Affairs officers that opted for early retirement) in city directories (i.e. *Where in Moscow* or *Where in St. Petersburg*) and make discreet inquiries about due diligence. If your means are truly limited, rely on instinct (you didn't hear that here), but read some of the good books on Russian character first (see Chapter 1).

Keeping a low profile when traveling. Is this important? Yes and no. It always pays to avoid ostentatious behavior and dress, particularly in a place where the magnitude of change has created a lot of resentment for those who "have more than their fair share."

But do not try to be something you are not. In many instances, you will derive negotiating and posturing strength from merely being a foreigner (this still carries considerable weight in Russia). Don't go native.

Interestingly enough, the huge influx of Western consumer goods and "new Russians'" ostentatious displays of wealth make it increasingly hard to stand out as a foreigner. And, given the incipient fear the average Russian has for "new Russians" (who all must be mafia connected, the thinking goes), this works to one's advantage, security-wise. Of course, if you don't speak Russian, your cover can be blown fairly easily... (See also Chapter 5.)

Avoid being targeted. There is surely no guaranteed way to avoid targetting by criminal interests. But it will behoove you to be street-smart and proactive. A bit of restrained paranoia about potential influences or infiltrations can help plug holes before they appear. And nothing works like research and networking for gaining insights into potential problems on the horizon: visit Russia several times before jumping in; make lots of local contacts; read and research with abandon. The best protection for both the up-side and down-side of this reality is to do your homework.

Business Etiquette

Good etiquette is, in most cases, a matter of simple common sense. The following guidelines for the business traveler (which also certainly can be extended to the independent traveler) to Russia should help you adjust to some of the cultural difficulties you may encounter.

DRESS

Most Russian business people have high expectations of Western business people. You will be judged immediately by the way you dress. Dress conservatively and well. Shoes are especially important, as is a nice hat in winter. Women should wear a hat or scarf if visiting an orthodox church. For dinners at someone's house, dress casually.

In winter, dress in layers. Buildings are usually overly-warm inside and you will want to be able to adjust flexibly. Take your overcoat off in public places (most have a place to check your coat).

DISCRETION

Few people are as critical of Russia as Russians. But do not mistake their remarks as an invitation for your criticisms. Russians are also very proud, and justly so, of their country. It may at times be easy to criticize Russia for its inefficiency. But it is a mistake to focus on the present problems and suffering, while overlooking the achievements of Russian and non-Russian cultures and the economic and social potential of these peoples.

MEETINGS

Allow extra time to be on time. Getting places takes a long time (and is subject to innumerable mishaps). While being on time may often not seem too important to your Russian contacts, it should always be very important to you.

Shake everyone's hand firmly when your greet them.

Defer to the senior official to lead the meeting, and wait to be given the floor. Be firm and polite at all times; don't be pushed. Try to get an agenda worked out before the meeting gets started or too far along.

Accept cookies and tea when offered. Tolerate smoking in meetings if you don't smoke (if you are completely intolerant of smoking, doing business in Russia is not for you). Ask first before lighting up to smoke and share your cigarettes generously.

A good translator avoids a thousand headaches. Do all you can to test your translator out in informal situations before you enter into formal situations. A simultaneous translator can be more efficient, but distracting.

BACKGROUND

When preparing for meetings, know who you are meeting with, how important this person is, what his/her background is, etc. Remember, this is a culture which is based on patronage and status. Before a meeting starts, know who everyone in the room is and why they are there — you will thus avoid stepping on egos. And be sure they know who you are and why you are there (and not someone else).

Know something about the company, association or department these people work in/for. As anywhere in the world, you will flatter people by showing them that what they do is known about by someone they previously did not know. You will also impress your hosts with your seriousness about working with them.

COMMUNICATION

Never underestimate the importance of written communications in Russia. The country runs on paper (and rubber stamps). Do not commit something to writing lightly. Retain any written records. When in doubt, notarize.

Written communication is formulaic and formal. Be sure you address the addressee formally. For letters in English, follow good Western business correspondence etiquette. Always type letters. Consult a knowledgeable Russian on writing any letter in Russian.

Fax your letters if your contact has a fax, or send it by email, which is growing rapidly in use. There is also telex, which is ubiquitous in the former USSR. Don't rely on the mail. Faxes, email and telexes will get the most reliable and timely responses – but also send copies through the mail. You can set up telex capability (and fax for that matter) on your PC with a modem (see Chapter 7, *Communications*).

GIFTS

There are three types of gifts. The first is the token gift you should bring along to hand out to business contacts. These souvenirs (lighters, pens, solar calculators with your logo on them) are essential and may be part of what is expected, particularly at New Year's.

The second type of gift is favors. There are things you will be able to provide that no one else can, that are either unavailable or unattainable in Russia. These run the whole gamut and you should try whenever you feel it is right to do all you can to help – you will rarely regret it.

The final type of gift is the bribe. Some would call this a bargain for exchange: VCR's for car registration, computers for an office lease, etc. Often these are unavoidable "given current conditions." Still, try to resist the argument that "this is how things are done here," if only because this is a cost of doing business that is impossible to write off legally (although, in the US – and even more so in other countries – small gifts to "grease the wheels" are deductible as a cost of doing business, gifts to get business are not legally deductible and "prosecutable" under the Foreign Corrupt Practices Act). If the arrangement is a *quid pro quo*, try to get your quo before handing over the quid. The best general slogan for doing business in Russia is: Believe it when you see it. Understand that you are engaged in trade (торговля– *torgovlya*), and if you do not get what was promised, you probably have no recourse.

BUSINESS CARDS

There is a ritual exchange of business cards at any business meeting or negotiation. Do not underestimate the importance of this event. Your business card may be all the information your Russian partner has on you. Make sure your cards say what you want to say about you and your firm – try to have them in Russian. See Chapter 1 for a list of companies that specialize in typesetting and printing bilingual, two-sided cards.

MONEY

You are bound to find yourself, while in Russia, in situations which involve significant financial outlays and yet your Russian counterpart may not have a well-padded expense account. What starts out as generosity can easily turn into exploitation. Think this issue out ahead of time and do not be extravagant unless this is the image you want to convey. Know where you are going, know what it costs (what currency), and know who is going to pay. In Russia, as elsewhere, typically the person inviting is the person paying.

AFTER WORK

While it is sometimes frowned upon to conduct business outside normal working hours, your host will often feel the need to take you out on the town, have a reception, etc. Feel free to discuss business insofar as your host takes the lead. But be better prepared at these times to show an interest in and knowledge of Russia, its history, politics, arts, and culture. Show yourself not to be all business.

Many foreign business people are not accustomed to consuming hard liquor (i.e. vodka and cognac) in the quantities and frequency which is accepted at dinners and receptions in Russia. Don't go overboard in your desire to fit in. Russian hospitality has a well-deserved reputation around the world. But know how and when to say no. If you need an out, be the designated driver.

CUSTOMS AND SUPERSTITIONS

Russian culture is steeped in superstition. Some aspects apply, quite seriously, to business. Russians will joke about these superstitions, but deep down they will also take these things very seriously. As well, there are some customs and points of etiquette which you should adhere to. Both customs and superstitions are listed below (you may judge for yourself which they are). You will avoid potentially embarrassing situations and/ or show yourself to be knowledgeable about things Russian by noting these.

- Never shake hands over a threshold: it will lead to an argument.
- Don't whistle indoors: you will blow your money away.
- Take off your shoes when visiting a home and your hat when indoors. Take off your suit coat in meetings only after asking if it is acceptable.
- Russia is still a very male-chauvinist society. Women in business should always dress conservatively or will end up being thought below their position. Women are not expected to pay for themselves or to be assertive in social situations.
- Always bring flowers or wine when invited to a Russian's home. Always bring an odd number of flowers; even numbers are for funerals.

- Russian personal space is much smaller than what is usual in the US or Europe. Expect more physical contact.
- Be careful when refusing food or drink when visiting friends; they will likely take it as a slight.
- Never pour wine back-handed. It is considered an insult to the person for whom you are pouring.
- Never gesture with your thumb between your first two fingers: this is an obscene gesture.
- Never put your feet up on furniture or show the soles of your feet when sitting: it is considered very rude.
- If you call someone on the phone and they don't recognize your voice, it means you will soon be rich.
- "Rough" language is frowned upon in "educated society."
- A black cat crossing your path is a bad omen taken very seriously.
- Never light a cigarette from a candle: it will bring bad luck.
- Before going on a long trip, sit down for a few minutes to collect your thoughts: your trip will go better.
- Be careful complementing something in a host's home; they may try to give it to you.
- Do not sit at the corner of a table: you will end up single.
- If you leave something behind when departing Russia, it is a good sign, it means you will be back.

TOLERANCE

You will probably meet with many situations in Russia which you would normally consider "intolerable." Tolerate them. Be flexible. If you want to be doing business in a comfortable atmosphere, your way, you should be doing business elsewhere.

⬢ FIRESTONE DUNCAN

Firestone Duncan began operations in Russia in 1993. At present our two offices in Moscow and Saint Petersburg employ 4 partners and over 40 staff. We offer fully integrated legal and tax services and specialize in the following areas.

- Corporate Law & Securities
- Currency Controls
- Intellectual Property
- Employment Law
- Real Estate Law & Title Searches
- Contract Law
- Customs Law
- Russian Corporate Tax Advice
- Tax Filing for Russian Companies
- Tax Filing for Foreign Companies in Russia
- Russian Payroll Planning
- Russian Personal Tax Advice & Filing
- Tax Dispute Resolution

- Registration of Russian Companies
- Accreditation of Foreign Companies
- Obtaining Licenses & Work Permits
- Russian Statutory Accounting & Audit
- Advice of Russian Accounting
- Due Diligence Review

FULLY INTEGRATED LEGAL & TAX SERVICES

Moscow:
21/1 Dolgorukovskaya St.,
Russia 103 006
Tel: +7 (095 or 501) 258 3500
Fax: +7 (095 or 501) 258 3501

Saint Petersburg:
12 Tambovskaya St., PO Box
362, Russia 192 007
Tel: +7 (812) 325 6440
Fax: +7 (812) 325 6441

Russian Business Law   9

The Investment Climate

Where there is opportunity, there is risk. In Russia opportunity abounds.

After eight years of haphazard reform and industrial decline, the Russian economy seems to be at the bottom of its trench. Monthly inflation rates are in the low, single-digits. Credit emissions from the Central Bank (a prime culprit of inflation) have all but stopped. Most importantly: private enterprise is firmly in control of the economy for the first time in nearly 70 years. Three-quarters of all Russians now work in the private sector, which currently is responsible for 76% of GDP.

Russian privatization, one of the most significant international economic achievements of the past several decades, has passed the point of no return. Nearly 100,000 enterprises have been privatized in three years. This, combined with legalization of land ownership means that, for the first time in 70 years, all manner of real assets in Russia can be bought and sold freely by foreign and domestic investors.

And, as the presidential elections of 1996 showed, while there will be continual disputes over the speed and content of economic reforms, it is clear that a broad consensus has formed around the direction and goals of reform: toward a pluralistic, democratic market economy. Real wages of workers have increased by more than ten times in the past three years. While prices are on the rise, store shelves are full in major cities and the average Russian now knows that, though times are tough, hard-working and enterprising persons can get what they need to take care of their families and even get ahead.

From oil and gas to rarer industrial and precious metals and minerals, Russia possesses a significant portion of available world supplies. But Russia's most underrated natural resource is its workforce. Very highly-educated and very inexpensive by Western standards, the Russian workforce can, with properly-focused investments and incentive, provide distinct comparative advantages in basic manufacturing, mining and refining industries. This workforce is grossly underemployed, eagerly awaiting investments that will make proper use of its capabilities.

Moreover, enterprises themselves are seriously undervalued. Their shares are now being sold off in search of investment – often at kopeks on the ruble.

In sum, if ever there was a time to buy low, it is now.

Yet one should certainly be aware of some land mines. While legal steps have been taken to grandfather business legislation, to reconcile competing legislation and centralize control over foreign investment legislation, much remains to be accomplished. Bureaucratic hindrances to enterprise registration, legislative uncertainty and excessive rates of enterprise and trade taxation are still matters of great concern.

It is legal and regulatory developments that will drive or destroy further reform in Russia. Certainly Russian Central Bank monetary policy, privatization efforts, organized crime, foreign aid and political reform will play supporting roles. But without a predictable, coherent and consistent legal environment, business people, be they Russian or foreign, will not make the long-term investments in infrastructure and manufacturing that are required to reinvigorate the Russian economy.

With this in mind, what follows is a summary of Russian legal acts relating to the most important aspects of business, trade and investment. Continual "adjustments" in this area are expected. This summary is *intended only as a thorough introduction*. For detailed and current appraisals of the legal climate, readers should subscribe to some of the legal periodicals reviewed in Chapter 1 and seek competent legal counsel (some Western law firms with offices in Moscow are listed in Ch. 1).

Russian Foreign Investment Law

Over the course of the past decade, the Soviet, and then Russian government has been attempting to build a legal framework for foreign investment where before there was none. In early 1987 there was no Russian securities market, no private foreign trade, no direct foreign investment. Now these things, and much more, exist. They exist, most observers would argue, in spite of (rather than because of) the government's efforts to construct foreign investment law in Russia. Certainly Russia's legal framework is as yet immature or, at best, maturing. And it does have a long way to go to provide investors with the levels of predictability and integrity expected of a major trading power. Liberalization is all fine and well, but without some assurance that trade will be free tomorrow, it is only so much good intention.

That said, if one takes stock of the great distance Russia has traveled in the past ten years (especially as regards privatization), one cannot but be encouraged about the prospects of Russia traversing the difficult road ahead. And, for all its faults, the legal environment for foreign trade and investment has in recent years become more stable and sure. Actions are being taken to grandfather in legislative changes, to level the playing field, and to weed out legal inconsistencies. This will all take time, but the course has been set. For now, Russian foreign investment legislation (as of June 1996), has the following characteristics.

EQUAL TREATMENT

The key statement is in Article 6 of the July 1991 law, *On Foreign Investment Activity in the RSFSR*: "The legal regime of foreign investments and investment activity may not be less favorable than the regime for the property, proprietary rights, and investment activity of legal entities and citizens of the RSFSR (Russia), with the exceptions stipulated by the present law."

The law puts foreign investors on an even footing with Russian business persons, granting the right to purchase shares in existing joint stock companies and privatizing state and municipal enterprises, to acquire various types of property and rights, including land and mineral use rights. It asserts, as is the case with all related Russian legislation, the primacy of the ruble for such transactions.

A September 27, 1993 presidential decree, *On Improving Work with Foreign Investment,* in addition to strengthening central government control over foreign investment and establishing a three-year grandfathering norm for investment legislation, further requires changes in government legal acts to ensure "the creation for foreign investors of equal conditions with Russian investors for participation in the privatization of state and municipal enterprises."

It is worth noting, however, that these provisos have yet to be tested thoroughly and dualistic legal norms have continued to surface (e.g. the Moscow government's establishment of higher transfer taxes on apartment sales to foreigners than for Russians, and higher minimum charter capital requirements for corporations with foreign investment).

INVESTMENT VEHICLES

Two types of *equity investment* are open to foreign investors as regards the establishment of enterprises: joint ventures* and wholly owned subsidiaries (see the notes under representations about affiliates). Two other forms of business activity *not involving direct equity investment* are also allowed: private (unregistered) business activity, and a representation. The procedures for establishing each and the laws that govern them are enumerated below.

The law explicitly allows resident investors and companies to maintain ruble accounts in Russia. Such monies, provided they are obtained from earnings within Russia, may be used to buy hard currency at auctions, to reinvest in the economy, and to buy shares in Russian companies, although foreign investors cannot use rubles to buy shares or securities if those rubles are acquired at rates lower than the MICE rate (see Chapter 5). There are some restrictions on the hard currency operations of any enterprise, and foreign representations (and nonresident investors) have some further restrictions on their ruble operations.

Certain activities (insurance, banking, brokering) require licenses. Otherwise, foreign investors can engage in any activity stated in their enterprise's statute, or which is not disallowed by existing legislation.

Joint Ventures

Russia does not have a law on joint ventures. The Russian law, *On Foreign Investment Activity in the RSFSR*, however, defines a joint venture as any registered Russian enterprise with foreign equity investment. Thus a joint venture is, *de facto*, any Russian enterprise which has a foreign investor, including an individual, regardless of whether that investor was a founder or has purchased shares in an existing enterprise. Meanwhile, joint ventures founded under the original 1987 Soviet law on joint ventures have since had to re-register as stock companies.

The implication is that *there are now few specific tax or other advantages accorded joint ventures*. The registration, activity and taxation of joint ventures is the same as for 100% Russian-owned enterprises, with but a few exceptions. These generally relate to import of equity contributions, foreign employees, avoidance of double-taxation, dividend repatriation and the like (in 1994 a new exception was added, extending a two year tax holiday to joint ventures with foreign investment in excess of $10 mn – see *Taxation* below). What follows therefore is a review of the different types of Russian enterprises. Where a particular aspect of their activity is or may be different when foreign investors are involved, this is noted.

The three most important types of Russian private enterprises (some have sub-types) provided for in Russian legislation are:
- joint stock company (open, closed)
- limited liability company (and additional liability company)
- partnership (full, mixed)

Each may also be classified as a "small enterprise," which, among other things, may enjoy some tax benefits. The new Russian Civil Code also introduced several other enterprise types, which are also dealt with briefly below.

Joint Stock Companies*

At the end of 1990, the Russian republic passed a joint stock company law which made it possible for the first time to found a company whose ownership was divided into transferable shares and which had liability limited to the extent of its assets. The Russian Civil Code provided further clarification.

The law allows for *open* and *closed* joint stock companies. In most instances, both types are treated identically under the legislation. There are exceptions. Shares in an *open* joint stock company can be sold or ceded to third persons with few restrictions. In a *closed* joint stock company, the founders retain preeminent right over the disposition of shares; a share-

---

* Note that we continue to employ the term joint venture here, even though there is no longer a law on joint ventures in force in Russia. The intent is to use the term in the broader sense, encompassing all types of investment (corporate or otherwise) which entail a combination of outside and local capital/equity.

holder may not sell or transfer his/her shares in the enterprise to a third person without the permission of other shareholders. Further, a new forced sale provision is now in force for closed joint stock companies, requiring a departing participant to sell his shares to the other participants. An open joint stock company is required to make its annual report public; a closed joint stock company may be so required.

The minimum statutory capital of joint stock companies is indexed to the minimum monthly salary (MMS), as are many other registration and tax payments. The minimum fee is 100 MMS's for closed enterprises, and 1000 MMS's for open enterprises.

CREATION AND REGISTRATION

• Companies may be founded by one or more participants, be they enterprises, establishments and organizations, state authorities or individual citizens. Article 11 explicitly allows foreign citizens and companies to be founders. Companies are established and operate on the basis of a Charter and a Founders' Agreement. An important exception is that a singular shareholder (whether through founding the company or buying it out) cannot itself be a legal entity with a singular shareholder.

• The Charter (устав – *ustav*) is the fundamental document. It sets out the legal name, address and type of enterprise being created, as well as the goals and objectives of its activity. It defines the management bodies and the procedures for their decision making (including a listing of decisions wholly within the competence of the board), the procedures for profit distribution and recovery of damages, and conditions for the organization and liquidation of the enterprise.

• The Founders' Agreement (учредительный договор — *uchreditelny dogovor*) is just that, a written agreement between the founders. In addition to reiterating the basic information about the enterprise, it enumerates the investments each founder is to make and how they are to be made, how this may affect distribution of profits, and how a founder may withdraw from the corporation. (This document becomes void once the enterprise is registered.)

• Article 34 of the law, *On Enterprises and Entrepreneurial Activity* (still in effect, even though the full law is not) and Article 7 of the law, *On Joint Stock Companies*, state that, to register an enterprise, you must submit the

---

* *The new Russian Civil Code reaffirmed, superceding a Moscow court's ruling, that joint stock companies did not, in fact, have to be "joint" – they could have a singular founder. Some observers have thus begun to call such companies simply stock companies. In point of fact, the literal translation of the Russian term* aktsionernoye obshchestvo *(often referred to with the shorthand AO) is shareholder society. Therefore there seems little justification for not simply referring to these entities as corporations. But the translation joint stock company was employed early on and, since this is still the prevailing tendency, we have chosen to employ the term here, overriding all linguistic and logical objections.*

following documents to the registration chamber (палата — *palata*) within 30 days of the enterprise's founding meeting:

❶ a notarized and certified **application** for the company's registration, which includes the company name, location, its objectives and the main types of activity of the company, the liability of the shareholders, the amount of statutory capital, the names and legal addresses of the founders and their citizenship, and the number of shares acquired by them (application forms are available at registration chambers);

❷ a notarized and certified copy of the company's **Charter**;

❸ a notarized and certified **minutes of the founding meeting** (unless the company has just one founder);

❹ proof that the enterprise's **registration fee** has been paid.

In reality, the following documents are also required:

❶ a copy of the **Founders' Agreement** (both this and the Charter should be supplied in multiple copies, usually six each);

❷ two copies of a notarized and certified guarantee **letter from the landlord**, attesting to the company's right to use the space at its intended legal address (a rental agreement may also be attached) – there are different forms this letter must take if the legal address is to be an apartment vs. a nonresidential space. While the law now says that this is no longer necessary, common practice shows that it is still required. *Important note:* enterprises cannot be registered in Moscow with residential addresses as their legal address – this will vary from city to city;

❸ a notarized power of attorney from the investor, on behalf of the local registration agent;

❸ *in the case of a joint venture or company with foreign participation,* **documents attesting to the liquidity/credit worthiness of the foreign investor** (ability to make the specific capital contributions) issued by the investor's bank or another financial institution (with certified translations of said documentation into Russian – documents may be apostilled in countries that are members of the Hague convention, i.e. US, UK, Japan, Holland; Canada is not a member);

❹ *in the case of a joint venture,* an **extract from the trade register** from the country of the foreign investor's origin, proving the legal status of the investor's company according to local law; if the foreign investor is an individual, then this means documents proving the right of the individual to conduct business activity in the country of his/her residence or citizenship (with certified translation into Russian or apostille);

❺ in cases where potentially harmful production processes are to be carried out, or in the oil and gas spheres, and particularly *in the case of joint ventures* in either case, an *expertiz* (examination) must be carried out by the responsible state authorities.

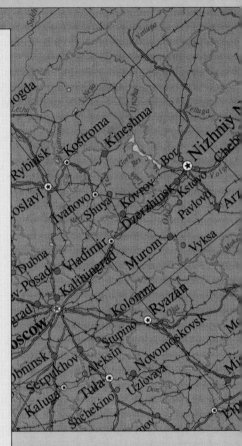

Other considerations:

• If the company is a *joint venture* in the oil sector or if the company is a *joint venture* with foreign investment in excess of 100 million rubles, the company must first be registered with the State Registration Chamber (which replaces RAMSIR in these functions), then locally. In all other cases, registration occurs first at regional, municipal or republic chambers (*palaty*).

• In all cases, a *joint venture* is registered with the Ministry of Finance after being registered with the local registration chamber.

• Half of the charter capital is due upon registration, the other half within one year of registration. If secondary contributions are not made, the enterprise must reregister with a lower charter capital.

• A joint stock company may be established by the conversion of a state enterprise (i.e. through privatization), but this requires a joint decision of the employees and the appropriately empowered state authority – see the section below on privatization. A state or municipal enterprise or body cannot be a shareholder in a joint stock company or any other private company.

• In addition to the right to found a joint stock company, foreign investors have the right, as explicitly stated in this law (Articles 3, 4 and 35) and the law, *On Foreign Investment*, to purchase shares in existing joint stock companies.

When compiling the Charter and Founder's Agreement, some general caveats to the process of drafting these documents should be noted:

• Avoid boiler-plate Charters or Agreements which can in no way account for the unique aspects of your enterprise; do not put anything but the name and type of enterprise on the title page of the documentation (i.e. do not write "small enterprise").

• Do not use the word Russia, Moscow or other geographical designations or words deriving from them without checking first to see if there are associated licensing fees or permissions required (as is the case with Russia and Moscow).

• The doctrine of *ultra vires* is enforced with some strictness in Russia. The company should have a very carefully worded statement of purpose. It should be broad and clear. Explicitly assert the company's purposes and rights in the foundation documents.

• Be very explicit in allocating responsibility, financial and otherwise, between the parties.

• Ownership protection and property rights regarding any inventions or new technology developed by the company should be carefully circumscribed in the documents.

• Set out a clear procedure for board access to enterprise finances including clear, regular procedures for supplying partners with information on profits and losses.

• Draft a clause that limits inspections or audits to specific circumstances or at least regular intervals.

• The reserve funds required by Russian law are the equivalent of costs and taxes that get careful consideration in the West. At a minimum, you should specify the amount of annual appropriations to these funds for each partner so that the cost is precise and predictable.

• Be sure all real estate and property issues (payment for facilities, utilities, pace of renovation, etc.) are explicitly enumerated. Be certain that the founding documents clearly and unequivocally state whether assets contributed by Russian partners (and Westerners for that matter) are to be directly owned by the new enterprise or merely within their purview – assets they have the right to control, but not liquidate.

• Retain significant Western partner input into and/or veto power over hiring and firing management personnel and spending beyond certain thresholds.

• Any employee profit-sharing programs should be included in the charter, with consideration of relevant tax and currency issues.

• Set out the exact dates for distribution of profits and the procedures for making those distributions.

• Draft a clear and unequivocal liquidation clause that allows each partner, at a minimum, to walk away with the equivalent of capital and equipment invested.

• Draft clear arbitration clauses, specifying the procedures for arbitrating disputes either via the Arbitration Court of the Russian Chamber of Commerce (whicih is gaining broad acceptance as a fair and inexpensive arbiter) or another court (i.e. Stockholm). It is also wise to include provisions for execution of arbitration awards within the actual contract and for collection in the event of either partner's insolvency.

SPHERES OF ACTIVITY

• No limits are placed on the areas of economic activity open to joint stock companies, as long as the activity does not violate the laws of Russia or its constitution. However, only the government is allowed to engage in certain types of activity (i.e. weapon production, tobacco and spirits production, processing of ores and precious metals). Certain other areas of activity require governmental approval (e.g. mining, fur, raw materials, timber).

Activity must technically be within the scope of activity defined in the Charter, yet transactions conducted beyond the scope of the Charter are legal insofar as they conform to existing Russian law.

• Joint stock companies have the right to establish subsidiaries in Russia or abroad. Establishing subsidiaries abroad, as well as investing abroad (including making simple bank deposits) requires approval of the Russian Ministry of Finance and/or the Russian Central Bank.

• All Russian enterprises, including joint stock companies, are forbidden from making hard currency settlements with other Russian enterprises, except in currency purchase and sale transactions. Joint stock companies can participate in currency auctions.

• A Russian presidential decree of October 27, 1993 strengthened rights of land ownership, allowing persons with title to land "to sell, bequeath, donate, mortgage, lease and change, and also to transfer land parcels or parts thereof as contribution to the authorized capital of joint stock companies, partnerships and cooperatives, including those with foreign investments." A subsequent June 1994 decree granted owners of privatized enterprises exclusive rights to obtain and/or decide the fate of land under and about the enterprise.

• In November 1993, the Moscow city government decreed that all foreign firms engaged in several business sectors, from food services to tourism to pharmaceuticals and consumer goods, obtain licenses for such activity from specified agencies. Other cities may have or may introduce similar requirements. Further, the Russian government requires licenses for business activity in many (over 100) spheres of activity, from tourism to alcohol production.

LIABILITY

• The joint stock company law invokes limited liability of the partners or founders of the joint stock company in the following manner (Article 8): "Shareholders shall be liable for the Company's obligations within the limits of their personal capital contribution." Yet, "wrongful acts" by company executives may require them to pay compensation for damage caused the company. There was worry that the Civil Code "pierced the corporate veil" of limited liability by creating a new "subsidiary liability" of company founders, although the new JSC Law indicates that this is only true for willful actions, i.e. a shareholder "knows that his actions will cause or are likely to cause the company's insolvency."

• A joint stock company created from the conversion of a state enterprise (i.e. via privatization) assumes the rights, responsibilities and liabilities of the state enterprise.

SHARES AND OWNERSHIP

• Unless specifically stated in the Charter, the sale or transfer of shares in a joint stock company does not require the consent of the company. Joint stock companies can issue registered, bearer, and preference (dividend) shares (up to 25% of the total value of charter capital). Joint stock companies can also issue bonds. Shares cannot be issued by a joint stock company until all charter capital has been paid in.

• In closed joint stock companies, participants enjoy priority right to buy shares which another participant wishes to sell or transfer. Further, the participant may cede a share or a part thereof to a third party or to other participants only with the consent of the other participants, unless stated otherwise in the Charter. Shares can be transferred to third parties only if the participant transferring the shares has paid his contribution in full. Further, dividends can be paid out only if shares are paid for in full.

Contributions to the charter capital must be made in full within one year of founding, with 50% contributions made within 30 days of founding.

• Sales of over 15% of shares of the company to a legal or natural person (who is not a founder) requires the consent of the Ministry of Finance. Sale of more than 50% of shares requires the consent of both the Ministry of Finance and the State Anti-Monopoly Committee.

• At registration, the company can create treasury stock, authorized for sale at a later date in order to raise capital. This new provision put in place by the 1995 JSC Law is important because previously the capital stock of the company could only equal initial share investments.

MANAGEMENT

Russian joint stock companies are to have a management structure not unlike that of Western corporations. Shareholders elect directors (optional for companies with less than 50 shareholders), who in turn elect/hire and oversee management. In addition, the company is to form an auditing commission to oversee and audit financial activities of the company. An audit can be demanded by shareholders holding 10% of all shares. A general meeting of shareholders cannot make decisions on issues not within its competence as under the law.

TAXATION & ACCOUNTING

• Joint stock companies are currently subject to a 13% federal **profits tax**, and up to 25% in additional local/regional profits taxes (up to 30% for banks and insurance companies), which are to be set by the different administrative subdivisions of Russia. If no rate has been set, a 22% rate applies, making the effective rate for most all companies 35%. Other taxes also apply (see the section below, *Enterprise Taxation*), among others: the value added tax, mandatory currency sales (which is, in effect a tax), property tax, advertising tax, social welfare and road taxes.

• In the absence of a tax treaty to the contrary, *in joint stock companies which are joint ventures*, the Western partner(s) will be subject to a 15% **transfer tax** on any dividends transferred to the Western partner's domicile. The new US-Russia Tax Treaty sets a maximum transfer tax rate on dividends of 10% (5% if the US company's equity share exceeds 10%).

• A joint stock company must maintain its books on model forms prepared by the Ministry of Finance, have its bookkeeping done by accountants directed by the Accountant General and file statistical reports in accordance with "established procedure." The good news is that Russian accounting standards are approaching internationally-accepted accounting standards, which means, in the case of Russian companies with foreign investment, eventually keeping only one set of books to satisfy both partners.

• Many types of businesses are required to submit annual audits (performed by licensed auditors): those with any amount of foreign investment, those with more than 100 shareholders, banks and other providers of credit, insurance companies, investment vehicles (funds, holding companies), extra-budgetary funds receiving monies based on mandatory payroll or tax deductions, humanitarian and goodwill agencies that rely on voluntary contributions, companies with annual earnings in excess of 500,000 minimal monthly salaries, companies with year-end assets valued in excess of 200,000 minimal monthly salaries.

• Imported equipment and supplies for production are exempt from customs, tariffs or taxation. Office supplies are not.

LABOR LAWS

• Under current Russian legislation, all labor issues of import in joint stock companies are to be decided in the process of negotiation of collective and/or individual labor contracts. But the legacy of Soviet labor law still imbues this process with certain expectations and realities. See the section on Labor Law below.

• Employees who are foreign nationals work under the same labor laws as Russian employees and must pay the same income tax rates, with the exception that many foreign nationals must obtain a work permit from the Federal Migration Agency. Exceptions are: employees with accredited representations, joint venture employees which are "highly qualified foreign specialists," foreigners who work in a Russian company for a short period under the terms of a management contract, members of the diplomatic corps, guest lecturers, students, clergy from registered religious organizations, journalists, crew members of sea or ocean-going vessels, persons whose work in Russia is governed by international or intergovernmental agreements. There is a nominal fee (<$10) for the work permit.

• All income taxes on all forms of income (rubles or hard currency) are payable in rubles. These taxes can be as high as 30% on net income (see the section on Individual Taxation below).

Limited Liability Companies

This new company type (*obshchestvo s ogranichenoi otvetstvennostyu*), along with a related *additional* liability company (*obshchestvo s dopolnitelnoi otvetstvennostyu*) first appeared in the new Russian Civil Code (October 1994). While they are treated there in some length, there is insufficient practical or juridical basis for judging the import of such companies. The Code does defer repeatedly to a law *On Limited Liability Companies*, which means one is likely forthcoming.

The Civil Code indicates that limited liability and additional liability companies are smaller than joint stock companies, that they cannot issue public shares and are, in essence closed 'societies' (*obshchestva*). In limited liability companies, participants' liability is limited to the extent of their investment; in additional liability companies, participants assume a *subsidiary liability* with personal property in an amount based on a predetermined share liability (set in the founding documents).

Partnerships

Russian law allows the formation of partnerships (товарищество – *tovarishchestvo*) as either legal entities or as temporary, task-oriented commercial arrangements. Partnerships can be between individuals or legal entities (companies) or a combination of both. The law defines two types of partnerships: general and mixed. A foreign citizen or foreign company can enter into a partnership as would a Russian individual or company. The resulting entity, however, would be a joint venture and require additional registration procedures. Unlike in English/American legal traditions, where a partnership need not be registered to be legal, in Russia, business partnerships need to be registered.

• A *full partnership* (полное товарищество – *polnoye tovarishchestvo*) is founded and operated on the basis of a founders' agreement, which contains the same basic information as for joint stock companies. The name of the partnership should be unique and include the phrase 'full partnership' or the name of one or several of the partners, the phrase 'and company,' plus the phrase 'full partnership.'

A full partnership entails *no limitation of liability* on the partners, and shares of ownership and profit are set in the agreement. Profits and dividends taken out of the partnership by a partner are taxed as individual income (or in the case of companies that are partners, profit taxes).

A person or entity can be a full partner in only one full partnership.

• A *mixed partnership* (товарищество на вере – *tovarishchestvo na vere*, literally a 'partnership based on faith,' also referred to as a *kommanditoye tovarishchestvo*, a 'sleeping partnership') combines the features of a general partnership with the option of allowing outside (sleeping) investors who do not take part in day-to-day administration. Such investors' liability is limited to the level of their investment, while the liability of other, full partners is not limited, yet they are not liable for other activities of the outside investor. A mixed partnership must register according to the procedures indicated above for joint stock companies, and must pay enterprise, profit and other taxes.

The name of the partnership should be unique and include the phrase 'sleeping partnership' or 'partnership in faith,' or the name of one or several of the partners, or the phrase 'and company,' plus one of the previous phrases.

A person or legal entity can be a full partner in only one mixed partnership; a full partner in a mixed partnership cannot be a full member in a full partnership, and visa-versa.

Other Enterprise Types

There are several other types of commercial and non-commercial entities which are of less interest to potential investors, but which are here worth a cursory description.

INDIVIDUAL LABOR ACTIVITY

Essentially, this entails self-employment, as a private contractor or private entrepreneur. Registration procedures require only a "patent" for conduct of individual labor activity (which requires submitting an application and proof of payment of the requisite registration fee). Income taxes are paid on earned income, and self-employed individuals or private contractors do not pay VAT on their activity. It allows the individual to obtain a bank account, credit and legal registration for business activity, as well as conclude any type of civil agreement allowed by law. A private entrepreneur cannot hire labor.

SUBSIDIARY AND DEPENDENT COMPANIES

A company is a subsidiary (*dochernoye*) of another when a predominant share of its charter capital is held by the other company. A subsidiary is not liable for the obligations of its parent company, but the parent company, together with the subsidiary company, is liable for obligations undertaken by the latter at the former's instruction. A parent company has subsidiary responsibility for the subsidiary company's debts in the event of its bankruptcy for reasons of its own doing, and participants of the subsidiary company can claim compensation for losses from the parent company if other provisions are not set in the law *On Companies* (*O khozyaistvennykh obshchestvakh*, which does not yet exist).

A company is a dependent company (*zavisimoye*) if another company owns more than 20% of its shares or contributes more than 20% of the charter capital. Any company which acquires such a share of ownership in another company is required to make announcement of same in accordance with the law *On Companies*.

PRODUCTION COOPERATIVES

Cooperatives were the first form of private enterprise in Russia and they continue to exist mainly in the law, as most cooperatives re-registered as partnerships or joint stock companies when the law allowed. Cooperatives (also now referred to as *artels*, hearkening back to the cooperatives of the pre-communist era) are commercial organizations of individuals who pool their work efforts toward a common productive end. A cooperative can have up to 5 members and cannot issue shares.

UNITARY ENTERPRISES

This is the new name for state- and municipally-owned enterprises.

NON-COMMERCIAL ENTERPRISES

The August 1995 passage of the law *On Charitable Activities and Charitable Organizations* brought clarity to this sphere of enterprise activity. While allowing non-profits and charitable organizations no favorable tax situation, vis-a-vis for-profit companies, the law did finally establish a legal basis for their existence (together with their acknowledgement in the Civil Code).

The law allows for many different types of charitable and non-profit organizations, from individuals to associations, institutions and foundations, but it may be read as somewhat restrictive (in socio-political terms) in delineating the scope of activities deemed as "charitable."

Non-profits may conduct business activity insofar as that activity is related to the achievement of the goals for which such organizations were created. All "profits" must be reinvested in the enterprise and the law seeks to prevent abuse of non-profit status through directors' siphoning off of high salaries, etc. Non-profits cannot support political parties, groups, etc. with its property or funds.

Small Enterprises

A small enterprise is a sub-classification of joint stock companies, partnerships or other legal entities. It is not a separate type of legal entity unto itself. The label merely denotes the scale of the enterprise. A small enterprise does, however, enjoy certain tax benefits.

SIZE

• Depending upon the sphere of economic activity in which an enterprise engages, restrictions are placed on the number of employees which may be employed by the enterprise and still be designated as *small*. If the enterprise engages in several activities, that activity which is responsible for the largest volume of goods or services provided is the operative sphere of activity. These limits are: Industry and construction – up to 200 people; Science and scientific activities – up to 100 people; Other branches of industry – up to 50 people; Non-manufacturing – up to 25 people; Retail sales – up to 15 people.

• Autonomous republics and localities may also place limits on the amount of total revenue which small enterprises of various sectors may earn and still be classified as small enterprises. Similarly, they may designate minimum numbers of employees for small enterprises.

TAXATION

• Certain types of small enterprises are wholly exempt from taxation during their first two years of operation. This applies to small enterprises engaged in agricultural production and processing of farm produce, consumer goods production, construction, maintenance/construction, building materials production, and to small innovation enterprises. Small enterprises engaged in other activities must pay only 25% of their normal tax rate in their first year of operation and 50% in the second year.

• Profits which are allocated to construction, modernization, retooling and renovation of fixed assets or training and retraining of personnel are tax exempt in an amount equal to 10% of the investment in fixed assets.

• All small enterprises must pay the full tax rate after two full years of operation (see section below, *Enterprise Taxation*). If a small enterprise ceases operations before it has been in existence for three years, it is liable for the full measure of taxes for the entire period of its operation.

Wholly-owned Subsidiaries

The Russian law, *On Foreign Investment Activity in the RSFSR* and some Soviet legislation which preceded it, laid a groundwork for legalizing registration and operation of 100% foreign-owned companies in Russia. On the surface, organization and registration of such companies is made to appear no more difficult than for Russian enterprises (which is, in fact, far from simple). As such, this is fast becoming the preferred mode of direct foreign investment in Russia. (A legal orphan, known as an affiliate or branch, was explicitly allowed in the Russian law, *On Foreign Investment*, and seemed to be a cross between a subsidiary and a representation. But, in actual practice, the procedures for registration and operation of affiliates do not fundamentally differ from that of a subsidiary, and thus have not been treated separately here.)

CREATION AND REGISTRATION

Typically, foreign companies are forming wholly-owned subsidiaries in Russia as joint stock companies, according to the procedures outlined above for such entities. But this does not mean that wholly-owned subsidiaries cannot be founded as other legal Russian enterprise types. In terms of the documentation required for registration, the law essentially treats wholly-owned subsidiaries as it does joint ventures. In any case, *in addition to the registration material and documents specified for the particular enterprise type*, the foreign company/investor must submit the following materials to the Ministry of Finance (via the registration chamber – *palata* – representing it – in some cases this may be the State Registration Chamber, see the notes on registration under joint stock companies):

❶ a **declaration**, signed by the director of the foreign firm which seeks to create the subsidiary, with a request to carry out its registration;

❷ a notarized and certified **copy of the decision** of the competent management organ of the enterprise to create the subsidiary;

❸ two notarized and certified copies of the **Regulations** which will govern the subsidiary;

❹ **documents attesting to the liquidity and credit worthiness of the foreign investor**, issued by the investor's bank or other financial/credit institution (with certified translations into Russian);

❺ an **extract from the trade register** from the country of the foreign investor's origin, proving the legal status of the investor's company according to local law (with a certified translation into Russian);

❻ an *expertiz* (examination) of the project in those cases required by law (when the investment targets certain "sensitive" areas and when investments are of a significant size).

Typically, temporary registration of such an enterprise can be achieved within one week from submission of the above documents. To achieve permanent registration, the enterprise must, within 30 days,

❶ open a bank account;

❷ deposit 50% of the charter capital therein;

❸ obtain permission for the company seal (stamp) described in the charter;

❹ register at the regional taxation inspectorate (and for import/export codes at the State Statistics Committee if desired).

Proof of these actions is then submitted to the registration chamber, which will issue a permanent registration certificate, which is then submitted to the State Committee on Foreign Investment.

TAXATION & ACCOUNTING

Wholly-owned subsidiaries are treated, for taxation purposes, as any other enterprise registered in Russia and therefore subject to a 13% federal profits tax and a 22-25% regional/local profits tax from the date of their founding. Other taxes also apply (see the section below, *Enterprise Taxation*).

Wholly-owned subsidiaries are subject to Russian accounting rules (see notes above under joint stock companies). In addition, subsidiaries must submit an annual audit of their financial operations.

OTHER CONSIDERATIONS

In all respects, a wholly-owned subsidiary operates according to Russian law and is a Russian enterprise. It therefore is subject to the same restrictions and rights with regard to property ownership, labor laws, etc. as Russian enterprises. Certain advantages may be available for creation of such enterprises in Free Economic Zones.

Representations

This entity, established in the late 1970s, and also known as an accredited office, is a holdover from the Soviet era. It allowed companies to maintain a quasi-diplomatic presence in Russia while doing business with Soviet ministries and enterprises. Its usefulness is, in many instances, dissolving, and most foreign representations are seeking to reformulate their presence into a wholly-owned subsidiary. Still, the notion of an accredited office does bestow immediate credibility on a firm (implying that the firm has been in Russia since the time when this was the only way to operate there), and it carries with it explicit governmental approval of the firm's activities in Russia. It also allows one to more easily obtain a multiple-entry visa, and does offer some other logistic advantages. Also, foreign news agencies which have no commercial purpose in country can operate as representations and be free of many taxes and reporting.

REGISTRATION

Registration of a representation is done through the State Registration Chamber. The foreign company must submit the following documentation to the Service:

❶ a written application;

❷ a notarized copy of the company's Charter;

❸ a notarized copy of the company's Articles of Incorporation or similarly valid documentation concerning the nature of the company and its activity;

❹ a notarized extract from the trade register from the country of the foreign investor's origin, proving the legal status of the investor's company according to local law (with a certified translation into Russian) or a copy of the company's registration certificate;

❺ a notarized document issued by the company's bank, attesting to the liquidity and payment capabilities of the company (with a certified translation into Russian);

❻ a power of attorney giving the representative effecting the accreditation the authority to act on the company's behalf;

❼ a least two letters of support from Russian companies with whom your company has done business in the past.

Registration entails a modest fee and may be renewed for up to three years. Upon accreditation, the company receives a Permission Certificate for opening an accredited representation in Russia.

SPHERES OF ACTIVITY

A representation, since it is not a Russian legal entity, is not allowed to engage in commercial activity (it was originally conceived to be like an embassy of the foreign company in the USSR) and may not hold bank accounts in Russia except for financial operations directly related to operation of its office. It may do business only on behalf of its parent company. Revenues from the representation's activity in Russia (i.e. sales of the company's output) must be transferred directly to the foreign bank accounts of the parent company.

TAXATION

Many representations are non-taxable, since some intergovernmental agreements specify that certain types of activity which are not directly commercial are not taxable. Russian law, however, specifies that, in cases where a company's net profits from operations are not readily ascertainable, it shall be liable for taxes equal to 25% of its total costs of operation. Meanwhile, the government's Tax Service has stated that income of foreign legal entities (including representations) earned from the provision of services (i.e. consulting, facilitation) are taxable, even where the provisions of permanent establishment (See Taxation, below) have not been satisfied. The only exemptions are those that may be provided by international treaties and for import/export activity by foreign legal entities, which is not subject to such taxation.

CUSTOMS

Recent legal acts have reaffirmed the right of representative offices to import equipment and supplies duty free, provided that the materials are not used for direct commercial purposes.

Private Business Activity

Russian law allows prospective investors to operate without legal status for a time while exploring the market and/or while managing the processes of registration, partner-search or negotiation. It does not entail the status of a legal entity, and does not allow hiring of staff (with the exception that foreign companies can contract with Russian individuals for the provision of services) or acquisition of legal premises (with the exception that private foreign citizens can both rent and purchase apartments from Russian citizens and companies). Taxation is entailed (and appropriate registration required), if a "base of operations" (also referred to as a "permanent establishment") is established at the rate set for Russian enterprises, and in any case for certain types of Russian-sourced income (i.e. rental income, licensing fees and interest). And, as noted above under representative office taxation, services provided in the Russian Federation by foreign legal entities are subject to taxation.

CHOOSING THE APPROPRIATE INVESTMENT VEHICLE

The type of investment vehicle appropriate for a particular venture is dependent upon the range of activities foreseen and the level of one's commitment to the Russian market.

The broadest range of commercial activity is allowed to "Russian" companies, be they jointly-owned by Russian and foreign entities, or wholly-owned subsidiaries of a foreign entity. Affiliates, representations and private business activity all have serious restrictions placed on the range of activities which they can undertake. And there are few tax benefits to *not* establishing such a Russian company. A Russian company, however, has the disadvantage of not being allowed to freely establish bank accounts, affiliates or investments overseas.

Choosing between a joint venture and a wholly-owned subsidiary depends primarily on the level of control and involvement (and of course, dividends) the foreign investor seeks from the investment in Russia. That the registration of joint ventures is declining and the registration of wholly-owned subsidiaries is on the rise is some indication that foreign investors are seeking a larger measure of control over their investments in Russia, something the law did not previously allow.

A joint venture or wholly-owned subsidiary is most often founded on the basis of a joint stock company. The obvious advantage of this being that joint stock companies limit investors' liability and allow a fairly free

Language

Literature

History

Art

Maps

Cooking

Business

Reference

Music

DIRECTORIES

Atlases

Videos

Travel

SOFTWARE

Culture

Accessories

transfer of shares. But joint ventures and wholly-owned subsidiaries can also be founded with or on the basis of partnerships or individual enterprises. Both the latter may, in fact, be better-suited for initial, small-scale investments or investments by individuals.

The representation, as noted above, offers few real advantages to the investor, now that real direct foreign investment is possible. The opening up of the Russian economy has, in a sense, caused the representation to outlive its usefulness, except for those entities not engaged in strictly commercial activity, such as press agencies or aid organizations.

LEASING AN OFFICE

If you are not relying on your Russian partners to provide office space for your venture, you will need to deal with this issue directly. The real estate market in Russia is, as yet, immature and overpriced, particularly in Moscow and St. Petersburg. Due to a lack of suitable commercial space, many Russian companies are housed in converted apartments (it is worth noting, however, that in some municipalities – Moscow included – it is not legal to operate an office out of residential space).

There are first-class office buildings being renovated and built in Moscow and St. Petersburg, although never enough to meet demand, and usually at prices only Fortune 500 companies can afford ($1000 per m^2 per year and up). Assuming that purchase of real estate is not the intention (see *Privatization* section below), this leaves the option of leasing from a Russian landlord. The following guidelines will help structure a safe lease. In any event, lean on the advice of an experienced Western lawyer based in Russia before signing any deal.

• Question one is who owns the property for lease. If it is owned by a state enterprise, that enterprise cannot sign a lease. Only the committee that is overseeing or will oversee the enterprise's privatization can do this.

• If the property to be leased is owned by either an individual or a company, it may be leased directly. Get unequivocal (or at least extremely convincing) proof of ownership at the outset of any discussions. An individual or company owns property (i.e. an apartment) if it has been privatized (ask to see the privatization certificate). If you are dealing with a company, be certain the person you are dealing with is properly empowered to lease this property on the company's behalf. Be sure any lease agreement is examined by your lawyer and fully notarized. The key proviso will be that which guards against unscheduled rent increases.

• If the person seeking to lease you the property does not own it, you must find out who does. Usually the property will be under lease or grant from a city or regional committee for property administration. With this body's approval, your future landlord can sublease the property to you. Note that in some cities, notably Moscow, apartments cannot be rented and used for office space.

• If you are signing a lease for a term of more than one year, it must be registered with the government to be legal.

• Consider the matter of who is covering the costs of liability and other business insurance on the property.

• Rent payable to a Russian landlord must be paid in rubles, by bank transfer. The VAT applies to rental payments (although some foreign entities are exempt from this – see the Enterprise Taxation section below). The landlord must pay taxes on rental income. If a landlord is a Western company or has a legal right to have a foreign bank account, the rent may be payable in foreign currency, but only via wire transfer. The many individuals and companies currently renting office or apartment space from Russians for cash foreign currency do so illegally and have no redress should the landlord demand a change in rental terms.

• Be sure you understand what is included in the rent. Who pays the electric bill? The phone bill? Water and heat? What type of renovation will be expected of the landlord? Does the contract include a provision for stopping rent payments if the space becomes uninhabitable.

• Commercial space should be inspected meticulously before rental. Ask to see the *tekhnicheskiy passport* for the space, which will help address zoning and use questions. If the space is a historical building, is being used for social welfare purposes, or requires capital repair, have your lawyer look into potential associated complications and additional approvals that might become necessary for you to use the space as planned.

Privatization

There has never in history been an effort to privatize state-owned assets on the scale of that undertaken in Russia. No significant private economic activity existed in Russia for over 60 years. This means there was no capital market to absorb massive divestment of state assets and no store of business knowledge with which to profitably manage new privatized enterprises. Nevertheless, privatization of the over 200,000 state-owned enterprises has occured. And is happened mainy by sheer force of will of the handful of ministers and deputy ministers overseeing the effort.

In June of 1992, privatization was launched when Russian President Boris Yeltsin issued a decree establishing a system of vouchers, and later investment funds, which was to form the foundation for a paper market. The immediate intent was to jump-start the privatization process, which had become bogged down for lack of any sense of urgency. The presidential decree required state-owned enterprises to choose a manner of privatization (from among three choices) and required vouchers to be distributed to all citizens by year's end. The voucher stage of privatization has now ended and the second, cash auction, stage continues at a much less frenetic pace.

ENTERPRISE PRIVATIZATION

Enterprise work forces have been, and will remain, at the center of the privatization effort. Enterprise employees enjoyed preeminent rights in both choosing the manner of privatization and, consequently, their share of ownership in the newly privatized enterprise. The first stage of any privatization allowed employees to buy shares at nominal value.

But the voucher system also allowed other citizens (and groups of citizens, through investment funds) to take part in auctions for the remaining enterprise capital (20-60%) not assumed by enterprise employees. Vouchers – each citizen received a single voucher, with a face value of 10,000 rubles – were the singular currency in these auctions during the first state of privatization. Upon completion of this first stage of privatization, enterprises are now able to use additional share issues (to be conducted as closed bid cash auctions) to raise needed capital and investment.

Stage 1

Three options: During the first stage of privatization, employees and management were offered three privatization paths, each entailing very different, resulting enterprise structures.

❶ *Limited control:* In the first variant, workers and management received 25% of non-voting shares free. Workers could also purchase up to 10% of voting shares at a 30% discount off the face value and management could buy an additional 5% of shares at face value. In this variant, therefore, outside investors could obtain from 60-75% of common stock through subsequent voucher and cash auctions.

❷ *Majority interest:* In the second variant, workers and management were to purchase, at 1.7 times the nominal price, 51% of common stock, with the balance to be sold via auctions or other competitive means.

❸ *Employee bail-out:* In the third variant, rarely adopted, a group of employees exercised the right to take control of the enterprise, pledging to make it profitable within one year. They were given an option on 20% of enterprise shares, for sale at face value, but had to put up personal assets as collateral, equaling a minimum of 200 times the current average monthly wage. Thus, through this variant, potentially 80% of shares could become available through public offerings.

In any case, final say on the amount of overall shares for sale by various means for vouchers was retained by the relevant councils of people's deputies and dealt with on a case-by-case basis.

As mentioned, the privatization options enumerated above applied to larger state and municipal enterprises (those with over 1000 workers or assets in excess of 50 mn rubles on January 1, 1992) that were transformed into open joint stock companies. Smaller enterprises (less than 200 workers or less than 1 mn rubles in assets), particularly those in the service and retail spheres, were privatized directly through auctions and tenders. Over 80,000 small enterprises were privatized in this manner.

Small scale enterprise privatization via auction stipulated some safety nets for employees of the enterprise. Employees could purchase shares in their own enterprises at 30% under the face value. If the enterprise were sold via tender and if conditions were attached to the sale, employees were potentially allowed a bonus of 20% of the final purchase price (or 15 times the monthly minimum wage each). If no conditions are attached to the sale of an enterprise and it goes on the auction block, employees may receive up to 30% of the final purchase price (or up to 20 times the minimum monthly wage each) as a bonus.

Stage 2
Whereas the intent of the first stage of privatization was to divest the state of its ownership in state enterprises and to distribute shares and ownership to the public at large, the second stage of privatization was intended to raise needed cash investments for these enterprises. Shares of these enterprises which remain in the hands of the state are to be sold off through auction –to the entity that offers the best combination of capital, equipment and expertise. At least 20% of the investment must be made in cash, no later than 30 days after the conclusion of the auction.

These auctions are to be competitive, closed-bid auctions, with the RFP, if you will, being an Investment Program drawn up by the target enterprise. A Competition Commission oversees evaluation of the bids, which occurs not less than 30 days from the date of announcement of the auction.

The winner of the auction receives the right to purchase the shares on offer and does so at par value. Proceeds from the sale of shares are transferred to the state property fund. Cash investments made in the enterprise are not treated as taxable revenue for the enterprise. It is, as yet, unclear how the state will treat equipment and in-kind investments in these enterprises: how the VAT, profits tax and property taxes will be assessed.

The Land Grab
Perhaps one of the most significant, but least-noticed developments in the wake of the first stage of privatization was a presidential decree granting privatized enterprises near-total discretion over the fate of the land on which the enterprise sits. The land can be purchased and potentially resold, or leased long-term from the state, thus retaining a first option to the land into the indefinite future.

PRIVATIZATION AND FOREIGN INVESTMENT
Given the present stage of privatization, there are a number of ways in which an interested investor can take advantage of the privatization process to obtain ownership of or shares in a Russian enterprise:
- Purchase, through negotiation, the assets of a bankrupt enterprise;
- Purchase securities on Russian exchanges;
- Negotiate directly with small and medium-sized enterprises that have privatized for investment and ownership of a portion or all of the enterprise;
- Negotiate directly for purchase of large enterprises already privatized, to re-register as a joint stock company with foreign investment or a wholly-owned subsidiary (in either case the new entity replaces the old);

- Purchase shares in Western investment funds (see listing in Chapter 1) that are actively and directly investing in Russian projects/enterprises;
- Take part in cash auctions for remaining shares in privatized enterprises;
- Purchase enterprise shares obtained through privatization by employees and management;
- Found a joint venture (joint stock company) with an enterprise that has privatized (in this case the privatized enterprise continues to function separately).

THE SECURITIES MARKET

The Russian securities market was set in motion during 1991 by the trade in vouchers and shares of funds or banks trading vouchers (publicly-traded commercial banks remain one of the best securities risks). It soon spread to the trade of shares in several large, privatized enterprises (e.g. in oil & gas, communications and heavy industry). While investment in securities can allow the foreign investor to benefit from the huge opportunities of investment in Russia without all the risks of local management, it does have significant risks of its own.

The first risk is confusion. There is a burgeoning market of bearer shares which are talked about as if they were securities, when in fact they are Russian junk bonds or lottery tickets (which ought to be warning enough). The widely-publicized MMM scandal and other pyramid scams have been based on such shares issued by private trading firms, grocery chains and investment funds. Trade in such shares is now technically illegal and certainly inadvisable.

The second risk is one endemic to the immature nature of the market. While several Western-financed efforts are underway, there is no centralized system for registration of shares. There is little policing of brokerage houses. And truth is highly relative when it comes to company disclosure during a stock issue.

The law currently requires all purchase and sale transactions to be validated by registration in the company's shareholder register. This means that, while one may effect the financial portion of a transaction in Moscow, one may also be required to travel to Simbirsk to effect the legal portion of the transaction. This offers many opportunities for fraud and the investor should require that their broker properly registers their share purchases and provides an extract from the company's register (most companies don't actually issue share certificates) to prove the sale. One way to circumvent this problem is to work with brokerage houses that offer nominee share holding. Another is to invest in the handful of Russian stocks that, through ADR, have shown up on the US over-the-counter market. Finally, one can invest in Western funds (i.e. Firebird) that invest in top-performing Russian securities.

The Russian business culture does not yet encourage, or require, full disclosure in business dealings. So due diligence can be a mighty task when assessing the value of a prospective investment target. The best bet is to rely on Western legal, financial and information services firms that are well-established in the market (see Ch. 1). They will have considerable experience in ferreting out the information you need to know.

This goes for getting information on your local broker, and you must have a local broker (except in the cases noted above). You should ask to see the broker's license if you have any doubts on this score. At the same time, find out on exactly which exchanges the broker is authorized to trade. Typical brokerage commissions are 3-5%, or lower on larger transactions.

These risks noted, the good news is that shares in Russian companies are seriously undervalued; centralized stock registrar systems are coming on line; foreigners are now being allowed to invest in lucrative GKOs (Russian Government Bonds or Obligations); standardized reporting of stock activity is taking hold (the best example of which is the *Moscow Times Index*); broker self-regulatory organizations are being put in place. While much of stock trading to date has been aimed at speculative trading, rather than long-term investments, that trend is expected to reverse.

Taxation

Dividends or revenues from securities trading that is received by individuals are treated as income and subject to the personal income tax (see below). Dividends received by companies are treated as business income and subject to profits taxation (see below). There is a 0.8% tax on most issues of stock by a company (excluding initial issues).

HOUSING PRIVATIZATION

Ever so quietly, behind all the noise about enterprise privatization, Russians have been seizing opportunities extended to privatize apartments and land. The amount of activity and that which is allowable differs region by region and city by city, but the process is mainly free and egalitarian, with each individual being allotted some 18m^2 of living space, plus an additional 9m^2 to each family (the average amount of living space for all Russians is 16.5m^2).

Meanwhile, housing auctions for unfinished construction, as well as private sales of apartments privatized, are taking place with some regularity. Real estate brokers are flourishing with abandon (before hiring one, see notes above about stock brokers) and a true real estate market (albeit wildly inflated) is taking shape. Foreign individuals are allowed to rent, lease or buy privatized apartments. Similarly, properly registered firms with foreign investment may acquire real estate in this manner.

Foreign Trade

Since January 1, 1992, there have been few legal restrictions on most foreign trade activity. All types of foreign trade activity, including barter, are permitted. All enterprises registered in accordance with Russian law may conduct import/export activity directly. Further, no special authorization or registration documents need to be submitted to the Ministry of Foreign Economic Relations or any State Licensing Committee (although there is still the need to show a customs official proof of valid registration of the enterprise, and the enterprise must be entered in the State Register of Enterprises, see below). However, importers and exporters are required to show proof of a hard currency bank account when executing contracts valuated in currency. For some operations an Export Passport is also required.

There are **export duties** on many goods (excluding those produced by joint ventures with over 30% foreign ownership), evaluated in ECUs, and payable in rubles at the market rate of exchange as set at the MICE.

Import duties are protectionist and are imposed at a *minimum* 15% of contract value, with rare exceptions (food items are excepted). The **VAT tax** (23% on almost all goods) applies to most all imports (see VAT section below), valued in currency and payable in rubles at the current rate of exchange.

Licensing of and **quotas** on imports and exports have almost wholly disappeared; now just some 5% of export items and 3% of import items are subject to licensing or quotas. The main items subject to quotas and licenses are goods of strategic importance, i.e. raw materials. Firms with greater than 30% foreign ownership are not subject to licensing on the goods they produce. Both general and single-use licenses are available; both are non-transferable and issued by the Ministry of Foreign Economic Relations. **Safety certificates** are required for import of many Western goods. The US company U.S. Testing has Russian government approval to issue such certificates (ph. 201-792-2400).

All fixed **currency ↔ ruble exchange** rates are abolished in the Russian Federation (although a ruble "corridor" has been in effect since mid-1995, whereby the Central Bank intervenes in the market to keep the exchange rate within the corridor). Banks may buy and sell rubles from foreign and Russian citizens at independently set rates; citizens are not required to prove the sources of any hard currency and have unlimited right of purchase and sale of rubles. Foreign citizens and companies may take part in currency auctions only via companies legally-registered in Russia. Hard-currency settlements between Russian enterprises is forbidden, except those involving currency ↔ ruble exchanges. Foreign legal entities may not conclude contracts with Russian enterprises for payment in rubles.

Since June 1992, by presidential decree, all enterprises, regardless of their form of ownership (i.e. including joint ventures) have been **required to sell 50% of hard currency earnings from export activity** (minus costs of transportation) within 14 days of receipt of revenues. Enterprises with over 30% foreign ownership may sell the entire 50% on the free market (see below, *Enterprise Taxation*).

Foreign trade contracts between Russian firms and foreign companies which involve shipment of goods from Russia abroad, must be paid off by the foreign firm within three months of shipment of the goods, or the Russian firm may suffer penalties.

CUSTOMS

While foreign trade has been greatly simplified since the Soviet period, this does not obviate certain customs formalities. These are outlined below.

Documentation and Registration

• To conduct foreign trade, an enterprise must be entered into the State Register of Enterprises. For enterprises with foreign investment, the list is maintained, and proof of entry is issued by, the Main Administration for Registration of Enterprises with Foreign Investment. After receiving a certificate of registration as an enterprise, such companies should seek registration with the Russian Registration Chamber. The paperwork required is: a notarized copy of certification of registration and of the Charter and Agreement; a certificate from Goskomstat attesting to assignment of registration codes; a certificate from one's bank attesting that an account has been opened and that 50% of establishment capital has been deposited. Registration is to take 21 days.

• To receive goods and property at customs and to officially register a shipment, the following documents are required (either the official recipient or a fully-empowered representative may present them):

❶ customs shipping declaration;

❷ permission of specified government organs, if the goods or property falls under the control of these organs;

❸ documents affirming payment for the customs procedure and, where necessary, for customs duties and taxes;

❹ other documents indicated in the declaration;

❺ a copy of the enterprise's establishment documents as proof of registration, if not already on file. Bank account certification may also be requested.

• Customs institutions may, as an exception, allow customs registration without a declaration. This is with the understanding that such a declaration will be presented within 15 days after customs registration. In such an instance, the declarant must affirm in writing that the declaration will be presented in the specified time period.

• Registration for export of "strategically important" goods and raw materials is done through the Ministry of Foreign Economic Relations (MFER). Strict quotas and licensing procedures apply. Firms seeking independent registration for such export activity must submit to MFER the following documentation: a notarized copy of the enterprise Charter and Agreement; a copy of the certificate attesting to registration as a legal enterprise; proof of the enterprise's maintenance of ruble and currency accounts in a Russian bank, together with a recommendation letter from the bank, attesting to the liquidity of the enterprise; a financial report of the company for the previous year and, if required, audit documentation proving the validity of the report; a list of contracts fulfilled in the previous year dealing with the concerned group of goods and indicating the basic terms of said contracts. Companies in this sector which have more than 30% foreign ownership need not obtain an export license on "independently produced output," but must first obtain certification of independent output from the Chamber of Trade and Industry.

Where to Receive Imported Goods

• Two main customs points are used in Moscow. Items shipped into Russia by air transit Sheremetevo II customs terminal. Goods arriving by truck typically transit Butovo customs point (on the Southern outskirts of the city). Goods arriving by train can be claimed at the train station. There are customs agents at all stations where goods can arrive from abroad. Declarations for train arrivals must be processed at Oktyabrskaya Tovarnaya Stantsiya, located at Komsomolskaya ploshchad. Private customs clearing houses and customs storage warehouses have been springing up as well, and these may prove more efficient means of receiving goods (see the Yellow Pages in our *Where in Moscow*); in fact, they can broker all customs formalities on your behalf.

• Under a July, 1995 customs order (#373), imported goods must be cleared at their point of entry into Russia. Thus, goods arriving by boat in St. Petersburg for transshipment on to Krasnoyarsk, must be cleared in St. Petersburg.

• In St. Petersburg, goods arriving by air transit Pulkovo customs terminal, those arriving by boat or truck transit Central Customs. For more detailed information, see our *Where in St. Petersburg*.

• Under current rules, goods and property can also be declared and cleared through customs:

❶ at the declarant's place of business, under the condition that the declarant assumes the costs of bringing the customs official to the site. The declarant may also request the assistance of the customs office in setting up an inspection committee (expert) or designation of a customs representative (see section below on *akt*);

❷ at the location of the customs office, whereby goods or property should be shipped to/received at that office;

❸ at other locations agreed upon with the customs office having jurisdiction for the declarant's region, provided other options are not possible.

The akt *of Receipt*

• When equipment arrives in Russia on contract, the opening of the shipment should be witnessed by an expert (or inspection committee) from customs or the Russian Chamber of Commerce. If the equipment arrives in unsatisfactory condition, the recipient will thereby be protected by a certified statement (*akt*) which will be jointly signed by the expert and the recipient, who will be able to take recourse for compensation with the party sending and/or shipping the equipment. A similar procedure is to be followed in the event damaged goods are received.

• For accounting and inventory purposes in a joint venture or other enterprise registered on Russian soil, any shipment received must be certified by an *akt*. This means drawing up a list of the items received, their quantity, and their value, and having the person who received the goods sign the list.

Processing Fees

• Processing fees for customs clearing are 0.1% of the contract value payable in rubles, plus 0.05% payable in the currency of the contract. Goods in transit are subject to the 0.1% fee only. Goods in transit to or from most CIS states are not subject to processing fees.

• No payment for processing is required if:

❶ the goods are being temporarily imported for cultural purposes (i.e. museum exhibits, archives, libraries, performances);

❷ property previously imported or exported on a temporary basis is being returned from whence it came (which is a broader category than the previous one);

❸ the goods or property are to be used for the official purposes of diplomatic or consulate representations of foreign states resident in Russia, of international intergovernmental organizations and the representatives of foreign governments which work in them, or of other international organizations which enjoy duty-free treatment on Russian territory (included are goods brought in for humanitarian purposes);

❹ a preliminary declaration is presented for shipments made upon a State writ;

❺ the goods are part of equipment under assembly and if a general declaration covering such goods has been previously filed. If such property subsequently becomes the object of a purchase, sale or barter and is re-declared as such, payment for customs processing follows the procedures specified above.

How to Pay for Processing Fees, Taxes and Duties

• Payment can be made in advance or at the time of customs clearing (if at a customs point such as Sheremetevo II or Butovo). If made in advance, payment should be made by bank transfer to the account of the Russian State Customs Committee. Ruble payments for duties and taxes can be paid to the account of the customs office through which goods are being cleared. The document which, for the bank's purposes, serves as the basis for payment, is the filled-in customs declaration. Proof of payment should accompany the declaration when it is presented at customs.

• Payment can also be made at the customs point, in cash. In general, payment should be made before customs will release the goods or property. Yet an organization or enterprise can present a guarantee letter (*garantiynoye pismo*) with the proper certification as proof that proper payment will be made.

FREE ECONOMIC ZONES (FEZS)

As a mechanism for encouraging foreign investment in targeted regions and industries, Russia has established Free Economic Zones (FEZs) in certain cities, regions and oblasts. Among these are St. Petersburg, Vyborg, Kemerovo, Novgorod and Nakhodka (see Chapter 1 for a complete list). The specific "privileged terms" for foreign investment and foreign trade are different for each FEZ (a general Russian law governing Free Economic Zones has yet to be passed), but all have certain elements in common.

• **Taxation is reduced.** In some cases, special tax holidays are extended to joint ventures; in others, caps are placed on the tax burden enterprises will have to bear (thus limiting some uncertainty). Generally, profits invested back into the FEZ's development are not taxed.

• **Import and export duties and taxes are reduced or eliminated.** In general, there are promises of "easing" the process of foreign trade, and quotas and licensing requirements are removed.

• **Local authorities are vested with greater authority** to register enterprises, set tax rates and terms of lease.

Labor Laws

State control over enterprise labor policy has loosened significantly since the demise of the workers' state. At present, collective and/or individual labor contracts are the primary basis for regulating labor-management relations, workers' rights, vacation time, etc.

This said, it bears noting that the RSFSR Labor Code (1983) is still technically in effect and, supposedly, has juridical weight greater than any individual or collective labor contract (at the time of publication, a very contentious first draft of a new Labor Code was being introduced to the Russian Parliament). The Labor Code, as a relic of the Soviet era, is significantly more "pro-labor" than is the currently accepted norm. In fact, recent court rulings have overruled the Labor Code, in favor of independently-negotiated labor contracts on issues of employee hiring and firing. The reasoning has been that the higher compensation inherent in such contracts sufficiently counterbalances any less advantageous working conditions (i.e. greater uncertainty) that the contracts might offer vs. what the Labor Code specifies.

The norms and expectations of Russian workers carried over from the Soviet period are still of great relevance, however, aside from the fact that they may be codified in the Labor Code.

• It is illegal to discriminate against employees or applicants on the basis of sex, race, nationality, or religious beliefs.

• The right to strike is not forbidden, nor is it allowed.

• Employees are expected, for the most part, to work a 40 hour, five or six day week. There are exceptions for teenagers and people employed at hazardous jobs; in fact persons under 18 years of age cannot be employed in "hard labor."

• An individual can be hired for a trial period (as specified in a labor contract), during or at the end of which they may be fired with or without cause or reason.

• It is now illegal to pay any salaries to Russian residents in foreign currency, even by wire transfer from abroad, as was previously permitted. It is, however, legal to pay non-resident foreigners in currency, if that is effected by wire transfer from abroad.

• There are seven holidays recognized as Russian national holidays when no one is expected to work. These are January 1-2, January 7, March 8, May 1-2 and May 9, June 12, November 7. Other regional or city holidays may also be celebrated. If a holiday falls on Tuesday, Monday is also a holiday and the previous Saturday is a workday. In addition, industrial, office and professional workers are entitled to at least 24 working days of leave (*otpusk*) per year with pay based on average salary for the past year.

• Jobs are typically classified according to skill grades and wage categories. Workers can be employed hourly or on a piece-work basis. Time-and-a-half is paid for overtime and double time for holidays.

• Management is expected to ensure occupational safety and health. It must satisfy the requirements of building codes. The facilities must meet with the approval of the state sanitary and technical supervisor, the trade union "technical inspectorate," the fire marshal, the trade union committee of the enterprise and any ministry or organization that may oversee the enterprise.

• Special clothing, instruction and safety equipment, as well as medical exams, are required in certain job categories. The enterprise is financially liable for disabilities to employees "arising from the performance of their duties."

• Female workers are afforded somewhat greater protection than males. For example, pregnant women and women with children under the age of one may not work at night (unless it is especially necessary). Pregnant women are guaranteed 112 days maternity leave with pay (140 days in the event of an abnormal birth). They may take up to a year with partial pay for child care.

• At least 2-3 days are to be given to workers getting married; 1-2 days for paternity leave; 2-3 days for a death in the family. There are, similarly, added protections for teenage labor. Special incentives often exist, such as a shortened work day, to encourage employees to continue with their education.

• Labor disputes in larger enterprises (where a labor union is present) are resolved, generally, before one of three tribunals:

❶ Labor dispute commissions are set up at the enterprise to hammer out differences internally.

❷ If the commission fails, the dispute is taken to a trade union committee with authority to overrule the commission.

❸ Either management or labor may appeal the trade union committee decision to district (or town) court.

• Cases of theft or property damage go straight to district court. Regarding theft, it should be noted that a doctrine similar to *respondeat superior* carries a special significance. Lost supplies or illegal use of equipment such as photocopiers may be the responsibility of the employer. Theft is very common. One way to avoid it is through adequate compensation and benefits. In some cases, employees' contracts can include a clause whereby they are individually or collectively liable for lost supplies. Joint ventures may also want to investigate insurance coverage for this problem or consider some sort of hold-back provision such as in construction contracts to cover losses.

• A labor contract in a large enterprise (with a labor union presence) often cannot be cancelled unilaterally by management. Cancellation is done only with the consent of the employees' trade union. If management wrongfully dismisses or transfers an employee, the management is personally liable for the damage sustained. Generally, employees in such enterprises cannot be unwillingly transferred to different jobs or different locations.

• While employment contracts are not required by law, if one is signed with an employee subsequent to their beginning work, the contract has retroactive force. The term for a labor contract must be either less than 5 years or indefinite in term. It must indicate the employee's salary, and the scope and duration of work to be performed. In point of fact, a contract can often be the employer's best defense against labor disputes, as it sets a definite end-date for the employee's work. And since, under Russian law, employees cannot be fired on notice, but only for 'cause,' this can be an important factor.

• Although the Labor Code says a place of work can keep an employee from leaving for two months in order to find a replacement, a worker is, in reality, free to leave at will. Likewise, the limits on a manager's ability to fire employees are much less strict than the written laws lead one to believe. One source on labor codes says that one acceptable reason for letting a worker go is "discrepancies of a worker in fulfilling his duties." The worker must be given one month's written notice.

• The following are generally accepted reasons for immediate firing of employees: liquidation or bankruptcy of an enterprise; drunkenness on the job; unauthorized absence from work or absence due to certain illnesses for more than four months; embezzlement; failure to perform; unqualified for the position; the company is rehiring an employee who was on leave and who previously held the position in question.

• A percentage of the income of large enterprises is typically earmarked for the cultural and sports activities of the trade union/employees. The enterprise also sets aside funds for all employees' "social insurance" (aside from the taxes in this area). These funds are used for disability, maternity leave, pensions, as well as medical treatment and dietary supplements.

Legal Status of Foreign Nationals

No single piece of Russian legislation regulates the status of foreign nationals in Russia. Rather, a complex interweave of laws and regulations concerning taxation, migration, currency and customs establish the fundament for foreigner's status and activity in Russia.

• Foreign nationals in Russia are supposed to enjoy the same rights and bear the same duties as citizens of Russia unless otherwise laid down in acts of Russian legislation. All of the labor laws are fully applicable to foreigners (even when they are on assignment in Russia for a foreign legal entity). This includes wages, taxation, contracts, leisure time and so forth. Likewise, the provision for maternity leave and other benefits are applicable. In reality, as noted above, labor contracts govern these and other benefits.

• Foreign nationals that work for Russian firms (including wholly-owned foreign firms) are required to have a work permit, which is obtained from the Federal Migration Service for a nominal fee (<$10) and good for one year. Foreign nationals working for representative offices or sent to work for a Russian company on a temporary basis are not required to obtain a permit.

• Foreign nationals who are permanent residents have the right, on the basis of and in the manner prescribed for Russian citizens, to receive accommodation in state and socially owned houses and in cooperative houses. Foreigners (excepting diplomatic personnel) further have the right to pay for accommodation in rubles.

• Resident foreigners are required to register with the local UVIR (visa registration) office within 72 hours of arrival.

• Foreign nationals who are permanent residents are entitled to the same free medical care as Russian citizens. Temporary residents are entitled to medical care as may be prescribed from time to time.

• Foreign nationals, temporary and permanent, must pay taxes (see section below, *Personal Taxation*), but are likewise entitled to pensions and other forms of social security.

• Foreign nationals may open bank accounts, purchase securities, own property and perform any business activity not expressly prohibited by Russian law.

• Foreign nationals coming to work in Russia for an extended period are extended extra allowances for import and export of personal items, the normal duty-free limit for which would be $2000. Extra allowances are granted on an ad hoc basis (a personal car can be imported for one year free of duties, but must be exported at the end of that period). See notes on the Personal Use Doctrine in Chapter 2.

• Foreign nationals have the same educational rights as Russian citizens. And, of course, they face similar obligations. They cannot vote, join political parties, and are not required to serve in the military.

• Foreign nationals may have their period of stay reduced if there are "no longer any grounds" for the stay. The period of stay may also be reduced for a violation of the law. It follows that, if the offense is serious enough, the period of stay can be extended. A foreign national's departure from Russia may be postponed until the fulfillment by him or her of property obligations to Russian citizens, organizations or the state.

• Foreign businesses in Russia should become familiar with the basic provisions of visa, customs and currency regulations (see the sections in Chapter 2, *Visas* and *Customs*), and should be certain their employees do the same. Employees in Russia should be briefed on criminal law, housing law, and the court system.

• When traveling in Russia, a foreign national should always have his passport with himself/herself. For instance it is illegal to board a domestic flight without a passport; purchase of train tickets and boarding trains often require display of some form of identification.

Personal Taxation

Businesses that are considering an investment in Russia need to consider a myriad of personal and enterprise tax issues and absolutely must have legal advice on these questions. This section on personal taxation, and the following one on enterprise taxation, can serve as an introduction to these issues but *cannot replace the advice of a competent lawyer or accountant* (see Chapter 1 for a list of firms active in Russia).

WHO IS A RESIDENT?

The first step in understanding Russian individual taxes is to understand the definition of a resident under Russian law. Only residents are required to pay Russian income tax and have it deducted at source.

A foreigner expecting to earn income in Russia and who will be resident in Russia **more than 183 days in a calendar year** is considered a resident. Note that this is for a calendar year. Thus, you could spend 364 consecutive days in Russia (the last 182 days in one year and the first 182 days the following year) and not be considered a resident.

If an individual reasonably expects to qualify as a resident, a declaration must be submitted within one month of entering Russia, stating the amount he anticipates earning. Taxes for the year are thus estimated and made payable in three equal parts of 25% of the estimated sum, on May 15, August 15, and November 15. A final declaration (and payment), with any changes, is to be made by March 1 of the following year. No declaration is required if one anticipates earning an annual salary within the lowest (12%) tax bracket.

A foreign national employed by a foreign legal entity (representative office or branch, diplomatic mission, etc.) is not subject to wage withholding and the company does not need to make the additional social welfare payments (in excess of 40% of the amount of the salary).

WHAT YOU MUST PAY

- Tax rates are based on annual income received each calendar year. The base tax rate is 12% and **rates on marginal income rise to 30%**. Every citizen who receives income outside of enterprises which deduct taxes from salaries shall be required, prior to April 1 of each year, to make a declaration at their local tax organ of revenues actually received and to provide adequate documentation of same.

- **Non-permanent residents** (less than 183 days) earning income based on business (i.e. rental income, royalties, licenses, services rendered) occurring in Russia are subject to a 20% income tax. This does not apparently apply to income from import/export activity.

- Salaries earned in hard currency must be valuated in rubles at the Central Bank rate. Taxes are payable in rubles or in hard currency via any Sberbank which handles currency operations (a 1% commission is charged). Thus, at the current commercial ruble rate, a foreigner earning greater than the equivalent of $12,500 per year must pay a 30% tax on all additional income. It therefore makes sense for any joint venture or subsidiary or representation to do some serious tax planning with full knowledge of what is legal and practical (i.e. through payment prior to departure or after one's return).

- Income tax is not due on money spent obtaining housing or a *dacha* or payment of financing for same. Up to 500 times the minimum Russian salary level earned from sales of such property is also non-taxable. There is no tax on income from sales of personal items (i.e. a car or other durables), provided the total such income does not exceed 50 times the minimum Russian salary level. There is also a standard deduction equal to one minimal monthly salary for oneself and all dependents.

- Income for a private company is considered to be income of the individual owning the company and is taxed as such. This requires a separate declaration from the one mentioned above.

- Taxable income is defined in the law as: wages and salaries, including fees, *per diem* and other compensations for living in Russia, compensation for education of children, for food, and for family members brought on vacation. Not included as part of taxable income are: payments for social insurance and pensions (made by the employer), compensation for rental of living quarters and a car necessary for business purposes, compensation for business trips.

- Many Soviet international tax agreements are still in effect, while some (i.e. with the US) have been or are being renegotiated. Most (including the US treaty) reflect similar treatment. Wages and other personal income that are earned by a person in one contracting state are not subject to taxation in the other state as long as (1) the person is not present in the other state for more than 183 days in any given calendar year, (2) the person's wages/salary are paid by the home office and not the local base of operations, and (3) the employer is not a resident legal entity.

The Russian treaties with Sweden, Cyprus, Finland and the United Kingdom provide that technical specialists resident in one contracting state will not be taxed in the other so long as they are not present in the other for more than 365 days in any two year period. It should be noted that, in some treaties, the tax treatment depends on the residency of the employer. To avoid double taxation, the taxpayer must declare tax payments made in other countries.

Enterprise Taxation

There are over 180 different types of federal and local taxes which may be levied on an enterprise, from customs taxes to property taxes to profits and VAT taxes. Only the most general and significant taxes are reviewed below. For a full understanding of tax obligations, consult a competent tax attorney or accountant (see Chapter 1 for a list of qualified law and accounting firms).

Investors should also be mindful of the fact that, as this edition of the guide was going to press, initial drafts of legislation to overhaul the Russian Tax Code were circulating. The most important elements of this new code will be simplification of the code and reduction in the number of taxes, redefinition of profits more in line with Western practice, simplification of the VAT, reduction of payroll taxes, lowering import duties, clarification and simplification of securities taxes, limitation of taxation exceptions and increasing the right to appeal tax judgements.

PROFITS TAX

All Russian enterprises, irrespective of their form of ownership (including foreign) are subject to a federal profits tax of 13%, plus regional/municipal taxes of up to 25% (up to 30% for banks and insurance companies). If the locality has not set a rate, the default rate is 22%. This is calculated based on total revenues, minus expenses, *excepting wages, advertising, training and entertainment expenses.* There are even higher rates for brokerage firms, trading services and middlemen, auctions, casinos, video/audio rental companies and companies offering video games. Taxes are payable on world-wide income of the enterprise, unless a double taxation treaty applies. Estimated taxes are to be paid quarterly with a final return due March 15.

A number of profits tax breaks can be sought. Specifically, companies will enjoy a deduction from taxable profits of: 30% of expenditures on environmental protection measures; 100% of the sum invested in health care centers, retirement homes, pre-schools, pioneer camps, cultural and sports centers, educational institutions and housing projects which are on the enterprise's balance sheet; 100% of the sum donated to certain charities;

100% of the sum devoted to agricultural and food processing improvements, to technical re-equipping and improvements in the oil and gas, medical/pharmaceutical and consumer goods spheres; 100% of donations to ecological, humanitarian, health, religious and other social organizations, but not more than 3% of overall profits in this case. This said, such deductions cannot reduce a company's taxes more than 50%.

Small enterprises are eligible for certain tax holidays during the first two years of their operation. See the section above in this chapter, *Small Enterprises*.

Enterprises with at least $10 mn in foreign investment and where the foreign investor owns at least 30% of the company now enjoy a two year tax holiday on the same terms as small enterprises.

Enterprises whose primary activity is as a religious or social organization, as a creative union or humanitarian fund, if properly registered as such, are freed from payment of the profits tax.

Non-profit and charitable organizations may enjoy tax benefits at the local or regional level; there are no benefits at the federal level.

Losses can be carried over for five years to diminish profits and the consequential tax burden.

The profits tax can be reduced by up to 50% for enterprises in which more than 50% of the workers are disabled and/or 70% of the employees are pensioners.

VALUE ADDED TAX

On December 6, 1991, the Russian Parliament introduced a value added tax (VAT) of 28% of the sales price or contract value of goods and services. The rate has since been lowered to 20% (10% for some food items, children's clothing, medicine and medical equipment), increased to 23%, and lowered again to 20% (in Moscow a 1% hotel accommodations tax has been set, so hotel bills reflect a 21% VAT). The amount of the tax is to be included in the price of goods sold, and the enterprise is to pay the government the amount of tax collected from goods sold, minus the amount it payed to suppliers (who also include the tax in their sales price). There are provisions in place to get back VAT on goods taken out of the country but, in practice, no one yet seems to be claiming VAT returns.

On imported goods, you must pay VAT on the "customs value" (in dollars or rubles) of those goods, which includes their market value plus insurance and freight (i.e. CIF), plus import duties and excise taxes. The VAT must be paid in rubles at the official Central Bank exchange rate on the date that the customs declaration is submitted.

Enterprises must pay the VAT three times monthly, monthly, or quarterly, depending upon the amount of income to be subjected to VAT.

There are many **exemptions to the VAT**, and these are ever-changing. At the time of publication, the following exemptions existed.

The VAT does not apply to:

- exports, but it does apply to imports (levied on the sum of the imports' value, plus any excise taxes and duties);
- rent (for offices or housing) paid by foreign citizens or companies (if there is a reciprocal tax treaty to this effect);
- foreign capital invested in Russian companies;
- purchase of securities and bank deposits by foreign nationals and foreign companies;
- loans to enterprises by foreign banks and certain Russian banks and from the Russian government;
- loans by foreign companies to a joint venture or wholly foreign-owned company in which they participate;
- transport for import/export or exported services, and on services which are provided to companies whose primary place of commercial activity is outside Russia;
- some types of equipment leases;
- self-employed individuals or private contractors;
- capital contributions to the charter capital of enterprises, if such contributions are made within one year of founding and, for fixed assets, when the assets are put into operation;
- grants from international organizations;
- payouts to shareholders upon liquidation or reorganization of an enterprise (as long as the amount disbursed does not constitute a capital gain – is less than or equal to the company's charter capital);
- financing based in the issue of company shares;
- medical services for individuals;
- import of periodicals, books and other printed matter;
- intra-company turnover;
- contributions to specified, allowable charitable activities.

EXCISE TAX

The sale of liquor, beer, caviar, luxury seafood, chocolate, tobacco, cars, tires, jewelry, diamonds, furs, high-quality porcelain and cut glass, rugs and carpets and natural leather garments is taxed with an excise tax. The tax does not apply to goods sold outside the Commonwealth (i.e. exported abroad). The rates are set by the Russian government and vary by the type of product.

EXCESS WAGES TAX

Enterprises, including joint ventures, which pay out a total amount in salaries that averages, per resident employee, more than six times the minimum wage, at one time had to pay an excess wages tax equal to the profit tax on the "excessive" sum. In effect, this meant that excess wages, so defined, could not be counted by the company as a legitimate cost of doing business. The tax was phased out in January of 1996.

EXPORT AND IMPORT TARIFFS

Export tariffs are established on natural resources, produce, agricultural products and arms. Two tariff rates are set. The first is the basic level of tariffs and varies depending on the item in question. The second is the level for goods which do not fall under the terms of mandatory currency sales (i.e. barter operations or non-currency operations), or *which are produced by* wholly-owned subsidiaries of foreign firms or joint ventures with at least 30% foreign ownership (which also are not subject to mandatory currency sales). The tariff on this second level is 50% above the basic level. The export tariff is valued in ECU, but paid in rubles at the current rate of exchange.

The import tariff is set at between 5-150% of the import value of the goods and applies mainly to excised items like alcohol, cigarettes and cars, but also to things like paper and canned food. The tariff is doubled for goods originating in countries with which Russia does not have mutuality of most favored nation status. Food and agricultural goods are no longer free of import tariffs. Tariffs are denominated in ECU and payable in rubles at the current rate of exchange.

SOCIAL INSURANCE TAXES

The social insurance taxes are add-on taxes and almost entirely employer-based; only 1% of employee wages are deducted for social insurance. The rest is paid by the employer such that, for every 100 rubles in salary paid to employees, there can be up to an additional 41 rubles in taxes to pay to the state.

Pension Fund: The amount payable to the national pension fund is based on total expenditures on worker salaries (including temporary contract labor or subcontractor labor). For enterprises, the amount due is 28% of paid salaries; for agricultural enterprises the tax is 20.6%. Persons engaged in individual labor activity, lawyers and some other activities must pay 5% of total revenues to the fund. 26% of author's honoraria paid must be paid to the pension fund. Employees pay 1% of their salary to the fund.

Other funds: all enterprises must pay 5.4% of all salaries to the social insurance fund, 2% of salaries to the unemployment fund, 3.6% to the health insurance fund, 1% to the education support fund and 1% to the transport fund.

CURRENCY EARNINGS TAX

Russian enterprises are required to sell to the Russian State Bank a set amount of all hard currency earnings from exporting (if that amount exceeds $500), excluding any costs of transport. Presently, Russian enterprises, including those with foreign investment, must sell 50% of such earnings through the centralized currency exchange, or banks participating in the exchange.

Wholly-owned subsidiaries of foreign firms and joint ventures with more than 30% foreign ownership are exempted from this requirement for goods of their own production. For other export operations, they are entitled to sell their currency through licensed commercial banks (whose rates are better than on the currency exchange). In any case, the sales must occur within 7 days of receipt of revenues.

There is no mandatory sale of currency obtained through its purchase on the currency exchange. Therefore, rubles gained from sales of currency that was earned from exports can be used to re-purchase currency on the exchange, and that currency may be repatriated or used as the enterprise sees fit. The difference in the amount of currency before and after this transaction, therefore, should be considered a tax on doing business in currency.

There is also no mandatory sale of currency which: (a) is part of an investment in the establishment fund of an enterprise; (b) is earned as a dividend from equity participation in an enterprise; (c) is earned from the sale of securities; (d) is part of credits borrowed or is part of payments for credits loaned; or (e) is received for humanitarian purposes.

OTHER MISCELLANEOUS TAXES

This section should really be titled, "What only the tax inspector really knows." Many seemingly incidental and minor taxes are introduced administratively by various levels of the Russian government. It is nearly impossible to keep 100% on top of current supplemental tax rates, thus it is highly advisable to rely on *both* the advice of your accountant and on an external advisor. What follows is a listing of some of the supplemental taxes known about at publication time.

• Banking and securities companies are subject to a 0.5% tax on issuance of securities; the buyer of such securities must also pay a 0.1% tax on the value of said securities.

• Resale of some items, such as cars and computers, is subject to a resale tax of 10% or higher.

• A tax on advertising is levied at up to 5% of the value of advertising services; payment is quarterly.

• There is a vehicle tax of 20% of the cost of the vehicle before VAT.

• A roads tax is assessed on all enterprises, valued up to 1.5% of sales.

• A property tax on enterprise assets can be levied at up to 2% of the assessed value of those assets (it is 1.5% in Moscow, 2% in St. Petersburg). Certain tax breaks are extended for social investments and account is given for reinvestment and depreciation. A land tax is assessed at 10 rubles per hectare and, for private farming plots, 1000 rubles per m².

• Capital gains are taxed at the same rate as corporate profits (35% or higher) or individual income (up to 30%), depending on the recipient.

• There is a 15% tax on interest income.

• There is a 6% tax on income from international transport services.

- Local governments (i.e. the Moscow City Government) impose taxes on buildings, motor vehicles, land, and any number of other objects. They are also increasingly introducing miscellaneous fees on certain types of trade and business activity (for example, there is a 1.5% profits tax to finance housing; there is now a tax on the purchase of apartments equivalent to 500 minimal monthly salaries (MMS) for non-Moscow resident Russian citizens and 5000 MMS for non-Russians).

- There is an investment tax credit law which can take some of the sting out of the above-mentioned laws, allowing a 10% tax deferment for 5 years on the total value of certain internal enterprise capital investments, with a ceiling of 50% of the total taxable amount. This law also allows privatizing enterprises to receive up to a 50% credit on profit taxes for interest paid on bank credit.

- Firms engaging in retail trade in Moscow (other cities should be expected to follow suit) must pay significant annual registration fees of 50 times the minimum monthly salary level; the fee is just 12.5 times this level for trade in non-excised food items. There are discounts for dealing in multiple items.

WITHHOLDING (TRANSFER) TAXES

There is a 15% transfer tax on the dividends a foreign partner repatriates from investments in Russia. This withholding tax will not be imposed if it conflicts with one of Russia's double taxation treaties (which, in most cases, are the soviet treaties). In the absence of an applicable treaty, the Ministry of Finance has the authority to waive this tax for a specific period of time or to reduce the rate. The Ministry of Finance is supposed to use this authority to encourage particular industries (medical equipment, high technology, consumer goods).

The US-Russia Treaty for Avoidance of Double Taxation of Income places a maximum 10% tax rate on dividends, at source (5% for investors with >10% ownership or voting stock in a company).

Treaty shopping (i.e. founding a joint venture using a subsidiary company registered in a third country) can provide access to more favorable provisions in other double taxation treaties. Several of these treaties (Austria, Cyprus and Finland, for example) provide that a distribution of profits and dividends are exempt from taxation in the country from which the dividends are remitted. Thus, dividends remitted by a Russian joint venture to a Finnish company would be free of the 15% transfer tax.

Of course, the big problem is whether or not these dividends can be remitted without incurring similar or even larger taxes in the other country. It obviously does not do any good to avoid a 15% transfer tax in Russia only to discover a 25% corporate tax in Austria.

Under the Cypriot-Russian Tax Treaty, dividends paid to a resident of Cyprus by a resident of Russia are not subject to taxation in Russia. Furthermore, it appears that under Cypriot law the income of companies that derive their income exclusively from sources outside Cyprus are subject to an income tax of only 4.25% and shareholders receiving a dividend from such a company are not subject to any tax.

It may also be advantageous to structure a deal in terms of licensing tangible or intangible assets to a Russian partner in exchange for royalties. Under the terms of the US-Russia Treaty (and those of Russia with other states), royalties of this type may be taxable only in one's home country, as is the case with interest payments.

Instruction 34

An Instruction of the Russian State Tax Service issued in July of 1995 added a new wrinkle to the tax withholding environment. The instruction states that companies with a permanent establishment (doing business from a fixed base) in Russia or which have given another organization agency powers to represent it, shall be taxed on net income from its business activities in Russia, at the prevailing rates. Permanent establishments, needless to say, must be registered and file and pay taxes.

The instruction further stipulates up to a 20% withholding tax (6% on freight), at source by the payor, for companies receiving income from Russia but which do not have a permanent establishment. This withholding at source does not apply to strictly foreign trade operations, i.e. exports of foreign goods to Russia, provided that income received from foreign trade operations are carried out exclusively in the name of the foreign legal entity (art. 5.1). Notably, companies with registered local subsidiary offices, with whom contracts are properly structured, also will not be subjected to the tax.

In any event, in the case of withholding taxes, as with all aspects of Russian business law, rely on the research and advice of a competent and informed lawyer to guide your decisions. This chapter can be but a thorough introduction to the many facets of Russian business law, with an emphasis on the more enduring aspects. Russian business law is constantly in flux, and needs to be carefully assessed, in specifics, at the time of your investment activity.

Index

Sources for facts on page 1 (aggregated): Business Central Europe Annual, Dec. 1995; *Transition,* Jan.-Feb., 1996; *Moscow Times,* 4/22/96, 7/2/96; *BISNIS Bulletin* 10/95; *Economist,* 2/29/96, 2/17/96; *East/West Executive Guide,* Feb. 1996; *Jamestown Monitor,* 1/31/96; *Russian Far East News,* 2/96; *Russia Review,* 7/1/96, 9/3/95, 2/12/96, 3/11/96; *VTsIOM,* 4/96; *OMRI Daily Digest,* 8/23/96.

S

SABIT. *See* Special American Business Internship Training
Safety certificates: for import of goods 207
Salans, Hertzfeld and Heilbron 60
Salaries 176; to local employees 212
San Antonio Capital 51
Sankt Peterburg hotel 89
Satellite phones 160
Savoy hotel 89
Scan Cargo Transport 168
Schenkers 168
Scott-European Corporation 62
Sea-Land Service 168
Securities 18, 205; systemic problems and 205; taxation 206; VAT and 219
Security companies 177
Security issues in Russia 49
SEEL—Survey of East European Law 28
Sergeyev Posad 93
Services: VAT exemption and 219
Shares: registration of 205
Shepard's/McGraw-Hill 27
Sheremetyevo airport 77, 102
Shippers 168
Shopping: Moscow 93; St. Petersburg 94
Sightseeing: Moscow 92; St. Petersburg 94
Simbirsk 41
Single-Entry Business Visa 66
Singles: on-line resources for 40
Slavyanskaya-Radisson hotel 89
Small Business Administration loans 43
Small enterprises 196; additional restrictions by localities 196; purposes of 196; size restrictions 196; taxation 196; tax benefits of 218
Smoking: tolerating 179
Smolensk Regional Venture Fund 51
Social Insurance Taxes 220
Socializing 181
Sokolniki 93
Sources of Finance for Trade and Investment in the 43
Souvenirs: customs regulations and 80; Moscow 93

Sovfracht 168
Soviet Archives 37
Sovtransservice 168
Sparrow Hills 93
Special American Business Internship Training 48
Speed limits 99
Sprint 157, 161; Global SprintFax 161
Sprint Express 159
Sprint Telemail 165
St. Isaac's Cathedral 94
St. Petersburg 41; orientation 93
St. Petersburg American Business Association 51
St. Petersburg Business News 36
St. Petersburg Chamber of Commerce 51
St. Petersburg Press 39
Stalco Forwarding Services 168
State enterprises: renamed 195
State Register of Enterprises 208
Statistics: east-west trade 46
Steptoe & Johnson 60
Street signs 98, 99
Subsidiary companies 195
Superstitions 181
Surviving Together 26
SWEEL 62

T

Tadzhikistan: embassy in the US 55; Web home page 40
Tadzhikistan Chamber of Commerce 56
Tajikistan Report 29
Tangent Graphics 61
Tariffs 220
Taxation, enterprise 217: advertising and 221; banking and securities tax 221; capital gains 221; carrying over losses 218; enterprise: profits tax 217; excess wages tax 219; excise tax 219; export/import tariffs 220; foreign nationals and 214; free trade zones and 211; international transport tax 221; international treaties and 222; investment tax credit 222; joint ventures: equipment and supplies 193; import/export taxes and duties 193; tax credits

217; local taxes 222; miscellaneous taxes 221; on currency earnings 220; personal: rates 216; private company income and 216; profits tax 192, 217; property and 221; registration fees 222; resale tax 221; residency status and 215; roads tax 221; royalties and licenses 223; social insurance taxes 220; transfer taxes 222; value added tax 218; vehicle tax 221; wage withholding tax 216
Taxation, personal 215; foreign nationals and 215; non-permanent residents 216; hard currency earnings 216; international agreements and 216; taxable income defined 216, 219
Taxis 95, 144; crime and 148; from airport 96; gypsy cabs 95; prices of 96
Technical Assistance: resources for 46
Tekhnicheskiy passport 202
TeleAdapt 162
Telecommunications 157
Telephones: cost of call from phone booth 157; dialing within the CIS: city codes 6; directory assistance 157; intercity dialing problems 158; international calls: cost of 159; international dialing 158; international dialing and 157; long distance within Russia 157; placing calls within Russia 157; setting up an office and 159
Telex 165; communication by 180; via electronic mail 163
Temperature: conversion chart 5; seasonal mean 4
Temporary business activity 200
The Global Monitor: Kazakhstan 40
The Kiev Letter 29
The New Moscow City Map and Guide 14
The New St. Petersburg City Map and Guide 14
The Ross Register of Siberian Industry 15
The Russia Desk 26